Nicholas Vincent has published half a dozen books and some fifty academic articles on various aspects of English and European history in the twelfth and thirteenth centuries. He has taught at Oxford, Cambridge, Paris and Canterbury and is now a professor at the University of East Anglia.

Recent highlights from the series

A BRIEF HISTORY OF

BRITAIN 1066–1485

NICHOLAS VINCENT

ROBINSON

Constable & Robinson Ltd
3 The Lanchesters
162 Fulham Palace Road
London W6 9ER
www.constablerobinson.com

First published in the UK by Robinson,
an imprint of Constable & Robinson Ltd, 2011

A copy of the British Library Cataloguing in
Publication Data is available from the British Library

UK ISBN: 978-1-8452-9396-3

Printed and bound in the UK

1 3 5 7 9 10 8 6 4 2

FOR HENRY MAYR-HARTING

CONTENTS

CONTENTS

ACKNOWLEDGEMENTS

Some years ago, a colleague of mine remarked, 'The thing is, Nick, that neither you nor I are ever going to write a book that anyone will want to read.' What follows is intended to test that statement. It is decidedly neither a 'textbook' (of which there are many splendid examples) nor a piece of undiluted scholarship targeted at a few dozen scholars, none of whom, save the reviewers (and even then not all the reviewers), will ever read it. It must open with an apology. My title and my task were given to me already formed. To all Welsh, Scots, Manx, Irish or Channel Island readers, it is necessary to point out that this particular brief history of 'Britain' focuses almost exclusively upon the history, indeed upon the 'Birth of the Nation', of England, with barely a glance towards other undeniably 'British' concerns. To trace the history even of England from the beginnings to 1485, is itself a daunting task. To have done so in tandem with a narrative of other British histories, themselves drawn from very different source materials, would have resulted in a story as confused and as set about with reefs and shipwrecks as the rocky western coast of Britain itself. Excellent histories of Wales, Scotland and Ireland already exist, and readers are urged to explore them. As for the English history which follows, I have both the privilege and the pleasure to belong to a history department at Norwich, and more broadly to a community of scholars, whose friendship and mutual support have ensured that medieval studies flourish today as never before, and that our connection with other scholarly communities, particularly in France, are stronger now than they have been at any time since the nineteenth century. Those who responded to requests for information or who talked over various of the issues in this book, not always aware of the fact that their pockets were being picked, include Martin Aurell, John Baldwin, Julie Barrau, David Bates, Paul Binski, Paul Brand, Christopher Brooke, Bruce Campbell, Martha Carlin, David Carpenter, Stephen Church, Alan Cooper, David Crouch, Peter Davidson, Hugh Doherty, John Gillingham, Chris Given-Wilson, Christopher Harper-Bill, Sandy Heslop, Jim Holt, Nicholas Karn, Simon Keynes, Edmund King, Tom Licence, Rob Liddiard, Roger Lovatt, Scott Mandelbrote, Lucy Marten, Gesine Oppitz-Trotman, Michael Prestwich, Carole Rawcliffe, Miri Rubin, Richard Sharpe, Henry Summerson, Tim Tatton-Brown, Alan Thacker, Tom Williamson and Andy Wood. There are a lot more who might be named, not least the many dozens of scholars whose contributions to the new Oxford Dictionary of National Biography I have mined with such pleasure and such a sense of my own essential ignorance.

All accounts of history are the product of their own time. It is no coincidence that after 1970 or so, historians began to explore the impact of inflation upon the politics of England in the 1180s, or that the 'ethnic cleansing' practised (or not practised) by the Normans after 1066 first became a burning issue after 1990, with the former Yugoslavia almost daily in the newspapers. The present book was written in a time of economic crisis, following the great 'credit crunch' of 2008, in the midst of warfare in Iraq and Afghanistan, and in the face of glib assertions from the usual quarters that if long-term educational, cultural and economic decline do not finish off the British, then environment and ecological factors almost certainly will. I began writing it in Caen, in November 2009, within sight both of the castle from which William the Conqueror planned his conquest of England and of the University, founded by Henry VI, one of the last acts of

English patronage in Normandy. Warfare and education have always sat rather well together. Most of the final chapter was written at Fontevraud or Poitiers in May 2010, the last pages at Rouen, within sight of the place where Joan of Arc was tried and executed. What I know of the period after 1300, I owe to the teaching of Roger Highfield and in particular to John Maddicott, who turned me from an early into a high medievalist but who failed to eradicate what he already suspected might be a populist streak in my prose. The book as a whole is dedicated to Henry Mayr-Harting, prince amongst teachers and an inspiration to the generations of undergraduates whom he has tutored.

Nicholas Vincent
Norwich
Midsummer 2010

MAPS AND FIGURES

1. Genealogy of the Kings of England 1066–1154

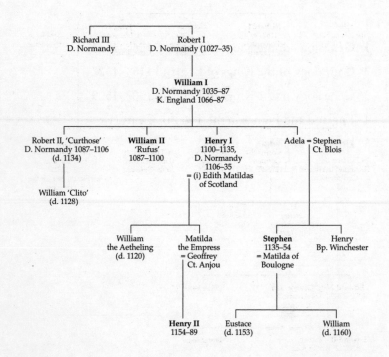

Richard III
D. Normandy

Robert I
D. Normandy (1027–35)

William I
D. Normandy 1035–87
K. England 1066–87

Robert II, 'Curthose'
D. Normandy 1087–1106
(d. 1134)

William II
'Rufus'
1087–1100

Henry I
1100–1135,
D. Normandy
1106–35
= (i) Edith Matildas
of Scotland

Adela = Stephen
Ct. Blois

William 'Clito'
(d. 1128)

William
the Aetheling
(d. 1120)

Matilda
the Empress
= Geoffrey
Ct. Anjou

Stephen
1135–54
= Matilda of
Boulogne

Henry
Bp. Winchester

Henry II
1154–89

Eustace
(d. 1153)

William
(d. 1160)

2. Genealogy of the Kings of England 1154–1327

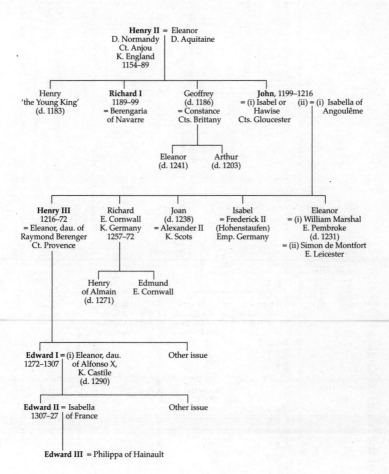

Henry II = Eleanor
D. Normandy | D. Aquitaine
Ct. Anjou
K. England
1154–89

Henry
'the Young King'
(d. 1183)

Richard I
1189–99
= Berengaria
of Navarre

Geoffrey
(d. 1186)
= Constance
Cts. Brittany

John, 1199–1216
= (i) Isabel or Hawise
Cts. Gloucester
(ii) = (i) Isabella of Angoulême

Eleanor
(d. 1241)

Arthur
(d. 1203)

Henry III
1216–72
= Eleanor, dau. of
Raymond Berenger
Ct. Provence

Richard
E. Cornwall
K. Germany
1257–72

Joan
(d. 1238)
= Alexander II
K. Scots

Isabel
= Frederick II
(Hohenstaufen)
Emp. Germany

Eleanor
= (i) William Marshal
E. Pembroke
(d. 1231)
= (ii) Simon de Montfort
E. Leicester

Henry
of Almain
(d. 1271)

Edmund
E. Cornwall

Edward I = (i) Eleanor, dau.
1272–1307 | of Alfonso X,
K. Castile
(d. 1290)

Other issue

Edward II = Isabella
1307–27 | of France

Other issue

Edward III = Philippa of Hainault

3. Genealogy of the Kings of England 1307–1509

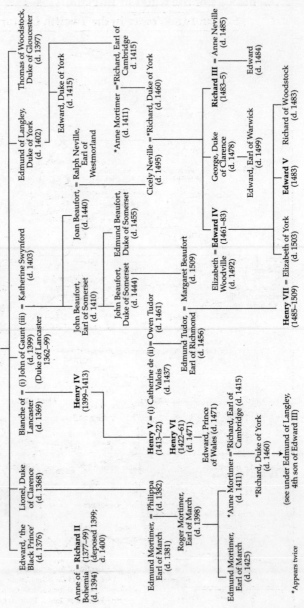

* Appears twice

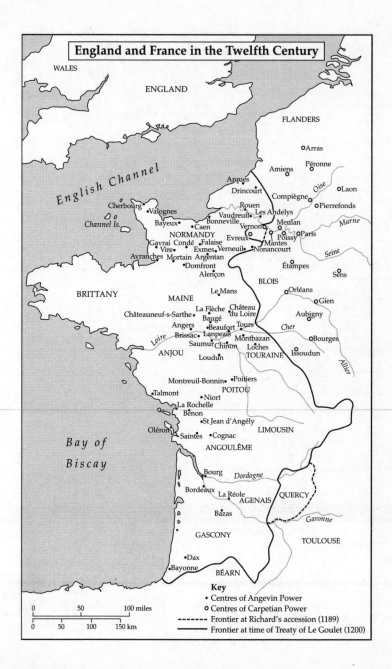

England and France in the Twelfth Century

WALES

ENGLAND

FLANDERS

English Channel

○Arras

Amiens
○

Péronne
○

Arques
●

Drincourt
●

Rouen
●

Les Andelys
●

Compiègne
○

Oise

○Laon

○Pierrefonds

Cherbourg
●Valognes

Channel Is.

Bayeux●

●Caen

Bonneville●

Vaudreuil●

Vernon●

Meulan
●

Marne

NORMANDY

Evreux
●

Poissy
○

●Paris

Gavrai ●Condé ●Falaise

Mantes
●

Seine

●Vire ●Exmes Verneuil●

Nonancourt
●

Avranches● ●Mortain Argentan
●

●Domfront

Étampes
●

Sens
●

Alençon
●

BLOIS

BRITTANY

MAINE

Le Mans
●

Orléans
○

Gien
○

Châteauneuf-s-Sarthe●

La Flèche
●

Baugé
●

Château
du Loire
●

Aubigny
○

Angers
●

●Beaufort

Tours
●

Cher

Brissac● ●Lanpeais

Bourges
○

Loire

Saumur● Chinon●

Montbazan
●

Loches
●

Issoudun
●

ANJOU

Loudun
●

TOURAINE

Allier

●Poitiers

Montreuil-Bonnin●

POITOU

●Talmont

●Niort

La Rochelle●

Bénon
●

●St Jean d'Angély

Oléron○

Saintes● ●Cognac

LIMOUSIN

Bay of

Biscay

ANGOULÊME

Bourg
●

Dordogne

Bordeaux●

La Réole
●

AGENAIS

QUERCY

Bazas
●

Garonne

GASCONY

TOULOUSE

●Dax

Bayonne●

BÉARN

Key

● Centres of Angevin Power

○ Centres of Carpetian Power

- - - Frontier at Richard's accession (1189)

—— Frontier at time of Treaty of Le Goulet (1200)

| 0 | 50 | 100 miles |

| 0 | 50 | 100 | 150 km |

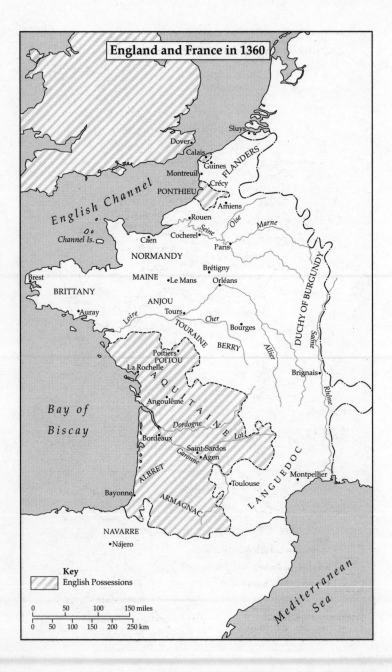

England and France in 1360

Dover
Sluys
Calais
Guines
FLANDERS
Montreuil
Crécy
PONTHIEU
Amiens

English Channel

Rouen
Oise
Seine
Marne

Channel Is.
Caen
Cocherel
Paris

NORMANDY

Brest
MAINE
Le Mans
Brétigny
Orléans

BRITTANY
ANJOU
Tours
Cher
Bourges

Auray
Loire
TOURAINE
BERRY

Allier

DUCHY OF BURGUNDY

Saône

Poitiers
POITOU
La Rochelle
AQUITAINE

Brignais

Bay of
Biscay

Angoulême

Rhône

Dordogne
Lot

Bordeaux
Saint-Sardos
Garonne
Agen

ALBRET

LANGUEDOC

Montpellier

Bayonne
ARMAGNAC

Toulouse

NAVARRE
Nájero

Mediterranean
Sea

Key
English Possessions

0		50		100		150 miles
0	50	100	150	200	250 km	

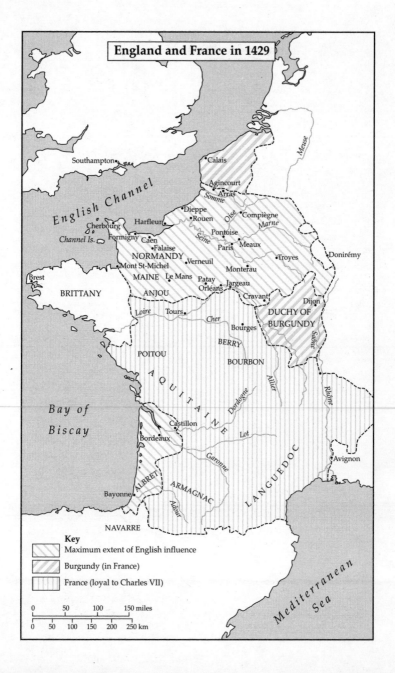

England and France in 1429

Southampton

Calais

Agincourt

Arras

Somme

Dieppe

Harfleur •Rouen

Oise •Compiègne

Cherbourg

Pontoise

Marne

Channel Is. Formigny Caen

Seine

Meaux

Falaise

Paris

NORMANDY

Verneuil

Montereau

•Troyes

•Donirémy

Brest

Mont St-Michel

MAINE Le Mans

Patay

Jargeau

BRITTANY

ANJOU

Orléans

Cravant

Dijon

Loire Tours•

Cher

DUCHY OF

BURGUNDY

Bourges

Saône

BERRY

POITOU

BOURBON

A Q U I T A I N E

Allier

Bay of

Dordogne

Rhône

Biscay

Castillon

Bordeaux

Lot

Garonne

LANGUEDOC

Avignon

Bayonne•

ALBRET

ARMAGNAC

Adour

NAVARRE

English Channel

Meuse

Mediterranean
Sea

Key
Maximum extent of English influence

Burgundy (in France)

France (loyal to Charles VII)

| 0 | 50 | 100 | 150 miles |

| 0 | 50 | 100 | 150 | 200 | 250 km |

I

THE ANGLO-SAXON PAST

By sundown on Saturday, 14 October 1066, events on a previously obscure Sussex hillside had decisively altered the course of English history, as indeed of world history. Surveying the scene of carnage, even those eyewitnesses who could hope to gain most from the day's events were appalled by what they saw. As William of Poitiers, in all likelihood a chaplain attached to the army of the Duke of Normandy, later put it, 'Far and wide the earth was covered with the flower of the English nobility and youth, drenched in blood.' Pitched battles were rare events in the Middle Ages. Too much could turn upon a single moment's hesitation, upon false rumour or an imperfectly executed manoeuvre. Only if prepared to gamble with fate, or absolutely certain of victory, would a general commit himself to battle. William of Normandy did precisely this in October 1066, not because he commanded overwhelming odds or could be certain of God's favour, but because he had just staked the wager of a lifetime. By crossing the Channel with a vast army of Frenchmen, not only his own Norman followers but large numbers of knights and mercenaries from as far north as Flanders and as far south as Aquitaine, he risked everything on a single roll of the dice. Should his army fail in battle, should the enemy refuse combat, cut off the possibility of retreat and leave the French to stew in their own mutual recriminations, then William would go down in history as one of the most reckless gamblers of all time. As it was, his outrageous manoeuvre succeeded not so much through his own skills but because of the hubris of his enemies.

The English commander, Harold Godwinson, had just celebrated victory in the north of England, having butchered an entire army of Norwegian invaders at the Yorkshire settlement of Stamford Bridge on 25 September. Clearly, God was an Englishman, and Harold was God's appointed instrument. In these circumstances, when news reached him of the landing of William's army at Pevensey, three days after his victory, Harold packed up his troubles and marched his army southwards for what he clearly expected to be yet another great celebration of English martial superiority. Not for the first time, nor the last, a sense of manifold destiny and of the invincibility of England in the face of foreign threat, lured an English army onwards to disaster.

Yet the battle about to be fought at Hastings would be a disaster unprecedented even on the scale of other such events, for example the English defeat at Maldon in 991 (when an English commander, once again convinced of his destiny and of the impossibility of negotiating with foreign terrorists, preferred his entire army to be massacred by Viking raiders rather than surrender to the heathens), or in Essex, at 'Assendon' in 1016 (when the English King Edmund 'Ironside' had been decisively defeated by Cnut of Denmark). In the whole of European history, Hastings finds few parallels either in the scale of the slaughter or the finality of the consequences. Like all such epics, it was fought on a scale and over a period of time that were appropriately vast. Like Waterloo, it was a close-run thing, lasting from about nine in the morning until dusk, nearly nine hours of fighting. At Hastings died not just Harold Godwinson but an entire civilization. Not just Harold's army but the whole 500-year-old panoply of Anglo-Saxon England went down before the swords of a new Norman invader. Why was this so, and what were the consequences?

The Dark Ages?

What we know about events in the Middle Ages depends upon a surprisingly narrow source base. We need to imagine a stage with ninety per cent permanently in darkness. An occasional spotlight flickers upon this corner or that, suddenly revealing details and colours that we might not otherwise imagine existed. A vague half-light enables us to discern some broader outlines, a few darker and lighter shadows. For the most part, however, we depend upon inference and imagination to establish what is there. It is no coincidence that those trained as medieval historians have occupied a disproportionately significant role in both MI6 and the CIA, precisely because the medievalist's training ensures that the bare minimum of detail is employed to the maximum effect in intelligence gathering. For the Middle Ages, a very large part of our intelligence emerges from one key source. Our spy network on the past is dominated by churchmen, which is to say by monastic chroniclers and the occasional bishop or parish priest, setting down their accounts of past events, virtually all of them men, most of them with a particular line to toe in respect to their own monastery or locality and their wider allegiance to the Church. Such men wrote not so much to illuminate the broader stage, to flatter kings, or to celebrate secular society, but for quite other purposes, above all to demonstrate the unfolding of God's plan for mankind, with the Church or churches as God's principal instrument.

Bede of Jarrow

To understand the Anglo-Saxon past and the society doomed to destruction at Hastings we need to go back to the eighth century, to Bede, Monk of Jarrow in the far north of England

and his great *Ecclesiastical History of the English Peoples*. Bede wrote almost three hundred years since the Angles, Saxons and Jutes had first crossed the North Sea from their German homelands, in the aftermath of the collapse of Roman rule. It was more than a century since at least some of these pagan invaders had first accepted Christianity, a Mediterranean religion closely associated with the pomp of Roman imperial government, reintroduced to a now pagan England via the more European-leaning parts of Kent. It was nonetheless Bede's historical narrative which for the first time attempted to impose a pattern upon this chaos of conquest and conversion. In the very opening lines of his *History*, he proclaimed that 'Britain is an island of the furthest west', deliberately echoing the words of the Roman geographer Pliny, and thereby setting the stage for at least two key concepts central to Bede's vision of Britain and its place in the wider world. Firstly, Bede believed that for all its physical insularity, Britain was linked intellectually and in terms of its peoples and their racial descent, to a mainland that had once formed part of the wider empire of Rome. Secondly, being an island supplied Britain with a compact unity that should have ensured, over time, a unified sense of purpose under a single monarchy.

Bede did not invent the idea either of Christian kingship or of nation. He nonetheless brought these two concepts into a new and powerful conjunction, arguing that through their acceptance of Christianity, and hence through their willingness to unfold God's master plan, the Anglo-Saxons had progressed to having one supreme King from having several. Kingdoms and peoples were pounded in the mortar of Christ's Roman Church to form a single 'England' under a single race of English kings. The English, like the Jews of the Old Testament, might have good or bad kings, but they were now a nation united under kingly rule. In turn, and with the advice of churchmen, their kings gave them laws, just as the kings of Israel had dispensed a Deuteronomy and the laws of Moses. Upon the pillars of kingship and the law was the nation founded.

There was much in this that was pure nonsense. But strongly expressed opinions often make for the most interesting writing about the past, and Bede, with his prejudices, racism and religious bigotry, was unquestionably a great historian, writing in a sophisticated and highly personal voice. According to his own lights, he was pursuing truth, on hunting down and verifying source materials that, but for his *History*, would be entirely lost to us. He wrote on an epic scale, and long books have always had the advantage in the bestseller lists. As a result, it was Bede's highly literary, highly prejudiced and resolutely misleading account of Anglo-Saxon history that was adopted as the master narrative. In due course, it was this same *History* that was fed back into the historical process, used by later Anglo-Saxon kings, especially the rulers of Wessex, to justify their own kingly authority. Faced with a Viking onslaught in the middle of the ninth century, King Alfred of Wessex responded by appealing to an English sense of identity, king, law and nation, founded squarely upon the twin pillars of the Bible and Bede. A phenomenon observable from Homer to *Mein Kampf*, a book of history became crucial in shaping the fate of subsequent historical events. Bede's *History* was translated into the vernacular English language at Alfred's court, and Alfred himself sponsored the writing of a new history in continuation of Bede, the so-called '*Anglo-Saxon Chronicle*', again in the vernacular, recording the events of more recent times on a year by year basis, copies of it being sent out to each of the major centres of West Saxon culture, the greater monasteries of Wessex, Kent and Mercia, from Winchester via Canterbury to Worcester.

The English

It would be easy to deconstruct large parts of Bede's narrative and the mythology founded upon it. For a start, the English had never been a single people. They were always, in Bede's day as later, a mixture not just of Angles and Saxons from across the North Sea, but of those already settled in the island long before the Romans came, most obviously the Celtic peoples, still independently ruled in large parts of Wales, Scotland and the Lake District. Even these Celts had been superimposed upon a population of far more ancient settlement. Unless we assume wholescale genocide, either when the Celts arrived in the fifth century BC, or again with the coming of the Germanic Angles and Saxons from the 400s onwards (and in neither case has the idea of genocide found favour with the scientists, from DNA or blood-test analysis), it seems certain that the population consisted for the most part of a mixture of long-established peoples, ruled over from the top end of society by war bands of Celts, Romans or, later, Saxons. To this already rich mix, the ninth and tenth centuries added further migrants. In the century after 800, most of England north of the Thames was conquered and settled by pagan Vikings, who established for themselves an entire 'Danelaw' independent of West Saxon control. The modern regions of Norfolk and Suffolk might continue to be known as East Anglia, after their original 'Anglian' settlers, yet for the entire period 800–1000, a period for which we have less than a dozen recorded 'facts' about this region, they were entirely overrun by Viking settlers. Indeed, it is questionable whether, for this period at least, East Anglia and large parts of the Danelaw are to be considered, in historical, linguistic or cultural terms, still parts of a political entity that we can call 'England'.

Even beyond the Danelaw, and here ignoring the Celtic enclaves of Wales or Scotland, the peoples of Cornwall continued to look as much to Brittany as to Winchester for ideas and leadership. Those of Cumberland, as late as the days of William Wordsworth, if not later, took few instructions from any authority beyond the Pennines and were more closely integrated with the worlds of Dublin, Strathclyde and even Norway than they were with those of Canterbury or London. This was a Britain, even an England, as it was to remain throughout the Middle Ages, of fiercely independent local identities, accents and even languages, in some ways more akin to modern-day Switzerland or to eighteenth-century France than to the peaceful and law-abiding chequerboard of green fields and pastures that is celebrated in myth and still visible, in places, from the air. Although by the year 1000 East Anglia and the Danelaw were Christianized and subsumed within the kingdom of Wessex, using precisely those dissolving myths of England's Christian destiny and kingly virtue which Bede had first employed to suggest a united 'English' kingship leading a united 'Engalond', it is questionable whether a united England itself became any sort of political or historical reality even then. England was a myth, constructed in the four hundred years either side of the Norman Conquest on the basis of a powerful series of ideas, of racial, religious, historical and linguistic cohesion, yet still a myth well beyond the comprehension of most of those that we would consider 'Englishmen' in 1066.

A Christian Nation?

The idea that 'England' was a fully Christianized nation, as opposed to an assembly of semi-Christian peoples loosely ruled over by Christian kings, is itself wishful thinking. The Roman Empire had no concept of England, not least because the 'English' themselves had yet to cross the German ocean to their new homeland. England as we now know it is contiguous with the two ecclesiastical provinces of Canterbury and York, and it might be supposed that, like other regional or national divisions, the formation of England was in some way the outcome of the formation of these two archbishoprics, from the sixth century onwards. Yet, through to the twelfth century, the archbishops of York claimed jurisdiction north of the border in what then, as today, was considered Scotland. The archbishops of Canterbury claimed authority not only over southern England but over Wales, not subjected to English rule until the late thirteenth century, and even then seen as a land distinct from England. Canterbury also claimed authority, albeit disputed, over the Church in Ireland. Furthermore, although the reader of Bede might assume that Church and nation were one indivisible unity, in truth the Church as often sought to oppose or ignore the dictates of kings as ever it did to encourage kingly authority. Anyone who supposes that the Church was a tame creature of secular authority, even in the centuries before the year 1000, ignores the fact that the Church was principally concerned not with political order but with eternal salvation. Christ's kingdom was not of this world, and the most influential political theorist of the early Middle Ages, St Augustine, had taught that it was false to identify any city or empire, even the Christianized empire of Rome, with the true City of God.

Laws and Hobbits

With regard to law, although we have law codes issued by successive Anglo-Saxon kings, from Ethelbert of Kent through to the Danish King Cnut, and although these codes are eloquent upon such matters as feuding and the control of violence, the punishment of arsonists and rapists and other 'public' crimes, they ignore ninety per cent of the law as we would understand it today. The vast majority of property disputes seem to have lain beyond the control of the King's courts, or at least beyond the competence of those lawyers and churchmen who wrote the King's law codes. Moreover, although the public declaration of law, through the courts of the counties and the hundreds, and through the regular reissuing of royal codes, was clearly of great significance, it is questionable to what extent it was actually the King's law that was applied in practice or at key moments of crisis.

There is perhaps a tendency to look upon Anglo-Saxon England through the rose-tinted lenses of one its most famous students, J.R.R. Tolkien. For nearly forty years as Professor of Anglo-Saxon at the University of Oxford, Tolkien occupied his time not so much in studying the Anglo-Saxons known to history as in inventing an entirely fictitious parallel universe in which the world of Beowulf rubbed shoulders with a peculiar brand of late-Victorian Catholic piety. Tolkien's vision continues to dominate much thinking about the Anglo-Saxons, relocated in a Tolkienesque England of well-governed and law-abiding make-believe: a Shire of freedom-loving hobbits writ large. Yet the definition of a law-abiding society must surely be one in which the law is widely known and applied, not only in peacetime but in time of disorder or war. The greatest crisis in the history of Anglo-Saxon England, which emerged in the 1050s and 60s over the question of an heir to the English King, was to be settled, not by lawyers or law codes, but by acts of violence and usurpation which themselves suggest that a large part of Anglo-Saxon law-making was mere window-dressing, intended to mask a rather more primitive and brutal reality. These were hobbits with swords and an attitude far from peaceable. Law codes, like the Deuteronomy of the Old Testament, gave the impression that the kings of Anglo-Saxon England were law-makers and law-givers in the mould of David or Solomon. Whether in practice such laws were applied, widely used or even widely read, remains a much more difficult question to answer.

English Wealth

If we remove the three pillars of a united kingship, Christian nation and law, then a very large part of the substructure imagined by Bede and his successors vanishes from our under-standing of Anglo-Saxon England. This leaves instead quite another unifying principle, one that in reality may have played a much more significant role in the idea of an entity named England. Just as modern Italy or Switzerland or Belgium are divided nations in terms of language, regional loyalties, culture or even administration, but united in the sense that they represent powerful trading communities with a single national economy, it is arguable that it was the wealth, rather than the religion or even the language of the English, that served as the principal unifying feature before 1066. England was preco-cious not only in terms of its sense of national identity, but in terms of its wealth. It was this potential bounty, over and above any other considerations, that first drew foreign invaders, Phoenicians and Romans of antiquity, Angles, Saxons and Jutes of the fifth century, Vikings of the ninth and tenth, and Normans and Frenchmen of the eleventh and twelfth centuries, to stake their claims to rule or own the land. There is every sign that England was extremely wealthy. There is very little proof of the source from which this prosperity derived.

It came perhaps from the mining of metals, above all tin, but lead too, and gold and silver, which, though now confined to a single gold mine in Wales, were in the early Middle Ages possibly abundant in the Mendips and the hills of Cumberland. These mineral resources probably first drew Britain into contact with the Mediterranean world, as long ago as the fifth century BC, when a Phoenician admiral reported the mineral wealth of Cornwall, long before Julius Caesar conceived of a Roman military conquest of Britain. The British Isles are formed of every conceivable rock and sediment heaved up from each of the great convulsions of the vanished continents of prehistory. England may have been the Gold Coast of early medieval Europe, dependent upon the export of those same two commodities, gold and slaves, upon which a much later British Empire was to be founded. Bristol was almost certainly a centre for the trade in slaves to and from Ireland and Wales, and perhaps for silver from Wales or the Mendips, long before it became involved in the trade in gold and slaves from Africa or sugar from the Caribbean. St Patrick, one of the most mythologized yet significant figures in Irish history, may have begun his life as a slave, captured in what is today south-west England and traded to the Irish *c.* 410 AD.

More likely, however, the wealth of the Anglo-Saxons derived from animal rather than from mineral or human resources, in particular from the export of wool. Wool exports can be meaningfully measured only from the late thirteenth century, but this was a trade in all likelihood much more ancient. It was English wool, spun and dyed, sometimes in England, more often by foreign weavers and dyers, that supplied the English with many of their best-known exports: Lindsey blankets, Worsted from Norfolk, and above all, the most precious of products made from English wool, Scarlet, woven with twisted yarns according to techniques originating in Central Asia, dyed white, blue, green but most often carmine red. If the Bayeux Tapestry was produced in England, as most modern commentators suggest, then the very variety of the colours supplies testimony, not only to the wealth that first drew William of Normandy to the idea of conquering England, but to the trade that already linked England to the European and Mediterranean worlds.

We have no firm proof that it was wool which made England rich before 1066. Nonetheless, there is powerful circumstantial evidence to this effect, not least the rise of neighbouring Flanders. If England was rich, then Flanders in the centuries before 1066 was growing richer still. Flanders itself was a great blank of flatlands and bogs, much of it undrained as late as the seventeenth century. Yet this unlovely corner of northern Europe already by the eleventh century boasted flourishing towns and an extraordinary density of knights, the elite 'haves' in a society of 'have nots'. Flemish knights, the 'Brabanters' and 'routiers' of the twelfth century, were to provide the staple of many a mercenary army in English and continental history. Flanders flourished probably as a consequence of its position on the trade routes between north and south, and in particular on the trade routes to England. In the two centuries after 1200, it was English wool, purchased by Flemish merchants, that fuelled the economies of both England and Flanders. There is every reason to suppose that this was a much more ancient phenomenon, and that the rise of Flanders tells us much about the rise of the English wool trade. Without sheep, and without Flemish merchants to trade their wool, the very idea of England might have been just one of those good ideas left unfinished on the cosmic drawing board.

By the eleventh century, across the continent, from northern France down to southern Italy, England was famed not only for its wools but for its role in associated luxury trades: precious metalwork, intricately painted manuscripts, and perhaps above all for the manufacture of '*Opus Anglicanum*', literally 'English Work': luxuriously decorated vestments, painted by needle with silks, pearls and the most precious of gold and silver thread, that through to the fifteenth century and beyond kept the English brand current upon the luxury export markets of the world. The Canterbury monk Eadmer, accompanying his archbishop to the papal court at Bari in southern Italy in the 1090s, was amazed to be shown a cope, a liturgical vestment, worn by the Archbishop of Benevento, trimmed all around with gold, apparently made of the most precious *Opus Anglicanum*. The cope had been presented to the archbishop in England many years before in part-payment for a most precious relic, the arm of the apostle St Bartholomew, sold to relieve a famine in Italy. That an Italian archbishop, in the 1020s or 30s, should regard England as a potential source of famine-relief tells us much about perceptions of English wealth. That he accepted and treasured such a gift for more than sixty years tells us that such gifts were particularly sought. In the same way, the English desire to acquire Mediterranean relics tells us much about England's cultural dependence upon Europe and in particular upon Rome, a much battered city but still viewed as the cradle of European civilization. An inventory of the Pope's treasures, drawn up at the end of the thirteenth century, lists no less than 113 pieces of English embroidery, exchanged for who knows what sort of reciprocal benefits to the English.

English Land

The wealth of England, like all medieval wealth, was ultimately invested in land. Buying or acquiring an estate was just as much a symbol of status and a guarantee of future prosperity as buying a house remains today. It was such land, inherited, purchased or acquired, upon which the sheep were fattened to supply wool, and from which grain was harvested to feed the men and women who sheared, milked and fed the sheep.

The land and the landscape of England into which William of Normandy came were, of course, very different from those which a visitor to England, even two centuries later, would have found. England in the year 1000 was above all a land of forests and woods. Some of the greatest of these stretched across the southern counties, from Kent through to Dorset. The Battle of Hastings was itself fought on the edges of the great forest of the Weald, known in the Anglo-Saxon period as 'Andredes weald', from the Roman name for Pevensey ('Anderida'), precisely the port where William of Normandy landed on his arrival in England in September 1066. Elsewhere, however, regions that we think of as sparsely wooded, not least the Cotswolds and the Wolds of Lincolnshire (derived from the same Germanic root, 'wald', as the Kentish 'Weald') took their name from the rolling hills left behind when ancient forests that had once rivalled the extent of the German 'Schwarzwald' or 'Odenwald' were cleared. The clearance of these forests was already a longstanding process, even before the Angles and Saxons first arrived. By 1066, nonetheless, it had made only a relatively minor impact upon a landscape that was still dominated by large, uncultivated tracts of land.

Within the woods themselves, an extraordinary variety of wildlife continued to thrive. Brown bears, hunted in Neolithic times, had almost certainly vanished from England under the Romans, but wolves and wild cat, boar and red deer remained. In the 960s, the English King Edgar is said to have imposed an annual tribute of 300 wolf skins upon the Welsh, and grey wolf populations, recorded in the 1160s, did not become extinct in England until the fourteenth or fifteenth centuries. Wild boar, threatened with extinction by the thirteenth century, were still maintained for hunting as late as the reign of Charles I. In the 1220s, the bishop of Winchester is to be found hunting for 'pigs', by which we can almost certainly assume 'wild boar', in his park at Taunton. In the wetland regions of the east, particularly in the fens, still undrained and inhabited by a semi-barbaric population, wildfowl flocked the air in numbers similar to those to be found today in the most remote wildernesses of the Danube estuary or the Carmargue. Custodians of the bishopric of Ely, in the thirteenth century, were regularly required to send vast quantities of wildfowl and fish for the King's feasts: 50 pike each of three feet, 50 of two and a half feet, 50 of two feet, 200 'steilung', 50 sticks of shaft-eels and 4,000 smaller eels for a single royal banquet in 1257. Besides kings, species such as the eagle owl, or even the European vulture, today confined to the northern and easternmost reaches of the continent, may well have fed upon this extraordinary diversity of English wildlife.

Population density

Dispersed across this landscape, the total extent of the human population cannot be estimated with any real accuracy. Population history is still very much a matter of guesswork, a sort of statistical witchcraft. Figures ranging from one to five million have been suggested for the English population in 1066, with the reality probably lying closer to the lower than to the higher end of this scale. For comparative purposes, the population of ancient Rome is estimated to have exceeded one million people. England was a far from densely populated land. More people lived in villages than in towns, though towns there undoubtedly were, and it was upon towns such as London, Winchester, Norwich and York that much of the economic activity of the countryside was focussed, not only because towns boasted markets, but because the urban population needed to be fed. Merely feeding the population of London, by the thirteenth century, was a major economic enterprise, consuming the surplus foodstuffs of Kent, Surrey, Hertfordshire and Essex and ensuring a large part of the prosperity of the south-east.

The Countryside

The countryside itself was looked upon with far cooler emotions than would be the case later, when English pastoral became a leading theme of English poetry. No one in their right mind would choose to live in the countryside, a dangerous place, thronged with werewolves, fairies and things that went bump in the night. Elves took delight in laming cattle and kidnapping the unwary. Arrowheads found in the fields (in reality Neolithic carved flints) were proof of their existence. Entire books of elf-charms, and of spells intended to counter elvish tricks, formed a substratum of Anglo-Saxon literature. Even after the Norman Conquest of 1066, which drove the elves into semi-retirement, revenants and spirits, almost invariably malevolent, are a constant theme in twelfth-century miracle stories. Against them, only the power of the saints could be invoked to any real effect. In the 1090s, an entire village in Derbyshire was terrorized by a pair of vampires risen from the dead, only appeased through the intercession of St Modwena of Burton.

The Village

By contrast to the open countryside, the life of the village implied civilization rather than small-mindedness, and neighbourliness or protection as much as confinement. From the seventeenth century, landowners planning their mansions began by removing peasants and their houses, opening up a prospect of park and woodland of which Horace or Virgil might have approved. In the Middle Ages, only the most ascetic and world-hating of monks behaved like this, for example the Carthusians, who lived as communities of hermits in near perpetual silence, and who, in establishing a monastery in the 1180s at Witham in Somerset, deliberately depopulated and dismantled the local villages, sending their peasants to live elsewhere. By contrast, up to 1100, most monastic communities tended to be established in or close to towns. Under Norman as under Anglo-Saxon rule, the greatest of aristocratic dwellings were built in proximity to villages, with lord and peasant established in close and deliberate symbiosis.

Roads and Transport

With few roads save for those last properly repaired by the Romans, and with only a few stone bridges, transport over long distances was not only difficult but expensive. Where possible, goods were transported by sea or river rather than by land. It was the extensive English coastline, and the access which its rivers supplied to inland markets, that rendered England itself a land so fit for trade, part of an island whose climate and geology permitted the production of an agricultural surplus, blessed with mineral resources, and with plentiful supplies of timber to serve as fuel, yet with no real extremes of climate, no insurmountable mountain chains, and with no part of the island further than a few miles from a navigable river leading ultimately to the sea. Cotton-in-the-Elms in Derbyshire, reckoned by the Ordnance Survey to be the most 'inland' spot in England, is in fact only five miles from the river Trent and only forty-five miles from the start of the river's tidal estuary.

England's rivers were not only full of fish but were a major source of power in driving water mills, by 1066 already a regular feature of the landscape. Moreover, in the temperate English climate, these were rivers for the most part free from disease and in particular from malarial mosquitoes. Just as the tsetse fly continues to hold back the agrarian economies of Africa, so in the Middle Ages the malarial swamps of southern France or central Italy served as a barrier to prosperity from which England was for the most part exempt, though tertian malaria or 'spring fever' was endemic in certain fenland areas until the nineteenth century. In the meantime, access to rivers and the sea meant that it was easier and cheaper, even in the twelfth century, to ship coals to London from Newcastle and the Durham coal fields, than it was, say, to sell Hampshire grain in the markets of Somerset, or Yarmouth herrings in

Warwickshire. Water-borne trade itself served as a major encouragement to the development of English shipping and ultimately of English naval strength. From the eleventh century through to the evacuation of Dunkirk in 1940, it was the small ships of the many dozens of havens and ports scattered along the southern and eastern coasts that served as the guarantors of England's defence.

Today, the journey from London to Ipswich by car is only sixty miles, about an hour's drive on a very dull road. From the air, however, the picture shows a ribboned and shredded coastline, one crucial to English history: many hundreds of miles of tidal mudbanks, monotonous to the eye, but dotted with havens where a boat can be landed, and with easy access to the Essex forests from which came the timber to build boats. It was within sight of these estuarial waters that much of the fate of eleventh century England was decided. It was here that the Viking fleets sought to hide, and it was here, at the battles of Maldon and Assendon, that Viking armies, themselves consisting of so many boatloads of marauders, decisively defeated English armies by land. The sea brought danger and foreign invaders, but it also brought wealth and an opportunity for nautical prowess. Even today, nearly a third of England's overseas trade enters and leaves via the single great port of Felixstowe. The well-kept lawns and rich wine cellars of the modern University of Cambridge are to a large extent maintained from the profits of Felixstowe's steel and concrete economy.

In the Middle Ages, it was no coincidence that it was another eastern town, Norwich, with easy access to the profits of North Sea trade, that was perhaps the richest in the kingdom. Nor should it be forgotten that Norfolk was the county of Nelson, himself raised at Burnham Market, within strolling distance of the oozing estuarial mudbanks of Burnham Stathe. Market, harbour and the defence of the realm form a highly significant trinity. The shipping of southern and eastern England was crucial not only to trade but to England's military reputation

overseas. In the eleventh century, one of the most vivid passages
in the contemporary life of Edward the Confessor describes a
great warship, given to the King. It was with gifts such as this
that political disputes were healed. The money to pay for ships
and their crews of eighty or more oarsmen was one of the more
significant tax burdens placed upon society. Galley service was
perhaps even more important to the Anglo-Saxon military
than service on land and, already by 1066, ports such as
Hastings were obliged to supply regular quotas of ships or men
to the King's service.

The English Diet

From ships came trade and a navy. The sea also fed the English.
As one historian has remarked, the herring served as the potato
of medieval England. Vast quantities of fish supplemented a
diet from which red meat, the 'roast beef of old England', was
almost entirely absent. Visitors from France to England in the
nineteenth century came to regard the English countryside as
one vast meat factory for the production of beef. But beef, in
the Middle Ages, was a luxury encountered more rarely than
venison or herring or eel. Cattle were expensive to feed, especially in the winter months when, before the introduction of
the turnip as a common winter crop, there was very little save
hay upon which they could be fed. Those that were kept were
as often used to pull ploughs and carts as for milk or meat.
Oxen were the tractors and trucks of medieval England. There
was also perhaps a sense, once again inherited from Bede, that
there was something rather awful and un-Christian about the
eating of beef. As early as the sixth century, Pope Gregory the
Great, writing to Augustine of Canterbury on the conversion
of the English to Christianity, had associated the eating of the
flesh of cattle with the feasts of the pagan rather than with the
Christian calendar.

Christianity was a Mediterranean religion, from a region
where the diet was principally vegetarian. Meat eating was
both a characteristic of the barbarian tribes and a symbol of

Germanic pagan allegiance. Only in the Celtic regions of Christendom, in Wales and in Cumbria, did cattle remain a staple element of diet, albeit prized as much for their milk as for their meat. Rents in Cumberland were still paid in 'cornage', as so many horns of cattle. The Welsh, in the 1260s, serving alongside Englishmen in the armies of the rebel baron Simon de Montfort, were horrified by the greed of the English for grain with which to make bread, just as the English craved to escape from the endless but breadless Welsh diet of cheese, milk and meat. As with modern commercial catering, poultry represented a compromise acceptable to most. Chickens and eggs were consumed in vast numbers. Church rents were sometimes payable as so many chickens, particularly at Christmas, and hard-boiled eggs were blessed in church before the Easter Mass, for distribution amongst the village community, a practice that by the fourteenth century was being condemned in some dioceses as a pagan superstition, but which together with the Christmas fowl has perhaps bequeathed both the modern phenomenon of the Christmas turkey and the Easter egg.

The English Myth

This was a world lit only by fire, fuelled by wood and water, fed and clothed for the most part from the produce of a few surrounding acres of plough and pasture, protected only by the small ships of the southern and eastern coasts, sustained in times of crisis by a myth of nationhood and Christian kingship devised by Bede and exploited by Bede's Anglo-Saxon successors. Elements of this world are still with us. In 1940, at the height of the last great crisis that threatened to overwhelm the English, Winston Churchill was able to make potent use of the myths of Englishness, of blood and soil, of the ploughman and the sailor of small ships, to conjure up a Dunkirk spirit, itself heir to the mythologizing of Alfred and of Bede. The advocates of English independence and the haters of European conformity, even today, pitch their stand on a similarly mythologized village green of Englishness, proclaiming England's particular historic destiny. No doubt, if one looked hard enough, it might still be possible to discover, kicking their heels somewhere in the far corners of England, the direct descendants not just of the Angles, Saxons and Jutes but of the Celts, and even of the aboriginals, if not the Neanderthals, who once inhabited this land. For the most part, however, even by 1066, long before the Normans landed their ships at Roman Pevensey, England was a land of myth and make-believe, its people a race of mongrels, its language and inhabitants already an uncertain mixture of German, Scandinavian and Welsh.

Crisis

At the top end of this world, within the narrow but rich seam between king and commoner, a small elite of church leaders and secular aristocrats dominated Anglo-Saxon society. It is the doings of these men that form virtually the only facts recorded in works of tenth- or eleventh-century history. What emerges from such accounts is a story of political crisis in England provoked by two great threats: firstly, of foreign invasion, and, secondly, of civil war. In the late tenth century, from the 980s onwards, during the reign of King Aethelred II, these threats combined to provoke a collapse in public order. Monastic chroniclers, having one eye always focussed upon God's dealings with mankind, and aware that the year 1000 was quite likely to mark a millennial watershed in human history, later blamed this collapse upon the King himself. What health could there be in the nation, if the King were a sinner or, in Aethelred's case, not merely sinful but un-counselled ('Unread' or 'Unready')? In reality, Aelthelred seems not only to have been well advised but a dynamic and bold military commander, changing his coinage in such a way as to advertise the need for men and weapons, a new portrait image of the King being shown on every one of his several million silver pennies, properly helmeted and armed. The problem lay not with Aethelred but with the coalition of enemies that he faced. Potential invaders from overseas now sought the assistance of traitors nearer to home.

St Brices's Day Massacre

In 1002, hoping to crush the threat from Denmark and the English Danelaw, Aethelred allowed, perhaps encouraged, a massacre of Danes within his English kingdom, timed for St Brice's day, 13 November: a pogrom, neither the first nor the last in English history, that was intended for political effect, to draw together friends in the mutual expression of hatred towards a common enemy. Following the destruction of much of Oxford in the ensuing massacre, Aethelred himself issued a charter justifying his actions. The Danes, so he argued, had to be rooted out from England like weeds ('cockles') from a field of wheat. Yet ethnic cleansing has never been an effective means of dealing with dissent. Those who choose murder and expropriation over negotiation generally sign their own death warrants. Far from advertising their racial superiority, they often draw attention to their own inadequacy. It is certainly ironic that England's greatest pogrom should have been timed for the feast day of St Brice, no Englishman but a Frankish archbishop from the Loire Valley, who achieved sanctity in part through his long residence in Rome. According to a much later source, it was the very attractiveness of the Danes to English women that led to the massacre of 1002. The Danes combed their hair daily and began to bathe every week to make themselves more seductive. It was the fact that 13 November 1002 fell on a Saturday, '*Laugar-dagr*', or 'Bath-day', in the Danish language, that determined its choice as a day of slaughter by the unwashed and sexually frustrated English.

Famine – and Apocalypse?

The massacre of 1002 was followed by a great famine, in which not just the cockles but the wheat itself came close to failing as the sense of crisis and apocalypse grew sharper. Aethelred's reign spanned the year 1000, widely believed to mark the imminent second coming of Christ. A fear of imminent apocalypse is inclined to provoke precisely the crisis which its prophets proclaim. Aethelred's own administrators and officials were disunited, and vied with one another for a greater share of power. The Danish King, Swein Forkbeard, mounted a full-scale invasion of England, no doubt hoping to seize his own spoils from the coming millennium. In 1013, he inflicted a crushing defeat upon Aethelred's armies, forcing the King himself to seek exile with his wife's family in northern France. A brief return in 1014 was followed by Aethelred's death, and the succession of his son, Edmund Ironside, himself fatally wounded at the battle of Assendon in 1016. London was handed over to the Danes.

Aethelred's former ministers scrambled to make their own settlements with the victors, including Godwin, a minor official from Sussex, now raised up as the greatest of English quislings under Swein and Swein's son Cnut. Godwin was married to Cnut's sister-in-law, and in due course gave Scandinavian names to his eldest sons: Swein, Harold and Tostig. The eldest of these claimed to be not Godwin's son but Cnut's, suggesting a degree of intimacy between the two families that extended beyond the council chamber to the royal bed. Cnut himself, meanwhile, had married Aethelred's widow, an act of sexual imperialism intended to stamp his authority upon the ruling English dynasty as upon England itself, now subsumed within a North Sea empire comprising large parts of Britain and Denmark and with ambitions towards the conquest of Norway. Most of those Englishmen whose careers prospered after the 1040s, and who were to play so crucial a role in the Norman Conquest of 1066, came to maturity in this period of Cnut's reign, in the aftermath of a Danish Conquest itself no less remarkable than that later mounted by William of Normandy.

The Godwins
In particular, the breaking under Cnut of the power of the old English administrative class paved the way for the emergence

of an even narrower political elite, founded upon only three or four key families: Godwin and his sons, as earls of Wessex and East Anglia; the Leofricsons as rulers over Mercia and the Midland counties; and the house of Bamburgh in Northumbria, itself locked into a bloody feud with the rival house of Aelfhelm of York. Much of northern England was divided between two great regional loyalties, to Bernicia in the north, and Deira stretching southwards as far as the Humber, divisions that themselves could be traced back to the age of Bede. Any idea that England had been welded into a united nation was given the lie by this division, as late as the 1040s and 50s, into a series of local earldoms themselves tracing their roots as far back as the divided kingdoms of Mercia and Wessex, Bernicia and Deira. Moreover, and as with any Mafia-style division of authority between a few oligarchic families of rich and powerful bosses, the fewer the families the greater the storms and hatreds brewed up amongst the elite, and the more vicious the jockeying for position. From this, it was Godwin and his sons who emerged as the richest and most successful players. In a lawless environment, the more powerful the protector, the more those in need of protection will commend themselves to his authority. When the wolves are loosed, the hobbits will run for cover. This is precisely what happened in respect to personal commendations to the Godwin family, England's greatest godfathers. Increasing numbers of lesser men, even outside the Godwin heartlands, began to commend themselves and their lands to Godwin lordship. As a result, when Cnut died and was succeeded by his son, Harold Harefoot, it was the Godwin family, in title merely earls, in reality the chief power behind the throne, who manipulated the situation to their own advantage.

By his wife, Emma, Aethelred left two sons, Edward and Alfred. These boys, the 'aethelings' or 'throne-worthy ones', had gone into exile at the time of Cnut's invasion, and had been brought up at the court of their mother's family, in northern France. In England, Emma had then been married to Cnut, and

had borne a son by him, Harthacnut. Harthacnut claimed to be
his father's only legitimate heir, Cnut's other son, Harold
Harefoot, having been born to an Englishwoman before Cnut's
marriage to Emma. The laws of marriage at this time were far
from rigid but it was nonetheless assumed as a matter of course
that only a legitimate son could succeed as king. From the time
of the founding of the West Saxon dynasty, back in the dim
distance of the fifth century, no declared bastard had sat upon
the West Saxon throne. Harold Harefoot, so the party of
Emma and Harthacnut alleged, was illegitimate and had only
seized power in England whilst Harthacnut was preoccupied,
in 1035, securing his father's kingdom in Denmark. Whether
this slur was true or not, into the turmoil that followed Cnut's
death stepped Alfred the Aetheling, Emma's son by her
marriage to Aethelred, clearly hoping for his own share of
power. Alfred, however, was deceived. Received by Earl
Godwin at Guildford, he was seized, taken captive and then
blinded, the traditional means, together with castration, of
rendering a potential heir unfit for royal power: a technique
imported from Byzantium, and in itself yet another indication
of England's contacts with the wider world. Alfred was sent in
captivity to Ely, where he soon died. The crime here was
horrific, and the taint of criminality extended not just to
Harold Harefoot but to Godwin and perhaps even to Emma,
who had first encouraged Alfred to enter England. For Godwin
to have permitted the seizure and mutilation of a guest of his
own hearth was regarded as a particularly vile act. To
encompass the death of a royal prince, sprung from the line of
Alfred the Great and the house of Wessex, merely compounded
the crime. Godwin and his sons were to be haunted by Alfred's
death for the remainder of their lives.

Edward the Confessor
Like most crimes, in the short term Alfred's murder had
distinct advantages for the criminals, consolidating Godwin's
authority in England. When Harold Harefoot died suddenly

in 1037, followed only five years later by Harthacnut, it was
Earl Godwin who brokered the next stage in this game of
kings and crowns, allowing for the return to England of
another of Aethelred's sons, Alfred's elder brother Edward.
Edward has gone down in history as 'The Confessor', a
milky-white, long fingered and semi-translucent embodiment of everything most saintly; an old man, famed for piety
and chastity rather than for worldly strength. Yet this reputation comes to us only from the later years of Edward's
reign, and in particular from the period after his death, when
historians were seeking an explanation for recent cataclysmic
events. In his lifetime, certainly through to the 1050s, Edward
was a more forceful and commanding figure, famed as much
for his rages as for his piety, keen on hunting, a jealous accu-
mulator of wealth and precious objects, a patron of the
military, not merely of the Church.

Edward's one overriding problem was his indebtedness to
Earl Godwin. Without Godwin he might never have negotiated his return to England, and yet Edward clearly resented
not only Godwin's role in the death of his brother Alfred, but
the extraordinary degree to which, over a period of thirty
years, Godwin had risen from virtually nothing to establish
landed wealth and a military authority rivalling not just that of
his fellow earls but the King himself. Like many princes who
come to the throne relatively late in life (Edward was at least 38
by the time of his accession), a sense of resentment may have
sounded as the keynote of his life. He clearly resented his
mother, who had abandoned him in childhood to marry his
father's usurper, Cnut of Denmark. So great was Edward's
sense of injury here that, after 1042, Emma was immediately
stripped both of power and of her very considerable wealth.
Even more bitterly, Edward resented Godwin. Although he
was persuaded in the short term to take Godwin's daughter,
Edith, as his queen, and although Edith and her family publicly
proclaimed the marriage to be all that it should have been,
Edward himself may have sought, from the moment he

succeeded to the throne, to work against the Godwins and ultimately to bring about their downfall.

His great opportunity came in 1051. The election of a new
archbishop of Canterbury, Robert of Jumièges, a Frenchman
from those regions of northern France where Edward himself
had been exiled before 1042, and the welcome that Edward
extended to Count Eustace of Boulogne, another Frenchman,
married to Edward's own sister and apparently given or
claiming some sort of authority over Dover and its defences,
provoked Godwin and his sons to the brink of civil war. With
the support of the other English earls, Edward forced the
Godwins into exile, Godwin himself to Bruges in Flanders,
Harold and others of his sons to Ireland. The precise motiva-
tions here are difficult to establish, but, in all likelihood, these
events were the outcome of long-fomented hatred. In
particular, the involvement of Eustace of Boulogne at Dover
and the promotion of a French archbishop of Canterbury
suggest a deliberate attempt on Edward's part to promote
northern French allies at the expense of the Godwins. They
also suggest that already, as early as 1051, there was a crisis
over the future succession to the English throne. Dover and
Kent were the keys to England, and it is difficult not to interpret
the offer of Dover to Eustace as in some way associated with
Edward's future plans for the throne. Certainly, after 1066,
Eustace was to lobby long and loud for possession of Dover
castle. In 1067, he was to attempt unsuccessfully to seize Dover
as a point from which to launch his own bid for power.

Succession Crisis?

If there was a succession crisis in 1051, then it was perhaps
already assumed that King Edward would have no legitimate
child to succeed him. The King was by now in his late 40s. His
queen, Edith, was much younger. Either Edward was judged
incapable of fathering children, or it was widely supposed that
he had no intention of producing an heir by a wife sprung from
the family of Godwin. Crucially, in 1051, at the same time that

Godwin and Harold were exiled, Edith herself was put away in a nunnery. Even her propagandists were forced to concede that her relationship with the King was more like that between father and daughter than husband and wife. In both political and personal terms the events of 1051–2 marked Edward's great bid for freedom. In both respects, he failed miserably. The Godwins returned. Rather than risk civil war, the other earls backed down, with the memory of Aethelred's reign constantly in their minds, fearing that the pursuit of vendettas amongst the ruling class might merely pave the way for foreign invasion. Edward was forced to receive back those he most hated, including Edith, now reinstated as queen.

Peering through the Mist

From this point onwards, our knowledge of the last fifteen years of Anglo-Saxon England is clouded, as the sophistication of our sources fails to keep pace with the complexity of events. What was recorded tended either to be too brief, as with the *Anglo-Saxon Chronicle*, or too verbose, as with the contemporary *'Life'* of Edward the Confessor. The three surviving versions of the *Anglo-Saxon Chronicle*, maintained in at least three different locations, become extremely patchy, in some years recording few events, in others none at all. The so-called *'Life of Edward'* (the *Vita Edwardi*), composed in the 1060s, either shortly before or shortly after the Norman Conquest, was the work of a Flemish monk hoping to please Queen Edith, writing in an obscure and poetic Latin which would be difficult to construe, even if the manuscript itself had survived intact, which it has not. These fragments can be supplemented by sources from across the Channel. But with the continental sources we have to be even more cautious. Virtually everything written about Edward's reign by foreign chroniclers was set down after the great cataclysm of 1066, on the whole to justify the Norman Conquest of England. It has to be read as propaganda rather than truth. Selecting which items of information to believe, and which to reject, becomes as difficult for the historian of late Anglo-Saxon England as it would be for a modern intelligence officer to construe the political development of China using nothing but official press bulletins.

Amidst the shadows, the outline of certain great events can be discerned. Firstly, although Earl Godwin himself died within a year of his return to England, on Easter Monday 1053 (as legend proclaimed it choking on a piece of bread after having challenged God to strike him dead should he have lied about his role in the death of Edward's brother Alfred), his power lived on, now invested in two of his sons, Harold who succeeded him as Earl of Wessex, and Tostig, promoted, apparently as the King's favourite, as Earl of Northumbria. Harold fought a series of prestigious and successful campaigns against the Welsh. Having killed the Welsh King, whose head was sent in tribute to King Edward, Harold then married the Welshman's widow, repeating a feat already associated with the Danish conqueror Cnut and in the process allying himself to another of the great aristocratic families of England, that of Leofric of Mercia. Tostig fared less well in his attempts to impose royal rule and royal taxation on the far north. In 1065, there was a violent rebellion against him. Tostig appealed for assistance from the English court, but then found himself sidelined, as he saw it betrayed by his brother Harold. Edward's own promise to suppress the rebels came to nothing. Tostig was left without an earldom but with a burning sense of personal grievance against his own family. Edward's own authority during these closing years of his life is very hard to assess. Certainly it was he who made earls and who continued to rule, in name at least. It was Edward who commissioned the rebuilding of the church of Westminster, intended as a monastic foundation, pledged in penance, so it was said, for his failure to fulfil a vow to make a pilgrimage to Rome. King Cnut had visited Rome, as probably had both Harold and Tostig. Was Edward's failure here an indication that the King himself was effectively a prisoner within his own court, able to hunt, to feast, to receive tribute, but in all practical respects eclipsed by his brother-in-law, Earl Harold?

Lacking positive initiatives, Edward seems chiefly to have exercised his authority through passive resistance, above all perhaps through his failure to nominate a publicly recognized successor to the throne. Edward the Exile, the son of Edmund Ironside, was invited back to England from his refuge in Hungary, but died in 1057, only a few days after his return. Some have suspected the Godwins of poisoning him. Edward the Exile left a son, Edgar the Aetheling, a mere boy, perhaps, five or six years old, now brought up at court, living in what appears to have been close contact with the King, but without any real power and without lands. There was certainly no official proclamation that Edgar was to be regarded as Edward's heir. On the contrary, contacts were maintained with Eustace of Boulogne, Edward's brother-in-law, and with Edward's mother's family in northern France. At no point was any one of these kinsmen promoted as Edward's clear and undisputed successor.

In 1051, at the height of his authority and with the Godwins exiled, Edward is said, according to one version of the Anglo-Saxon chronicle, to have received a man named 'Count William' from overseas, generally identified as William, Duke of Normandy, great-nephew of Emma, Edward the Confessor's mother. Many historians have supposed that this visit by William in 1051 formed part of William's own bid for the English throne. Contemporary Norman chroniclers, although they mention no visit by William to England, claim that specific promises were made to William in respect to the throne, not only by King Edward but by Harold. One such Norman version of events, famously shown on the Bayeux Tapestry, implies that, at some time in the 1060s, perhaps shortly before Edward's death, Harold crossed to France and there was persuaded to take oaths to William, sworn on the holy relics of Bayeux Cathedral, no doubt promising to recognize William as Edward's heir.

The problem with all of these stories is that they date from after 1066, when the Normans had not only scooped the jackpot but were in a position to rewrite the history of recent events, if necessary burying the truth in order that their own actions might be justified. Even the story of Count William's crossing to England in 1051 is open to dispute. Did the Anglo-Saxon chronicler intend to imply here that William was specifically offered the throne? If so, why did he not mention the fact? Why do none of the Norman sources written immediately after 1066 refer to any visit paid by William to England before the Conquest, especially when we bear in mind the very great incentive that such writers would have had to include something so significant and supportive of Norman claims? Could it be that William of Normandy came to England in 1051 not to receive a promise of the English throne but to render homage to his elder and richer cousin, the newly empowered King Edward, for his own lands in northern France?

Certainly, William's rule over Normandy was especially insecure at the time, with his enemies gearing up towards a great rebellion. Might it even have been another 'Count William', not William of Normandy, who made the visit? In 1051, there was at least one other northern French aristocrat, William, Count of Arques, William of Normandy's uncle, who might have had an incentive to visit the English court. William of Arques was either already in rebellion or about to rebel against his nephew, William of Normandy, and would in 1051 be forced to seek exile in the territory of another of the players, Eustace of Boulogne. In some ways, William of Arques fits the bill for the 1051 visit to England even better than William of Normandy.

As this suggests, we have very little idea of the reality over which all of the chroniclers, English and Norman, were so keen to varnish. What we do know is that, from the 1050s onwards, the various dukes, counts and lords of northern France began to occupy a more significant place in English history than had previously been the case. It is time therefore that we turn our attention from Anglo-Saxon England to events on the other side of the Channel, and in particular to the rise of one northern French dynasty: the dukes of Normandy.

Normandy

Normandy enters our story here for the simple reason that Emma, the mother of Edward the Confessor and the wife both of Aethelred and Cnut of England, was of Norman birth, the daughter of Duke Richard I of Normandy, himself the grandfather of the future William the Conqueror. Edward the Confessor and William of Normandy were therefore related in the third degree of kinship as second cousins, with Richard I of Normandy, Emma's father, as their common ancestor. A series of highly significant facts should be stressed here. Edward and William were cousins, but not close cousins, and not a drop of the blood of the West Saxon dynasty flowed in William's veins. From the 1050s onwards, there were many others who could claim far closer patrilineal kinship to Edward the Confessor, not least Edward the Exile, son of Edmund Ironside, and the Exile's son, Edgar the Aetheling. To some extent indeed, in the 1040s, Edward the Exile, already aged twenty-five in 1040, might have been promoted as a more plausible candidate for the English throne even than his cousin Edward the Confessor. Secondly, William of Normandy was a bastard, born of an extramarital liaison between his father, Duke Robert, and a woman, Herleva, whose own father has traditionally been identified as a tanner from Falaise. Tanning is a trade that in the Middle Ages, as in parts of the Third World even today, involved the use of large quantities of human urine and dog dirt. These less than dainty agents were employed to depilate and soften the hides of animals. What remained thereafter of the rotted flesh and bone was rendered, very messily, into glue. No one who has been near even the most hygienic of animal-glue factories is likely to forget the experience. One of the smelliest and most disgusting of trades, tanning was entrusted to workers generally placed beyond the bounds of decent society, in locations as far removed from town or city centres as the local population could ensure. Find the tanneries in any medieval town, and you will generally have found the most squalid of slums.

As a bastard, born to a woman descended from tanners, William would have been even less plausible a candidate for the English throne than Harold Harefoot in the 1030s. By contrast to William, Harold Harefoot was merely alleged to be a bastard: he himself might have denied the charge. Recently, it has been suggested that William's grandfather was not a tanner, but a furrier, a tailor or more likely an undertaker or embalmer. None of these trades would exactly raise the family to the highest levels of aristocracy. Finally, although we now remember Normandy as a cradle of civilization and as one of the most dynamic regions of eleventh-century Europe, the focus of an entire academic sub-industry of Norman studies, things might easily have been otherwise. Normandy's rise, whatever William's propagandists might suggest, was very far from inevitable or straightforward.

Between 900 and 1100, during two hundred years in which the inhabitants of that part of western Europe that we now call France were deprived of strong central monarchy, many regional dynasties emerged. Some of these new families enjoyed the most dramatic and impressive of debuts but few of these dynasties survived for more than a couple of generations in anything other than a very localized position of power. Only the dukes of Normandy, through their conquest of England, prolonged their greatness and came indeed to rival the French kings not only in terms of wealth and majesty but in the sheer extent of the territories over which they ruled. In many ways, however, this was to lend Normandy an artificial significance which but for the accidents of 1066 it would never have possessed. Had it not been for the catalogue of errors that culminated in the Battle of Hastings, Duke William, the tanner's grandson, and Normandy itself might seem as insignificant to us today as the once powerful counts of Vermandois or Ponthieu.

It was against this background that Normandy first entered English history. It was from Normandy that Aethelred chose his bride, Emma, and it was to Emma's family that he fled in 1014, after his initial defeat by Swein. Thereafter, it was in

Normandy that Aethelred's sons by Emma, Alfred and Edward, were raised after Emma's return to England to marry Cnut. In later life, Edward the Confessor commemorated the more than twenty-four years of his exile in Normandy by grants of land in England to the monks of Mont-St-Michel, Fécamp and Rouen. Fécamp came to possess land in Sussex, some years before Edward's death, including an estate at Hastings, a remarkable indication of the ties that already bound the Confessor's court to the religious institutions of Normandy, many years before the Norman invasion. St Michael's Mount in Cornwall and its monastery, placed under the protection of the monks of Mont-St-Michel on the Norman–Breton frontier, constitutes another surviving relic of Edward the Confessor's exile in Normandy before 1040. St Michael himself had battled with Satan and from the high places of the world had thrown him down to hell. Those appealing to the memory of St Michael tended, in the Middle Ages, to have battle in mind. Edward's gift of a Cornish island to the Norman monks of St Michael, made in the mid-1030s on the eve of his return to England, already describing Edward as 'King of the English', thus suggests not only a familiarity with Cornwall (the two 'mounts' in Normandy and Cornwall could be mother and daughter) but an intention on Edward's part to use his Norman alliances to mount an armed campaign against the forces of evil led by Harold Harefoot.

It was Edward's connection with Normandy, the facts that William of Normandy was his cousin, and that Edward had passed most of his life before 1042 at the Norman court which allowed Norman claims to enter the debate over the succession to the English throne. Whoever Edward actually intended as his heir (and there is no real proof that he opted decisively for any one candidate during the more than twenty years that he sat on the English throne, after 1042), it seems reasonable to suggest that, in the early 1050s, Edward deliberately made use of his Norman connections in an attempt to build up a following for himself in England independent of the English earls. Not only was the archbishop of Canterbury Norman, but other northern Frenchmen, including the bishops of Wells and Hereford, were granted bishoprics or lands in England. Ralph of Mantes, Edward's nephew, son of Edward's sister and the Count of Vexin, was granted estates and an earldom in Herefordshire. There is some possibility that, in the 1050s, Edward's court was partly French speaking. If so, the collapse of Edward's short-lived period of independent rule, after 1052, would have been even more clearly marked since it led to the expulsion from England of most of his former French protégés. It did not, however, put an end to the claims advanced by William of Normandy for his succession to the English throne. To understand why, we need here to consider the situation of Normandy and its ducal family.

Superficially, by the 1060s, a casual observer might have found little to distinguish Normandy from England. Indeed, for ninety per cent of the human population, bonded to the land in the age-old rhythms of agricultural labour, it is doubtful whether, apart from language and the name of one's particular lord, there would have been much to distinguish Bedfordshire from Bayeux or St-Lô from St Ives. Normandy's landscape is similar to, indeed originally was physically attached to that of southern England. Both places have extended coastlines and many rivers allowing access to the sea and hence to seaborne trade. Both were lands of forests as well as of richly productive agricultural land. England came to be defined as the two ecclesiastical provinces of Canterbury and York. Normandy's frontiers were for the most part coterminous with those of the single ecclesiastical province of Rouen.

Rollo and the Vikings

England had suffered from Viking attacks from the ninth century onwards, still ongoing in the time of the greatest Viking of them all, King Cnut of England and Denmark. Normandy owed its very formation to the Vikings, since it was a Viking raider, Rollo, accustomed to wintering his ships in the estuary of the river Seine, who had first carved out independent rule over the region around Rouen, negotiated in a series of treaties with the kings of France according to which, by the 920s, the whole of the province of Rouen, from Eu and the river Somme in the far north, to the bay of Mont-St-Michel and the frontiers of Brittany and Maine in the south-west, was placed under the power of Rollo and his heirs, ruling now as independent counts, later as dukes, no longer directly answerable to the heirs of Charlemagne. Just as English history had been founded upon myths of nationhood, so the Normans commissioned their own national history from a French monk named Dudo of St-Quentin. Dudo deliberately followed Bede in his presentation of the Normans as a people united under one ruler through God's providence and through that ruler's wise decision to embrace Christianity. Like Bede, he thus glossed over the fact that the Normans were never a racially distinct people, and that their war bands ruled over a local population still to a large extent made up of the aboriginal Gallo-Roman or Frankish peasantry who had for centuries inhabited this particular corner of France.

Normandy and England

William of Normandy's own history to some extent mirrored that of his elder cousin in England, Edward the Confessor. Like Edward, William had been orphaned at an early age. His father, Robert of Normandy, had died in 1035, returning from a penitential pilgrimage to the Holy Land, when William was only seven or eight. Like Edward, William was dependent during his youth upon much older and more powerful men. Like Edward, William clearly suffered his own share of indignities, not least the murder of some of his closest counsellors in the ducal court, acts of public violence which suggest, like the murder in England of Edward's brother or the upheavals of 1051–2, not only a society loosely governed under the law, but one in which the ruler struggled hard and often ineffectively to make his rulings stick. Such was the fear of assassination that

William himself had to be hidden by night in the cottages of the poor, to escape the plots of his enemies.

Here, however, the comparisons between England and Normandy end and the contrasts begin to assert themselves. The rulers of Normandy, like those of England, exercised the same late-Roman proofs of public authority: for example, jurisdiction over roads, public crimes such as murder, rape or arson, the minting of coins and the disposal of treasure. Even today, much of the authority invested in the person of Queen Elizabeth II – over the Queen's highway, treasure trove, the Queen's counsels and the law courts in which they act, the royal mint – derives from far more ancient precedents than the Roman emperors or even the rulers of ancient Babylon might have recognized as specifically 'royal' prerogatives. Yet, in the eleventh century, there was a considerable contrast between Normandy and England, both between the extent to which such prerogatives were exercised and between the instruments by which they were imposed.

Normandy could boast nothing like the wealth of England. The English coinage, for example, with its high silver content, stamped with a portrait of the reigning English King, regularly renewed and reminted as part of a royal and national control over the money supply, has to be contrasted with the crude, debased and locally controlled coinage of pre-Conquest Normandy, at best stamped with a cross, at worst resembling the crudest form of base-metal tokens, the sort of token that we would use in a coffee machine rather than prize as treasure. In Normandy, the dukes had local officials, named 'baillis' or bailiffs, but nothing quite like the division of England into shires, each placed under a shire-reeve in theory answerable to the King for the exercise of royal authority through the meetings of the shire moot, the origins of the later county courts. In particular, whilst in England kings communicated directly with the shire by written instruments, known as writs, instructing that such and such an estate be granted to such a such a person, or that justice be done to X or Y in respect of their claims to land or rights, there is no evidence that the dukes of Normandy enjoyed anything like this sort of day-to-day control of local affairs. Not until the twelfth century were writs properly introduced to the duchy, fifty or more years after the Conquest and in deliberate imitation of more ancient English practice. Norman law itself was for the most part not customized or written down into law codes until at least the twelfth century. Above all, perhaps, the dukes of Normandy were not kings. Although they underwent a ceremony of investiture presided over by the Church, intended to emphasize their divinely appointed authority, they were not anointed with holy oil or granted unction as were the kings of England, raising kings but not dukes to the status of the priesthood and transforming them into divinely appointed ministers of God. The Bayeux Tapestry shows William of Normandy wielding the sword of justice, sometimes seated upon a throne, sometimes riding armed into battle. By contrast, both in the Tapestry and on his own two-sided seal, Edward the Confessor is invariably shown seated, enthroned, carrying not the sword but the orb and sceptre, far more potent symbols of earthly rule. William had to do his own fighting. Edward the Confessor, as an anointed king, had others to fight for him.

Thus far, the contrasts between England and Normandy seem all to be to the advantage of England, a much-governed and more ancient kingdom. Yet there is another side to the story. Precisely because they were newcomers, parvenus, risen from the dregs of a Viking pirate army, the heirs of Rollo were spared much of the dead weight of tradition that tended to gather around any long-established dynasty. To take only the most obvious example here, in England no king could afford to ignore the established power of the great earldoms of Mercia, Wessex and Northumbria. Earls were in theory the appointed delegates of the King. In practice, when Edward the Confessor attempted to appoint his own men to earldoms – Ralph of Mantes to Herefordshire, Odda of

Deerhurst to western Wessex, Tostig to Northumbria – the fury of local reaction was such that these appointments were either swiftly revoked or risked head-on confrontation with local interests. Normandy had a secular aristocracy, but it was one that had emerged much later, for the most part in direct association with the ruling dynasty, in most instances from the younger sons and cousins of the ducal family. By the 1050s, under William, most of the higher Norman aristocracy were the duke's own cousins or half-brothers. This tended to intensify the rivalries within a single, all powerful family, and William faced far fiercer and more frequent rebellions against his rule than ever Edward the Confessor faced from the English earls. Yet the very ferocity of this competition tended to focus attention and an aura of authority upon William himself as successful occupant of the ducal throne. The more fighting there is over a title, the greater the authority that such a title tends to acquire. From both of the great crises of his reign, in 1046 when there was concerted rebellion against his rule in western Normandy, and again after 1051, when the malcontents within Normandy threatened to make common cause with outside forces including the counts of Anjou and the King of France, William emerged victorious. At the battles of Val-ès-Dunes in 1047, Mortemer in 1054, and Varaville in 1057, he himself triumphed over his enemies, in the process gaining not just an aura of invincibility but significant practical experience of warfare. Edward the Confessor, by contrast, for all his fury and petulance, had never fought a battle and emerged in 1052 from the one great political crisis of his reign with his authority dented rather than enhanced. There was no Norman equivalent to the Godwins, threatening to eclipse the authority of the throne.

William of Normandy enjoyed distinct advantages, not only in respect of the secular aristocracy, but in his dealings with the Church. In England kings were anointed as Christ's representatives on earth. Patronage of the greater monasteries and the appointment of bishops were both distinctly royal preserves. King and Church, Christian rule and nationhood had become indivisibly linked. Even in his own lifetime, Edward was being groomed for sanctity. As early as the 1030s, there is evidence that the King, by simple virtue of his royal birth, was deemed capable of working miracles and in particular of touching for the king's evil (healing scrofula, a disfiguring glandular form of tuberculosis, merely by the laying on of his royal hands). There was nothing like this in Normandy. William, as contemporaries were only too keen to recall, was descended from ancestors who had still been pagans almost within living memory. Ducal patronage of the Church was itself a fairly recent phenomenon: William's tenth-century ancestors had done more to loot than to build up the Norman Church. And, yet, in the century before 1066, it was this same ducal family that went on to 'get religion' and in the process refound or rebuild an extraordinary number of the monasteries of Normandy, previously allowed to collapse as a result of Viking raids.

They also introduced new forms of the monastic life, above all through their patronage of outsiders: men such as John of Fécamp who wrote spiritual treatises for the widow of the late Holy Roman Emperor, and the Italian Lanfranc of Pavia, one of the towering geniuses of the medieval Church, first a schoolmaster in the Loire valley, later prior of Bec and abbot of St-Etienne at Caen in Normandy, promoted in 1070 as the first Norman archbishop of Canterbury.

In England, the West Saxon kings might have their own royal foundations and their own close contacts with monasteries such as the three great abbey churches of Winchester, or Edward's own Westminster Abbey, but members of the ruling dynasty were not promoted within the church. To become a bishop, a man had first to accept the tonsure, the ritual shaving of a small patch of scalp. Perhaps because the tonsure was associated with the abandonment of throne-worthiness (in the Frankish kingdoms it had been the traditional means, more popular even than blinding or castration, of rendering members of the ruling dynasty ineligible for the throne), there is little sign that any West Saxon prince was prepared to accept it.

In Normandy, by contrast, William not only patronized the church and founded new monasteries, but promoted members of his own family as bishops. At Rouen, for example, the ecclesiastical capital of the duchy, Archbishop Robert II (989–1037), son of Richard I, Duke of Normandy, and founder of a dynasty of counts of Evreux, was succeeded by his nephew, Archbishop Mauger (1037–54), himself son of Duke Richard II. William the Conqueror's half-brother, Odo, was promoted both as bishop of Bayeux, in all likelihood future commissioner of the Bayeux Tapestry, and as a major figure in ducal administration. As the Tapestry shows us, not only did Odo bless the Norman army before Hastings, but he rode into the battle in full chain mail. For priests to shed blood was regarded as contrary to their order. Odo therefore went to war brandishing not a sword or spear but a still very ferocious looking club. The Tapestry shows him at the height of battle, as its contemporary inscription tells us 'urging on the lads'. In the aftermath, Odo was appointed Earl of Kent. His seal showed him on one side as a bishop, standing in traditional posture, tonsured, dressed in pontifical robes and carrying a crozier. On the other side, however, he is shown as a mounted knight riding into battle with helmet, lance and shield, unique proof of the position that he occupied, halfway between the worlds of butchery and prayer.

William himself might not have been anointed as Duke of Normandy, but in the eyes of the Church he commanded perhaps an authority not far short of that wielded by the saintly Edward the Confessor. In particular, the fierce penitential regime of William and his father lent an aura of religiosity to what might otherwise be construed as their purely secular acts of territorial conquest. William's father, Duke Robert, died whilst returning from a penitential pilgrimage to Jerusalem, the *ne plus ultra* for anyone concerned to advertise their Christian piety and remorse. Jerusalem at this time, of course, was still firmly under Islamic rule. To visit it, and to walk in the places where Christ had trod, was both an arduous and an expensive undertaking. William himself, by marrying his own cousin, Matilda of Flanders (thereby forging an alliance with the greatest of the magnates on Normandy's northern frontier), was obliged to undergo penance by the Church. It was penance, however, that both broadcast a particularly powerful image of the duke himself and paved the way for further acts of territorial expansion. To atone for his sins, William built the massive Benedictine monastery of St-Etienne at Caen. Matilda, at the same time, paid for the construction of a sister house, a no less massive monument on the other side of Caen, intended for nuns, the abbey of La Trinité. In the space between these two great monasteries, William laid out a vast ducal castle, surrounded by ramparts, the whole complex of abbeys and castle itself surrounded by a new town wall. As an advertisement of ducal power, the planning and construction of Caen took place on a truly epic scale. To lead his new abbey, William promoted the outsider Lanfranc: a clear bid to demonstrate his commitment to the reforming party within the Church as a whole, and a means of strengthening ties between Normandy and the reforming Church in Rome.

By the 1060s, the Norman Church basked in papal approval. The English Church, however, became ever further severed from continental tendencies, not least through the promotion by Queen Edith of Stigand, Bishop of Winchester and a member of the Godwin affinity, as Archbishop of Canterbury. Thereafter he ruled both Canterbury and Winchester as a pluralist, against the dictates of the Church, and, more seriously still, blessed as archbishop of Canterbury not by the rightful pope of the reforming party but by a rival, whom the Roman aristocracy had briefly established on the papal throne. In the eye of the papacy, Stigand was a scandal. William of Normandy, by contrast, was later to claim that his invasion of England was undertaken as a holy war, intended to cleanse the polluted Anglo-Saxon Church and to bring enlightenment to a nation sunk in sin. The Pope, Alexander II, certainly sent William a banner, as a token of friendship and special favour. Whether Alexander realized that William would use this banner to lead his men in the conquest and slaughter of fellow Christians across the English Channel is another matter entirely. The banner, like William's close relations with Rome, was a powerful tool of propaganda. Propaganda itself, however, does not necessarily accord with 'truth'.

Edward's Death and the Eve of 1066

So to 1066 itself, and the sudden conjunction of political crisis in England with Norman ambition and Norman military might. So far as we can tell, the reign of Edward the Confessor ended in chaos and confusion. The expulsion of the King's earl, Tostig, from Northumbria, was followed by no effective royal counterattack. Edward may have raged against the treachery of the northerners, as the *Anglo-Saxon Chronicle* tells us that he raged, but he was powerless to act. His rage indeed may have brought on the final illness from which he died, at Westminster, on 5 January 1066. From here on, we can trust neither the English nor the Norman account of events, since both were written posthumously, after the Battle of Hastings, and with a clear intention to justify what took place.

King Harold

According to the English, and to some Norman sources, on his deathbed Edward commended both his widow Edith and his kingdom to the keeping of Harold Godwinson, Edith's brother. Harold was duly crowned King, probably within a day or two of the late King's death, but certainly not at Easter 1066, despite the fact that Easter was the traditional, some have argued immutable date of Anglo-Saxon coronations, being the feast of the risen Christ and therefore the most suitable feast-day for the crowning of Christ's representatives on earth. Harold was crowned perhaps on 6 January, the feast of the Epiphany, associated with kingship since it marked the arrival of the Magi, the three wise men from the East, at Christ's nativity. Even so, the failure to observe an Easter coronation suggests a sense of urgency, perhaps of panic, about Harold's crowning. Not just the mythologized King Herod who had tricked the Magi, but the flesh and blood rulers of several northern European peoples were now likely to turn murderous eyes upon the English. The Bayeux Tapestry, as if to signal such panic, reverses its otherwise standard chronological narrative at this point, placing Edward's funeral cortège before his death, and on this unique occasion superimposing two scenes, of deathbed and funeral, immediately before Harold's coronation in a way that may have been intended to emphasise the speed and sudden disjunction of events. Under its depiction of the crowned Harold, the border of the Tapestry reveals a scene of three ships, unmasted, ghostly, yet clearly the threat of an invasion fleet that the English not only feared but expected. Harold himself is shown inclining his head to the right, as a courtier whispers in his ear news of the sighting of Halley's Comet, always an omen of change and ill-fortune. As he listens, Harold's crown tilts sideways, threatening to slip from his head. The portents here were far from favourable.

From the moment of his crowning, Harold faced at least two threats of invasion. The first, led by his disgruntled brother Tostig, in alliance with Harold Hardrada, King of Norway, was both the first to materialize and the first to be suppressed. The Norwegian army was cut to pieces by Harold at Stamford Bridge, eight miles east of York, on 25 September, five days after their short-lived victory against the northern earls Edwin and Morcar at Fulford, just across the Ouse from the modern York racecourse. No one claimed that the Norwegian invasion was anything other than opportunistic, provoked no doubt by Harold Godwinson's mishandling of his brother, Tostig.

With the Norman invasion that burst upon England a few days later, things were rather different. Across northern

Europe, virtually everywhere except within Normandy itself, Duke William's attack was treated as an act of violent usurpation, an unprovoked onslaught upon a Christian opponent, the rape rather than the conquest of England.

Within Normandy, however, William's propagandists rapidly got to work to justify the invasion according to the laws both of God and of man. Edward, so it was argued, had promised the throne to William since long before 1066 (a claim for which there is no real proof). Harold had sworn oaths to William, shown indeed on the Bayeux Tapestry, placing his hand on holy relics, perhaps in the presence of the consecrated host, the body of Christ, promising to support William's claims. Harold may well have crossed to Normandy at some time shortly before King Edward's death, but quite why and with what outcome remains unclear. Possibly he went to negotiate not over the succession but over the release of hostages, including his own younger brother, held by William apparently since 1052, given up by Earl Godwin not in respect of the succession but in the aftermath of his return to court as guarantors for his own future good behaviour in respect of Edward the Confessor. If so, if William were holding English hostages against the will of the English King, and if Harold was forced to swear an oath rather than volunteering to do so, then even under canon law and the tenets of the Church, nothing that Harold had been made to do in Normandy could be held against him afterwards. An oath sworn under compulsion, like a marriage into which either of the parties was forced, was not in any way to be considered binding. 'He made me do it' has always been an acceptable excuse for misbehaviour, whether in the playground or a court of law.

In any event, and despite the subsequent Norman claims, Harold's visit to northern France might not have been intended to take him to Normandy. Even the Bayeux Tapestry seems to imply that Harold's ship drifted off course and that his landing in the county of Ponthieu, at the mouth of the Somme, was unplanned. Perhaps, rather than being sent to swear oaths to William, Harold went to France on his own account, to negotiate alliances with other northern French magnates, the Count of Boulogne perhaps, or the Flemings to whom his father, Godwin, had fled at the height of the crisis of 1051. Rather pathetically, one English source later alleged that Harold was not heading for France at all, but rather blown off course on a fishing trip along the Sussex coast. If so, and given that the Bayeux Tapestry shows Harold's men loading hawks and hounds on board his ship – traditional aristocratic gifts offered to foreign princes – one has to wonder what sort of fish he was hoping to catch. What is perhaps most surprising about Harold's brief period as king, from January to October 1066, is that he secured not only coronation but the apparent assistance of the other English earls, most notably the earls of Mercia, against both of the foreign threats now facing England. This does indeed suggest, contrary to Norman propaganda, that Harold's claim to the throne was widely acknowledged and that the deathbed dispositions of Edward the Confessor were treated as a legitimate bestowal of the late King's succession.

Preparations for Invasion

In Normandy, meanwhile, the preparations for invasion involved an immense expense of money and effort. Alliances with other French lords had to be negotiated to secure an army sufficient to the task. One modern commentator has calculated that an army the size of William's represented a logistic miracle. Allowing for 10–15,000 men, and 2–3,000 horses, the force that waited throughout August and early September on the estuary of the river Dives to the north of Caen would have consumed a phenomenal quantity of grain and other foodstuffs. Had the troops slept in tents, then these alone would have required the hides of 36,000 calves and the labour of countless tanners and leather workers. The horses would have produced 700,000 gallons of urine and 5 million tons of dung. We seem to be back in the world of the tannery, far from the more exalted claims that were advanced on William's behalf and a long way from the shadow of the papal banner under which William's army is supposed to have marched. Even if we treat these figures as inflated or wildly speculative, the sheer scale of the operation cannot be ignored. That there was indeed an epic quality to William's preparations is suggested by the *Life of William* by William of Poitiers, which deliberately echoes the words of both Julius Caesar and Virgil in its account of William's Channel crossing, here likened to the expedition of Caesar to conquer Britain, and to Aeneas' flight from Troy to Rome, to the foundation of a new world order.

An even more ancient myth may have been present in William's own mind. In June 1066, shortly before embarking for England, William had offered his own infant daughter, Cecilia, as a nun at the newly dedicated abbey of La Trinité, Caen. Was he thinking here, perhaps, of the sacrifice of a daughter by an earlier king, by Agamemnon of his daughter Iphigenia, intended to supplicate the Greeks and hence to supply a wind to speed the Greek expedition against Troy? If so, then by associating himself with the Greeks, outraged by the abduction of Helen, William not only broadcast his own sense of injury against the treacherous King Harold but trumped even Virgil in his appeal to classical mythology. Aeneas had founded Rome as an exile from ravaged Troy. William would be the new Agamemnon, precursor to the exploits of Alexander, fit conqueror not just of Troy or Rome but of the entire known world.

Medieval rulers were rarely blind to the classical footsteps in which they trod, or blithely unconscious of the epic nature of their deeds, and the Norman Conquest of England was certainly an expedition of epic scale. Having mustered his army in early summer, and camped at the mouth of the river Dives for over a month, presumably on the river's now vanished inland gulf, protected from attack by sea, some say waiting for a wind, others for news that Harold's fleet had dispersed or been diverted northwards, William moved his army to St-Valéry on the Somme and from there set sail on the evening of 27 September, hoping that a night-time crossing would enable his fleet to slip past whatever English force was waiting for them in the Channel. Once again, it was surely no mere coincidence that his landing at Pevensey took place on 28 September, the vigil of the feast day of Michaelmas, commemorating the same warrior Saint Michael, the scourge of Satan, whom Edward the Confessor had honoured thirty years before, while in exile in Normandy, in the hope of Norman support to secure him the English throne.

The Normans in England

The ensuing campaign, in so far as there was one, can be briefly told. William immediately embarked on a scorched-earth policy, harrying and foraging as was the general rule for medieval warfare, burning villages, terrorizing the local population, advertising his own position and at the same time assembling the sort of resources in food and provender that would be required to maintain his vast army should the enemy refuse immediately to engage. The harvest was newly gathered in, so resources were not hard to find. But the prospects, if the English held back, were not propitious. A Norman occupation of Sussex might dent Harold's pride, not least because his own family stemmed from precisely that part of England, but would not in itself have delivered a fatal blow to the English state. By contrast, the chances that William's army could be held together for any period of time without proper supplies and without engaging the enemy, were slim indeed. Even the greatest warriors have to eat, and no lord in the eleventh century could afford to leave his own estates unprotected for long, especially at harvest time when the pickings were richest. The Norman army was now in entirely foreign territory. Very few, even of its leaders, had any experience of England. Without the benefit of Ordnance Survey maps or signposts, they would have depended entirely upon local spies and intelligence-gathering, but the local people no more spoke French than William's soldiers could read Anglo-Saxon.

William moved east towards Hastings, building a temporary castle at Hastings itself, positioning his own army across the main road to London. Hastings was already a major centre of English naval operations, and its occupation was to some extent equivalent to the later seventeenth-century Dutch burning of the Medway dockyards. But this in itself was not sufficient to provoke Harold to battle. Rather, hubris persuaded Harold, having just marched his army southwards from Yorkshire, to leave the safety of London and immediately embark upon another campaign, risking the third pitched battle in three weeks. Perhaps precisely because battle was so rare, and because Stamford Bridge had proved so total a victory, Harold, the experienced commander of more than a decade of warfare in Wales, believed himself invincible.

The Battle of Hastings

Given the number of books describing the Battle of Hastings in the minutest of detail, it may come as a disappointment to learn that the vast majority of our 'facts' concerning the battle are nothing of the sort. The Bayeux Tapestry, combined with the account by William of Poitiers and the Latin 'Song of the Battle of Hastings', generally attributed to Guy, bishop of Amiens, and written very shortly after 1066, give us the main gist of the action but surprisingly little specific detail. We cannot even be sure of the ground or the extent to which the battlefield has been altered out of all recognition since October 1066. One of the more important contemporary accounts, by William of Jumièges, threatens to overturn all traditional understanding of the battle by claiming that Harold was killed early in the day, rather than at the battle's final climax. Nonetheless, if the high altar of Battle Abbey was indeed built on the site of Harold's final stand, then we can assume that the two armies faced one another across a shallow valley, with Harold and his shield wall of housecarls and axemen to the north, blocking the road to London. It is clear that William was obliged to take the offensive and that the first charges by both cavalry and infantry failed to strike home. The cavalry charge misfired to such an extent that the Bretons on the Norman flank panicked and came close to causing a rout. We should remember here that the Bretons were traditional enemies of the Normans, and they enlisted in 1066 as temporary allies only from mutual self-interest. It would have been perfectly natural for Norman writers to have blamed the Bretons for any failings in their own attack.

The English may have sought to exploit the disorder caused by poor discipline within the French army by pursuing the fleeing horsemen, allowing William to launch a second attack against the now weakened English defences. Rumours circulated that William himself had been killed, but he was deftly able to reassure his troops by raising the visor of his helmet, a scene very clearly shown on the Bayeux Tapestry. Had the stakes not been so high, and had the French the possibility of a retreat to recoup their strength, then it is possible that the battle might have ended at this point, as an inconclusive draw. Desperation alone drove William on to a final attack upon the English position which now, at the very end of the day, began to crumble.

Harold was killed still fighting in the shield wall. Precisely how will never be known. The Bayeux Tapestry famously shows him, or someone near to him, blinded by an arrow in the eye, but this detail was not necessarily recorded in the Tapestry when it was first embroidered. It may be the result of repairs and restitching as recently as the eighteenth century. Several twelfth-century chroniclers, including the Norman poet Wace, refer to Harold's blinding. Wace, writing in the 1170s, had almost certainly seen the Tapestry in his role as a canon of Bayeux, but, like modern commentators, he may have misinterpreted the Tapestry's meaning, already a century old by the time that he saw it, which in any case seems to show merely that Harold was blinded, not killed, by the arrow. The blinding, indeed, may be

yet another Biblical echo, of the story of the Hebrew King
Zedekiah, blinded by Nebuchadnezzar for violating an oath of
fealty, thereby, like Harold after him, bringing destruction upon
himself and his people. The 'Song of Hastings' and most twelfth-
century accounts state that Harold was killed by the sword, the
'Song' paying particular attention to the three French knights
who in company with William of Normandy butchered his
body. With night falling, the Normans found themselves victorious by sheer desperate persistence.

Around them lay the dead and dying. Before the discovery
of penicillin, even a flesh wound could prove fatal. Internal
injuries or anything that risked peritonitis or blood-poisoning
were more likely to kill than to be cured. The physical effects
of several hours of head-on violence, in which two groups of
heavily armed men sought to bash the life out of one another
with sharp pieces of metal, are difficult for us to imagine, in
spite of Hollywood images of gore and guts. The psychological
consequences are perhaps easier for us to grasp. Some modern
writers suggest that medieval men came, if not from a different
species, then certainly from a different psychological universe.
Emotions such as anger and grief, or such physical states as
exhaustion or jubilation, they say, might have been experienced and expressed in quite different ways a thousand years
ago. Much of this sort of writing reeks of poppycock. We must
never shut our ears to the differently pitched voices of the past,
but no more must we close off our capacity for emotional
engagement with humanity's common experience. The dehu-
manized, unemotional history of which some modern historians dream, the desire to assess the past as if it were a set of
data to be graphed and computed, seems to be an utterly inadequate response to events such as the Battle of Hastings.

First after the battle came a sense of relief for William's
army. A victory had been won that to those still living seemed
epic in its proportions. This was no ordinary battle, and the
victors were well aware of the fact. Most chroniclers in northern
Europe, from the Loire to the Elbe, recorded the events at

Hastings in some way. After the relief came exhaustion. William's army seems to have halted in Sussex for a full two weeks. The assumption has been that they were waiting for what remained of the Anglo-Saxon leadership to offer their surrender. In reality, sheer exhaustion combined with the after-effects of anxiety, injury and disease provides a more likely explanation. A large number of the Norman army had been killed. The dead had to be buried. There were many arrangements to be made. Eyewitnesses to another bloody victory, at Waterloo in June 1815, report a similar sense of aftershock, anticlimax and grief. Perhaps already William himself had begun to fall ill. Dysentry as a result of weeks of insanitary camp life and almost unbearable tension might explain the sickness that now gripped the army as a whole. Disease might also, to the medieval mind, symbolize sin and its consequences. Certainly, whatever rejoicing took place on the evening of 14 October would have been tempered with a sense of the need to give thanks to God.

William is said to have pledged the battlefield itself to religion, even before the battle began. The site was subsequently given to the monks of Marmoutier on the Loire, on the understanding that they would found there an abbey to commemorate the day's events. Within a few years, penance was officially imposed upon all of those who had fought at Hastings. We know the precise terms here, and they speak of a Norman army as much bewildered by its own success as boastful of its victories. For every man that he had slain in the battle (and we might note here that Hastings was already being described not just as a battle but as 'The Great Battle'), the killer was to fast on bread and water for a year; for every man struck but not necessarily killed, forty days of penance; for everyone not sure of the number that they had slain, a day of penance for every week remaining to them for the rest of their lives. Those who fought motivated only by greed were to be treated as murderers, sentenced to three years of fasting. No doubt there were many at Hastings who had kept no exact tally of the number they had killed or wounded, or who were not entirely sure, even in their own minds, whether they had fought for personal gain or for the glory of God. To such people, perhaps the majority of William's army, the battle was a great victory, but a victory earned only at peril to their immortal souls. Summing up the guilt and bloodshed of Hastings, a monk of the monastery later founded on the battle site reported that 'the fields were covered with corpses, and all around the only colour to meet the gaze was blood red. It looked as if a river of blood filled the valleys.' The blood shed at Hastings was to stain the next four centuries of English history.

2

NORMAN ENGLAND

William the Conqueror

Everyone knows, or thinks they know, what happened as a result of the Battle of Hastings. The Norman Conquest of 1066 ushered in a century of Anglo-Norman rule, in which William of Normandy, his sons and grandson, established a powerful feudal monarchy in England. For the first time since the Romans departed, England was brought into direct conjunction with continental Europe. French became the dominant language of the court and of an aristocracy itself now more French than English. Ruthless Anglo-Norman efficiency triumphed over the ramshackle 'mucking along' of Anglo-Saxon England. This is the gist of the matter. In reality, however, each part of this equation could be deconstructed and disproved.

Norman Conquest?

What happened at Hastings was not a 'Conquest' but merely a Norman victory in battle followed by the coronation of

William as King of England on Christmas Day 1066. Christmas, the festival of Christ's nativity, was an appropriate date for the birth of a new monarchy and all the more appropriate given that it had been on Christmas Day, in the year 800, that Charlemagne, King of the Franks had chosen to be crowned not just as King but as Emperor (the origin of the so-called 'Holy Roman Empire', successor, after a hiatus of more than 300 years, to the vanished western empire of Rome). Once again there was a self-consciousness about Norman actions in 1066 that speaks volumes about their sense of treading in the footsteps of the great. William's Christmas coronation was undoubtedly a significant event. In all likelihood it served as the final climax of the Bayeux Tapestry, now sadly mutilated at its further edge, but originally perhaps recounting the story of the Normans, from an image of Edward the Confessor enthroned and issuing instructions to Harold, via the coronation of Harold near its centre, through to the coronation of William in the aftermath of the great battle.

Yet coronation, even a coronation on Christmas Day, was a long way from Conquest. The English had lost one king, Harold, widely regarded as a usurper, only to acquire another whose usurpation had been even more sudden, more public and more violent. William was a foreigner, a bastard, and some would say a murderer. No less than Macbeth, whose real historical exploits had only recently erupted upon the stage of Scottish history, his path to the throne had been drenched in blood. Even in territorial terms, as a result of Hastings William controlled little English land save for those parts of Sussex and Kent through which his army had marched during the past three months. Like Swein after 1013, or Cnut after 1016, he might have been expected to temper invasion with accommodation. The English earls would retain their lands, now serving a Norman king rather than a Danish or an English one. The royal court would become a bilingual Anglo-Norman affair, closely linked to northern France, just as after 1016 the court of Cnut had looked as much to Scandinavian as to native English affairs. England itself would endure. Regime change would not provoke any more permanent upheaval. To this extent, there was a Norman coronation in 1066, but no Conquest. Conquest only came afterwards and was to occupy William and his men for at least a decade after the Battle of Hastings. Hastings itself, and the events of 1066, are known to us in a detail quite remarkable by the standards of medieval reportage. The events of the later 1060s and 70s, by contrast, still remain largely mysterious. We can write the history of the Norman invasion with some confidence. That of the Conquest remains conjectural and still hotly disputed.

Feudalism

Whatever the schoolbooks may claim, William did not introduce feudalism into England, let alone 'feudal' monarchy. 'Feudalism' is a modern rather than a medieval concept, invented in the eighteenth century and from the start invested with a pejorative meaning, intended not merely to describe but to castigate a system of lordly privilege and peasant subjection already, by the 1750s, on the eve of passing away. The French revolutionaries after 1789 proclaimed the destruction of feudalism to be one of their principal intentions. Even today, those invested with the French *Légion d'honneur* swear an oath in which they proclaim their determination 'to combat any enterprise which strives to reintroduce the feudal regime, and the titles and qualities which were its attributes'. In this scenario, feudalism is as far removed from the sort of strong and centralized monarchy that William of Normandy introduced into England as Socialism is from the policies of most Socialists. By scooping up not only the traditional lands of the English kings and queens, the so-called royal 'demesne', but also the lands of the vastly wealthy Godwin family and their supporters, in the aftermath of Hastings William laid the foundations of a royal estate that entirely eclipsed the wealth and power of any ruler of Anglo-Saxon England before 1066, rivalling indeed the sort of accumulated spoils of conquest to which Julius Caesar or the Roman emperors of antiquity had laid claim.

The limited resources of Edward the Confessor had ensured that, before 1066, the King struggled to keep pace with the power and wealth of his greatest subjects, above all with the Godwins. The combined wealth of the three greatest earls in England, before 1066, had been far more than anything that the King alone could muster. Hence Edward the Confessor's dependence upon negotiation, in 1042 at the time of his succession, and again in 1051–2, when alliances with the earls had enabled him to exile Earl Godwin but thereafter failed to make that exile permanent. By contrast, after 1066 William 'the Conqueror' obtained more land, more wealth and more raw power than most other rulers in English or indeed in European history. Nothing in this was 'feudal', at least not in the sense in which French historians would apply the term to a society dominated by aristocratic privilege, tending towards the breakdown of public authority, poised on the cusp of a 'feudal anarchy' in which the wishes of the few prevail over the interests of the many. Were we to think of England in terms of this sort of feudalism, then it is clear that William did not introduce feudalism to England. On the contrary, by curbing the power of the over-mighty English earls, he strangled feudalism at birth.

European Connections

The idea that William brought England for the first time into proper or natural connection with European affairs is highly misleading. England, before 1066, had never been an island entirely sundered from the European main. During the century that preceded 1066, it had faced crises provoked by Danish, Norwegian, Norman and northern French neighbours. Its laws were a combination of Germanic and late Roman. Its Church, first implanted by Frankish missionaries, looked to Rome as its ultimate authority. Edward the Confessor built Westminster Abbey and dedicated it to St Peter in direct commemoration of Rome and the prince of the apostles. He was buried there in 1066 wearing eastern silks and a pectoral cross (or 'encolpion') clearly of Byzantine workmanship, carrying images of the crucifixion and housing a relic of the True Cross, itself advertised as the greatest relic of the Christian world, acquired for the city of Constantinople in the fourth century by Helena, mother of the emperor Constantine the Great, herself reputed to have been a native of Colchester in Essex.

Edward's Queen Edith, daughter of Earl Godwin, patronized the German bishop of Wells, and may well have played a part in the election of other foreign bishops. In 1050, she had supported the removal of the south-western bishopric from Crediton to Exeter under the rule of the continentally educated bishop Leofric. Even Harold Godwinson had visited Rome and the Holy Roman Empire in Germany. His religious patronage was directed chiefly towards the canons of Waltham in Essex, living under a discipline derived from the reformed clergy of the Rhineland (the central region of the medieval Empire, named Lotharingia by association with Lothar, one of Charlemagne's grandsons). To present Harold as patriotic defender of the national cause against the foreigner, William of Normandy, is significantly to miss the point. Harold's own family owed its rise not to its Englishness but to the patronage of the Danish King Cnut. Harold's brother, Tostig, had no qualms in making common cause with the Norwegian King, Harold Hardrada, and Tostig's widow was subsequently remarried to Duke Welf of Bavaria, scion of one of the greatest aristocratic houses of eleventh-century Europe. The Battle of Hastings itself derived its name from a Sussex port where land already belonged to the monks of Fécamp, a Norman monastery which for much of the eleventh century had been ruled by a succession of Italian or Burgundian abbots.

If England, before 1066, was a great deal less isolated from Europe than is sometimes supposed, then afterwards it retained a peculiarity that does not accord with the generally accepted idea of a French-speaking aristocracy dragging the English reluctantly into the European limelight. Two great conflicts came to dominate the affairs of Europe in the late eleventh century: the disputes between popes and emperors (the so-called Investiture Contest), and the summoning of a crusade after 1095 to 'liberate' Jerusalem from the hands of the Islamic infidel. Normans, particularly the Normans of Sicily, played decisive roles in both of these conflicts. Englishmen, or indeed Norman lords with English connections, were almost entirely absent. It was the very isolation of England from the papal–imperial disputes of the 1070s and 80s, that rendered those disputes so bitter in England when they did belatedly cross the Channel. Then, as today, the English economy and English politics marched to a significantly different rhythm to that sounded elsewhere in Europe. Even the idea that the French language somehow ousted English as the mother-tongue of William's new realm fails to account for the extraordinary way in which the English language itself mutated after 1066, and in which the Normans came to adopt an early form of Franglais in their daily dealings.

English Languages

The English had long been a bilingual, or even a trilingual people, speaking in various dialects of the Anglo-Saxon language inherited from their Germanic ancestors, writing in a highly stylized dialect of West Saxon that bore little relation to living speech (historians of language would call such a split identity 'diglossic'), instructed in God's mysteries and reserving many of their more profound thoughts for Latin, the language of the Church, and required frequently to deal with peoples from Wales, Cornwall, the Scottish lowlands or Cumbria, who themselves spoke a bewildering variety of Celtic dialects. True, only those at the upper end of society were forced actively to engage with this multitude of languages. As throughout history, the ability to communicate in more than one language has always been one of the accomplishments of the educated and powerful. Even so, like French peasants who even today can converse both in patois and in standard French, the peasantry of England would have been forced to adopt at least two registers of speech, to neighbours and to outsiders. The accents of Newcastle or Yarmouth would have been as incomprehensible in Kent as the King's West Saxon writings were gobbledegook to the inhabitants of Derbyshire. The tendency when dealing with the Middle Ages is to assume that we are dealing with a more 'primitive' society than our own. On the contrary, it is clear that regional diversity encouraged a more sophisticated approach to the comprehension of language than anything which the modern BBC would credit to the British population. In our crudely post-Freudian age, those who speak in two accents, or who reserve particular thoughts for particular languages, are likely to be dismissed as frauds or victims of an 'identity crisis'. The Middle Ages knew better than this. In the eleventh century, not only the elite but anyone living on the frontiers with a region of different language or dialect would have been required to exhibit the same sort of skills that today we assume to be confined to 'impersonators' or to the bi- or trilingual inhabitants of a country such as Switzerland.

After 1066, French was added to this already rich mixture. Rather than entirely replacing English, either amongst the elite or the peasantry, French acquired an English flavour in England just as the English now acquired an entire new vocabulary of Franglais. To English speakers William might be 'royal' in his French pomp, but he was still an English 'king'. His Norman 'barons' ate French 'mutton', but it came from English 'sheep' owned by a 'lord' who ate his 'beef', whilst the lesser cuts, like 'ox tail', were left to his English servants. The English 'horses' of the Normans made them 'knights', rather than 'chevaliers', and the chief local representatives of royal authority, although assigned to Francophone 'counties', also known from the old English as 'shires', were named 'earls' not 'counts', 'sheriffs' rather than 'vicomtes'.

At Peterborough, despite or perhaps precisely because of a massive and deliberate implantation of Norman knights under a new Norman abbot, the monks continued to maintain their own version of the *Anglo-Saxon Chronicle*, written in the language of Alfred or of Aethelred for a century after the 'Conquest' of 1066. By the time that this archaic relic was finally discontinued, in or shortly after 1154, new forms of English were already being recorded, not just for use by the illiterate peasantry but for the entertainment of those far higher up the social scale, written in the new Middle English tongue that made its first appearance less than a century after Hastings and whose chief characteristic was its strong regional diversity. This was an English far closer to the language actually spoken in the shires than the highly formalized Anglo-Saxon of Wessex used in most vernacular writing before 1066. Far from destroying the English language, the Norman Conquest vastly enriched and transformed it.

In our haste to uncover the roots of the modern English language, we should not ignore the effects that Anglicization had upon French. The Normans of 1066 already spoke and wrote a language that was subtly different from that of the inhabitants of other parts of France. The Conquest greatly heightened this distinction, so much so that within a hundred years it is questionable whether a Norman or French baron learning his French in England would have been anything but a laughing stock had he spoken in his native accents in Paris or the fairs of Champagne. Dialects carry with them a multitude of social and economic presuppositions, so that the assumptions made by a modern German about someone speaking in Dutch or Viennese dialect or Swiss-German will be clouded by all manner of cultural assumptions, just as the accents of modern-day Devon or Glasgow or Essex evoke very different reactions amongst English-speakers. In the twelfth century, even the son of an English king, of French birth but brought up in England, was apparently mocked because he spoke French not after the school of Paris but after that of Marlborough in

Wiltshire. Chaucer's prioress, two centuries later, was equally ridiculed for speaking French after the school of Stratford-atte-Bow, perhaps the first recorded instance of an Essex or estuarial accent, 'because French of Paris was to her unknown'.

Like the English in India, not only did the Normans in England acquire a series of English loan words, the eleventh-century equivalent of the 'bungalows' and 'tiffins' of the Raj, but the language which they themselves bequeathed to their English subjects as Norman French was itself just as strange and foreign to Frenchmen of the twelfth and thirteenth centuries as is the English spoken today in many foreign call-centres. By 1200, Norman French itself was fossilizing into a high-status language, used in noble speech and writing, rather like the written language of Anglo-Saxon Wessex: no longer a true vernacular, but a high-status acquisition taught in schools and learned from books rather than from living speech.

Norman Efficiency

Finally, the idea that 1066 ushered in a new phase of Anglo-Norman 'efficiency', with (in the words of the nineteenth-century sage and reactionary Thomas Carlyle) the 'pot-bellied equanimity' of the Anglo-Saxons easily mastered by the 'heroic toil' of their new Norman drill serjeants, is itself badly in need of rethinking. The military caste of the Norman Conquest has undoubtedly led to the portrayal of the Normans themselves as a warrior nation, dressed in chain mail even when in bed, plotting lordly proto-Thatcherite schemes to impose order upon a chaotic society. Out went the hobbit burrows of the Anglo-Saxons and in came the newly pre-fabricated efficiency of castles, counting houses and dungeons. Norman hard tack was substituted for Anglo-Saxon cakes and ale.

In reality, the myth of Norman administrative efficiency is precisely that: a myth. To cope with Viking attack, Anglo-Saxon England had developed a sophisticated concept of social respon-sibility in which many within society were required to contribute to the burden of society's defence. The King served as collector of taxes such as the Danegeld (intended to buy off the Danes), Heregeld for the payment of ships and their crews, pontage for the building and maintenance of bridges, and wall-money (later known as 'murage') for the building and upkeep of town defences. By contrast, after 1066, the tendency was for the new Norman kings to treat such revenues as perquisites from which their own expenses could be met and, so far as their greater lords were concerned, as obligations from which favoured friends might be exempted. The outcome was a rapid decline in the capacity of taxation to raise the funds necessary for the task in hand, and consequently the imposition of an ever heavier burden upon an ever dwindling base of potential taxpayers.

There are parallels here with the history of taxation in the last years of the Roman Empire, when increasing demands for taxation were placed upon an ever dwindling number of tax payers. Thanks largely to the fact that England experienced no threats comparable to that posed by the Vikings to the kings of Wessex, or by the Germanic tribes to the Roman Empire, public works after 1066 somehow muddled through. Responsibility for bridges, for example, particularly for those such as Rochester's, which had an annoying tendency to fall down, was placed unfairly but with some degree of success upon the local people with most interest in maintaining communications, which in practice meant those owning land on either side of the bridge. This is nonetheless far from arguing that the state became more rather than less interventionist after 1066. On the contrary, in many respects, save when the King himself could hope to gain from the proceeds of taxation, justice or public works, there was less attention paid after 1066 to even such seeming social necessities as the maintenance of roads and bridges, which were, to a very large extent, as before the seventh century, left to take care of themselves.

Domesday
Set against this miniaturist view of the Norman state, we have one massive and seemingly incontrovertible piece of evidence:

Domesday Book, still proudly displayed in the Public Record Office in London as the greatest archival monument to the Norman Conquest. As is widely known, there are at least two books now stored in the Public Records described as 'Domesday': 'Great' Domesday and 'Little' Domesday, the first covering most of England and parts of Wales, the second covering East Anglia in particularly close detail. A third volume, housed in Exeter Cathedral, known as 'Exon Domesday', appears to supply an earlier stage of the survey of the western counties, which were later revised in Great Domesday. Other such 'satellites' record various stages in the inquest as it proceeded in the various part of England. As has become apparent in recent years, we badly need to distinguish the Domesday survey itself from the 'Book' in which it resulted. As has become equally apparent, the survey would have been inconceivable had it not been for Anglo-Saxon precedent. Far from testifying to Norman efficiency, Domesday actually reveals an enormous amount about the wealth and sophistication of the old English state. The fact, for example, that every manor could be assessed at a valuation applied not only to 1086, the year in which the survey was made, but to the date of the death of Edward the Confessor in 1066, and that such valuations were available for each of the shires of England, speaks volumes about the sophistication of Anglo-Saxon record keeping, and in particular about the need by the Anglo-Saxon state to maintain regular geld rolls, reporting the potential financial obligations of each local unit of assessment. Had Domesday Book not survived, it is highly unlikely that historians would be willing to credit its existence. Certainly, no such detailed accumulation of information survives for any other part of eleventh-century Europe. We would need to look to ancient Rome for a similar level of sophistication and to eleventh-century China for a contemporary regime capable of compiling records on this massive scale and with this degree of detail. Both the extent and the detail of Domesday are chiefly functions of Anglo-

Saxon traditions of local government and record keeping rather than of Norman 'efficiency'.

The fact that the survey was made at all testifies to the limited number of royal officials involved in its making. If such surveys were to be completed, they were best made in haste. Anything more deliberate or involving larger numbers of officials was likely to remain unfinished, as kings were to discover in the thirteenth century, when both King John and King Edward I embarked upon much more ambitious surveys than Domesday, both of them so extensive and involving so many pairs of hands that neither was ever completed. Domesday as passed down to us was made by about seven circuits of commissioners, each comprising no more than half a dozen persons, written up in the case of Great Domesday Book, for most of the shires of England, by a single editorial hand. In short, it took a 'government' of less than forty persons, virtually none of whom was permanently in 'government' employ, to make both the survey and the book. What we have is evidence of a tiny and hence easily managed bureaucracy, not of a massive appa-ratus of state. Nor was Domesday by any means a complete survey of England: it omits most parts north of the Mersey and the two largest cities, Winchester and London. Even within those parts that were surveyed, the apparent monotonous uniformity of each entry – who owns what land, who owned it previously, what is it worth, what was it worth in 1066, how many hides of land, how many tenants, mills, acres of woodland or pasture, etc. – masks very considerable variation between one circuit of surveyors and another, and even between one estate and another. It is apparent, for example, that the greater ecclesiastical barons, such as the bishop of Worcester or the abbot of Bury St Edmunds, were responsible for making their own returns and in the process for exaggerating or playing down their own particular rights and resources.

Far from being a monument to Norman efficiency, Domesday is a highly fallible resource made possible only by the solid Anglo-Saxon foundations upon which it was based.

Perhaps most remarkably of all, despite the identification of its principal scribe as a clerk in the service of the bishop of Durham, despite intensive statistical analysis of the social and economic information that it supplies, and despite more than a hundred years of scholarship that has produced a small library of books and articles devoted to nothing but Domesday, we still have no very certain or agreed idea of why the survey was made or what purpose it was intended to serve. Was it, as early commentators supposed, a Geld Book, intended as part of a reassessment of national taxation? Was it linked to the invasion scare of 1085 and to the need to assess individual baronial resources so as to billet vast numbers of troops in a realm threatened by the King of Denmark? Was it intended as a vast confirmation charter, recording in documentary form the state of landholdings built up piecemeal since the 1060s, in order for the holders of these estates to render homage to the King, by oaths taken at Salisbury in the summer of 1086? None of these explanations has proved entirely satisfactory.

What is clear is that neither the survey nor the book marked an end to the process of Norman colonization in England, and that far from being some sort of valedictory offering or successful shareholder statement presented to King William towards the close of his reign, Domesday testifies to a real flesh and blood process of conquest and to real suffering on the part of those whose land was conquered and who now, in many cases as jurors to the inquest, were called upon to report the process of their own dispossession. What one modern historian has described as the 'tormented voices' of history's poor and put-upon do occasionally whisper their sad tales from Domesday's folios. Such is the case of the Buckinghamshire tenant of William fitz Ansculf, who according to the local jurors held his land at Marsh Gibbon 'harshly and wretchedly'. The most detailed documentary monument to Norman success is itself a mausoleum to the vanished hopes of the Anglo-Saxons without whose assistance it could never have been made.

Fate or Accident

There is a natural tendency when writing about the past to assume an inevitability or internal logic to past events, that what was had to be. Attempts to challenge such comfortable assumptions generally take the form of 'counterfactuals', or 'what ifs?', of which, for England after 1066, two questions pose themselves ahead of all others: what might have happened had Harold won the Battle of Hastings, and what would have been the outcome had Normandy and England remained divided realms despite William the Conqueror? The first of these questions invites images of a long-haired line of Harold's descendents, buoyed up by victory at Hastings, but surely, in the longer term, brought low either by foreign invaders (the King of Norway, the King of Denmark, the Count of Boulogne, or any others of those who, even before 1066, had expressed an interest in acquiring the wealth of England), or by civil war provoked by the Godwins' own hubristic hoarding of wealth. Ireland might provide an apt comparison here. Theoretically united by the late eleventh century under a race of native high kings, one of whom is reputed to have fought alongside Tostig at Stamford Bridge, Ireland was in practice divided between the various claimants to high kingship, which led, sooner rather than later, to foreign intervention and, a century after Hastings, to a full-scale English invasion. The destinies of Scotland and Wales, as we shall see, followed a similar pattern. The eleventh and twelfth centuries, indeed, can be regarded in general as a period during which European and above all French traditions of lordship were extended across the North Sea world, not just through the Norman conquest of England, but through the conversion of Iceland to Christianity, the Danish conquest of Norway, and the forced incorporation of the Baltic regions of Prussia, Lithuania and Sweden into European affairs.

The Godwinsons were not entirely exterminated by the Norman victory in 1066. Though Harold, Leofwine and Gyrth, sons of Earl Godwin, were all killed at Hastings, three weeks after the death of their brother Tostig at Stamford

Bridge, Harold left a mother, at least two women claiming to be his widow and several children by both of these marriages. In 1068, his mother fled to Flatholme in the Bristol Channel and thence into exile at the court of her nephew, Svein of Denmark. Harold's sons by his first marriage attempted armed landings from Ireland in 1068 and 1069. A son by his second marriage, also named Harold, was as late as 1098 engaged in attacks by the Norse King Magnus 'Barefoot' Olafson against the Norman settlers of Anglesey. Meanwhile, Harold's daughter Gytha had been married to Vladimir Monomakh, prince of Kiev, becoming sister-in-law to the Holy Roman Emperor, Henry IV, kinswoman to the emperors of Byzantium, and the begetter of several dynasties of princes and princesses across Russia. There is some suggestion that Harold, via Gytha and her Russian offspring, was the ancestor not only of the future queen Isabella of England, wife of King Edward II, but of the composer Modest Mussorgsky and the aristocratic Russian anarchist, Peter Kropotkin. Another of Harold's daughters, lover of Count Alan Rufus of Brittany, gave birth to a daughter who married into the Norman family of Aincourt and thus produced a minor line of Nottinghamshire gentry, more than happy, within forty years of Hastings, to commemorate their English royal ancestry.

At much the same time that the Aincourts were raising a funeral monument to Harold's granddaughter, Harold himself reappeared in England, or so it was alleged. Far from dying at Hastings, being interred on the seashore at the high tide mark or carried off for royal burial at his foundation of Waltham in Essex, he had recovered from his wounds and, after a period of continental wandering, returned to live as a hermit outside Dover, eventually moving to Chester where he died in 1176 or 1177, presumably aged about 170, his identity confided to only a close circle of initiates. As late as 1332, a Welsh chronicler reported that the body of Harold, dressed in golden spurs and crown, had been found at Chester, still incorrupt and smelling as sweetly as the day on which it was buried: a clear sign that

Harold was now amongst God's saints. Such reports fit into a common pattern of survival myth that can be traced from the legends of King Arthur, to ideas of the survival of members of the Russian imperial family after 1917, of Adolf Hitler after 1945, or even of Elvis Presley restored, beyond the grave, to perfect voice and waistline. Ultimately, such legends derive from the love of a good story and to some extent from religious impulses, specifically from the idea of Christ the risen king, triumphing over death. What is most interesting about the survival myth of King Harold is that it should have been confined to Chester and a very narrow audience: those disconcerted by the new style of kingship pioneered after the 1150s by Henry II. If in Wales Harold was remembered as a saint, in England he was commemorated, not as a threat to William I and his heirs, but chiefly as a mighty warrior against the Welsh. Many inscribed stones had been raised by him on the Welsh Marches, so it was alleged, still visible when Gerald of Wales toured the region in the 1180s, stating that 'Here Harold defeated the Welsh'. To this extent, both the Welsh and English began to take comfort from Harold's memory. Harold himself, meanwhile, had become an irrelevance. Rather than threaten the foundations of Norman or Plantagenet kingship, he and his family had been fully subsumed within English myth.

Far more intriguing from a counterfactual perspective is the question of what would have happened had William of Normandy died soon after 1066, leaving England and Normandy once again to go their own separate ways. Here, no doubt, much the same would have happened as in the reign of King Cnut: a brief period of North Sea imperialism, the promotion of various foreigners to land and power in England, but thereafter the rapid collapse of this empire and a restoration of the status quo. It is here that the truly momentous nature of the changes in English society after 1066 come into focus. There seems little doubt that, to begin with, William's intention was to govern England from Normandy, rather as Cnut had ruled from Denmark, treating England as an imperial fiefdom subject to foreign control. William had already shown a willingness in Maine, where he had extended his authority, to work in harmony with the local aristocracy who retained their lands and wealth, albeit under a new Norman administration. Like Julius Caesar before him (and we should remember here that there were many at William's court who had read Caesar's *Gallic Wars*), William used the English earls as local 'feodati' to control English tribal loyalties. Meanwhile, he retained a number of the old king's officials, most notably the chancellor, Regenbald, who now issued writs and charters in the name of King William just as he had previously issued them for King Edward and King Harold, composed both in Latin and in the English vernacular. At Christmas 1066, William was crowned in the old English style albeit, like Harold, in Westminster rather than at Winchester, the traditional coronation church of the West Saxons. It is symptomatic of William's later difficulties that the Norman soldiers standing guard outside the coronation misinterpreted the shouts of acclamation raised by the English assembly within, assuming that the crowd was baying for his blood. A massacre of the English by the Normans was only narrowly averted.

Rebellion

After 1066, there were numerous rebellions or threats of rebellion in England, and almost as many invasion scares. The widespread fear of an English uprising, or that Danish, Flemish or Irish war bands were about to repeat William's coup at Hastings, tells us a great deal about the insecurities and guilt-ridden nature of the first twenty years of Norman rule. A millennium later, and Hastings appears as a mighty and permanent paragraph break in English history. At the time, there was no guarantee that the victors of Hastings would not themselves be swept away in the subsequent chaos of plunder and revenge. In fact, none of the rebellions or invasions attempted after 1066 amounted to much. Their failure has been blamed upon the incompetence or churlish indifference of the

English themselves, with Carlyle's heroic Norman toil once again triumphing over Anglo-Saxon 'pot-bellied sloth'. In fact, the failure of the English resistance can be traced to a number of different causes. It was poorly coordinated, reminding us of the deep personal and regional divisions that had long been apparent in English society. It was launched by families that had themselves been traumatized by the events at Hastings and which in many cases had already been robbed of their strongest or most dynamic male warriors. In a single day at Hastings, William had cut off not only England's head but its strong forearm.

The outcome was a series of rebellions, inadequately prepared and poorly led, beginning at Exeter in 1068, via risings in the north in 1069 brutally suppressed by William, through to the so-called revolt of the earls in 1075, when a rising by the Northumbrian Earl Waltheof, the Breton, Ralph, Earl of East Anglia, and Roger, earl of Hereford, was decisively crushed by King William's loyal viceroy, Lanfranc, Archbishop of Canterbury, without the King even having to set foot in England. This did not entirely end resistance. As late as 1085, there were fears that Cnut IV of Denmark, cousin of the late King Harold and son of Danish King Svein Estrithsson, who had attempted invasions of England in both 1069 and 1070, would mount a major expedition to England in league with his father-in-law, Count Robert of Flanders. In the remote fenlands, at Peterborough in 1070, and then in a final desperate stand at Ely in 1071, a local landowner named Hereward earned a heroic reputation for himself as a captain of English 'freedom-fighters'. Like the Jews in their great fortress at Masada in the histories of Josephus (one of the most frequently read ancient histories, not least because it appeared to supply an alternative history of Christ's Judea to that available from the Bible), Hereward and his men were forced to watch from Ely as the Normans slowly built a causeway towards them, eventually taking the island with great bloodshed. According to the later semi-fictionalized account of these events, known as the *Deeds of Hereward*,

Hereward himself was pardoned by King William. Another early historian, however, tells us that he was murdered in France by a band of disgruntled Norman soldiers. In any event, like Harold Godwinson, Hereward very rapidly faded from reality into myth. According to the *Deeds of Hereward*, one of his first acts of heroism was to fight with a ferocious bear, offspring of one of the last talking bears in the north, from whose acts of rape were descended the kings of Norway. After that as an introduction, anyone who believes much else in the *Deeds of Hereward* does so very much at their peril.

English rebellion itself slowly faded from violent reality to distantly remembered legend. Modern historians, who like to speculate on what might have happened in 1940 had the Germans crossed the Channel, may find the events of the 1070s instructive. The English did attempt resistance, and very brave resistance it must have been. William the Conqueror, for all his claims to be the heir to Caesar or Charlemagne, was a brutal enemy. In the 1050s, when the men of Alençon in southern Normandy had rebelled against his ducal rule, manning the walls of their town and banging on pelts to taunt William for his ancestry as a tanner's bastard, William exacted a vicious revenge, having their hands and feet cut off. In the winter of 1069, when he led an army across the Pennines to suppress northern resistance, almost unimaginable horrors were unleashed: pillage, deliberate starvation, all of the more ghastly accompaniments to military action against a civilian population. This was a war against English terrorists, conducted with all the brutality that such wars tend to engender. According to the chronicler Orderic Vitalis, himself of mixed birth as the son of an English mother and a Norman father, raised in Shropshire and later a monk of St-Evroult in Normandy, this 'harrying of the north' was a crime in which William succumbed to the cruellest promptings of revenge, condemning more than 100,000 Christian men, women and children to death by starvation, besides countless others slain by fire or the sword. Though Orderic's statistics are not to be

relied upon, before the days of war-crimes tribunals or the
Geneva Convention, brutality and terror were not disguised
but, on the contrary, deliberately advertised as the hallmarks of
successful warfare.

William certainly brought a brutal enthusiasm to the task in
hand, but it is arguable that the English themselves were inured
to brutality. The north of England, even before 1066, had
seethed with vengeance killings and blood feud between the
houses of Bamburgh and York. Even at the English royal court,
there had been murders and conspiracies that rendered England
in many ways a far less chivalrous society than the supposedly
brutal society of pre-Conquest Normandy. With their songs
of Roland and Charlemagne, it is arguable the Normans were
already acquiring a veneer of chivalry and polite manners,
imported for the most part from further south, from the
princely courts of Aquitaine and ultimately from Spain, from
the court of the Arab caliphs. It was the distant civilizing
influence of Islam in the eleventh century which ultimately did
most to smooth away the brutalities of European warfare. In
particular, wars between equals were henceforth to be
conducted openly and according to some sense of legal
propriety. Peasants and lesser peoples might be tortured,
starved and treated as the brute animals that they were
perceived to be, but women, children and high status prisoners
were not deliberately to be harmed. Even the most significant
of noble enemies were to be imprisoned or ransomed, not
mutilated or murdered.

These were rules obeyed as much in the breach as the
observance. William did not order the execution of any close
member of the ruling dynasty of Wessex or even of the
Godwinsons. Indeed, he seems to have striven to preserve a
fiction of courtesy, even when members of these families
were caught in the most blatant of conspiracies. But when
Earl Waltheof of Northumbria rebelled in 1075, the outcome
was judicial execution. Waltheof's beheading was treated in
some circles as an act of martyrdom, yet another reason,

perhaps, for William to tread a more chivalrous path in future, to deny rebels either the crown of martyrdom or the oxygen of publicity. Henceforth, for unmitigated brutality we would need to turn away from civil war or disputes between Christian knights, to the frontiers of Wales or the more distant parts of Scotland and Ireland. Here, the Normans behaved as if the local population lay quite outside the rules of Christian warfare. Being barbarians, who themselves failed to observe the chivalric niceties, such peoples were to be suppressed with maximum prejudice. Long before American frontiersmen invented the rituals of scalping, English soldiers on the Welsh Marches had turned head hunter. In the early 1060s, Harold Godwinson had sent the head of the Welsh King Gruffydd to Edward the Confessor. After 1066, this brutal trophy-collecting remained a regular feature of Anglo-Welsh warfare. By the 1230s, the English crown was paying a bounty of a shilling a head for all hostile Welshmen decapitated on the Marches.

Collaboration

In England, meanwhile, the earliest phase of violent pillage after 1066 eventually yielded place to accommodation and collaboration. The English themselves were tamed. They were also renamed. The new spirit of collaboration is perhaps most clearly marked in personal naming patterns adopted after 1066. Even within families of pure English descent, the Alfreds, Aethelreds and Edwards of the 1060s, within twenty years were naming their sons Geoffrey, Richard and above all William, adopting the names of England's new Norman master race. By the 1170s, so ubiquitous were such names that the eldest son of King Henry II was able to hold a special session of his Christmas court at which only men named William were allowed entrance. There were more than 110 knights at this feast. How many English children, one wonders, might have been christened Napoleon or Adolf had later invasion plans come to fruition? How many Caribbean children might not

now be named Wesley, Washington or Winston were it not for
the accidents of imperialism?

Only in the remoter parts of England, and in the lowest
levels of society, did old English personal names survive.
Cumberland in the twelfth century could still boast men named
Uhtred, Gamel or Orm, according to pre-Conquest tradition.
One of these Orms, a priest from the East Midlands, wrote
what today is the very first surviving book composed in the
new Middle English, a highly indigestible collection of rhyming
homilies known as the '*Ormulum*'. In East Anglia, likewise,
old English names survived. The shrine of St William of
Norwich was attended, from the 1140s onwards by a succession
of pilgrims with names like Lewin, Godric, Gilliva, Godiva,
Glewus, Colobern, Godwin Creme and Stanard Wrancbeard:
names that are defiantly English rather than Norman, and
which transport us to a world far removed from the cosmopolitan fashions of the Anglo-Norman court. At the court, no
son of a king of England received an English baptismal name
for nearly two hundred years after 1066. Then in the 1230s,
things began to change.

Reverse snobbery inclines today's upper classes to name
their children Harry or Jack or Gus, favouring estuarial earth-
iness over parvenu pretension. The Right Honourable
Anthony Wedgwood Benn Viscount Stansgate is transformed
into Tony Benn the people's friend. In the 1230s, a combination of piety and patriotism led the English King Henry III
to turn away from Norman or French to English naming
patterns. Henry's eldest sons, themselves the great-great-
great-great-grandsons of William the Conqueror, were
named Edward and Edmund, in commemoration of Edward
the Confessor, venerated at Westminster, and St Edmund,
king and martyr, of Bury St Edmunds, the greatest royal
saints of the Anglo-Saxon past. Perhaps nothing so clearly
marks closure to the violence and inter-racial strife of the
Norman Conquest than the fact that in 1272, two hundred
years after the death of Edward the Confessor, one of these

English-named sons of Henry III, King Edward I, ascended the English throne.

The Cataclysm of the Conquest

In the meantime, we should never underestimate the cataclysm that overwhelmed English society after 1066. The phrase 'The Norman Conquest' should not be allowed to reduce events to euphemistic miniature, masking a period of violence and expropriation never to be repeated in English history, even at the height of the Tudor 'revolution' of the 1520s or the Civil War of the 1640s. The 'Conquest' after 1066 invites comparison not so much with the later history of England as with the nineteenth-century 'Scramble for Africa', with England as the land raped and pillaged by foreign colonialists. In part through simple greed, in part from fear of an English backlash, the victors of Hastings very rapidly shifted from accommodation to conquest. Within twenty years, they had dispossessed all but a tiny number of the greater English landholders. Our chief reference point here, the Domesday survey of 1086, makes plain that, by the 1080s, mostly during the 1070s, something like ninety per cent of land held in 1066 by English thegns or English lords had been seized by King William and his followers.

The process of seizure was neither uniform nor well-documented. Some of the greater honours carved out from the spoils of 1066 were centrally organized. Thus in Sussex, guarding the Channel approaches, in Holderness, protecting the Humber estuary from the threat from Scandinavia, or in Cheshire and the Welsh Marches, looking towards the threat from the Welsh and the Irish, massive new estates were created for William's most trusted followers. The King's half-brothers Robert of Mortain and Odo of Bayeux obtained vast swathes of land, for Robert in Devon, Cornwall and Dorset, for Odo in Kent. Hugh of Avranches was granted not only Chester and the northern parts of the Welsh March but land in twenty English counties, the origins of the future great earldom of

Chester. Roger of Montgomery, another of King William's
closest lieutenants, scooped not only two of the new divisions
of Sussex, known appropriately enough as the Sussex 'rapes'
(from the Anglo-Saxon word for the 'rope' which marked out
the meeting place of a local court), but a large part of Shropshire
and the town of Shrewsbury, protecting the central Welsh
Marches. All of these estates, known then and since as
'honours', were royally approved. The honours system, then
as now, depended upon the crown. Today it involves the
bestowal of medals and titles. In the 1060s and for many
centuries thereafter it involved the much more solid resource
of land.

Even so, not all of the great post-Conquest honours were
created or even necessarily sanctioned by the King. In some
parts of England, in Yorkshire, for example, following the
brutal harrying of the north, equally vast estates were carved
out by Norman lords acting on their own initiative, grabbing
what they could, evicting the former English landlords, and
where necessary defending their plunder against other
Normans who might otherwise seize the spoils. This was a
Darwinian struggle, in which dog ate dog. It was still in full
progress as late as 1086, when the Domesday survey reveals
large numbers of manors still disputed between two or more
Norman lords. Indeed, one purpose behind Domesday may
have been the identification and regulation of such disputes,
with the survey, made as the result of cooperation between
king and barons, being intended to draw a line under the
chaos of the 1060s and 70s and to lend a veneer of royal
approval to a process that, at the time, had lain far beyond the
control of the King, in the hands of many dozens of greedy
and unscrupulous local land-grabbers. If the Battle of
Hastings marked a Norman victory rather than a Norman
'Conquest', then in the 1070s and 80s there was not so much a
single Conquest as a whole host of conquerors seizing what
spoils they could. This was the greatest seizure of loot in
English history, speedier and even more intense than the

process by which the Angles, Saxons and Jutes had conquered post-Roman Britain five centuries before.

In the process, many of the territorial divisions of late Anglo-Saxon England were melted down and entirely reforged. Some of the Norman newcomers laid claim to the estates of particular English lords. In Northamptonshire, for example, the lands of an Englishman named Bardi were claimed virtually in their entirety by the new Norman bishop of Lincoln. Those of a woman named Gytha formed the nucleus of the new Northamptonshire honour of William Peverel, those of a thegn named Northmann, the estate of Robert de Bucy. More often, however, the tenurial map of 1066 was simply torn up and new estates created from the manors and lands of a diversity of Anglo-Saxon landholders. In Suffolk for example, the lands previously held by one of the greatest of Anglo-Saxon thegns, Eadric of Laxfield, were divided between at least four major new Norman honours. In the process, there was a massive transfer of land out of the hands of the late Anglo-Saxon earls and into those of the King and his immediate circle. Whereas the landed resources of Edward the Confessor had been dwarfed by those of the Godwinsons and the earls of Mercia and Northumbria, King William by 1086 was far and away the richest landowner in England, with ten times the wealth even of his half-brothers who themselves, with £5,000 of land, held twice as much as the £2,400 of the next richest landholding family, the Montgomeries.

The outcome was a total reversal of the baronial stranglehold over royal action that had done so much to create the inertia and tensions of the 1050s and early 1060s. By the 1080s, it was the King rather than his earls and barons who held the clear balance both of wealth and power. The more successful baronial families acquired estates across England, scattered collections of manors, rents and lands which thereafter had somehow to be controlled by a single lord. One unintended consequence of this shattering of the landscape into many thousands of family holdings was to emphasize and enhance the significance of royal authority. The primitive institutions of the state and of royal government, the sheriff, the hundred bailiff and the courts of the hundred and county were the means by which an intensely localized society could be made to respond to the needs of landlords with estates now scattered not only across England but on either side of the Channel.

Barons holding directly from the King are known as tenants-in-chief. They could be super rich, modestly wealthy or relatively poor. Thus there was a vast distinction to be drawn between a man like Hugh of Avranches, ancestor of the later earls of Chester, with over £1,000 of land recorded in Domesday Book, and a humble serjeant like the ancestor of Roland the farter, confined to a few hundred acres of land in the Suffolk manor of Hemingstone, held for the service of making a leap, a whistle and a fart before the King every year on Christmas Day. The services attached to such serjeanties are often peculiar – keeping the king's hounds or hawks, polishing the king's boar spear – and some have survived even into modern times. At the coronation of King Edward VII in 1911, for example, the Dymoke family continued to advance claims to serve as King's champion. The office of champion was a relatively modern one, first recorded at the coronation of Richard II in 1377. Even so, serjeanties held for service as baker, cook and crossbowman were already in existence by the 1080s.

Such men were small fry, of course. England after 1066 was dominated by between a dozen and twenty great families, many of them closely related to the King. Between them, these families, of which about a dozen were in due course granted title as earl, controlled more than half of the wealth of England. Inequality has always been an English characteristic, and the vast disparities in landed wealth between rich and poor were far greater in the eleventh century than in the early twentieth century when inheritance taxes were first devised, in theory as a means of levelling the playing field. As earls, the first being the King's half-brothers Odo, Earl of Kent, and Robert, Count of Mortain, and his cousin William fitz Osbern, Earl of

Hereford, such men had an obligation to oversee the King's affairs in their own particular region or county. In practice, the duties of an earldom were far outweighed by its privileges, save at moments of particular national crisis.

Beneath the tenants-in-chief, reaching downwards to the humblest of freemen and those barely distinguishable from peasants, stretched a vast array of lesser tenants, holding some-times, as with the serjeants, directly from the King, more often from one or other of the greater tenants-in-chief. The most significant of these subtenants were the knights, holding their lands in return for military service. By the last decade of the eleventh century, such landholdings were already being described as 'fees' or 'knights' fees', and in theory their holders were obliged to send a knight for forty days of military service each year whenever summoned to do so by their lord. Once again, however, theory and practice swiftly diverged. Some knights' fees represented extensive landed estates, the bare minimum required to support a knight, his horse and his armour being assessed at about £5 of land. In practice, almost as soon as the knight's fee first emerges into the light of day, in the returns to a survey conducted on the estates of the Archbishop of Canterbury, we find men assessed not just for whole but fractional fees: a half, a quarter, later sometimes as little as an eighth or a twentieth of a knight's fee. Clearly, someone holding an eighth of a fee was not responsible for supplying an eighth of a physical knight to serve in his lord's army. What was being assessed here was not a military but a fiscal unit.

Military Organisation

In other words, although we seem after 1086 to find a classic system of landholding in which tenants hold land from barons and barons hold from the King, all owing military service rather than money and all bound together in a feudal 'pyramid' with the King at its top and a broad array of knights at its base, this classical formulation had very little to do with the way that armies were actually raised, even as early as the 1090s. Money rents were already a factor in landholding, and what appear to be military units of land are often best regarded as simple fiscal responsibilities. William the Conqueror paid mercenaries to accompany him to England in 1066, and a mercenary or paid element made up a large element of the professional side of the King's army ever after. Knights' fees go entirely unmentioned in the Domesday survey, and the very first reference to the emergence of fixed quotas of knights owed by each of the major tenants-in-chief, in a writ supposedly sent by William I to the abbot of Evesham, occurs in what is almost certainly a later forgery concocted long after the events which it purports to describe.

In reality, we have no very clear evidence for the emergence of this quota system until the reign of Henry II, after 1154. We may assume its existence at an earlier date, not least because by 1135 it appears that the majority of the greater barons expected to answer for round numbers of knights, generally measured in units of ten, answering for twenty, fifty or sixty knights. That such quotas ever served in the field, however, or that they were used as the basis for levying taxation on barons who did not themselves serve, remains unproved until the 1150s. One scenario, rather likelier than the traditional presentation of such things, is that barons and the greater churchmen answered for fixed numbers of knights to the King, and were responsible for ensuring that a certain number of men turned up in their retinues whenever summoned, if necessary by paying mercenaries to make up their 'quotas'. This would explain why lists of such 'quotas' begin to appear in monastic records, for example at Canterbury by the 1090s and why the King had cause to complain, again at Canterbury in the 1090s, not of the quantity but of the poor quality of the knight service that was being supplied. Only at a later date, and only really with nationwide effect from the 1150s, did kings begin to charge a tax (known as 'scutage' or 'shield money') on barons who failed to supply the requisite quota of knights, arranging for this money to be paid to fully professional mercenary soldiers rather than have the baron make up his service by paying any old rag-tag or bobtail retainer.

The classic formulation of the 'feudal' pyramid ignores other inconvenient or untidy aspects of reality. With the barons holding from the king, and knights holding from barons, it was clearly necessary for the barons themselves to recruit large numbers of knights. To begin with, in the immediate aftermath of the conquest, such knights were often drawn from the tenantry who in Normandy already served a particular baron. Thus knights with close links to the Montgomery family in Normandy naturally gravitated to the estates of the Montgomeries in Shropshire (amongst them, the father of the chronicler Orderic Vitalis, which explains Orderic's later move from Shropshire back to St-Evroult and the Montgomery heart-lands in southern Normandy). Those Bretons who distinguished themselves in England after 1066, such as the ancestors of the Vere family in Essex, future earls of Oxford, or the future earls of Richmond in Yorkshire and East Anglia, tended to recruit other lesser Bretons into their service. The honour of Boulogne carved out in England, especially in Essex after 1066, recruited large numbers of knights originally associated with the north-ernmost parts of France or southern Flanders. It has been argued that the consequence here was the emergence of a series of power blocks based upon pre-existing French loyalties. The Bretons stuck together. Normans from the valley of the river Seine tended to stand apart from those from lower Normandy and the Cotentin peninsula. Such may have been the case for a gener-ation or so after 1066. Surveying the rebels of 1075 who had joined the Breton Ralph, Earl of East Anglia in rising against the king, Archbishop Lanfranc was able to describe them collec-tively as 'Breton turds'. What is more significant, however, is that such regional identities very swiftly began to break down in the melting pot of post-Conquest England. Normans consorted with Bretons, Bretons married English or Norman wives. By the reign of Henry I, after 1100, it is clear that, within England, those of diverse Norman and Breton background fought

together or, on occasion, on opposing sides, without any clear
pattern imposed by pre-existing regional loyalties in northern
France. Why was this so?

The most obvious answer lies in a shortage of appropriate
manpower after 1066. The King had to ensure that those to
whom he gave great estates were both loyal and competent.
Hence, for example, the extraordinary way in which Roger of
Montgomery was promoted not only to command two of the
rapes of Sussex, Arundel and Chichester, in the front-line of
defence against attack by sea, but also to a vast estate in
Shropshire, on the Welsh Marches, clearly in reward for past
service but carrying with it future responsibility for the defence
of yet another strategically vital frontier. Roger, accustomed to
the frontier fighting of southern Normandy, was chosen to fill
the shoes of three men presumably because he was one of the
few men whom the King could trust. If loyal commanders were
few and far between at the upper end of society, then lower
down, too, it was hard to find the competent knights that any
great lord would be anxious to attract to his service. In the rebel-
infested regions of the fens, within the estates of the monks of
Ely and Peterborough, where the English had several times
mounted armed resistance after 1066, a deliberate attempt seems
to have been made to swamp the countryside with Norman
knights. Enormous numbers of small estates were carved out,
burdened with knight service and handed over to practically all
comers from northern France. A similar and deliberate mass
importation of outsiders might explain why the West Country,
yet another forum of rebellion, was colonized by knights, many
of them from the frontier regions of south-west Normandy,
granted in England the so-called 'fees of Mortain', held from
their overlord, William the Conqueror's half-brother, Count
Robert of Mortain, and possessing the value of only two-thirds
of an ordinary knight's fee elsewhere in the country.

These lesser knights of eastern and south-western England,
probably from the very start, lacked the landed resources ever
to serve effectively on campaign. It was their sheer quantity

rather than their particular competence which won them their English land. As this suggests, there was never a shortage of land-hungry knights, younger sons, ambitious outsiders or thrusting members of the lower ranks. As a simple commodity, knights were, if not quite ten a penny, then certainly bred up in enormous numbers within eleventh-century society. A treaty between England and the Count of Flanders, first negotiated in 1101 and thereafter renewed on a regular basis throughout the next seventy years, provided for the King of England to pay an annual subsidy to Flanders in return for a promise of the service of no less than 1,000 Flemish knights, should he require it. Figures for the total number of knights settled in England by the thirteenth century vary between a parsimonious 1,200 and a profligate 3,000. Of such men, however, relatively few would have been any use in a fight.

As today, the obligation to pay taxes, which in the twelfth and thirteenth centuries were used chiefly to support the King's military endeavours, does not imply any ability on behalf of the taxpayer to discharge the functions for which such taxes pay. We may grumble about our taxes paying for tanks and guns, but we ourselves would not know one end of a bazooka from the other. Even the equipment necessary for fighting – a mail coat, a sword and shield, a helmet and, in particular, the expensive war horse that the Bayeux Tapestry depicts carrying the Normans into battle, a sleek and priapi-cally masculine creature – all of this lay beyond the means of a large number of those who in technical terms appear in England after 1100 described as knights. In a society organized for war, founded upon war, and with war as its chief sport and future ambition, the professional players could be attracted only at a very considerable premium.

Landholding and Loyalty

Hence the fact that, by the 1080s, we find so many of these 'real' knights holding land from large numbers of Norman lords, all of whom were keen to attract the very best of subtenants. If we take just a couple of examples from the Domesday survey, we might begin with a man named William Belet, literally 'William the weasel'. By 1086, William, whose nickname is clearly French and probably Norman, held the manor of Woodcott in Hampshire, a substantial estate at Windsor in Berkshire and several Dorset manors, all of them directly as a tenant-in-chief of the crown. In addition to these tenancies-in-chief, however, William had also acquired at least one subtenancy in Dorset from the major baron, William of Eu, principal lord of the Pays de Caux, north of Rouen, in which the Belet family lands in Normandy almost certainly lay. In turn, since William Belet's heirs are later to be found as tenants of several other manors held from the descendants of William of Eu, William Belet can almost certainly be identified with an otherwise mysterious William, without surname, who at the time of Domesday held most of William of Eu's Dorset estate as an undertenant. Furthermore, by the 1190s, the Belet family is recorded in possession of the manor of Knighton House in Dorset, held at the time of Domesday from another baron, King William's half-brother the Count of Mortain by another mysterious William, again almost certainly to be identified as our William Belet.

In this way, with a little detective work, we can very rapidly put together a picture of a Domesday Norman knight who held from at least three lords, including the King, and whose heirs were to remain a considerable force both in local and national politics for two hundred years thereafter. Rising at the court of the Conqueror's son, King Henry I, William Belet's son or grandson, Robert Belet, acquired the manor of Sheen in Surrey for service as the King's butler. As a result, the Belets became hereditary royal butlers, responsible for the procurement and service of the king's wine, the Paul Burrells of their day. Michael Belet, a leading figure at the court of Henry II, is shown on his seal enthroned on a wine barrel with a knife or bill hook in both hands, testimony both to his proud office and to his close access to the royal court. His seal, indeed, can be read as a deliberate mockery of the King's own seal on which the royal majesty was displayed enthroned, carrying the orb and sceptre in either hand. Michael Belet and his sons were a major presence at the courts both of King Henry II and King John, founders of Wroxton Priory in Oxfordshire, later the residence of that least successful of British prime ministers, Lord North, of American Independence fame. Yet even by the 1180s, the Belet family was quite incapable of personal military service to the King. Michael Belet, the butler, was a courtier, a King's justice and lawyer, not a warrior. The family estates in Dorset had by this time been so divided and dispersed amongst several generations of brothers, sisters and cousins, that the Dorset Belets were merging into the ranks of the free peasantry.

To see how common a pattern this is, let us take another example, again more or less at random. In Domesday, we find a knight named Walter Hose, literally Walter 'Stockings' or Walter 'the Socks', tenant of the bishop of Bath for the manors of Wilmington and Batheaston in Somerset, and holding land in Whatley of the abbots of Glastonbury. In 1086, Walter was also serving as farmer of the royal borough of Malmesbury, paying an annual render of £8 to the King, probably already as the King's sheriff for Wiltshire, an office which he held until at least 1110. A close kinsman, William Hose, held other lands in Domesday of at least two barons, the bishop of Bath and Humphrey, the King's chamberlain. The Hose family remained a major force in Wiltshire politics thereafter. Henry Hose or Hussey is to be found fighting in the civil war of the 1140s, in the process acquiring a castle at Stapleford in Wiltshire and establishing a cadet branch of his family at Harting in Sussex. One of these Sussex Hoses returned to Wiltshire after 1200, joined the household of William Marshal, Earl of Pembroke, and fought in Marshal's wars, acquiring a major Irish estate in the process. As a result, the chief Hose or Hussey fortunes were transferred to Ireland. The family in England remained, like the Dorset Belets, as a reminder of vanished glories, not without resources and not without land, but no longer at the cutting edge of the military machine.

What do such stories teach? To begin with, they should remind us that competence has always been a rare quality, and that the able and the talented, in this case knights, can command a high price for their services. From the very start, however, there would be a problem with any model of 'feudal' society that attempted to assign either the Belets or the Hoses to a particular rank or position within society. Both families began with knights, but knights who held both from the King and from other lords. We can assume that William Belet was a wealthy man, with estates scattered across at least three English counties, one of the premier league players in the game of Norman conquest. Walter Hose was the King's sheriff for Wiltshire, one of the leading figures in local administration. Yet neither of these men, if rather more than mere knights, were barons. Moreover, even by the 1080s, their loyalty to the lords who had rewarded them was very far from clear. If the Count of Mortain should rebel against the King, in the case of William Belet, or if the bishop of Bath should seek to seize land from the abbot of Glastonbury, in the case of Walter Hose, which lord would William or Walter support?

At least William and Walter were fighting men whose support was worth purchasing, but what of their sons and grandsons? The hereditary principle ensures that, once a landed family becomes established, it is relatively hard to divide it from its land or wealth. But this is no guarantee that the children of such a family will continue to dream of battle and the clash of arms rather than the pleasures of the wine cellar, the counting and spending of their money, or, dread thought, such ignoble pursuits as farming, reading and even writing. Military ability or general intelligence, unlike wealth, cannot be guaranteed by inheritance. Loyalty is most certainly not a genetically transmitted trait. Just because a family ancestor was loyal to the Count of Mortain or the Bishop of Bath, this is no guarantee that the children or grandchildren of such a man would remain loyal to future counts of Mortain or bishops of Bath in the years, indeed centuries, yet to come. The great, the kings and counts, earls and bishops of this world, have always had to repurchase the loyalty of their servants and cannot rely upon tradition alone to buy them either brain or muscle.

Status and Title Deeds

The 'following' (historians tend to call it the 'household' or the 'affinity') of a great man, was what distinguished a truly powerful baron from his inferiors, in the eleventh century as in the eighteenth, or indeed as is still the case amongst the modern-day affinities of pop stars or Hollywood egoists. A man who travelled with twenty knights, forty servants and a menagerie of hangers-on, up to and including a clown and a pet monkey, was to be accounted a great deal better than someone who travelled alone or with a smaller retinue. We begin to get lists of these affinities and of the knight service of the great from the late eleventh century onwards, because listing them was one way of boasting of wealth and status. The letters and charters, the documents by which kings and barons conveyed their instructions and gifts, are the most common historical sources because they have been carefully preserved. All manner of deeds and documents might be discarded from an archive, but not the charters by which land had been acquired, the jealously guarded title deeds to an estate. In themselves, such deeds often display the pride and power of the barons who issued them. Not only are they written instruments from a time when writing itself was a rare accomplishment, but they are authenticated with wax seals, generally showing a stylized figure of a warrior riding into battle, with lance or sword and shield, his horse being the chief symbol of lordly authority. From horseback, it is very hard not to look down upon pedestrian concerns, just as today the pedestrian finds it hard not to look up to a mounted police officer.

As a second guarantee of authenticity, medieval documents were also witnessed, not, as in a modern marriage register, by one or two close friends, but by a great list, sometimes as many as twenty or thirty of those present at a charter's award. It is from these lists that we can reconstruct the affinity of the greater barons, always bearing in mind, of course, that the lists themselves were intended, even at the time, to give an impression of the strength, number and authority of a baron's hangers-on. In this way, the witness lists to royal charters are our best, indeed sometimes our only guide, to who was or was not at the King's court. The witness lists to the charters of barons and bishops tell us who was in, and who was out, amongst a baronial or episcopal affinity.

What do such lists tell us about the connection between knights, land and loyalty in post-Conquest England? Firstly, they suggest that within one or at most two generations of the Norman Conquest, not only had the division between Normans and other Frenchmen from various parts of northern France been largely smoothed away, but that a new gulf was beginning to open up, dividing those who held land on either side of the Channel. Not all Normans with lands in Normandy participated in the Conquest of 1066. In the aftermath, even those families which gained land in England might choose to divide their estate on the death of its founder, with the Norman patrimony remaining with the eldest son, the newly acquired English lands passing to a separate branch stemming often from a younger son in England. The effects of this over time, as we shall see, were to prove momentous. Secondly, they suggest that even by the 1130s, within less than a century of 1066, barons were being required to bring new men into their affinities, either because the ties of loyalty between them and the descendants of the tenants to whom their fathers and grandfathers had given land had begun to fray, or because the specific requirements that they placed upon their followers could not be discharged from within the pool of talent supplied by their existing tenantry. Within a further half century, indeed, it becomes increasingly hard to find any tenants regularly attached to the household of a great man whose ancestors were that great man's original followers in the aftermath of Hastings. The military tenantry of the greater estates tended to solidify into nothing save a tax-paying rump. The actual knights serving a baron would be recruited by other means, in return for money, less often in return for land. Land was the ultimate goal of such men, but after 1100 it was in much shorter supply than had been the case during the great bonanza years of the 1070s and 80s.

Moreover, lords had learned their lesson: to grant land in one generation was to risk indifference or even disloyalty in the next. If we take a particular example, a Wiltshire knight of the 1140s, descended from men who had arrived in England only shortly after the Conquest of 1066, inherited little land from his father so went abroad to carve a reputation for himself on the tournament fields of northern France. He became so famous as a knight that kings vied for his service. Eventually, aged nearly 50, he was allowed to marry a great heiress in the King's gift. Shortly afterwards he was granted the ceremonial belt that conferred title as an earl. In his new estates, however, he was a stranger to his tenantry, unknown to those whom he now ruled as lord, none of whom had owed him any sort of allegiance before his rise to greatness. Instead, he turned back to the Wiltshire friends of his youth and began to import large numbers of these cronies, or the sons of these cronies, into his household, some of whom, when land became available, were richly rewarded from his new estate. The man in question was named William Marshal, and he will reappear later as one of the leading figures in English, Irish and Anglo-French history towards the end of the twelfth century. In the meantime, his story is significant in disproving two persistent myths that continue to attach themselves to the Normans and the Norman Conquest of England.

Myths of the Conquest
The first is that mercenaries or knights serving for money fees played no real role in English military organization prior to the

late thirteenth century. On the contrary, not only were large numbers of mercenaries maintained even for William of Normandy's army of conquest in 1066, but thereafter the mercenary was a standing feature of most armies. A list of the payments made from the household of William de Mandeville, Earl of Essex, as early as the 1180s, records a whole series of money fees paid as annual retainers to unlanded knights, conveniently divided between those attached to the earl's household either in England or in France, supplying yet further proof of the tendency, within a century of the Conquest, for the two parts of the Norman empire to go their own separate ways. Secondly, although, after 1066, the baronial honour and its court served as a significant instrument of social control, and although, on a local scale, such courts functioned in many ways as royal courts in miniature, we should not exaggerate either their cohesion or their sense of group loyalty. Once a generation had passed, the original loyalties upon which they had been formed soon dissolved in forgetfulness and changeability. Like all revolutions, the Norman Conquest of 1066 did not establish an unchanging social order of its own. On the contrary, it led inexorably towards yet further and more profound social change.

Names and Nicknames

Before we leave our model Norman knights, William 'the weasel', and Henry 'the socks', their names deserve brief mention. Before 1066, both in England and Normandy, Christian names were only rarely accompanied by nicknames ('Eric the Red'), trade names ('Windy the Miller' and 'Postman Pat') or place names (what the specialists would call toponyms, 'Eadric of Laxfield'). Below the topmost levels of the aristocracy, it was virtually unknown for such names to survive more than one generation or to become in any way 'surnames' or family names as we would understand them today. Within any particular family, a limited number of Christian names might be favoured, which can sometimes help us to reconstruct family descent, but even here there was no certain rule. Surnames, sometimes derived from a nickname or place name, sometimes from the Christian name of an ancestor, only began to develop in Normandy on the very eve of 1066. Nonetheless, our William Belet 'the weasel' and Walter Hose 'the socks' as early as 1086 had joined that select group of men whose families were henceforth identifiable by true surnames. Names that might be thought to be dismissive or pejorative, 'the weasel', 'the fat' (Gros, or Crassus), the 'fat headed' (Grosseteste, name of a famous future bishop of Lincoln), 'the beaky nosed' (Becket, name of a yet more famous archbishop of Canterbury), even, notoriously from Domesday Book, Humphrey 'Goldenbollocks' (like Robert 'the Perverted', or 'Tesco' of Colchester, one of the more bizarrely named of the Essex tenantry), not only began to proliferate but to be carried by successive generations as proud badges of descent. By the 1130s, families such as the Fitz Geralds, descended from an ancestor named Gerald, began to adopt not just patronymics, those names beginning Fitz This and Fitz That (son of X or Y) that clutter up the 'F' section of the indexes to books of medieval history, but true family names so that the son of Henry fitz Gerald was named Warin fitz Gerald not Warin fitz Henry.

What is perhaps most interesting here is the extent to which the Norman Conquest itself forced families to adopt these new badges of self identification. Newly established in England, families held on to the place names of their Norman birth and the personal names of their Norman ancestors long after they had ceased in all other terms to be anything other than English by birth, breeding and outlook. This great explosion of surnames, for the most part derived from Norman place names, ensures not only that we can attempt to trace the precise geographical origins of large numbers of families established in England after 1066, but that, throughout English history, the names of the greater English baronial or aristocratic families have a distinctly French ring to them. The definitive form of the document known as Magna Carta, first issued in 1215, comes to us from the reissue in 1225 and claims to have been witnessed by twelve bishops, twenty abbots and more than thirty barons. This list of barons begins with the names of a dozen earls or officials known by the names of their English counties, all but one of them from French families and with their French family names specified in Magna Carta in no less than six cases. Of the remaining twenty-two barons, four have 'Fitz' names, three have names derived from English places. The other fifteen all have Norman or French toponyms, in the vast majority of cases commemorating the names of places which the barons themselves had never so much as visited but which had cradled their ancestors. England's greatest constitutional document is therefore to a large extent French. Like later colonialists, scattering 'Hotel Bristols' or 'High Streets' or bungalows named 'Windy Ridge' across the Indian subcontinent, the descendants of the colonialists of the 1060s and 70s remained Norman in name long after they had ceased to be in any way Norman in person.

The arrival of dozens of Norman barons, hundreds of Norman knights and thousands of Norman settlers spelled disaster for the English landholding class. Most of those English thegns not killed at Hastings were dispossessed in the ensuing rebellions or slowly marginalized by their new Norman neighbours. Not everyone lost their lands. There were rare survivals, the quislings of their day, such as Edward of Salisbury, sheriff of Wiltshire, or Thorkell of Warwick, son of a sheriff of Warwickshire, who still appear in Domesday as tenants-in-chief. A list of the knights of the archbishopric of Canterbury from the 1080s includes men named Aethelwine, son of Brithmaer, and Deorman, both of them undoubtedly of Anglo-Saxon descent. Both were Londoners, Aethelwine appearing amongst the witnesses to a charter crucial to our understanding of the role played by the Norman bishop of Rochester, Gundulf, in the building of the White Tower of the Tower of London. In 1125, a man named Ordgar fitz Deorman is still to be found amongst the London 'Cnihtengeld', the city's guild of knights. For the majority of the English land-holding elite, after 1066, there were nonetheless few alternatives save for dispossession or exile.

The Varangian Guard

One outlet for frustrated Englishmen lay in the east, reached only after an arduous journey via the trade routes that traversed the North Sea, the Baltic and thence via the Dnieper and the land of Rus to the Black Sea and Byzantium. The elite imperial troops of the city of Constantinople were traditionally recruited from amongst the peoples of the north, the so-called Varangian Guard, 'the men of the pledge', 'the axe-bearers'. As early as the 1040s, John Raphael, the Byzantine emperor's 'protosparthios', commanding a Varangian regiment in southern Italy, was in correspondence with England; his lead seal was rediscovered fairly recently in an archaeological dig at Winchester. The events of 1066 led to a great increase in the number of displaced or dispossessed Anglo-Saxons seeking refuge on the coast of the Bosphorus. By the 1080s, perhaps as many as 1,000 Englishmen were attached to the Varangian guard. Some of them are said to have established a settlement, known as 'New England', in the Crimea. Long before the Pilgrim Fathers sailed for America, England may already have spawned its first 'colony' as a direct result of the Norman Conquest.

In the aftermath of much later events in the Crimea, following the Crimean war of the 1850s and the setting up of the English camp at Scutari on the Bosphorus, the tombstones of various of the Varangian exiles from England, inscribed with their names and epitaphs, were discovered still lying about, more or less neglected in the city of Constantinople. The inscriptions were copied, but the copies were then burned in a fire in 1870. By the time that anyone returned to the stones themselves, hoping that they might be taken to Scutari for safe keeping, they had been smashed up for rubble. Thus perished, in the shadow of Florence

Nightingale's new English hospital, the last vestiges of the old
English aristocracy itself forced into Byzantine exile by the
ancestors of the very men who in the 1850s commanded Queen
Victoria's Crimean expeditionary force, the lords Raglan (son of
the Duke of Beaufort), Cardigan (of the Brudenell family, introduced from France in the thirteenth century) and Lucan (alias
George Bingham, an English name, although a grandson of the
distinctly French-sounding Earl of Fauconberg, derived from
Fauquembergues to the east of Boulogne, from whence came the
Fauconbergs settled in Yorkshire by the early twelfth century).
So tenacious was the aristocratic hold over land, and so close the
connection between Norman ancestry (even spurious or
conveniently invented Norman ancestry) and aristocracy that in
popular mythology the Charge of the Light Brigade risked the
shedding of almost as much Norman blood as William the
Conqueror's great charge at Hastings.

In the meantime, in the 1080s and 90s, the Varangians,
including the Anglo-Saxons amongst their ranks, would have
witnessed two highly poignant encounters, in October 1081
(fifteen years almost to the day since the Battle of Hastings), at
Durazzo on the shores of the Adriatic, when, in a rerun of
earlier events, the Varangians serving the Byzantine emperor
clashed with and were defeated by a Norman fleet now seeking
their fortunes in southern Italy, and again in 1096, when
Bohemond of Taranto and his Normans were received in
Constantinople, together with Duke Robert, the eldest son of
William the Conqueror, King of England, at the start of that
great venture known as the First Crusade. The frosty reception
extended by Byzantium to the French-speaking crusaders
perhaps owed something to the bitterness with which the
Anglo-Saxons now exiled in Constantinople regarded their
Norman guests.

Castles and forests
In England, the dispossessions and conquests of the late
eleventh century have left an impact not just upon aristocratic

DNA and naming patterns but upon the modern English land-scape. The *Anglo-Saxon Chronicle*, still croaking away in its archaic English prose, reported the death of King William I in 1087 not in a spirit of vengeance or hatred but in something approaching wonder. This King, the chronicler wrote, built castles and sorely oppressed the poor. He also so loved the wild beasts of England, the hart, the hare and the boar, that he protected their habitat with new laws.

William was not the inventor either of the castle or the idea of the forest. Castles of one sort of another had been known in England as long ago as the ice-age, and the remains of Roman military encampments still litter the English, Welsh and Northumbrian countryside. In the 1050s, one of the conse-quences of Edward the Confessor's encouragement of Normans at his court was the building of castles, by the Norman Oswin Pentecost in Herefordshire and by Ralph the Staller in Essex, with Eustace of Boulogne probably planning one at Dover, all of them powerful symbols of foreign authority within regions theoretically controlled by the Godwin family. As for forests, hunting was the great joy of the young Edward the Confessor, and large parts of England, including the Mendip Hills, were probably already regarded as special royal hunting reserves even before 1066.

The Normans after 1066 nonetheless vastly extended the reach of both castles and forests. Even before the Battle of Hastings, with the construction of a castle on the Sussex coast, William introduced a new concept to the English: a baronial or royal fortress established not just in towns or cities but across the English landscape, defensible in time of war, and capable of serving as a centre of baronial law and tax gathering. This, the dungeons and dragons view of the castle, is one side of the coin. Certainly, some castles were places of fear and torture. But the shadows cast by castles were not always dark. In time of war, the castle could serve to shelter the local population, not just to terrorize them. It could also serve as a symbol of sophistication and cosmopolitan taste, not merely as a brutal reminder of

Norman violence. The White Tower, now the oldest structure within the Tower of London, or Colchester Castle, or, slightly later, Norwich Castle built around 1100, were amongst the largest and most impressive buildings raised anywhere in medieval Europe. They served as administrative centres and as symbols of authority. Colchester Castle, for example, was deliberately founded on the ruins of the Roman temple of Claudius, reusing a site and materials originally intended to celebrate Caesar's successor as imperial conqueror of the English, its walls banded with darker and lighter layers of masonry in a deliberate echo of the imperial walls of Rome and Constantinople. Nearby, the King's steward Eudo Dapifer established a new monastery, one of the largest and richest Benedictine houses founded anywhere in northern Europe after 1066, described specifically in one of its early charters as a 'basilica' , literally as a church worthy of a 'basileus' or emperor. The Roman military camp at York, reputedly the spot where Constantine first declared his intention to rule as sole Roman emperor, was itself incorporated within the precincts of York Minster.

Castles undoubtedly performed a military function, serving as outposts of lordly or royal authority, impregnable shards of resistance buried deep in the flanks of any army attempting to advance across country, guarding towns, cities and the greater roads and river crossings. But not all were principally of military significance. Many were intended to symbolize power, even when left ungarrisoned, as at Corfe Castle in Dorset, or to serve as lordly residences, posed in a carefully planned landscape. At Castle Acre, for example, one of the principal residences of the Warenne family, the castle itself was built in conjunction with a priory of monks, imported from distant Cluny on the Rhône, and with a park and pleasure grounds surrounding it, as part of a deliberately planned landscape of lordship. Nearby Castle Rising, symbolizing the rise to power of the Aubigny family, was sited on a false crest above the Babingley river, chosen not for military or defensive purposes but for display, dangerously vulnerable to higher ground to the south, but impressively visible both from the sea and by all traffic up and down the river, its keep built in deliberate imitation of the great royal castle at Norwich, itself one of the most impressive stone structures then existing in northern Europe.

Castles such as Arundel or Belvoir or Alnick still impress the spectator, even today, because their sites were selected precisely in order to strike awe into the minds of those who viewed them. So spectacular was the site of Belvoir, that the family which built it, natives of Brittany, chose to use an image of their massive new stone keep on the seal that they employed to authenticate their letters and charters. If we imagine a visitor to England, tacking up the Channel from Sussex to the Thames, the sight from sea first of Pevensey, then Hastings, then Dover, then Richborough, Reculver and Rochester, would have evoked an extraordinary and potent combination of Norman Romanesque combined with more ancient classically Roman architectural monuments, for the most part on a scale that even the kings of France or the Holy Roman emperors of Germany would have been hard put to match. No wonder, then, that the building of castles, by the King and by his barons, was one of the changes after 1066 seared into the memory of the Anglo-Saxon chronicler, whose fellow Englishmen and other semi-slave labour would have been required in vast numbers to raise the earth mounds on which such structures rested, and to hew the stones from which their massive walls and keeps were constructed. These were public works, built from the sweat and toil of the defeated English, proclaiming the Normans as the new imperial master race.

In the shadow of the castle stretched the forest. What changed after 1066 was not the royal or aristocratic taste for hunting. Hunting, and the deliberate, often highly ritualized taking of life, had always been a royal sport, be it in ancient Babylon, where the lions' den in which Daniel was accom-modated implies huntsmen to capture the lions, or Judea where King David could compare himself to a partridge

hunted upon the mountains (1 Samuel 26:20). Edward the
Confessor had probably passed a great deal of his time in the
1050s and 60s hunting in the ancestral parks of the West
Saxon kings, and as early as the reign of Cnut not only had
hunting in the king's parks been forbidden to all save the
King and his guests, but certain wild creatures – whales,
porpoise and sturgeon for example – were recognized as
lordly perquisites, reserved for the table of king or earl. It was
not merely the King's right but his duty to shed blood.
Capital punishment, into the twentieth century, remained
one of the crown's particular concerns, so that the possibility
of the King or Queen's pardon, from a very early date,
certainly by the twelfth century, became a regular aspect of
the last days of those condemned to death for homicide.
Kings who did not hunt or who refused to shed blood shirked
one of the greater obligations of royalty, as teachers in the
schools of Paris were later to declare.

What changed after 1066 was not the significance or regularity of the king's hunt but the environment in which it took
place and perhaps the procedures of the hunt itself. Large parts
of the country, by no means all of them thickly wooded, were
set aside from the ordinary laws of England and declared to be
'forest': a newly defined legal concept that came to denote a
region in which the preservation of the king's beasts was the
overriding concern. Within such regions, no one might cut
green trees and plants, the vert, in which wild beasts lived, or
clear waste land and cultivate it, or keep hunting dogs or in any
way injure the wildlife, the venison of the forest, under pain of
the most draconian punishments, such as cutting off hands or
feet and other judicial mutilation. In all likelihood these legal
restrictions already applied, before 1066, albeit in slightly
modified form, to the greater ducal forests of Normandy. The
effect in England was drastically to reduce the proportion of
the population entitled to hunt or consume game, from hares
and herons to foxes and deer. The hunting of such creatures
was now restricted by law to a tiny elite.

Not surprisingly, as successive kings placed more and more of England under forest jurisdiction, the King's foresters and forest laws became one of the more blatant and resented symbols of raw royal power. It is remarkable how many of the saints venerated by Englishmen in the twelfth century earned their reputation for sanctity in part by resisting the power of foresters. St Anselm, Archbishop of Canterbury, who saved the life of a hare from pursuing hounds is matched in this respect by St Hugh, bishop of Lincoln in the 1180s, who kept a pet swan at his manor of Stowe, thereby taming and possessing one of the most regal of wild birds, and who regularly ignored royal prohibitions to excommunicate the king's foresters guilty of pillage and worse. In the meantime, the creation by the Norman kings of vast wastelands known as forests, policed and set about with the cruellest of punishments, was not only resented by those who inhabited or owned land in such regions, but was regarded as one of the greater sins of pride to which the Norman conquest had given rise.

The creation of the New Forest, for example, not only forced the expulsion and resettlement of large numbers of peasants previously bonded to land now set aside for the king's deer, but ensured that many of those who held manors within this region, the bishop and monks of Winchester for example, could not properly exploit such land, clear new fields or extend the area under cultivation without incurring heavy fines for their encroachments upon the vert. Not surprisingly, the fact that two of William the Conqueror's sons, Richard in the 1080s, and William Rufus in 1100, himself King of England, met their deaths as a result of hunting accidents in the New Forest, Richard in a fall from his horse, Rufus shot with a crossbow bolt fired at a deer, was widely interpreted as God's vengeance. The Normans were punished for their pride by the death of a king and a king's son in the thick of the English greenwood. Robin Hood, that archetype of the English rebel, cocking a snook at Frenchified sheriffs, was in good company in doing so from the depths of the forest, making his home and his dinner from the vert and venison theoretically reserved for a foreign elite.

Into these forests and in the shadow of their castles, the Normans introduced new and exotic creatures not previously known to the English. Pigs fattened on forest acorns became a far more common element of upper-class diet, clearly reflecting a particular Norman taste for pork. Pea hens and peacocks, already shown in the Bayeux Tapestry as a feature of Duke William's court in Normandy, now screeched raucously across the lordly English countryside. Fallow deer, smaller than the native red deer, were introduced to the woods, to begin with as something almost as exotic as llamas or ostriches to the modern millionaire. They came ultimately from Turkey, perhaps via the Norman colony in Sicily, and seem to have been introduced to England long before they arrived in France or other parts of northern Europe. The bishop of Norwich, a Norman named Herbert Losinga, wrote a bitter letter of complaint when his own fallow deer, apparently a single specimen, fell victim to local poachers. Rabbits, known to the Romans but thereafter apparently hunted to extinction in England, were reintroduced from Normandy, although perhaps not in large numbers until later in the twelfth century. The word 'warren' is a Norman import and the warren itself was carefully protected, with special warreners to guard it and terriers trained to control its rapidly multiplying population. In regions of sand or marginal soil, rabbits bred for their fur as much as for their meat henceforward became a common feature of the English landscape, so common indeed as to be virtually invisible to archaeologists. Those excavating early rabbit warrens have sometimes published their findings as if they were investigating not man-made rabbit burrows but ritual labyrinths or even the burial chambers of prehistoric midgets.

Jews

After 1066, the human population was also leavened with exotic new imports, if not with anything quite so bizarre as two-foot bunny-men. The Anglo-Saxon world knew of the Jews only through the Old Testament, there being no Jewish settlement in England. After 1066, perhaps in the last decade of the eleventh century, Jews previously settled in Rouen and other parts of Normandy were deliberately transported to England and settled in English towns under the direct supervision of Norman lords. The Jews of this new Diaspora were victims of a particular paradox within Christian society. The Bible laid down strict prohibitions against usury, the lending of money or goods at interest, rules which the Jews had long observed and which Christians, as the heirs to the Old Testament, themselves sought to emulate. Such prohibitions did not, however, extend to loans made between members of one religious confession and another, so that, even in the strictest application of theory, a Jew might charge interest on loans made to a Christian just as a Christian might charge interest when lending to a Jew. As a result, moneylending very quickly became a Jewish speciality, as essential as it was unpopular in a world in which the ready availability of credit was a precondition for economic success.

Furthermore, since the Jews were the focus of millenarian beliefs, their conversion to Christianity being awaited as a sign foretelling the end of days, and since there was a sense, expressed by the Pope himself, that the Jewish community must be protected rather than destroyed, if only so that the Jews might serve as a reminder of the fate that awaited all of those foolish enough to deny the divinity of Christ, Jews in England as in Normandy were placed under the direct authority and protection of the King. From this it was only a short step to the royal taxation and exploitation of the Jews, with royal officials demanding the right to collect the arrears of debts owed to the King's Jews, meanwhile actively discouraging the Jews from engaging in any enterprise save for moneylending. Within a century of the Norman Conquest, the so-called Exchequer of the Jews was a major source of revenue to the English crown, with massive though for the most part

unspecified sums of money being collected from the debts of
such plutocratic Jewish money lenders as Aaron of Lincoln or
Isaac, son of the Rabbi Josce of York.

Women

As the rampant biting stallions of the Bayeux Tapestry most
splendidly illustrate, this was a violently male society.
Historians indeed are hard put to find any role for women
within this environment save as heiresses or passive trans-
mitters of cultural memory. The old legend that Duke William's
wife, Matilda, sat at home embroidering the Bayeux Tapestry
whilst her men-folk went to war, is no longer credited. The
Tapestry itself was probably designed within a monastic environment, St Augustine's Abbey at Canterbury being the most
favoured of the various suggested workshops, planned and in
part executed by men rather than women. Even so, to ignore
half of the human population merely because they make little
impact or noise amidst the record of warfare and kingship
would be a foolish dereliction of the historian's duty. It was via
a woman, Emma, the mother of Edward the Confessor, that
the Norman claim to the English throne was first transmitted.
It was from the circle of another woman, Edith the Confessor's
queen, that we obtain our most detailed record of the
Confessor's reign, the so-called '*Vita Edwardi*'. Women, such
as William of Normandy's daughter, Adela of Blois, played a
crucial role in transmitting Norman propaganda to other parts
of France, and it was via marriage to English heiresses that at
least some of the Norman conquerors laid claim to their new
English estates.

The greatest of these heiresses, Matilda, the wife of the
Conqueror's youngest son, the future King Henry I, was not
only the great-great-granddaughter of King Aethelred but the
daughter of a female saint, Queen Margaret of Scotland
(d.1093). Such was the significance of Matilda's marriage into
the Norman ruling dynasty and the consequent merging of the
blood of Norman and Saxon kings, that courtiers after 1100 are

said to have referred to the King and Queen as Godric and Godgifu, precisely because they affected to behave like the low-born English. It was via the children of Henry and Matilda that the bloodlines of England and Normandy were truly united. Not a drop of English royal blood had flowed in the veins of William of Normandy or of King Henry I. By contrast, Henry I's daughter and grandsons were the direct descendants not only of Rollo of Normandy but of Alfred, Aethelred and the English kings of yore. Even for those Norman lords who did not marry English heiresses, English women may have played a significant role. It was possibly via English wet nurses, recruited from the middling or lower levels of English-speaking society, that the English language itself was communicated to future generations of bilingual Norman lords.

Buildings

Although Anglo-Saxon England bequeathed some of its language to the Normans, the greatest of its bequests was paid not in words but in cash. The Conquest of 1066, followed by the looting of England and the emptying out of the strong boxes and treasuries of the Anglo-Saxon aristocracy released more liquid wealth into the European economy than arguably any single event since the fall of Rome. The barbarians who had toppled the Roman Empire after 450 AD turned their wealth into treasure, into gold and silver objects to be hoarded and admired but for the most part later to be melted down and entirely lost to posterity. The Normans took their spoils in cash, and used the money to buy themselves some of the most impressive and long-lasting monuments ever raised in the history of the world. English tourists today who flock to view the great pyramids of Cairo or the Aztec ruins of Mexico would do well to reflect that on their own back doorstep there are man-made stone structures just as impressive as anything that the ancient civilizations of America or Egypt can boast.

The great cathedrals raised in England after 1066 were built on a scale to dwarf not only the relatively modest stone structures of the Anglo-Saxon Church but even to rival the greatest achievements of Rome. By 1100, a traveller to western Europe, seeking out the longest, widest and tallest stone buildings would have been well advised to book a ticket for England. Listed in terms of length, breadth and volume, the greatest buildings in Christendom were the churches of St Peter and St Paul in Rome, the church of Hagia Sophia in Byzantium, and the Roman Pantheon, at least judged in terms of its height. On the Rhine our tourist could view the massive cathedral at Speyer, constructed as the mausoleum of the Holy Roman emperors of Germany. On the Rhône stood the abbey of Cluny, in some ways the most impressive monastic building ever raised. Thereafter, all of the greatest monuments lay in England, all of them constructed from their foundations upwards in the thirty years since 1066. They included the cathedral churches of Winchester, Ely, Canterbury and Norwich, shortly to be joined by Durham, and by the great abbey of Bury St Edmunds. Norwich and Canterbury were planned to be exactly the same length as the pope's church of Old St Peter's in Rome. Winchester and Bury were quite deliberately made longer still. These were buildings on a scale unknown to the Normans before 1066. Indeed, most of the cathedrals of Normandy, even those constructed after the Conquest, could have been fitted twice over into the great nave of Winchester.

This is not to suggest that the Normans of Normandy, as opposed to the Normans now settled in England, reaped no benefits from the conquest of 1066. On the contrary, the duchy experienced an economic miracle. Stone-quarrying in particular became a new boom industry, particularly for the oolitic limestone quarries in the vicinity of Caen. Caen stone could be easily carved and retained the crispness of its carving. It was also a pale shade of whitish cream that clearly appealed to those who built with it. This alone does not explain why Caen stone was imported in such vast quantities into England, not just in the immediate aftermath of 1066 but for more than two centuries thereafter. Caen stone was still being used in the 1180s, for the facing of Henry II's great keep at Dover Castle, and in the 1270s for Henry III's rebuilding of Westminster Abbey. The Norman export of stone cannot be explained simply by the lack of high quality native stone in England. On the contrary, Purbeck stone from Dorset or Barnack stone from the vicinity of Peterborough were both perfectly respectable building materials. Rather it seems that the use of imported building materials was a deliberate gesture by the new Norman patrons of the English Church, intended literally to set the conquest in stone.

Wealth Flows into Normandy

As this suggests, wealth flowed in huge quantities from England into Normandy. Much of it, we can assume, was squandered on wine, women and song, as popular after 1066 as after any great military campaign. Even so, a great deal of treasure still came to rest in Normandy. Many of the best and most luxurious Anglo-Saxon manuscripts survive today not in English but in Norman libraries, acquired by Norman monks and their patrons after 1066 and sent back as souvenirs of conquest to the home country. For the Norman economy, we have few reliable statistics, but those we do possess suggest a vast influx of cash into the duchy. Receipts from tolls on the bridge of St-Lô, where the bishop of Coutances constructed a new 'bourg' or trading settlement, are said to have increased from 15 livres to 220 in the period between 1048 and 1093.

Without displaying quite that degree of megalomania and vulgarity that led the church builders of England to besiege heaven with their vaults and towers, the Church in Normandy acquired many new buildings and new religious foundations. Large quantities of land in England were given over directly to Norman monasteries or to the greater monastic confederations of the duchy. The abbey of Bec, for example, acquired land in nearly twenty English counties and on several of these estates founded priories directly dependent upon Bec's rule, from St

Neots in Huntingdonshire to Chester on the border with Wales. The significance of this influx of wealth to Normandy can perhaps best be judged by the effects upon the Norman Church, a century and half later, when these English resources were suddenly cut off. The register of Archbishop Odo of Rouen, recording the archbishop's year by year perambulation of his diocese from the 1240s onwards, provides vivid testimony to the collapsed towers, the leaking roofs and the ruinous state of a large number of religious houses in Normandy that had previously depended upon revenues from their English estates, now difficult or impossible to raise. As for the building programmes undertaken in England, the *folie de grandeur* of those who undertook them even now threatens to bankrupt English Heritage or whatever other public body is entrusted with the care and upkeep of the greater cathedrals raised on the spoils of the Conquest. A rationalist would no doubt have had them all pulled down and something more convenient, and less expensive to heat and light, raised in their place. Precisely these sorts of plan were entertained by the Cromwellians of the 1640s, who did indeed draw up a scheme for the demolition of Winchester Cathedral, in some ways the whitest elephant of them all.

Wealth and Rents in England

The release of hoarded wealth after 1066 allowed the Norman conquerors to indulge the most lavish and in some cases megalomaniac of schemes. In England, although Domesday Book suggests that some areas of the country may have suffered heavily as a result of plunder and destruction, most obviously after the harrying of the north in 1070, which Orderic Vitalis tells us was accompanied by a deliberate policy of famine and depopulation probably no less violent than that attempted by Lenin and the Bolsheviks of the 1920s in the Ukraine; by 1086 even in parts of the north, some estates were rendering higher rents than they had paid twenty years before. No doubt this was in part the result of an increasingly predatory style of lordship. The Norman newcomers were able to extract rents and services which their Anglo-Saxon predecessors had been unable or reluctant to demand. Above all, they tended to rent out their land for money rather than exploiting it directly. There is an entire technical vocabulary that historians employ for this process, but in essence we are dealing here with the renting out of resources to farmers who paid an annual cash fee or 'farm' for the land that they cultivated, rather than with the direct exploitation of a landlord's resources, his 'demesne'. Most lords retained some sort of demesne, sometimes hundreds or even thousands of acres, but the majority of land, both of the barons and the Church, was farmed for cash. The effect here was to ensure that the Normans had the necessary cash resources, from their rents and from the profits of war, to invest in new ventures, not just in the great cathedrals and monasteries but in such commercial enterprises as mills and tanneries, mineral extraction and iron works.

In Normandy, the mill was one of the great symbols of lordly authority, with a monopoly over the milling of all or nearly all of the grain grown by the neighbouring peasantry and hence the right to charge heavily for the flour that constituted the chief staple of peasant diet. Other lordly monopolies included the right to control clearance of waste land on the fringes of the cultivated zone, a process known as 'assarting', from the French 'essarter', to grub up. Lords also extracted labour services from the peasants on their land, so many days a week a year of work on the lord's demesne, and fixed dues such as the 'heriot', the best beast payable when the son of a peasant inherited his father's lands, or 'merchet', the right to payment when the peasant's daughter married and thereby deprived the lord of that portion of her future labour now devoted to her husband's family. Depending upon the extent of such services owed, the peasant was regarded as more or less free, ranging from the semi-slave condition of peasants forbidden to leave their lands, to the relatively free peasantry of the Danelaw regions of Lincolnshire and East Anglia, where the peasant not only possessed the right to buy and sell land but to leave it should he wish.

Peasant Life

Much debate surrounds the degree to which the Norman Conquest impacted upon peasant life, and a lot of this writing has been influenced by more recent political debates. The old story, for example, that the Normans introduced the concept of the 'lord's first night', the right to deflower all peasant virgins at the time of their marriage, is little more than an eighteenth-century libel, broadcast by the enemies of lordly privilege on the eve of the French Revolution to blacken the reputation of the old regime. It would in fact be possible to argue that the conditions of large numbers of peasants improved as a result of the Norman Conquest. Henceforth, outright enslavement of prisoners or captives like brute animals was forbidden by the Church. These rulings were first enacted, ironically enough, at the same Council of Westminster in 1102 which saw the introduction to England of draconian legislation against sodomy. As this suggests, one set of freedoms is generally gained only at the expense of another. The romanticized, Tolkienesque idea of the Anglo-Saxon peasant living in close proximity and joshing sympathy with his social betters, the sort of peasants of whom Trollope or Tolstoy would have approved, is very largely a myth. There were massive social divisions before 1066, however much the Church might attempt to gloss over the gulf by describing those who toiled, those who prayed and those who fought, the three orders of society, as parts of an indivisible and symbiotic whole. Even so, after the Conquest there was an increase in lordly privilege, an increasingly legalistic definition of social standing, and a rush towards the identification of lordly privileges and perquisites that undoubtedly depressed the standing and prospects of as much as ninety-five per cent of the population.

Villeinage, serfdom, the peasant economy, became a legal as well as a human reality, hedged about with new restrictions and obligations that bonded the peasant to his land and made escape from the manor or from the condition of serfdom increasingly difficult. Sir Walter Scott, whose *Ivanhoe* supplies perhaps the most powerful nineteenth-century vision of post-Conquest England, was indulging in gross exaggeration when he portrayed his English peasants after 1066 choked with massive metal collars as the symbol of their slavery. The good old English lords of *Ivanhoe* are portrayed oafishly drinking themselves to death whilst a new generation of brutal and domineering Normans, the Reginald Front-de-Boeufs of the Conquest, lord it over a cowering and conquered land. Scott was influenced here by events of his own day, by a romanticized vision of the symbiosis of Scotland's lords and peasants, by the experience of Napoleonic conquest that gave the French a less than perfect name as imperialists, and by his loathing for a cosmopolitan and urban conformity that he saw corroding the old verities of locality, place and position. Medieval history has sometimes been written by radical reformers, seeking to parody the iniquities of the present in the brutalities of the past, sometimes by political conservatives, such as Scott, keen to contrast the good old days with present day inequality and ruin. Neither party is likely to do full justice to the reality of the past.

As in more recent times, after 1066 the withering away of liberties and the sharpening of social divisions between haves and have-nots went hand in hand with a general upsurge in prosperity. The most prosperous times are often those that witness the greatest erosion of the liberties of the many faced with the privilege of the few. It is another general rule of agrarian economies, not least of the Ukraine after the great famine of the 1920s, or most of western Europe after the terrible trans-continental wars of the 1640s, 1750s, 1800s or 1940s, that agriculture recovers relatively rapidly even after the most severe looting or conquest. Livestock or seed grain may be stolen or driven away, barns may be burned and the harvest ruined, but the land itself abides. All that is required for its recultivation is sufficient new investment, and this is generally forthcoming from the profits of conquest, no matter who wins the war. The Conquest, for all the obligations it placed upon peasants to remain bonded to their land, did little or nothing to stifle social mobility or to deter economic migration.

Towns

Towns, already a feature of the Anglo-Saxon landscape, not least as a result of King Alfred's deliberate encouragement of walled 'burhs' such as Oxford or Wallingford as outposts of West Saxon defence against the Danes, did not cease their expansion after 1066. On the contrary, the forced wanderings of many hundreds of dispossessed Anglo-Saxon landlords, the chaos and disruption of the rebellions and disturbances in places as widely dispersed as Ely or Exeter, all contributed to the likelihood that many thousands of peasants would uproot themselves and seek refuge and a new life in the town.

Rather like the Third World cities of today, the towns of the Middle Ages were towns within towns. On the one hand stood the privileged townspeople or 'burgesses', renting or owning their own burgages or stalls and houses, in legal terms regarded as free men and women. On the other stood the migrant workers, the incomers and those on the fringes of society, often resented by the established population. The slums of Dickensian London, the tenements of early twentieth-century Glasgow, or indeed the modern shanty towns of Calcultta, Rio or Istanbul give us some idea of the degree to which the official picture of a city and its population often fails to account for the vast numbers of people settled on its semi-legal margins. To this extent, attempts to use official records such as Domesday to calculate the population either of towns or villages are little more than educated guesswork. Migrants and economic refugees very rarely impact upon such statistics. What must be apparent is that England, after 1066, was thrown into turmoil, not merely for a year or two as William established his rule, but for most of the period up to 1086 when the Domesday survey at last allows us to view the scene, to some extent with the dust now settled upon it. To this extent, the Conquest provoked perhaps the greatest hiatus in English history before the social disintegration brought about by the Industrial Revolution of the eighteenth and nineteenth centuries.

As in any time of revolution or vast upheaval, it is hardly surprising that the Normans sought to secure the verdict of posterity by establishing permanent monuments to themselves. It generally takes a fire, a war or a revolution to replan any city, and in the longer term there is no more conservative city or nation than one (e.g. Paris or Vienna) that has regularly been replanned. Most of what we today assume to be the age-old symbols of an unaltered past are in reality the visible stone icebergs thrust upwards from periods of profound turmoil and disintegration. Revolutionaries build on a massive scale because they are only too aware of the fragility of human achievement. In much this way, the great buildings of post-Conquest England, today read as symbols of calm endurance, the backdrop to Barchester and the sweet mutterings of church choirs, were in reality shocking statements of the new. Via their imported Caen stone and their massive proportions they proclaimed a new social order and the achievements of a new master race, content to think of itself, and to be thought of, in the most grandiose and epic of terms. The great churches of post-Conquest England were imperial symbols, every bit as politicized and controversial as the hammer and sickle of communist Russia, English post boxes in Ireland, or the mycelium-like spread of MacDonalds and Starbucks across the modern Third World.

Fashion and Lifestyle

Other badges came to signify the Normans and their 'Normanness', or as they would have called it, in Latin, their 'Normannitas'. We cannot peep inside the wardrobe of William the Conqueror, though, so far as we can tell, the basic repertoire of clothing, shirts, vests, cloaks, hose for the men, longer more flowing garments for the women, were much the same in England before 1066 as they were in Normandy. The Bayeux Tapestry, our chief source here, nonetheless suggests that there was a quite deliberate distinction between Norman and English ways of dressing hair. Hair itself is a major though often neglected aspect of human history. From the hairy Esau to the smooth Jacob, and from Christ depicted without a beard to the bearded kings and emperors of the twelfth century, shifts in the aesthetics and cultural significance of hair may tell us a lot about more profound social change. Norman men, it is clear, wore their hair short and in a style that today one associates with those too mean or too mad to pay a barber, with the back of the head shaved a long way upwards towards the crown. The Bayeux Tapestry and contemporary Norman chroniclers tell us that the Anglo-Saxon aristocracy wore their hair long, combed and anointed 'nancy boys', as one highly idiomatic modern translation of the *Song of the Battle of Hastings* puts it. Certainly, the Normans regarded long hair as a sign of effeminacy. The court of William the Conqueror's son, William Rufus, became notorious for allowing its men to grow their hair parted in the middle so that their foreheads were shamefully bared, for encouraging them to wear absurd shoes with pointed toes curling backwards at the tip like scorpion tails, and for dousing the lights so that all manner of crimes might be committed after sunset. We have already encountered the 1102 sanctions against sodomy, enacted two years after William Rufus' death, and it was almost certainly as a sodomite that the chroniclers sought to portray Rufus, albeit posthumously.

Like gay-bashing through the ages, this in fact tells us as much about the writers of such reports as it does about those whose deeds they reported. If for the Normans moral corruption was associated with effeminacy (and we need to remember here that women in general were believed tainted with the sin of Eve), then moral strength lay in the masculine and the manly. If jests and absurd dress were the qualities of a sodomite, then only those who took themselves very seriously indeed could hope for redemption. Despite the wealth released by the Norman Conquest, the Normans themselves were not to be tempted into luxury or ease. In their own eyes, they were more Spartans than Romans, Greeks rather than lazy Trojans blinded by Helen's beauty. Seriousness and a refusal to laugh at oneself are qualities essential to any would-be empire builder. From the Pharoahs to Cecil Rhodes, and from Nebuchadnezzar to Mussolini, the would-be imperial court is a place where laughter has to be concealed behind a scowl and where the absurd has to be accepted, at least in public, with absolute seriousness. Such places also tend to pose very stark alternatives between good and bad, loyalty and treason, the ins and the outs. Time is short, and empires, even on the map, are generally not coloured in shades of beige.

Norman Empire

There is no doubt that William the Conqueror, whether by accident or more likely by design, built an empire for himself. By 1066, he had already campaigned on the southern and western frontiers of Normandy, in Maine and Brittany. After 1066, not only did he add England to his conquests, but the Normans continued to press southwards towards the Loire, establishing a frontier against the rival power of the counts of Anjou. William's son and successor, William Rufus, was to die in 1100 dreaming of a vast campaign of conquest that would carry Norman authority southwards to Aquitaine and Bordeaux. This official record of conquest was only part of a much wider story of heroic Norman endeavour. At almost precisely the same time that the Normans were conquering England or pushing southwards into Maine, groups of exiles, either no longer welcome or unable to prosper at the ducal court, many of them from the frontier regions of southern Normandy, took their ambition elsewhere, to southern Italy where, from the 1050s onwards, they began to carve out what would eventually become the Norman kingdom of Sicily, comprising not just Sicily itself but a large part of mainland

Italy, as far north as Naples and the southern hinterlands of Rome. One of the reasons why the Pope was so anxious to appease William the Conqueror, both in 1066 and thereafter, was that on his own back doorstep the papal lands were menaced by the rise of this new Norman power in the south.

The Norman conquest of southern Italy was guaranteed in 1071, when the Byzantine empire was at last forced to abandon its outpost at Bari, and finally crowned in 1130, when the last of the Norman dukes in Apulia began to style himself not merely as a duke but as King. In the meantime, both from their northern and their new southern lands, the Normans of Normandy, England and Sicily played a glorious part in what was widely portrayed as one of the more glorious episodes in the history of Christendom: the 'liberation', after 1095, of the Holy Places of the East, culminating on 15 July 1099 with the capture by the army of the First Crusade of Christ's own city of Jerusalem. No matter that, like a lot of Norman enterprise, this was a bloody affair, and that the fall of Jerusalem was followed by a massacre, not just of its former Islamic occupiers but of all those members of the population foolish enough to have swallowed their valuables in the hope of preserving them from harm. The crusaders (if reports are to be believed, although these reports are themselves merely copied from the Jewish writer Josephus, describing what the Roman imperial army had done in Jerusalem after its capture in 70 AD) made a large bonfire and reduced the bodies to ash, in the hope of extracting precious metals and jewels from the pyre. Like many such 'liberations', the liberation of Jerusalem by the crusaders might be read as something closer to an enslavement of those it supposedly freed. From a Norman perspective, what mattered here was that the Normans had played so prominent a role in yet another great conquest. From Hastings, via Bari to Jerusalem, they were now indisputably the greatest warrior-race that Europe had experienced since the Romans or the Huns.

And here, of course, hubris began to lurch inexorably towards nemesis. The idea of the Normans as a master race, as we shall see, was a myth no less attractive and no less fictitious than any others of the myths that the now-conquered Anglo-Saxons had once told about themselves. From their reading of Virgil or Caesar, the Normans learned how to behave like imperialists, how to carve out an imperial destiny for themselves. From the very monuments and methods of their success, however, they perhaps acquired that delight in irony and the absurd that has ever afterwards been a central feature of the English sense of humour. To what extent, one wonders, did the Normans themselves ever truly believe in their own invincibility? Seriousness often begets self-mockery and the very richest talent for irony.

3

FROM HASTINGS TO HENRY II, 1066–1154

The deeds of kings and the plotting of their advisers constitute only one small aspect of human history. We know about such things in a detail and with a clear chronological trajectory that we lack for the broader and deeper transformations within society. Hence the fact that stories of the wars of good and bad kings occupy so prominent a place in books of history: a rule that applies not just to medieval England, but to the Old Testament books of Kings and Chronicles. Throughout the Bible, and hence throughout the Christian Middle Ages, dynastic narrative served to underpin mankind's understanding of the past. Kingly history cannot be avoided; indeed, deployed wisely it can lend a structure and coherence to the broader canvas of events that might otherwise be lacking.

The deeds of the kings and queens of Norman England can be briefly told. In many ways they are less significant than the background of conquest and colonization against which they were played out. They carry us, via the last twenty years of

William the Conqueror, through the reigns of his sons Robert in Normandy and William Rufus in England, to the death of Henry I, the last of these sons, in 1135 and the accession of a grandson of the Conqueror, Stephen of Blois, in circumstances that led to civil war and the division of England into a series of hostile camps. The civil war of the 1130s and 40s was resolved only in 1154, nearly a century after Hastings, with the accession to the throne of a new dynasty, the Plantagenets, formerly counts of Anjou and hereditary arch-enemies of the dukes of Normandy. In turn, the Plantagenet succession, as we shall see, far from resolving the problems of the first century of Norman rule merely posed further problems of its own.

Surviving records

Fundamental to all this were questions raised and never properly resolved by the Conquest after 1066. How were the descendants of William the Conqueror to legitimize their rule and succession when their title to the throne had come to them only through bloodshed and main force? How were such kings to resolve the lopsided realities of a dominion or empire, divided by the Channel, ruled by Normans yet powered by England's wealth? Our knowledge of events is sketchier than we might wish. Only for William the Conqueror and King Stephen do we have contemporary 'lives', and, compared with modern day ideas of biography, both of these leave a great deal to be desired. The 'Gesta Guillelmi' or 'Deeds of William' by William of Poitiers was written to sanitize William's part in the violent overthrow of Anglo-Saxon England. In its present state, it breaks off, incomplete, shortly after William's accession. The 'Gesta Stephani' describing the deeds of King Stephen was written to demonstrate the King's recovery after the disasters of the early years of his reign. The fact that Stephen, far from recovering his reputation, then went on to even more ignominious failure perhaps explains why the author seems thereafter to have abandoned all interest in the King's cause.

The only surviving manuscript of William of Poitiers has been lost, burned in the great fire of 1731 that destroyed so much else of the library of Sir Robert Cotton. We need to remember here that our knowledge of the past is based upon small fragments of information, salvaged when the great bulk of medieval writing was destroyed, sometimes by accident, sometimes, as in the Dissolution of the Monasteries of the 1530s, by design. Cotton was one of those antiquaries who set out to salvage what he could from the scatterings of monastic archives. It was into his library, and those of his contemporaries such as Matthew Parker, Archbishop of Canterbury, that an extraordinary proportion of the surviving chronicle and charter evidences for medieval England were gathered. The accidental burning of a large part of the Cotton library in 1731 destroyed an inestimable quantity of such materials, as can be seen, for example, from the blackened vestiges of Cotton's copy of Magna Carta, still displayed in the British Library, its seal reduced to a formless lump, like a half-chewed toffee.

Fortunately, in the world of manuscripts there are always discoveries to be made as well as losses to be reported. Another perhaps much better copy of William of Poitiers' chronicle, said to have existed in the 1620s, has never been traced and may still lurk, unrecognized, on the shelves of a private library in France. Stranger things have come to light even in the past few years. It used to be believed that both the 'Vita Edwardi', our principal source for the life of Edward the Confessor, and the so-called Encomium, a sort of life of King Cnut, survived in single manuscripts, in one case incomplete. Then, within a period of only a few months in 2009, not only did a second complete and indeed extended copy of the 'Encomium' emerge from a library in Devon, but a large chunk of the 'Vita Edwardi', previously unknown to scholarship, turned up in the British Library, copied out by a sixteenth-century anti-quary whose papers had never been properly surveyed. Medieval history is not just about making patterns from small pieces of evidence. It involves hunting down the evidence itself, often to strange or unexpected places.

For those unfamiliar with such sources, it is important to bear in mind that medieval biography omits an enormous amount that today we would take for granted. It rarely includes dates. It may supply only the briefest and most stylized of descriptions of personality, personal appearance, personal taste or friendships, indeed of all of those qualities that we would today assume essential features of a human life. Sexuality, let alone psychology, lay well beyond the bounds of what biographers could describe. Even if mentioned, most often through the delineation of sexual misdeeds, adultery or fornication, references to the king's sex life are generally to be read in a moral rather than a literal sense, as an indication of the degree to which a fallible individual failed to heed God's imperatives. The models for this sort of writing lay partly in the Bible, partly in the work of classical historians, above all of Suetonius, the highly scandalous, highly moralizing biographer of the Roman emperors. As a result, we cannot expect medieval biographies, particularly royal biographies, to supply anything other than the crudest and most distorted of portraits. Even when their details seem authentic, we must take care that they are not simply copied from Suetonius or some account of an Old Testament king.

A fragmentary account of William the Conqueror, for example, supposedly written by a monk of Caen, tell us that the King was very abstemious in his use of wine and rarely drank more than three times at a meal. This is, in fact, a detail copied directly from Einhard's *Life* of the Emperor Charlemagne, and in turn, by Einhard from Suetonius' life of the Roman Emperor, Augustus. It tells us nothing reliable about the drinking habits of William the Conqueror, though it may potentially tell us a great deal of the imperial models which William and his biographers were keen to ape. For the rest, we depend upon chroniclers such as William of Malmesbury, Orderic Vitalis and Henry of Huntingdon, all of whom had particular axes to grind, all of whom set out to moralize their histories, chiefly by pairing off good against bad kings, and most of whom were writing long after the events they described, in an attempt to explain to themselves and their own bewildered contemporaries how such a cataclysmic event as the Norman Conquest had come to pass. The surviving letters and charters of the kings themselves may sometimes assist us in establishing who was at court, or where exactly the King was, but these charters are rarely dated, leaving even such matters as the King's day-by-day movements, his 'itinerary', largely hidden from us. For the entire period of William I's reign, for example, from 1066 to his death in 1087, we know the King's precise whereabouts for only 42 days out of about 7,500.

William the Conqueror's first five years as king were spent dealing with the rebellions and invasion scares that convulsed the English after 1066. In 1070, re-enacting his coronation of Christmas 1066, he was crowned King by papal legates, at Easter, the feast of Christ's rebirth, in an attempt to set a seal of papal approval upon the Conquest. In the same year, at the Council of Winchester, all but one of the surviving English bishops were removed from office, including Stigand, the scandalous archbishop of Canterbury. This paved the way for William to promote Lanfranc as head of the English Church. In 1072, having put down risings at Peterborough and Ely, William was able to lead a joint land and sea operation against the Scots and their king, Malcolm Canmore, resulting in the so-called peace of Abernethy. Malcolm recognized William as his overlord and surrendered hostages for his future good conduct. In 1068, William had already visited Cornwall, being perhaps the first King of England to do so in the past century, putting down the rebellions that had troubled Exeter and the West Country and appointing a Breton as earl. In 1070 during the harrying of the north, he had built castles at Stafford and Chester intended to offer future protection against the Welsh. In the 1080s, he intervened in disputes between the rival Welsh princes of Morgannwg and Deheubath, personally travelling as far west as St David's, in theory as a pilgrim, in practice as part of an itinerary intended to emphasize his political authority. His successor, William II, in the 1090s, kept up the pressure on the Scots and Welsh, expelling the local ruler appointed to Cumbria by the Scots king, refounding the Roman garrison town of Carlisle as a new outpost of Norman rule and, on the east coast, pushing his rule as far north as Bamburgh and the Tweed. These were the actions of an imperial regime, extending Norman rule to the furthest corners of what might be regarded as England and beyond.

Having dealt with the Scots, William I retired to Normandy where he remained for all but a few months of his final years, troubled by disputes in northern France, where Flanders now emerged as an enemy rather than an ally. Maine, on his southern frontier, was only with difficulty restored to Norman control, henceforth disputed by William's powerful southern neighbours, the counts of Anjou. In 1074, the collapse of a rebellion by Edgar the Aetheling, last of the surviving great-grandsons of King Aethelred, and in the following year, the brutal suppression of the rebellion led by the earls of East Anglia, Hereford and Northumbria, appeared to usher in a new period of stability in England. At Christmas 1075, as if to symbolize the end of the old order, William attended the funeral of Queen Edith, the widow of Edward the Confessor and sister of Harold Godwinson, laid to rest in Westminster Abbey. The execution of Earl Waltheof of Northumbria, however, and the subsequent miracles said to have been worked at his tomb in Crowland Abbey, where he was venerated as a martyr, merely paved the way for yet further Anglo-Norman hostilities. Orderic Vitalis blamed the death of Waltheof, the last of the English earls, for all of King William's subsequent troubles.

These troubles took a predictable and familiar form. The question of succession and legitimacy had long loomed over English history, from the death of Aethelred in 1016, through to Edward the Confessor's failure to nominate an heir in the 1050s and 60s. In 1078, the same issue re-emerged, this time as a result of quarrels within the family of William the Conqueror. William had at least four sons, one of whom died young, killed, as we have seen, in a hunting accident widely interpreted as God's punishment for Norman pride. The eldest of the sons, Robert known as 'Curthose' ('short legs' or 'short stockings'), had been promised the succession to the duchy of Normandy from at least 1063, aged only thirteen. With his father refusing to relinquish control over Normandy's affairs, Robert increasingly considered himself cheated of his rightful position and authority. In 1078, he rebelled, so Orderic Vitalis tells us as the result of a family quarrel in which his younger brothers, William Rufus and Henry, playing dice in a room above Robert's lodgings, jokingly urinated on Robert and his attendants. Henry was only ten years old at the time, Rufus eighteen. We seem to be here in the same sort of 'broken society' of binge drinking adolescents that modern politicians claim to be so anxious to 'heal'. Like many absurd family quarrels, this one had serious consequences. In the ensuing family war, Robert personally wounded his father in a skirmish fought outside Gerberoy to the north-west of Beauvais. William was only saved through the intervention of an Englishman, Toki of Wallingford, a remarkable instance of the way in which a Norman king could now trust to the loyalty of the very people that he had met and defeated in battle less than twenty years earlier.

Although relations between William and Robert were thereafter patched up, tensions between father and son were widely reported by contemporaries and never entirely resolved. After 1084, Robert once again broke with his family and spent the next three years, through to his father's death in 1087, as an exile from Normandy. Such dissension was only increased in 1082 when William arrested and imprisoned his half-brother, Bishop Odo of Bayeux, accused of plotting to succeed as king or even of attempting to buy himself the papal throne in Rome. The purchase of holy office, associated with the New Testament sinner Simon Magus mentioned in the Acts of the Apostles, in the eleventh century had come to be seen as the most serious of crimes: simony, a sin which cried out for a root and branch reform of the Church's affairs. The fact that Odo was accused not just of simony but specifically of attempting to use simony to gain the papal throne suggests a deliberate campaign of propaganda against him and the raking up of the most outrageous charges that any enemy could devise. Meanwhile, William's arrest of Odo, the man responsible for commissioning the Bayeux Tapestry, still today the most optimistic and forthright statement of the Norman claim to the English throne, is a fitting symbol of the slide of William's family towards disputation and the politics of revenge.

Death of William the Conqueror

The Conqueror died in 1087, as the result of a riding accident. In his final years William is reputed to have grown enormously fat. Assaulting the French town of Mantes, on the frontier between Normandy and France, he slipped in his saddle. The pommel rode up into his distended stomach, and he suffered fatal internal injuries. On his deathbed, although displaying traditional pious regard for the redemption of his soul, he failed to make any definite provision for the succession. As a result, there was yet another succession crisis, the first of many still to come. Between 1066 and 1216, a period of 150 years, no king of England came to the throne as the first born son of his predecessor, and not until 1272 did the succession of such a first-born son occur in peacetime and apparently without dispute.

William Rufus

From the events of 1087, the Conqueror's second son, William known as Rufus, the 'red', emerged with the greatest of the spoils. Crossing immediately to England and with the assistance of Archbishop Lanfranc, Rufus seized the treasury at Winchester and had himself crowned King in Westminster Abbey. Robert Curthose, still in disgrace and therefore absent from his father's deathbed, found himself deprived of the larger part of his potential inheritance. The outcome was warfare between Robert as Duke of Normandy and Rufus as King of England. The vastly superior financial resources of England enabled Rufus to root Robert out of Normandy, at first under threat of military conquest, thereafter by the liberal disbursement of cash. After 1096, and in return for a massive payment of 10,000 marks, Rufus bought out Robert's claim to Normandy. Robert himself used the money, itself an indication of the vast superiority of English over Norman wealth, to raise an army for the First Crusade. In theory, his arrangements with Rufus were set to last for three years. In practice, it was not expected that Robert would return from the East. As both parties were aware, Robert's grandfather, the father of William the Conqueror, had embarked for Jerusalem in the 1030s and had never come back. In Robert's case, however, not only did the First Crusade lend him enormous prestige but, returning via the Norman colony in southern Italy, it brought him a wife. The wife in turn brought him a son and heir, and a very considerable dowry with which once again to finance war against his brothers.

Henry I

Henry, the youngest of these brothers, and the only one of the Conqueror's sons conceived after 1066 and hence born 'in the purple' as the son of a ruling king of England, had meanwhile outmanoeuvred Robert. In October 1100, hunting in the New Forest, William Rufus was accidentally shot through the heart by an arrow fired by one of his fellow huntsmen. Quite who fired the shot was never resolved, although most people blamed Walter Tirel, lord of Poix near Amiens. Attempts to expose a conspiracy have enjoyed little support. Henry, Rufus' younger brother, was an unpleasant, ambitious and libidinous young man, but even he is unlikely to have stooped to fratricide. This did not mean that he was above scheming or making the very most of a God-sent opportunity. Without even waiting for Rufus to be buried, Henry rode pell-mell for Winchester to grab the family treasury, and then to London where he was crowned in Westminster Abbey only three days later, not, as was customary, by the Archbishop of Canterbury, but by the relatively junior bishop of London. His speed here, and the fact that he immediately issued a 'coronation charter', promising to revoke various of the more serious abuses of Rufus' regime, indicate the panic of the moment. There was still no agreed procedure for royal succession and the victor in any succession dispute was likely to be the person closest to the scene of the late King's death, with the fastest horses and the speediest access to the royal treasury.

Henry's seizure of the throne of England was a *coup d'état* just as dramatic and controversial as Rufus' accession thirteen years earlier. Once again, Robert Curthose was deprived of what he believed to be his right. For the next twenty years, a large part of Henry's energy was to be devoted to warfare, first against Curthose, then, following Curthose's defeat and capture in the Battle of Tinchebrai in 1106, against William 'Clito' ('the heir'), Curthose's son. Clito was aged only four when his father disappeared into captivity but thereafter, backed by Henry's principal enemies, King Louis VI of France and the counts of Anjou and Flanders, he emerged as the focal point for resistance to Henry's rule. In 1119, at the Battle of Brémule on the frontiers between Normandy and the Ile-de-France, Henry defeated Louis VI. Clito fled from the battle-field, abandoning even his war horse, later returned to him by Henry I, fully equipped, as a gesture of deliberate and chivalric condescension. In return for peace and the freeing of Robert Curthose, Clito now offered to set out for Jerusalem with his father, and, this time, not return. The offer was refused. Instead, the death of Henry I's only son, accidentally drowned in 1120, and the outbreak of yet further rebellion in Normandy, once again placed Clito, now in his early twenties, at the head of a coalition of rebels. As before, however, Henry's superiority both in resources and generalship, led to the rebels' defeat in battle, at Bourgtheroulde in 1124.

Refusing any suggestion that he now recognize Clito as his
heir, Henry I declared that the throne of England and, with it,
rule over Normandy should pass to his daughter Matilda,
married to Geoffrey of Anjou, son of Count Fulk, in a gesture
intended to end hostilities between Normandy and Anjou.
Clito protested, and for a while seemed to have gained the
advantage, when the murder of Count Charles of Flanders
and interventions by Louis VI as overlord to the Flemings,
led to Clito being appointed Count Charles' heir. News of
Charles' murder in Bruges is said to have reached London
only two days after the event, giving some idea of the possible
speed of communications across the Channel. As a grandson
of Matilda of Flanders, the wife of William the Conqueror,
Clito had at least some hereditary claim to the Flemish
succession. With Flemish wealth and Flemish knights to back
him, all seemed set for a major onslaught upon Normandy.
Instead, Clito's mishandling of his new authority, and the
emergence of a rival claimant, Thierry of Alsace, backed by
the financial support of Henry I led to civil war in Flanders,
and in July 1128 to Clito's death, assaulting Thierry's castle at
Aalst. Clito died childless. His father, Robert, outlived
virtually every other member of his family, dying, still in
captivity at Cardiff Castle, in February 1134, aged well over
eighty. Robert had spent nearly thirty years in prison in
relative comfort, writing poetry and learning Welsh, the
futility of these pursuits signalling that essential lack of ruthlessness which had led to his being passed over as England's
king. Twenty months later, he was followed to the grave by
Henry I, his younger brother and the last of the Conqueror's
sons.

Family Quarrels

All told then, from the 1070s through to the 1130s, the wealth
and energy of the kings of England was devoted principally to
warfare and foreign alliances and specifically to warfare
provoked by family quarrels, fought out in Normandy and

dragging in broad coalitions of northern French noblemen, from Flanders to Anjou, and from the kings of France to the counts of Alsace. An inestimable quantity of English silver and human life was expended in a quarrel provoked originally by a couple of teenagers urinating on their elder brother. There was a great deal more to the reigns of both Rufus and Henry I than just this narrative of family squabbling, but not surprisingly their contemporaries looked to moral or cosmic explanations to explain the turmoil. Both the Bible and classical antiquity are full of the contentions of sons against fathers, of brother against brother, and of the moral causes that were believed to explain such sickness within the body politic. To those seeking explanations, the rebellions of Curthose and the fact that the ruling family was increasingly given over to internal squabbling could only be interpreted as proof of the illegitimacy of Norman claims in England; fit punishment for the violent usurpation with which William the Conqueror had despoiled the Anglo-Saxons. In turn, this carries us back to another overriding theme in English history after 1066, the guilt that the Conquest had inspired.

The Norman Myth

As so often in human history, the apparent pride and arrogance of an imperial people masked deep-rooted anxiety as to the justifications for empire. Superficially, after 1066 the Normans seemed to be riding high. Not just in England but in southern Italy, and from the 1090s, in the Holy Land and Jerusalem itself, they carved a swathe across Christendom that their rivals and contemporaries regarded as little short of incredible. Like the Huns in the fifth century, or the armies of Charlemagne in the eighth, the Normans seemed to have erupted into human history fully formed and invincible. Beneath this veneer of invincibility and racial superiority, however, there were more troubling and complex realities. The Normans sought to present themselves as a master race of warriors, unbeatable in war, the chosen people of God.

This, the so-called 'Norman Myth', was questioned even at the time and ever afterwards has fuelled the speculation of historians. In reality, the Normans had never constituted a race or a single bloodline. Like most other European tribal allegiances, with the possible and bizarre exception of the Basques, they comprised a mixture of Viking, Gallo-Roman and Frankish elements even before they emerged onto the historical stage. Their culture was the adopted Latin Christianity of Rome, and even their language was borrowed from France with only a small smattering of Scandinavian loan words, often for the technicalities of the sea by which the Vikings had first come south.

The Christian culture of which they made so much, and by which they claimed their status as a chosen people of God, was itself compiled from a kaleidoscopic palette of Lombard, Lotharingian, Burgundian and Roman elements, as foreign churchmen, none more famous than Lanfranc, the first 'Norman' archbishop of Canterbury, were welcomed to the ducal court. Even the building style that they came to adopt in England after 1066, was not a truly native Norman style, but acquired, like the Norman war horse, in part from Spain, in part from Lotharingia and the German imperial lands of the north. Just as the Normans ransacked the libraries of conquered England for their most precious Anglo-Saxon books, so the books that they themselves introduced were for the most part copied not from Norman exemplars but from other centres of learning. The works of St Augustine, acquired by the new Norman cathedral at Sarum (later Salisbury) were copied from exemplars supplied from Flanders and Lotharingia, not from Normandy.

In learning, in building, even in their warfare, where, after 1066, at their battles such as Tinchebrai or Brémule they adopted King Harold's technique of riding to battle but fighting on foot, the Normans were the most brazen and parasitical of plagiarists. Their greatest thinkers, first the Italian Lanfranc, then the equally Italian Anselm, were outsiders. As with the later American acclamation of immigrant intellectuals and artists, from Rachmaninov to Einstein, it was as if the Normans lacked confidence in their own native talent. Like the British imperialists of the nineteenth century who insisted that their greatest musicians all have German or Italian names, as if no one named Smith or Jones could compete with a Hallé or a Melba, the Normans may have harboured something of a chip on their shoulder about their relative lack of cultural sophistication. Normannitas or Normanness was chiefly something related to warfare and the ability to win battles. Real culture, the Normans seem to have felt, was to be found somewhere other than Normandy itself.

So far so good. Most modern historians have been happy to puncture the 'Norman Myth'. Deeper than this, however, the Normans after 1066 experienced real problems over the definition of authority. In recent years, it has become fashionable to suggest that their lack of confidence led them increasingly to resort to law and to legal arguments as a means of legitimizing their conquests. Law and law-making, which were to emerge as vital themes in the history of twelfth-century England, were pursued by the first generation of Norman settlers as a means of discovering legal justifications for the violent seizure of English land. One such justification could be obtained from the canon law of the Church, which sanctioned succession blessed from one generation to another in the way, for example, that bishops succeeded bishops, tracing their origins back to the first apostles and hence to Christ as their first originator. In this way, perhaps instructed by Archbishop Lanfranc, William the Conqueror deliberately presented himself as the legally nominated successor to the Anglo-Saxon kings and specifically to Edward the Confessor as his 'antecessor' or immediate predecessor.

This is all very well. However, there is actually precious little evidence that the early Norman kings saw themselves as law-makers as opposed to law-keepers. It was the laws of Cnut that were supposedly renewed by both Edward the Confessor and William the Conqueror, and even the so-called 'Laws of Henry I' turn out, on inspection, not to be newly forged statutes but a procedural guide, perhaps written at a very local level, for one of the bailiffs of the hundreds of the county of Surrey, as to how existing laws might best be administered. Rather than fortify their claim with jurisprudential justifications, the Normans possessed a far simpler and more easily understood explanation for their victory, as an act of God. God had sanctioned the Normans as conquerors to purge the sins of the English, and perhaps specifically the failings of the English Church. God had permitted the Normans to seize England, just as the crusaders subsequently laid claim to Jerusalem, and just as in centuries gone by the Romans or the Arab conquerors of much of the known world had claimed their lands, by right of conquest.

God, Normans and Anglo-Saxons

God remained a potent force in English law for many centuries still to come. He is named in the opening clauses of Magna Carta as the first beneficiary to whom King John granted his charter, and his activities, even into the nineteenth century, have led to wranglings in English law courts over what precise instruments God was accustomed to use in his dealings with mankind. If a man were killed by a bull, a falling tree or a mill-wheel, for example, even as late as the 1840s, such animals or objects were in theory to be confiscated by the crown as 'deodands', God's gifts and the instruments of divine wrath. Bulls and mill-wheels are clearly a great deal more costly to replace than dead trees, but there was no real attempt to do away with medieval legal practice until the invention of the railway train and the consequent risk that such expensive machinery might be confiscated or made liable to a massive fine every time that it accidentally flattened a pedestrian. As a result, deodands are now a thing of the past, although insurance companies continue to exclude 'Acts of God' from virtually every policy that they issue. Even in our modern and largely godless world, God remains part of the equation of man's dealing with nature and the law. In the eleventh and twelfth centuries, God's footsteps in the garden of humanity were far more readily detected.

The Normans had conquered because God wished them to. As with all such simple formulas, there were nonetheless major problems that emerged from this very simplicity. To begin with, if God was on the side of the Normans, then he could just as easily turn against them. Any defeat in battle, any sign that a Norman king was no longer victorious in his wars, could be interpreted as proof of the loss of divine favour and hence lend support to rebels or the discontented keen to undermine royal authority. In short, anyone who lives by the claim that his victories signal divine favour is likely to perish by evidence that he is no longer victorious. Beyond this, there arose the nagging question of why God should wish a particular king or people to prosper. Medieval Christianity was founded upon a keen and imminent sense of the approaching end of days. It would surely not be long before God began to pack up the theatre of human history and initiated that process, described in the New Testament Book of Revelation, by which signs and wonders would foretell the imminent Apocalypse. Just such signs and wonders were looked for around the year 1000, that great millennial milestone in human history. When the year 1000 passed more or less without event, and then the decade of the 1030s, marking the thousandth anniversary of Christ's crucifixion, and then the 1070s, marking the thousandth anniversary of the destruction of the Temple of Jerusalem, some began to wonder whether humanity would enjoy a much longer lease of life. One reason for the upsurge of learning and for the new intellectual optimism of the twelfth century was quite possibly the realization that humanity was no longer doomed to imminent destruction or condemned to the power of Satan. At the same time, there were others who continued to look for signs of the imminent second coming of Christ. Few such signs were written up in gaudier or larger letters than the Norman

Conquest of England followed very shortly thereafter by the
Norman Conquest of southern Italy (in the process defeating
the Byzantine empire, the eastern empire of Rome) and then
the truly apocalyptic liberation of Jerusalem in 1099, once
again won largely through the strength of Norman arms.

It was widely believed that the Apocalypse, when it came,
would begin in Jerusalem, and in particular at the site of
Christ's crucifixion and burial, marked since the fourth century
by the church of the Holy Sepulchre. Hence the popularity of
copies of the Holy Sepulchre across Europe. One of them was
even built in the fenland town of Cambridge, at this time a
dreary port dominated by a Norman castle, itself controlled by
a particularly tyrannical Norman sheriff named Picot
(described by nearby monks as 'a ravenous lion, a prowling
wolf, a cunning fox, a filthy pig and a shameless dog', which
rather overdo the animal metaphors). Here a local guild of
pilgrims built themselves a round church in deliberate though
inaccurate imitation of the Holy Sepulchre in Jerusalem. The
Cambridge Round Church still stands. What though did the
reconquest of Jerusalem and the Holy Sepulchre foretell? If
those who reconquered it were agents of a divine power, was
that power itself for good or for evil? Were the conquests of
the Normans won through the power of God or of Satan?
Indeed, to what extent were the Normans, and their pride,
infernal rather than agents of the divine?

This was an age of Christian knighthood and consequently
of attempts by the Church to control violence, certain sorts of
violence (such as the Crusade) being sanctioned, other sorts
(such as indiscriminate pillage) being forbidden, most notably
through the so-called 'Truce' or 'Peace of God' movement
which enacted legislation to forbid certain types of armed
conflict and to limit the periods of the year in which fighting
could take place. William the Conqueror introduced the Peace
of God to Normandy and strove, so far as we can tell,
throughout his reign both in Normandy and England to be
presented as a Christian warrior, aware of the new customs

governing warfare, themselves fast crystallizing into what would later be known as a 'chivalric code'. As instruments of God, however, were the Normans to be accounted a blessing, like the Christian armies of Charlemagne, or a curse, like the Huns of the fifth century or the Mongols of the thirteenth? Were the Normans themselves blessed or cursed by God?

The answer to this question would clearly be determined by the Church. Hence it was vital to the image of Conqueror and Conquest that the Church be brought under Norman control. At least to begin with, it was by no means clear that such control would be achieved. As after the fall of Rome, when the Church had served as a repository of Roman imperial memory, preserving Roman traditions of literacy, administration and even of late imperial dress and diet, in the midst of barbarian military triumph, it was quite possible that the English Church after 1066 would retreat into its own past, not only urging the victors to penance but demanding that the vanquished repent of the sin which self-evidently explained the speed and violence with which they had been conquered. Even though its highest positions, as bishop or abbot were henceforth reserved for Frenchmen, the Church offered one of the few remaining opportunities for the sons and daughters of Anglo-Saxon land-owners dispossessed by the Conquest to enjoy a high-status lifestyle. Such men and women joined communities of monks and nuns which themselves were exclusively and self-consciously English and which, on occasion, could explode in outrage against foreign abbots or bishops. At Glastonbury, for example, three monks were killed and eighteen wounded in a riot brought about when the new Norman abbot attempted to force them to abandon their own traditions of singing for a style of Gregorian chant pioneered in Dijon and favoured in Normandy. The new Norman abbot of Abingdon sat at table with his friends mocking the Anglo-Saxon saints whose relics the abbey housed. He was punished immediately afterwards, much to the satisfaction of the local English chronicler, being found dead in the lavatory.

To begin with, at least, the Church served as a mausoleum of Englishness, and it is no coincidence that it was English monks or clergy who offered some of the most trenchant criticisms of the new Norman regime. Englishmen seeking explanations for 1066, such as Eadmer, a monk at Canterbury, or Henry, archdeacon of Huntingdon, used their pens as weapons to revenge themselves on their new Norman masters. To the half-English, half-Norman William of Malmesbury, there could be little doubt that the Norman Conquest was God's punishment for English pride and specifically for two failings still familiar themes today: the drunkenness of the English, and their willingness to sink vast sums of money into sub-prime housing stock. According to William, the English 'passed entire nights and days in drinking parties' and 'consumed their whole substance in mean and despicable houses, unlike the Normans and French, who live frugally in noble and splendid mansions'. Not surprisingly, after 1066 there was a vast upsurge both in the quantity and the quality of historical writing produced in English monasteries. Where previously the English Church had depended on Flemish monks to write its history, historical writing now became one of the great exports of England. Once again there are modern parallels here, to the way, for example, in which some of the best writing about international affairs since 1945 has been produced by English historians, unable any longer to celebrate a British empire, yet controlling the means by which other empires, American, Russian or Chinese, are perceived. In just such a way, English monks now controlled access both to the English and to the Norman past.

Yet even in this rewriting of the English past there were the first signs of accommodation between conquered and conquerors. Bede's *Ecclesiastical History* was widely regarded as the greatest work of Latin history written by any Englishman before 1066. Not surprisingly perhaps, as a celebration of the Anglo-Saxon past, it enjoyed an extraordinary vogue after 1066, newly made copies of this very large book finding their way into libraries across England and northern France. But copying was more than an act of nostalgia. It led to imitation and imitation in turn leads to innovation. In the north of England, where monasticism had virtually expired in the centuries between Bede and Edward the Confessor, Bede's *History* was used as a blueprint for the refoundation and implantation of monastic houses by the Normans after 1066. The new monastic communities established in such places as Durham, Hexham, Whitby and York, represent a sort of retro-fashionable rediscovery of the world of Bede.

Not only this, but the decision, after 1070, to refound many of the English dioceses and to move them from small Anglo-Saxon sites into larger towns or monasteries itself owed something to the perception that the English Church as celebrated by Bede was pre-eminently a church ruled by monks. In 1066, only three of the fifteen English bishoprics were served by monastic chapters (Canterbury, Winchester and Worcester). By the time that Ely was selected as the site of a new fenland diocese in 1109, there were a further six monastic cathedrals established (Durham, Bath, Chester/Coventry, Rochester and Ely). Various of the traditions that Bede declared to be peculiarly English, in particular the daily celebration of Mass, were widely adopted by the English Church after 1066, no doubt in a deliberate effort to stress continuity with the past. In just this way, the new Norman church hierarchy came enthusiastically to adopt such peculiar English observances as the feast of the Conception of the Virgin Mary (8 December), supposedly celebrating the immaculate conception of Jesus' mother. Elsewhere in Europe, the doctrine of the immaculate conception of Mary (the idea that, through the operation of the Holy Spirit, not only Christ, but Mary herself was born without sin) was less than enthusiastically received. The great Cistercian polemicist, St Bernard of Clairvaux, for example, declared the very idea of Mary's immaculate conception to be impudent and new-fangled nonsense. It was not fully accepted as Catholic dogma until 1854. In England, however, within living memory of the Conquest of 1066, Norman abbots such as Anselm at Bury St Edmunds or Osbert of Clare at Westminster helped preserve what they regarded as a peculiarly English devotion. Even before 1100, Norman barons with lands in England were already beginning to make awards not just to their own religious foundations in Normandy or England, but to established pre-Conquest English monasteries such as Bury St Edmunds or Ely. Some were even choosing to be buried in English churches rather than in their native Norman soil. After about 1100, such Anglo-Norman patronage of English monks and burial in English rather than Norman graves became the rule rather than the exception.

This change in attitudes, from hostility against the English Church towards admiration and deliberate emulation, can most clearly be signposted from Norman approaches to the old English saints. The very first generation of Norman church leaders did their best, as with Abbot Ethelelm at Abingdon, to ridicule the English saints, to purge the church calendar of their feast days and to consign their relics to the obscurity of a box in the attic. Within less than a generation this attitude had changed to one of acceptance and open celebration. The new and magnificent monastic cathedral built on the great rock above the river Wear at Durham was consciously planned as a monument to the cult of the English St Cuthbert. At Canterbury, the Norman cathedral was dedicated to the Holy Trinity, that most cosmopolitan and least nationalistic of cults, yet the relics of the old English saints Dunstan and Alphege were deliberately assigned altars in the east end, flanking the high altar of the Trinity. The same generation of English monks who in their historical writing sought explanations for the horrors of Conquest was now called upon to rewrite the old English legends of the saints, producing updated versions now rebranded for cults directed towards an Anglo-Norman rather than an exclusively English audience. In the process, a large number of these hagiographical makeovers sought to stress the close relations that had always existed between saints and the King, indirectly legitimizing William the Conqueror's role within the Church by emphasizing the degree to which his Anglo-Saxon predecessors had dealt with the Anglo-Saxon saints.

Archbishop Lanfranc

As this suggests, after 1066 William the Conqueror and his sons did their utmost to assert their control over an institution, the Church, vital not only to the self-image that they conveyed to the outside world but to the salvation of their own eternal souls. The chief instrument of royal policy here was the first of the post-Conquest archbishops of Canterbury, Lanfranc. In 1075, at a Church council held in London, it was Lanfranc who sought to issue new legislation for the disciplining and reform of the English Church, and it was undoubtedly through Lanfranc's diplomacy that England and King William were able to stand aloof from the convulsions of the papal–imperial dispute that shook the rest of Europe throughout the 1070s and 80s. At his Council of London in 1075, Lanfranc issued statutes that appeared to treat the late Anglo-Saxon Church as a hopeless cause, sunk so deep in corruption that only root and branch reform could save it. Bishoprics were moved at will, so that in due course the former see of Dorchester-on-Thames was relocated one hundred miles further north to Lincoln, the bishopric of Sherborne was translated to a new royal compound at Sarum, and in due course the former see of East Anglia, so obscure that even its precise location before 1066 remains disputed, was moved into Norwich. In each case, a powerful royal castle loomed over the newly constructed cathedral, at Sarum in such close proximity that the cathedral's canons were later to complain that they could not enter their building without permission from the King's soldiers.

Yet even this drastic shake-up was not conducted without a thought for the Anglo-Saxon past. At Norwich, for example, the focal point of the cathedral became precisely the bishop's 'cathedra' or throne, an Anglo-Saxon object, supposedly the stone chair carved for the seventh-century St Felix, first

Christian missionary to the East Angles, now translated into
the new building as the cathedral's most precious relic. Others
of Lanfranc's rulings at the Council of London might suggest
that the Anglo-Saxon Church was abandoned to superstition
and to semi-pagan customs such as the use of animal bones to
ward off cattle plague, or divination and the prediction of
future events, henceforth placed under the strictest of prohibitions as works of the Devil. A series of notes preserved in a
manuscript in Cambridge nonetheless reveals that Lanfranc,
like all post-Conquest bishops and archbishops blessed in
Canterbury Cathedral, was invited to conduct precisely such
an act of divination, opening the Gospels at random at the time
of his consecration, to see what a particular scriptural passage
might foretell of his future rule. Lanfranc's passage came from
Luke (11:41), 'Give alms and behold all things are clean unto
you.' Odo of Bayeux, that most treacherous of the Conqueror's
half-brothers, can hardly have been pleased to find his own
prognostic taken from Christ's words about Judas (Matthew
26:23): 'He that dippeth his hand with me in the dish shall
betray me.'

In some senses, Lanfranc sought to pose as a harsh discipli-
narian. He played a leading role, as the King's vice-regent, in
the suppression of rebellion in 1075, and for the monks of his
own cathedral church at Canterbury he issued constitutions
intended to do away with former abuses such as the risk that
older monks might take advantage of child or teenage novices
making their way by night, without candles, through the
monastic dormitories. There is a deliberately militaristic caste
to the metaphors in Lanfranc's letters, offering to do battle
against Satan and to employ the shield of righteousness against
the sword of iniquity, a reminder that Lanfranc himself was the
agent of a military dictator. Even the ablutions of the
Canterbury monks were subjected by Lanfranc to a new sort
of military discipline, with as many privies supplied for the
monastic community as there were monks then established in
the convent, the apparent intention being that each monk

should not only pray, eat and sleep, but conduct his other bodily functions in concert with his fellows. Not even the most senna pod-obsessed of preparatory-school headmasters could have imagined so disciplined a community. Yet as this extraordinary boom in lavatories should remind us, the period after 1066 was one in which the sheer number of monks increased out of all recognition. Over such a body of potentially unruly Englishmen, many of them recent entrants with only a bare minimum of religious instruction, it was only right that severe discipline be maintained.

Moreover, like all great monastic leaders, Lanfranc was prepared to temper discipline with forbearance. So many women had fled to nunneries to escape the Norman Conquest that the nunneries themselves struggled to cope with the influx. This great flight to religion has generally been presented as an attempt by Anglo-Saxon women to escape from forced marriages. In fact we now know enough about the practices of victorious armies, not least in Berlin in 1945 or Bosnia in the 1990s, to appreciate that it was not so much marriage as rape that was feared. Lanfranc was willing to relax the religious vows made by such women to a life for which they had no proper vocation. The most famous of these reluctant nuns was herself a member of the former West Saxon royal dynasty. Matilda, the daughter of Malcolm III, King of Scots, via his marriage to the English princess Margaret, a granddaughter of Edmund Ironside, had been entrusted, probably in the late 1080s, to the rough discipline of her aunt, Christina, a nun at Romsey in Hampshire. Either at Romsey or at Wilton, Matilda was compelled to dress as a nun even though she never officially took vows and despite the fact that this was strongly disapproved of by her father, who is said to have torn the veil from her hair. Almost certainly she was veiled to escape the attentions of King William Rufus, who soon came calling at Wilton, pretending that he had entered the cloister only to admire the rose bushes and other flowering shrubs. Rufus, who never married and who was allegedly not a ladies' man, was not the only suitor to appreciate the potential advantage of marrying an English princess with dynastic links to both the West Saxon and the Scottish thrones. In the end, and after an official ecclesiastical process had released her from her religious profession, Matilda was married not to Rufus but to his younger brother, King Henry I.

As this implies, the Church had a major role to play as mediator between Norman and English identities after 1066. It also, of course, as the richest of all medieval institutions, played an equally significant role in the economic exploitation of post-Conquest England. This can be demonstrated from such well-documented instances as Peterborough, a pre-Conquest abbey, founded in 966, exactly a century before the Conquest, by Aethelwold, the great reforming bishop of Winchester. As a result of the Conquest, not only did the new abbot of Peterborough swamp his lands with knights imported from Normandy and from amongst his own kin, but he encouraged a massive new clearance of the Northamptonshire woodlands, assarting or grubbing up at least a thousand acres of previously uncultivated land now laid to the plough. Abbot Thorold's activities as entrepreneur were themselves, at least in part, urged on by tensions between English and Norman elements at Peterborough. The importation of sixty or more knights to the Peterborough estates was a direct response to the revolt of 1070/71 by Hereward, a former Northamptonshire thegn. It was at Peterborough and at nearby Ely that the legend of Hereward was most keenly cultivated, and it was at Peterborough, after 1100, that the *Anglo-Saxon Chronicle* continued to be written up, year by year, in the Old English vernacular: an important reminder that even those religious institutions most keenly involved in the Normanization of England, in the clearance of ancient woodlands and the draining of England's fenland wildernesses, also continued to admire and to commemorate the old English past.

The new bishoprics founded after 1070, at Lincoln and Sarum, might look to the first of their new Norman bishops as potential patron saints, setting a trend whereby the calendar of saints came to be filled by an increasing number of Anglo-Norman bishops, canonized as much for their administrative skills and their patient learning as for any more dramatic accomplishments. Yet the very first post-Conquest saint generally to be recognized in England was almost certainly Waltheof, at Crowland in the Lincolnshire fens, an Anglo-Saxon earl executed, some would say martyred, for rebelling against Norman rule. After 1066, a great mass of blood lay spilled behind the English throne. The Church did as much to advertise as to conceal this fact.

King and Church

It was the Church that imposed penance upon those who had fought at Hastings or who had afterwards, even in time of peace, killed and looted their way to English wealth. It was the Church, in the form of gifts to monasteries, that served as the chief repository for the Normans' own burden of sin. Like many newly enriched vulgarians, unsure of their entitlement to prosperity and uncertain whether they themselves were to be accounted instruments of God or the Devil, the Normans were lavish in their almsgiving. Their new cathedrals and the fifty or so new abbeys and priories established in England by the 1130s testify to this generosity born of guilt. At the same time, the Church was also prepared to support the claim of the Norman kings to be vicars of Christ rather than tools of Satan. The elaborate, imperial elements introduced to the English coronation service (no one is quite sure when, but certainly before the death of Henry I); the ceremonial crown-wearings in which the King regularly displayed his authority, majestic on his throne; the introduction both to Normandy and to England of the ritual performance of the 'Laudes', elaborate hymns in praise of the King and his monarchy sung regularly on public occasions, all of these were ritual acts by which the Church and its leaders acknowledged that the King was more than a mere warlord, more indeed than a mere man: a semi-sacral representative of

Christ on earth. At his coronation, the King was anointed with chrism, the same oil mixed with myrrh from the sap of trees native to the Yemen and Arabia, by which priests themselves were consecrated to their holy offices. At a time when the papacy, especially Pope Gregory VII, was seeking to draw an ever clearer distinction between the superior power of the Church and the inferior authority of lay rulers, this deliberate insistence in England that kings ranked amongst the chosen ones of God was highly provocative.

Perhaps the clearest sign of the King's self-perception comes from his seal, the blob of beeswax attached to all royal letters and charters, as a means of authentication more majestic (and in an age of secular illiteracy more convenient) than any sort of signature. William I's seal copied that of Edward the Confessor in two respects. It was double-sided, which itself implies a deliberate attempt to emulate the double-sided seal of the Holy Roman emperors, and on one of its sides it carried an image of the King enthroned in majesty. Where Edward had been shown carrying a rod and a sceptre, however, the two symbols of royal authority with which the King was ritually invested according to the new imperial coronation ceremony, William was shown carrying a sword and an orb, symbols of dominion (the world encompassed in a metal ball) and of justice imposed at sword-point. On the other side of his seal, the change in emphasis was even clearer. Where the Confessor had employed merely a second version of the image of enthronement, William the Conqueror's seal introduced an entirely new portrait of the King on horseback with helmet, lance, shield and pennant. The majesty or throne side carried his titles as King of England, the equestrian side his titles as Duke of Normandy.

In essence, this same juxtaposition of majesty and warlord has been maintained on the great seals of all successive kings and queens of England over the past thousand years. Under Henry I, the lance on the equestrian side was replaced with a brandished sword. Thereafter, despite growing progressively larger (from three and a quarter inches in diameter under the early Norman kings to five inches for the second seal of Henry IV), and more elaborate in their decoration and setting (including the use of ever more garishly coloured wax), there were to be no fundamental changes here until the second seal of Henry VIII (after 1538), when a greyhound was introduced to the scene of the king on horseback, transforming it from an image of war to one of hunting. Even Queen Victoria, however, continued to use a two-sided seal, the equestrian image striking a neoclassical pose in which the Queen carries a sceptre rather than a sword. All of this imagery, from the 1060s through to the early twenty-first century, conveys two unmistakable messages, firstly, that the monarch is invested with authority from God, and secondly, that such authority should be imposed, if necessary, from horseback and under the threat of a very sharp and heavy piece of iron. Sacrality and the sword were here merged into a single image of the King as a warrior ruler blessed by God. Those who consider such traditions of sacrality inappropriate to our desacralized age are in for a nasty shock, when King Charles III or King William V receive coronation on the Confessor's throne in Westminster Abbey.

Something of the impression that the conqueror made on contemporaries can be recaptured from a story told in the *Life of Lanfranc* attributed to Milo Crispin. On one of those great festivals when William was seated in majesty, wearing his crown and royal robes, a jester, seeing the King resplendent in gold and jewels, cried out 'Behold, I see God!' Archbishop Lanfranc, standing beside the throne, reproved the King, saying 'Don't allow such things to be said of you' and demanding that the jester be flogged. Superficially, this story suggests that contemporaries were persuaded to identify William with the Almighty. Beneath the surface, however, it can be read in a more ironic sense. The jester, being a jester, was mocking rather than praising a King who dared clothe himself like God, and Lanfranc was determined not that William should project a less majestic image, but that he should punish those who mocked his majesty. The Church supplied the props to the theatre of monarchy, but never abandoned its right to discipline any actor who misplayed the role of King.

Religious faith in the Middle Ages remains a difficult subject to probe. In general, the kings of England, and most of their subjects, are written off as 'conventionally pious', which is the historian's way of admitting that we can never really probe the depth of their religious sincerity. The most outspoken of religious invocations in wills may have been dictated by the clergy rather than by the dying believer. Gifts to a monastery might have been undertaken in true faith. Alternatively, as for example with William I's patronage of the abbey of St-Florent-de-Saumur on the Loire, they might represent an attempt to intrude political influence via the back-door of gift-giving and patronage. The most emotional outbursts of personal penance have to be treated with a degree of scepticism, as confessors were reminded at the time, since many people are capable of acting out a remorse that they do not themselves feel. God alone could tell whether a penitent's tears were genuinely contrite. Even so, it is clear that protestations of Christian belief were the norm, and that outright atheism was something attributed only to the most inveterate of sinners. Some Christians, as today, were more enthusiastic than others, but essentially this was a religiously minded society, for whose members Christianity offered the conventional, and in many cases the only possible explanations for a whole series of eventualities.

In an age of high child mortality, of violence, of fire and potential famine in which there were no insurance companies to offer compensation and no doctors aware of the true causes of most disease, a belief in the supernatural was an entirely rational recourse. So much in the world made so little rational sense that the frontier between the natural and the supernatural was blurred. Recovery from disease, the destruction of crops, thunder and lightning, even the sudden death of children, could best be explained as divinely ordained eventualities. The sinner uncertain as to whether it was an incurable tumour or bad indigestion from which he was suffering, the woman who mourned the death of a child, the King who sought to probe the secrets of the future or the hidden thoughts of his courtiers, all of these could find a degree of comfort within the Church. We should add to this list of the comforts of religion the facts that man is perhaps by nature a religious animal, that the Church was massively powerful and attractively adorned, and that, in an age without properly equipped medics, let alone psychologists, the clergy, or on occasion the saints working from beyond the grave, were often those best-equipped or at least most willing to discuss 'personal' issues. Tears and chatter were the two great driving forces of monastic spirituality.

As for the clergy living in the world rather than the cloister, even the humblest of parish priests could command authority within village communities whose lords were frequently absent. The parish church, after all, was in general the largest of village institutions, and, with its bells and its bell tower, the loudest and best advertised. Although not necessarily educated beyond the simple needs of reading and some writing, the priest could on occasion serve not just as spiritual but as practical community leader. In the 1130s, when the north of England was threatened with a Scots invasion, it was the parish priests of Yorkshire who gathered together a militia to oppose invasion. As the first teacher of the village's young, on occasion teaching as much by the whip as with words, and as the repository of much secret knowledge about his parishioners, long before lay confession became a universal adult obligation after 1215, the priest was a figure of awe, even if, like various priests in medieval fiction, he himself were merely the poor vicar of a much richer absentee rector, his robe roughly darned and his farmyard worse kept than those of his parishioners. The priesthood of rural Ireland as imagined by nineteenth- and twentieth-century writers is not a million miles from that of the medieval English village. It is not difficult to understand why this was an age in which faith was a great deal more than just a superficial or ritual affair.

Amongst the early Norman kings of England, one alone
stands out as a figure for whom religion meant less than it
did for most. William Rufus was not only branded a sensu-
alist and a sodomite by his opponents, but reported openly
to have mocked the Church. Warned that he should not
cross the Channel in the middle of a storm, he replied that he
had never heard of a king being lost in a shipwreck, joking
that the sea and the wind would obey his royal commands.
Told that a group of fifty Englishmen had been acquitted of
forest offences by the ordeal of hot iron – in effect a way of
testing God's judgment by making the accused hold a
red-hot piece of metal and then estimating his innocence or
guilt from the severity of the burns – Rufus declared that
anyone who believed God to be a just judge deserved to be
damned. His favourite oath, 'By the Holy Face of Lucca',
was intended as a jibe against one of the eleventh-century's
most venerated yet least plausible relics, a full-sized wooden
image of the crucified Christ, said to have been carved by
Nicodemus, one of the attendants at Christ's burial, and to
have floated miraculously from the Holy Land to western
Italy, arriving there after a voyage that must have lasted
nearly a thousand years.

Towards the English Church in general, Rufus was
mercenary and unyielding. He demanded knight service from
its lands and left vacant for long periods any bishoprics whose
incumbent died, meanwhile reserving their revenues for his
own royal coffers. To profit from the Church in this way, and
to make over resources intended for spiritual purposes to his
own very secular needs was a provocative gesture, not least
because this was an age in which simony, the offering of money
in return for holy office, was considered the worst of all crimes,
worse even than sodomy. Within the Church, Rufus' closest
henchman was his confidential clerk, Ranulph Flambard ('the
torch-bearer'), eventually promoted bishop of Durham.
Flambard was a sinner of such notorious lasciviousness that
young girls, even those vowed to religion like the future saint,

Christina of Markyate, were well advised to lock their doors whenever he appeared.

Yet, like other noisily irreligious men, Rufus was perhaps more aware of his own sinfulness than many of those who outwardly posed as believers. The most hardboiled of sinners often make for the best and most tearful of penitents. This is precisely what happened at Easter 1093, when Rufus lay ill at Gloucester, clearly believing that death was upon him. Rather than appoint a worldly man to fill the archbishopric of Canterbury, vacant since the death of Lanfranc, he suddenly and without apparent warning demanded that it be given to a visitor to his court, the abbot of Bec, an other-worldly old man who had recently heard the King's confession. The abbot was named Anselm and he was already approaching sixty. An Italian by birth, he had found refuge with Lanfranc at Bec and had stayed on there after Lanfranc's departure for higher things, attempting largely unsuccessfully to manage the financial affairs of the abbey. Like many of the greatest intellectuals, Anselm was a late starter. He published virtually nothing into his forties. He was widely regarded as a charismatic and holy pastor of monks, willing to spend time not just lecturing but listening to the young and the troubled. He was also a visionary.

Anselm Finds God

Listening to matins one day, and allowing his mind to wander, he had come upon what he believed to be an irrefutable proof of the existence of God. This, the so-called 'ontological proof' (from 'ontology', the pursuit of the essence of things) continues even today to fascinate theologians. For present purposes it should serve to remind us that English history is far more than a mere catalogue of facts, dates and battles: Englishmen (or in this instance Norman-Italians later resident in England) once had minds and thoughts that captured the imagination of Europe. In essence, Anselm argued, if 'God' is a concept that embodies the greatest thing that can be imagined, and if God exists in the imagination, then it must be greater for him to exist in reality than merely in the mind. Therefore he must really exist. This is an argument unthinkable a century earlier, derived from two developments in Western thought that were to have profound future consequences: a rediscovery of classical philosophy, and in particular of the teachings of Plato on the relationship between ideas and reality, and a new delight in human language as a means of exploring the purposes of God. Language, linguistic terminology, and the organization of language statements into self-evident 'truths', still underlies a great deal of philosophical enquiry. Anselm is surprisingly close in this respect to twentieth-century philosophers. At the time that he was writing, the three skills deployed here – grammar, logic and rhetoric – constituted the very basis of education, being drummed into the heads of all schoolboys attempting to grapple with Latin as a European-wide language of learning.

It was through grammatical analysis, more than through recourse to classical philosophy, that Anselm's former teacher, Lanfranc, had sought to oppose those who taught that the Mass was little more than a commemorative re-enactment of Christ's last supper and that nothing akin to transformation of the elements of bread and wine into the substance of the body and blood of Christ took place at the moment that a priest consecrated them. The technical terminology, and the understanding of the precise operation of this transformation, what would later be known as 'transubstantiation', had yet to be established. For a modern audience it is nonetheless important to notice that what Lanfranc and others argued was not a literal, physical transformation of bread and wine into flesh and blood. This would have been an abomination, akin to cannibalism. Instead, we are once again here in the realm of words, grappling with realities that could only be expressed through ideas clothed in language. In such an environment, it could be argued that the substance, the inner nature of the bread and wine, was changed into that of the substance of Christ himself without this involving any obvious change to the accidents, the outer appearance of the elements of bread and wine.

To many people at the time, as indeed to many people even now, such arguments seemed too abstract and, like the onto-logical proof advanced by Anselm, to depend upon a false identification between words, ideas and realities. Hence the numerous miracles reported by the more literally minded of the faithful, in which the bread or wine was seen literally to transform itself into bleeding flesh, into images of Christ the lamb, or to become incandescent with an inner light revealing the light of God in ways less subtle than those proposed by the philosophers. But to Lanfranc, and later to Anselm, the possi-bilities that language and philosophy opened up to the explo-ration of divine truth seemed both new and tremendously exciting. To Anselm, who in his meditations could declare with deep self-knowledge, 'My life terrifies me,' language, properly used, seemed to offer solutions even to such deep-rooted secrets as the distinction between truth and justice, or the inner reality of good and evil.

Whether a thinker such as Anselm was ideally suited to the administration of a great church such as Canterbury is quite another matter. Even as abbot of Bec, he had struggled to supply the daily needs of his monks in food and drink, and had been so poor, at one point, that he had attempted to improvise a seal for his abbey by re-using two parts of a silver mould. The two parts being of different sizes, this experiment did not succeed. At Gloucester in 1093, Anselm had literally to be forced to accept office as archbishop, with the sick King urging on his attendant bishops to force the pastoral staff into Anselm's hands. Shortly afterwards, Anselm did homage to the King for the lands of his archbishopric. Virtually every aspect of this process – the King's nomination, the refusal of any voice to the monks of Canterbury Cathedral who in theory had the right freely to elect their arch-bishops, the insistent investiture with the pastoral staff, and the taking of homage by the King – was contrary to the new spirit of canon law which the popes, since Gregory VII, had been prepared to risk international warfare to promote. All might still have been well had Rufus done as was expected and died at the scene of Anselm's promotion. Instead, Rufus almost immediately began to feel better.

Far from expressing gratitude to Anselm as God's agent who had brought about this recovery, Rufus seems to have felt only annoyance that he now had to deal with so other-worldly and conscience-ridden an archbishop. But Anselm did some things of which the King would heartily have approved. For the first time, for example, he began to emphasize the particular authority of Canterbury over not just the bishops of southern England but the whole British Church, including the bishops of Wales and, more surprisingly, those in Ireland. Lanfranc had gone to great lengths to emphasize his own superiority, termed his 'primacy', over the other English archbishropic at York. Anselm not only maintained this claim to primacy but assumed the right to act as papal legate in England, even though he had not as yet obtained recognition for his election from the Pope, and even though the Pope sought to appoint a legate of his own to regulate the affairs of the English Church. In all of this, Anselm's actions ran directly counter to the most recent tendencies in papal thinking.

The papal line was increasingly one of obedience and order, with the Church of Rome now placed at the centre of all European Churches. A chain of command extending via the archbishops to the bishops and the simple clergy, like the spokes radiating out from the centre of a wheel, with the hierarchy closest to the hub supplying commands to the order directly below, would ensure what in modern management-speak would be termed 'line management'. Should any of his subordinates disobey the Pope, or should the Pope himself wish to discipline those at a lower level of the chain of command, then the Pope was entitled, as Christ's chief representative on earth and as the direct successor to St Peter, to intervene, to control each level of the structure, and if necessary to stir up the lower clergy, even to stir up the faithful laity, against bishops or archbishops who disobeyed his commands. Anselm's vision derived from a more conservative world, in which each of the great Churches of Europe, be they archbishoprics, bishoprics or abbeys like his former home at Bec, possessed a special dignity of its own, to be handed down intact and undiminished from one generation to the next.

Not surprisingly therefore Anselm found himself at odds both with the King and with the Pope. The result was two extended periods of exile, the first from 1097 to 1100, when Rufus granted him permission to seek counsel from the Pope in Rome, the second from 1103 to 1106 when, having fallen out with Rufus' successor, King Henry I, Anselm once again sought direct papal advice on whether kings could or should invest bishops with their sees. The outcome was a compromise: the King might take homage from bishops for the 'regalia', the lands and rights that they held directly from the crown, but might not any longer invest them with their offices by granting bishops their pastoral staff and ring. Across Europe, similar compromises were reached between papal ambitions and day-to-day reality. Within an English context, what mattered far more was that Anselm's periods of exile set a trend for future archbishops of Canterbury. Exile, even self-imposed exile, had not been a tradition of the Anglo-Saxon bishops, even though the Anglo-Saxon Church had been prepared on occasion to criticize its kings. Between 1097 and the 1240s, by contrast, at least four archbishops of Canterbury were to spend prolonged periods overseas, at odds with their king and seeking refuge either with the popes or with the King of England's enemies in France.

As a symbol of the increasing divorce between ecclesiastical and secular power, this is significant. It also marks the emergence of an institution still with us today. From the 1090s onwards, the kings of England either issued or deliberately withheld letters of protection for churchmen travelling outside the realm. Here we have the origins of the modern idea of the passport, without which the traveller is deprived of official protection. The question of protections or passports both for Archbishop Theobald in the 1140s and Archbishop Becket in the 1160s was to loom large as an issue in their disputes with the crown. Elections to bishoprics nonetheless continued to be tightly controlled by England's kings, and the granting of licence for election and subsequently the acceptance or withholding of the homage of the elect was a powerful tool in royal oversight of the episcopate, still one of the prerogatives of the crown today, albeit exercised via a Crown Appointments Commission and the Prime Minister's Office, rather than by the sovereign in person.

Having to some extent established his authority over the Church, and with the battles of Tinchebrai and later Brémule promising him victory in his succession dispute with his brother and his nephew, King Henry I in theory ranked amongst the richest and most powerful Kings in Christendom. His patronage and his silver were sought by monks from as far away as Toulouse and the Holy Land. He was recognized to be a far-better-educated man than either his father or his elder brothers had been, certainly capable of reading and writing. His cruelty – in the 1090s he had personally pushed a rebellious Rouen merchant from one of the city's highest towers, henceforth known as 'Conan's Leap', and he was known for blinding and mutilating prisoners, especially those convicted of offences against forest law – came to rival the sophisticated sadism of the Byzantine emperors of the East, but was tempered with a respect for English law. Henry himself had succeeded to the throne only after issuing a so-called 'coronation charter' which, in a standard political manoeuvre, sought to blacken the reputation of the previous king, William Rufus, in order to emphasize Henry's own good rule. Henry promised henceforth not to keep churches vacant or to seize their revenues during vacancies, not to charge excessive or unreasonable fines from his barons when they came to inherit their lands (a payment known as a 'relief'), not to marry off heiresses without their consent, and to restore the good laws of King Edward the

Confessor together with whatever legal reforms William the Conqueror had made with the assent of his barons. The fact that Edward the Confessor had not issued any sort of law code did not prevent Henry's contemporaries from inventing such a code and, although the King kept the promises of his coronation charter more in the letter than the spirit, for example by filling poor bishoprics almost immediately but leaving such great cash-cows as Canterbury or Durham vacant for prolonged periods, the charter itself was significant not only as the first written promise by an English king to obey the higher authority of the law, but as a step on the road towards curbing the absolute sovereignty of kings, intruding law and justice as principles even higher than the personal authority conferred upon kings by God.

During Henry's reign, the apparatus of royal government, if not newly invented, for the first time begins to emerge from the confusion and translucence of the historical record. This is thanks in part to the survival of a far larger number of the King's letters and charters than survive for his predecessors, almost 1,500 compared with the 500 of his father and elder brother, but above all due to the preservation of two unique documentary records. The first is a Pipe Roll, or annual summary of the King's income and expenses, covering the year 1130. Known as a Pipe Roll because its large parchment sheets were originally rolled up and stored in a pipe, it is the earliest survivor of a series of such rolls that would originally have stretched back to the occasion when the King's Exchequer or accounting office first began to keep written records of its dealings with the individual officers, the sheriffs of the twenty-six or so English counties, responsible for collecting and disbursing the King's ordinary revenues.

The Exchequer itself, which may already have been in existence from the reign of Rufus, was named from the chequered cloth, literally the chess-board, that was used as a simple sort of abacus for the calculation of receipts. As this implies, Henry's court was a place of some learning and sophistication, capable of grasping the usefulness of such exotic devices as the abacus or the astrolabe, recently imported from the Arab world, addicted to what had originally been the Persian game of chess, itself a training not only in military strategy but in manners and maths. The 1130 Pipe Roll reveals something of Henry's wealth, since it appears to show the King in receipt of at least £23,000 in cash from the English counties, itself only a small and uncertain proportion of the King's overall revenues, incalculable from the surviving records but undoubtedly including revenues from Normandy, from the shadier aspects of bribery and the sale of justice, and in large part from the profits and tribute of war. Even so, at £23,000, Henry I's ordinary income was a great deal higher than that recorded for any king of England for the next forty years.

Besides the Pipe Roll we also have a report, entitled 'The Constitution of the King's Household' which purports to list the chief offices of the King's establishment, from the chancellor and treasurer down to the bakers who baked the King's pastries and the huntsmen and kennel keepers who cared for his hounds and his sport, remunerated not just in money but in wine and candle ends. The combination here of candles and alcohol should remind us that, unlike the households of more humble Englishmen, the King's was an establishment that functioned even after darkness fell. Something of the murkier side of these night-time activities emerges from the fact that, besides fathering two legitimate children by his first wife, Margaret, a direct descendant of the Anglo-Saxon kings, Henry I was also father to at least twenty-four illegitimate children, sired on a number of women, many of them high-born ladies recruited from the immediate vicinity of the King's hunting lodges at Clarendon and Woodstock. Henry's lechery rivalled that even of such later royal Casanovas as Henry VIII or Charles II, and, like Charles, in the 1670s, Henry did his best to promote his children both to high office and, in the case of the girls, to prestigious marriages, where possible to the leading families on the frontiers of his dominion. In this way two of the King's illegitimate sons, both named Robert, were promoted, in one case as Earl of Gloucester with control over the border region of Glamorgan and the greatest of the West Country fortresses at Bristol, in the other as a Devon land-holder with eventual control over the hundred knights' fees of the honour of Okehampton.

These promotions themselves suggest that, within a gener-ation of the events of 1066, Henry I was hard put to maintain the loyalty of those families first granted lands by William the Conqueror but now inclined to forget from whom their rewards had first flowed. Much of Henry's warfare in France was directed not merely towards the resolution of his succession dispute with his elder brother, Robert Curthose, but for the eradication of Robert de Bellême, son of William the Conqueror's loyal servant Roger of Montgomery, now attempting to establish himself as an independent power on the frontiers between Normandy and Anjou. In turn, the need to buy new supporters of his own led the King to confiscate the estates of those he could not trust, to grant away a significant proportion of the estates that had once been held by his father, and to reward a series of newcomers, newly promoted at court. The Welsh Marches were used for the promotion of families, such as the Clares in Ceredigion or Brian fitz Count (illegit-imate son of the Count of Brittany) in Abergavenny, licensed to acquire what land they could get by conquest from the native Welsh. To similar ends, a community of Flemings was installed in Pembrokeshire rather as English government in the seventeenth century was to install lowlands Scots in Ulster, as a guarantee against native resistance.

Other families newly promoted by Henry I ranged from the scions of great French noble houses such as the Beaumont twins, Henry and Robert, earls or counts respectively of Warwick and of Meulan to the south-east of Paris, down to the humbler level of such families as Clinton (whose name derived not from Normandy but from Glympton in Oxfordshire), Chesney and Clifford. Contemporary moralists, remembering the corruption that Roman historians had attributed to the rise of 'new men' untutored in the proper ways of patrician society, tended to dismiss such figures as 'risen from the dust'. In reality, they were all of them relatively well born, even when their immediate ancestry is uncertain, recruited from amongst the branches of families long established at court, each such family tree being populated by an entire host of lesser members twittering and pecking at one another for promotion in the King's service. For more than thirty years, Henry I proved a canny and careful patron of such men. In the process he not only encouraged the first emergence into the historical record of families that were later to gain even greater prominence in English (or in the case of Clinton, American) history, but promoted the development of specific court offices, as justiciar or vice-regent (an office held in effect by the former royal chancellor, Roger, bishop of Salisbury), and as treasurer (deputed to Roger's nephew, Nigel, bishop of Ely). These, amongst the first great offices of state, speak of a government that was becoming increasingly bureaucratized even though still entirely dependent upon the King's personal favour.

Henry also sent justices into the English counties to dispense royal law at a local level. The intention here was not to do good so much as to be seen to do good. As the principal authority for the regulation of disputes the King could hope to collect the fines and profits that inevitably arose when justice was done. Office as justice, then as in the eighteenth century, was an extremely lucrative one, and we have letters of a slightly later date, in which the King's travelling justices, by then known as justices 'in eyre', boast of the sums that they had collected for the King but fail to mention the bribes and douceurs that we can assume they collected for their own private profit. Bribery, like corruption in general, is one of the most persistent aspects of medieval government yet also notoriously difficult to quantify. The house historian of the abbey of St Albans, for example, tells us that his abbot paid over £100 to the King, in the twelfth century a very large sum of money, for the confirmation of the abbey's rights. No mention of this sum appears in the corresponding royal account rolls which in this respect are often no more informative than the accounts of Enron or Elf-Aquitaine as a means of assessing total income or expenditure.

Virtually everyone in royal employment, from the sheriffs down to the most humble of estate bailiffs was involved in syphoning off as much as they possibly could from royal revenue for private gain. The extent to which the proceeds of the agricultural harvest disappeared before ever being entered in written accounts is impossible to quantify but in all likelihood rivalled the extraordinary levels, more than 50 per cent of production, that came to typify the late Soviet economy of Russia. Judges in particular, those expert delayers of the law, had an especially evil reputation. A vision of Hell, reported in 1206 by an Essex farmer named Thurkel, listed the punishments inflicted upon a lawyer and former justice of the Exchequer, forced by demons to swallow and then to vomit red hot coins in an endless cycle of pain. At St Augustine's Abbey in Canterbury, as late as 1314, the monks drew up proposals on how best to influence the King's justices with weekly distributions of bread, wine and ale, firewood, straw for their horses and regular invitations to dinner. Such gifts were regarded as perfectly normal, well below the level at which accusations of bribery or undue influence might have been triggered.

Stephen and Matilda

Henry I, despite his wars in France and on the frontiers with Wales, achieved peace in England in all but the first two years of his reign. Peace, however, did not spell an end to the disputes over succession that had dogged English kingship since at least the time of Aethelred. Henry's legitimate son and heir, William the Aetheling, was the first member of the ruling dynasty since 1066 to have had the blood of both King Alfred and the dukes of Normandy flowing in his veins. Marriages arranged between William and a daughter of the Count of Anjou and, even more prestigiously, between William's sister Matilda and the German emperor Henry V, appeared to promise not only stability on Normandy's troubled southern frontier but the merging of the bloodline of the kings of England with that of the greatest rulers in Christendom. That neither marriage prospered was judged by some contemporaries to have been due to the blood of the Conqueror still tainted by the violence of 1066. William the Aetheling was drowned, in 1120, attempting, after what seems to have been an especially drunken party, to race his father back across the Channel. Embarking on one of the greatest of the court's transports, the *White Ship*, from the port of Barfleur in Normandy, William's vessel struck a submerged rock and sank, taking with it not only the heir to the kingdom but a large number of courtiers, including the Earl of Chester. The sole survivor left to tell the tale was a drunken Rouen butcher who had been carousing with his social superiors when the ship went down. With shades of the modern morality of news gathering, this butcher was regarded as beneath contempt by the chroniclers, who nonetheless hung on his every word when it came to the details of the disaster.

With no legitimate son to succeed him, and with no children born to a second marriage hurriedly arranged in 1121, Henry was forced to entertain alternative strategies for the succession. The outcome in the longer term was to provoke civil war. On the one hand he promoted at his court his nephew Stephen of Blois, a grandson of William the Conqueror, already recognized as Count of Mortain in south-western Normandy and as lord of the English honours of Lancaster and Eye (in Suffolk), who in 1125 married the heiress to the immensely well-connected county of Boulogne. Stephen was an affable man, now in his mid-thirties. He had escaped the disaster of 1120 only by divine providence, having been prevented by a sudden attack of diarrhoea from joining his cousin on board ship. Even so, Stephen was not even the first-born son of his father, the Count of Blois, having two elder brothers, the first perhaps an idiot, the second a capable if dull representative of his line. Even if Stephen began to harbour ambitions for the English throne, his hopes were surely dashed in 1125 when the emperor Henry V died, leaving his childless widow, King Henry's daughter Matilda, to return to England. As a widowed empress (a title which she now adopted and used to the end of her life, forty years later, despite the fact that she had never been crowned or recognized as such by her late husband) Matilda commanded enormous prestige. In 1127, she was betrothed to the fourteen-year-old heir to the county of Anjou, Geoffrey Plantagenet (whose name perhaps derived from the broom plant used as a family device, adopted in memory of a golden flower which the Pope had bestowed on one of Geoffrey's ancestors). At the same time, Henry I had Matilda proclaimed as heir to his lands both in England and Normandy, Stephen of Blois vying with Robert, Earl of Gloucester for the honour of being the first to swear an oath to uphold this settlement.

The marriage between Matilda and Geoffrey proved tempestuous. Despite a reconciliation in 1131, a second series of oaths that Matilda would be recognized as Henry's heir, and the birth of a son, named Henry in honour of his grandfather, in 1133, daughter and father quarrelled, in the months immediately before Henry I's death, to such an extent that Matilda was not at her father's deathbed. Henry himself died after a meal of lampreys, a particularly disgusting sort of eel-like parasite with a cylindrical toothed mouth, accustomed to sucking the blood of other aquatic creatures. Henry I's lampreys supplied an apt metaphor, to those looking for such things, that it was the luxury and parasitical greed of the Conqueror's sons that would prove their downfall.

Stephen of Blois, despite his earlier oaths to recognize Matilda, now seized his opportunity. Like Rufus in 1087, or Henry I in 1100, he happened to be in the right place at the right time, in a position to make a dash for the English coast and coronation. Whereas Rufus and Henry had made first for the royal treasury in Winchester, Stephen could rely on his younger brother, Henry of Blois, bishop of Winchester since

1129, to manage affairs in the old West Saxon capital. Instead, recognizing the increasing significance of a new capital city, Stephen made his way to London. Having, like Henry I before him, offered a charter of good government, promising to limit the extension of forest law and to allow free elections to the English bishoprics, he was crowned at Westminster Abbey on 22 December 1135, exactly three weeks after the death of his uncle, the late King. Across England as a whole, Henry I's former subjects responded to the news of his death with a wholesale slaughter of the King's deer and the breaking down of newly erected forest fences: a clear sign that Henry I's administration of the forests was resented and oppressive.

All now seemed set for a repetition of the *faits accomplis* of 1087 and 1099. Stephen secured papal approval for his coronation, and bought off his elder brother with a promise of money. When the Scots invaded the northern counties and seized Carlisle and Newcastle, the Welsh rose in rebellion, and Baldwin de Redvers, a former servant of Henry I, fortified Exeter castle on behalf of Empress Matilda, Stephen reacted with laconic affability. A peace was agreed with the Scots. The garrison of Exeter, besieged for three months, had no sooner surrendered than they were allowed to go free. Apparently, Stephen believed that he commanded such vast resources and had so many friends and allies at his disposal that he could afford to be magnanimous. This was a disastrous miscalculation. The velvet glove of Rufus or Henry I had proved effective precisely because it concealed a massive iron fist. Stephen lacked the requisite ruthlessness. A characteristic story, told much later but nonetheless relevant to the events of the 1130s, describes Stephen's siege of the castle of Newbury in Berkshire. When the castellan, the former Marshal or chief adjutant of Henry I, refused to surrender, Stephen seized his five-year-old son as a hostage, threatening to execute the boy should the castle not be delivered up. The garrison ignored this threat, even when the boy was displayed on a siege catapult, and the King, far from executing his young hostage, was later found in his flower-strewn pavilion playing at knights with the boy, using dolls made of straw.

The result of such clemency was a mounting series of crises, as Stephen gradually became aware that something more forceful was required from him. An expedition to Normandy in 1137 failed to prevent an invasion of the duchy by Geoffrey of Anjou. It should be remembered here that Stephen, with his connections to Blois and his army of Flemish mercenaries recruited via the county of Boulogne, was no more a natural friend to the Norman barons than Geoffrey and his Angevins. In the following year, troubled by the oaths to his half-sister Matilda that he had signally failed to respect, Robert, Earl of Gloucester, the greatest of Henry I's illegitimate sons, rose in rebellion at Bristol. A second Scots invasion was only narrowly defeated at the Battle of the Standard fought near Northallerton in August 1138, led on the English side not by the King but by the Count of Aumale, William 'the fat', assisted by a rag-tag militia apparently recruited by the Archbishop of York, parish by parish for national defence. Even then, Northumbria and Newcastle were definitively ceded to the Scots.

Stephen's response, like that of many weak men, was intended to appear decisive, but in fact seemed merely tyrannical. When the Pope in 1139 failed to absolve him from the oaths previously sworn to Matilda, adjourning any decision rather than pronouncing a firm verdict, Stephen arrested three of the English bishops, Roger of Salisbury, the former justiciar of Henry I, and his two nephews, Alexander, bishop of Lincoln and Nigel, bishop of Ely. The move was intended to calm rumours of rebellion. In reality it merely turned the Church against Stephen, who could now be portrayed as a tyrant as well as a usurper and perjurer. Even the King's brother, Henry of Blois, wavered in his loyalty.

All of this came, almost literally, as a Godsend to the Empress Matilda, who landed in England in the autumn of 1139 and who, rather than being attacked in Sussex, where she had established herself, was granted safe-conduct to join her half-brother Robert at Bristol. Demonstrating all the subtle idiocy that one associates with modern masters of warfare, Stephen apparently reasoned that it was better to concentrate his enemy's forces in one location, rather than have them spread out across southern England. The bringing together of Matilda and Robert was the tipping point after which there was no real hope of peace so long as either Matilda or Stephen lived. Bristol henceforth was an impregnable Angevin fortress, and, for the first time in English history, Robert began to use Welsh mercenaries from his Glamorgan estates, 'a dreadful and unendurable number of Welshmen' as the contemporary *Deeds of Stephen* puts it, as a key element in war.

It would be tedious to pursue the individual campaigns of the ensuing civil war. In essence, 1141 proved a year of wonders. First, King Stephen was taken prisoner in battle at Lincoln in February, and consigned to prison at Bristol. The Empress Matilda was installed as 'Lady of England' but then alienated the Londoners through her haughtiness and her insistence upon remaining seated whilst her subjects appeared before her. In the subsequent flight from London and then Winchester, Robert, Earl of Gloucester was himself taken prisoner by an army mustered by Stephen's queen. An exchange of prisoners, in which both the King and Earl Robert were released, in effect placed Stephen back on the throne within a year of his imprisonment.

Thereafter, England itself became divided between a series of campaigning fronts, the most bitterly contested lying along the Thames valley from Oxford to the outskirts of London. Normandy went its own way, finally conquered by Geoffrey of Anjou, who in April 1144 was installed as duke. Gloucestershire and Bristol served as the chief Angevin redoubt in England, with the local financier Robert fitz Harding, himself of Anglo-Saxon descent, as banker to the Empress and her party. Robert fitz Harding, an Englishman, followed shortly afterwards by the Flemish financier William

Cade, deserves to rank as the first state banker in English history, founder of a line of ill-omen yet supplying a necessary service at a time when royal income had dwindled to unsustainable levels. Stephen himself held out in London, with London and the counties of Essex and Kent sufficient to supply his financial needs despite his loss of nearly everything else. Both parties issued their own coins, as did the Scots at Carlisle and Newcastle and a number of magnates and earls, including the bishop of Winchester in the south.

Alliances between individual barons were negotiated and committed to writing, in an attempt to limit warfare in the localities. Even so, many dozens of temporary castles were built. At least two of the greatest earls in England, Geoffrey de Mandeville, Earl of Essex and Ranulf, Earl of Chester, were arrested at Stephen's court, even though in theory under safe-conduct. Although few if any barons were killed in combat, the fear of treachery became near universal. The death of Robert, earl of Gloucester in 1147, and the refusal of the Archbishop of Canterbury, Theobald (yet another monk of Bec), to crown Stephen's eldest son as King during his father's lifetime, in effect brought stalemate to both parties. This was resolved only by the emergence of Henry Plantagenet, the son of Geoffrey of Anjou and Empress Matilda, as leader of the Angevin party. Geoffrey's death in 1151 brought Henry enthronement as Duke of Normandy and Count of Anjou. His marriage, the following year, to Eleanor, only three weeks earlier divorced from the French King Louis VII, brought him the entire duchy of Aquitaine stretching from the Loire to the Pyrenees. Probably at this time, or shortly afterwards, Henry began to issue coins on which he proclaimed his title as '*Henricus rex futurus*', 'Henry the future king'.

In 1153, he returned to England determined upon a final showdown. In the midst of negotiations and threats, Stephen's son Eustace died, some said poisoned by the monks of Bury St Edmunds where he had recently stayed. Like many accusations of poisoning, this cannot be taken at face value. Sudden deaths, often within a few hours of dining, were frequently attributed to poison when other causes should be sought: heart attack, stroke, or, in the case of intense stomach pains, acute appendicitis, for which there was neither diagnosis nor cure. The death of Eustace nonetheless opened the way to a final peace. For the rest of his lifetime, Stephen would retain his title and authority as King. Henry of Anjou would be acknowledged as his heir. The barons of England would swear homage to both men. The King's younger son, William of Warenne, would be compensated with a vast estate, which Henry would guarantee to respect just as he would respect the greatest of Stephen's grants to the religious, most notably Stephen's foundation of a new abbey at Faversham, where the King himself intended to be buried.

Stephen was approaching sixty. None of the post-Conquest kings of England had so far lived beyond that age. Even so, death came more suddenly for Stephen than was expected. Staying with the monks of Dover, from where he hoped to conduct negotiations with Flanders, Stephen was suddenly seized with violent stomach pains and a flow of blood, 'as had happened to him before', remarks a local chronicler, clearly anxious to avoid the sorts of accusations of poisoning that had been levelled at Bury St Edmunds a year earlier. Stephen died on 25 October 1154. Anglo-Norman kingship, which for the past ten years had not even been Anglo-Norman but Anglo-Flemish-French, died with him.

King Stephen and his reign have provoked an unusual degree of attention from modern historians. Since the Second World War, whilst Rufus has attracted only one biographer, and most medieval English kings only two, there have been at least five full-scale biographies of Stephen as well as a whole series of related studies, down to and including the work of Ellis Peters and her tales of the twelfth-century monastic detective, Brother Cadfael. It is as if, afraid of being accounted dull, English historians have emphasized the eccentric and the extraordinary reign of Stephen, albeit with a comfortable sense that they themselves are lucky not to have lived through such interesting times. For the history of England, and the wider story of Britain, does this period of warfare and confusion have any deeper significance?

It has been suggested that Stephen's reign mattered chiefly because it ushered in a new and more secure sense of the ownership of land. Barons and knights whose inheritances had previously lain at the disposal of the King were now able to ensure that land passed from father to son with no real possibility of upset. In reality, although a firm legal basis for the possession of land (what lawyers would call 'seisin') and for its inheritance developed only after the 1150s, in terms of possession and the practicalities of inheritance nothing much had changed. For reasons only loosely related to politics, dictated far more by a desire to secure the financial profits of justice, the kings of England after 1154 began offering legal procedures (established by enactments known as 'assizes') whereby their subjects could stake a claim, quickly and without undue quibbling, to land that had recently been seized from them, or to land in which they claimed ancestral right. If Stephen's reign did not usher in a new approach to landholding did it perhaps draw a decisive divide between England and Normandy? Once again, there is little to suggest that this was so. In the decade after 1144, it is true, the King of England had no real authority in the duchy, but then this was equally true of Henry I before 1106. Moreover, after 1144, as under Henry I, the breach proved only temporary. The families divided by the civil war of the 1140s were very rapidly reunited, and Normandy passed together with England into the hands of Henry II.

There is one further reason to attribute particular significance to Stephen's reign. It witnessed the first real outbreak of xenophobia and the hatred of foreigners permitted since the conquest of 1066. Xenophobia was to become one of England's greatest exports: an expression of national identity that could be channelled through public violence, the destruction of foreign property and, in extremes, the murder of foreigners. The St Brice's Day massacre of 1002 supplied only a foretaste of the pogroms yet to come. Under Stephen there were two incidents that suggest a growing unrest over national identities. The first was the mistrust expressed towards Stephen's Flemish mercenaries, and in particular against his mercenary captain William of Ypres. The community of Englishmen, since 1066 unable to vent more than eighty years of frustrations over the compromises forced on it by accepting Norman lords, was perhaps all the readier to seek scapegoats in other communities, with the Flemings and the Welsh high on the list of potential victims. Anger over Henry I's harsh government had already been expressed through the deliberate destruction of forests and the killing of deer. Perhaps the Welsh and the Flemings came to represent an alternative target of attack, regarded as less than civilized and in extreme cases as less than entirely human.

Anti-Semitism: William of Norwich

One other incident of Stephen's reign supports this suggestion. Like the deer of the forest, the Jews of the greater cities were in theory placed directly under royal protection. In 1144, according to later and highly unreliable testimony, rumour spread that a twelve-year-old boy named William, apprenticed to the skinner's trade in the city of Norwich had been lured into the house of a Norwich Jew where he was ritually tortured and crucified, his agony lasting from the Tuesday in Holy Week until Good Friday. Thus far, the story depends very much upon an identification between William of Norwich and the infant Christ, and should remind us that the twelfth century was an age in which Christ and his sufferings were viewed in increasingly human terms. William's body was then disposed of in woods to the south of the city, where it was discovered by a local forester, keen to ensure that no one illegally gathered timber from the bishop's wood. After a procedure that is described in baffling and highly improbable detail, the Jews were accused in the bishop's synod but bribed the local sheriff, John de Chesney, to grant them refuge in Norwich Castle. The body itself was dug up and reburied in the cathedral precincts by the cathedral's monks. Lacking any obvious saint of their own, the monks were anxious to supply themselves with a potentially miracle-working cult. The cult itself took several years to promote, and William's body had to be exhumed and ceremonially reburied no less than three further times, in April 1150, July 1151 and April 1154, before miracles became widely reported, set down in a long account of events and miracles by the chief guardian of the shrine, a man named Thomas of Monmouth. What is particularly significant here is that Thomas accused the Jews of a conspiracy that reached from one end of Europe to another, controlled by a line of Jewish princes living in Narbonne in southern France, by whom the Jews were committed to the annual sacrifice of a Christian boy-child in deliberate and mocking emulation of the crucifixion of Christ.

This is the first known appearance of the so-called 'blood libel', the idea that the Jews were ritually committed to the kidnapping and murder of Christian boys, a vile accusation that in certain unsavoury quarters even today still poisons relations between Christians and Jews. After the Norwich incident, the very next appearance of the blood libel also comes from England, from Gloucester, where in the 1160s another young boy, named Harold, was likewise said to have been done to death by Jews. The chief church in Norwich market place, dedicated to St Peter, was a dependency of Gloucester Abbey, which no doubt explains the connection. From Norwich and Gloucester, the libel spread far and wide, to France, and thence to most parts of Europe, where it came to form one of the cornerstones of European anti-Semitism. For present purposes, what is particularly interesting about this great British export is that, in origin, it seems to have been both anti-foreign and anti-royal. The King's sheriff was amongst the villains of the piece. Most of those involved in disclosing the 'truth' or in finding healing at William's shrine bore unmistakably English names. Even William, despite his Norman Christian name, was of sound Anglo-Saxon birth, descended from what seems to have been an extensive, well-heeled, and at this time still just-about tolerated family of priests.

Anarchy under Stephen?

Historical debate on the reign of Stephen has too often descended into sterile point-scoring over the extent to which this was a period of 'anarchy'. Like 'feudalism', 'anarchy' is an anachronistic term, invented only in the eighteenth century. Lacking any sort of 'anarchy-meter' for the 1140s, historians have debated the relative significance of coinage, baronial castles, peace treaties and charters as if these can somehow be calibrated into a verdict for or against the 'anarchic'. In reality, the blood libel may be a much more significant and, in European terms, easily the most baneful of the legacies of King Stephen's chaotic reign. Two other legacies are worth mentioning, not just of Stephen's reign, but of the interaction between Church and secular society over the first fifty years of the twelfth century.

Monastic chroniclers, most famously the compiler of the *Anglo-Saxon Chronicle* still being written at Peterborough, tended to play up the disasters of the 1140s, writing of Stephen's reign as the nineteen years 'when Christ and his saints slept'. In fact, far from being a time of inactivity, this was a period when the public face of both Christ and the Church was transformed. The internecine warfare of Stephen's reign undoubtedly left a bitter legacy of property disputes, with two or more families ever afterwards convinced that they had proper title to the same estate. Land was the chief symbol of wealth and status, and its confiscation or violent dispossession, as in the late 1130s or 40s, was all the easier to effect given that there were few major landholding families in England whose title to their land, by 1135, was more than seventy years' old. One set of violent seizures, after 1066, only paved the way for another, after 1135.

Some of these new disputes were resolved via the law courts and the new assizes of Henry II's reign, whose effect was principally to reward those who could prove long-standing possession. In other cases, where two or more families had longstanding claims, a resolution was more difficult. It might be achieved by political persuasion, by the King's friendship, or by simple bribery. More often, it led to endless bitterness and litigation via the sorts of process that activate several of the more law-ridden novels of Trollope or Dickens. Jarndyce versus Jarndyce, give or take a bit of armour and quite a lot more physical violence, is easily rivalled by such cases as those of Stuteville versus Mowbray for possession of Kirby Moorside, fitz Harding versus Berkeley for the honour and castle of Berkeley, or the earls of Gloucester versus the earls of Chester for possession of Chipping Camden. All of these disputes had their origin in the reign of Stephen.

The Cistercians

For those who believed they had title to land, who were aware that such title was likely to be disputed, and who either wished to atone for their sins or to avoid interminable vendettas, one solution was to grant such land to religion. By using a disputed estate to found a monastery and by settling it with monks keen to defend their title to the land, a landholder could hope to profit from the monks' prayers and spiritual intercessions without himself risking the costs of litigation or warfare. Hence the fact that so many monasteries were established on land encumbered with pre-existing legal disputes, and that monks were amongst the keenest and most active litigants in the king's courts. The consequence here during the reign of Stephen, a period of particular instability in the possession of land, was the foundation of a quite extraordinary number of new religious houses, perhaps more than 180 all told in the nineteen years from 1135 to 1154, doubling the number of monasteries in existence in England.

A large number of these new foundations were Cistercian, ultimately imported from eastern France and from a revived and ascetic spirituality that had led large numbers of French monks, from around the year 1100, to seek God in the deserted places in forests and mountains. One of the earliest abbots of Cîteaux (the monastery near Dijon in Burgundy that came to symbolize and to control this new order) was an Englishman by birth, Stephen Harding, who, as a child, had been vowed to the monastic life at Sherborne in Dorset, perhaps one of those children placed in monasteries when their Anglo-Saxon fathers were disinherited as a result of the Conquest. In the later retelling of their history, it was Stephen Harding who was credited with writing the constitution of the new Cistercian order, placing each successive foundation under a meticulous system of supervision and discipline, presided over by a General Chapter of all Cistercian abbots meeting at Cîteaux in October each year. A great deal of this historical account represents later twelfth-century make-believe. In reality, it was a slightly later recruit to Cîteaux, the Frenchman Bernard, himself for thirty years abbot of Cîteaux's daughter house at Clairvaux, who transformed the order and gave it both its intellectual and its institutional coherence. As a result, there is still much dispute as to the circumstances in which Cistercian monasticism was introduced to England, probably via the first of the Cistercian abbeys established at Waverley in the Surrey forest in 1128, thereafter demonstrating a particular affection for the high places of Yorkshire and the north, with Rievaulx and Fountains both established before the death of Henry I in 1135.

Precisely how and in what circumstances these abbeys were subjected to specifically 'Cistercian' customs remains a controversial, though in many ways less significant fact than their encouragement of a new spiritual discipline in which contemplation and the deliberate imitation of Christ were paramount impulses. Not surprisingly, the humanity of Christ loomed large in Cistercian thinking, and in particular the relationship between Christ and his mother, the Virgin Mary. All Cistercian houses, at least from the 1120s onwards, were dedicated exclusively to the Virgin Mary and, although Bernard himself disapproved of such Marian devotions as the feast of the Conception of the Virgin Mary, it was the Cistercians who did most to broadcast the cult of the human Christ, bound by love to his human mother. At almost exactly the same time that the Jews of Norwich were being accused of crucifying a twelve-year-old boy in cruel imitation of the crucifixion of Christ, Ailred of Rievaulx, the greatest of the English Cistercian writers and himself of impeccable Anglo-Saxon descent, was composing a treatise on 'Jesus at the Age of Twelve', deliberately emphasizing the humanity of the infant Christ as a model to those seeking the life of prayer.

As with most religious reformers throughout the ages, there were paradoxes and a tinge of hypocrisy to Cistercian spirituality. Ailred of Rievaulx might have sought a life of poverty and a deliberately spartan diet, but he himself was of high birth and he owed his promotion as abbot to his contacts with the Scots royal court where he had served as steward. The Cistercians, as at Rievaulx, might seek out the deserts of the world, but they swiftly transformed such places into a machined landscape for the generation of cash. The sheep runs of north Yorkshire were treasure trails from which came the wool, itself sold according to new and sophisticated credit arrangements, to merchants prepared to stake large sums of money as advance payment for the next year's crop. Although, in the 1150s, the Cistercian General Chapter stepped in to forbid monks from acting as middle men, from buying up the wool crop of surrounding farmers and selling it on at a profit, the practice by no means disappeared. Large-scale sheep-farming and the futures market in wool remained especially Cistercian enterprises.

As late as the 1320s we learn from the notes kept by an Italian named Pergoletti, wool buyer for the Florentine merchant house of the Bardi, that it was from such Cistercian abbeys as Tintern and Abbey Dore in the Welsh Marches that the best and most expensive raw wool was to be purchased. At £18 the sack of twenty-six stone, the best Cistercian wool was priced at more than three times the value of wool to be had from lower quality suppliers. The whole Cistercian enterprise, from the monks' sheep runs to their massive and well-stocked barns (the barn of Beaulieu Abbey at Great Coxwell in Oxfordshire being a particularly magnificent example), from their artificial water courses to their industrialized structures of prayer, was a monument not just to asceticism but to the pursuit of virtue through the profits of hard work. In Wales in particular, the Wild West of twelfth-century Britain, it was the Cistercians who brought commercialized agricultural practices to valleys previously farmed according to very different pastoral traditions. All of this within a century of the Norman Conquest, and in the 1140s, in the midst of a brutal civil war that might be supposed to have consigned England to a dark age of violence and 'anarchy'.

Like a lot of religious ascetics, Ailred of Rievaulx had diffi- culties with human sexuality. According to his chief biog- rapher, who clearly thought of Ailred as a potential saint, he used to immerse himself for hours in a cold bath, placed in a secret chamber under the house of the novices, in order that he might master the Devil's urges and so that he might ease the symptoms of the kidney stones with which he was plagued, some of them the size of beans, requiring recourse to his bath up to forty times a day. Rather like the High Church reformers of the nineteenth-century Oxford movement, the Cistercians were sometimes suspected of being distinctly unmanly in their celebration of the spiritual love between man and man. In reality, they were belligerent supporters of Christian warfare. St Bernard of Clairvaux was at the forefront of crusading rhetoric and one of the first patrons of the Templar knights, themselves introduced to England during the reign of Stephen. Nonetheless, a story told by the court wit Walter Map, said to have drawn laughter from King Stephen's successor, Henry II, related how St Bernard had prayed for a miracle, seeking to restore life to a young monk who had recently died. Bernard threw himself on the boy, with prayers and entreaties, but when Bernard got up, the young monk, being still dead, did not. 'That is odd,' said Walter Map, 'because I have often heard of older monks throwing themselves on boys, but when the monk gets up, generally the boy does too.'

Henry II

In the aggressively heterosexual humour of Henry II's court we perhaps see yet another response to the pathetic affability of Stephen's reign. Testosterone-charged masculinity is often a feature of conquering or restored monarchies, be it in the rampant Norman stallions of the Bayeux Tapestry or the notorious womanizing of King Charles II. Just as the bloodshed at Hastings was still wet to the touch in 1135, so the confusions and disputes of the 1140s further dented the already tarnished reputation of England's kings. To Henry II, determined to rule in a very different way, the reign of Stephen was something to be struck from historical memory. After 1154, Henry II's new regime chose to look back to the circumstances of the reign of Henry I, Henry II's grandfather, deliberately consigning the intervening period to oblivion, described as the 'shipwreck' of Stephen's reign (with deliberate reference, perhaps, to the *White Ship* disaster of 1120).

We can see this in Henry II's approach even to the tombs of his ancestors. Henry I's resting place, at Reading Abbey in Berkshire, was richly endowed by the new king. Faversham, where Stephen was buried, was effectively ignored. A vast ground plan, laid out by Stephen was never completed and the abbey's lands, grudgingly confirmed by Henry in accordance with his promises to the late King, led to no great prosperity. We can see precisely this same contempt for Stephen even in the timing and arrangements for Henry II's coronation.

Stephen died in October 1154. Henry waited almost two months before crossing to England. The date he chose for his crossing, the night of 7–8 December, was the vigil of the feast of the Conception of the Virgin Mary, a feast day intimately connected to English identity, sacred to the memory of the mother of Christ, herself ' the star of the sea' and the patron of all mariners. When he next returned to France, it was for a crown-wearing in Rouen cathedral on 2 February 1156, the feast of the Virgin Mary's Purification, and it was on 14 August, the vigil of the feast day of the Virgin's Assumption, that he crossed to Normandy again in 1158.

Meanwhile, on his first landing as King, Henry did not immediately seek coronation at Westminster. Instead, he waited until Sunday, 19 December, the 4th Sunday in Advent, precisely the same day of the liturgical calendar on which Stephen himself had been crowned in 1135. The symbolism was obvious. The coronation of 1135 had been a mistake, to be re-enacted nineteen years later more or less to the day, now with the rightful claimant rather than a usurper installed on his grandfather's throne.

4

THE FOUNDATIONS OF A DYNASTY, 1154–1189

The Plantagenets

Henry II

The red-haired and fiercely energetic young man who succeeded to the throne of England as King Henry II was the son of Empress Matilda, daughter of Henry I of England. On his father's side, he was descended from the counts of Anjou, the Plantagenets, who had held sway over the city of Angers and the Loire valley from at least the tenth century. It was this paternal inheritance that historians have in mind when they assign the label 'Plantagenet' or 'Angevin' to Henry and his successors. Henry II was vastly to extend his ancestral inheritance. Contemporaries greeted him as the fulfilment of a prophecy, attributed to Edward the Confessor, in which the green tree of England would only flourish again once the split parts of its trunk were rejoined. As the grandson of Queen Matilda, the wife of Henry I and a direct descendant of the

Anglo-Saxon kings, Henry II was the first ruler with the blood of Alfred flowing through his veins to have sat on the English throne since 1066. Certainly, Henry did his best to emphasize his own kinship to Edward the Confessor, ensuring the official papal canonization of Edward and the translation of his relics to a new shrine in Westminster Abbey in 1163. The feast day assigned to the Confessor was 13 October, the eve of the anniversary of the Battle of Hastings. Like the reign of King Stephen, Harold Godwinson was to be airbrushed from historical memory. Meanwhile, Henry II was equally keen to stress his kinship to the Norman dukes, in 1162 at Fécamp presiding over the reburial of the bodies of dukes Richard I and Richard II, the grandfather and great-grandfather of William the Conqueror, in new and elaborately carved stone sarcophaguses almost certainly provided at Henry's expense.

By his marriage to Eleanor, heiress to the duchy of Aquitaine, Henry had already, two years before he became King of England, acquired dominion over the whole of south-western France, stretching from the Loire down to the Pyrenees. Through a process of political coercion, by the mid-1160s he was to project his authority westwards into Brittany and Wales, and northwards to seize back the counties of Westmorland, Cumberland and Northumberland occupied for the previous twenty years by the King of Scots. In 1171, stepping into the maelstrom caused by the conquest of Leinster by an army of freebooting marcher barons commanded by Richard 'Strongbow', Earl of Pembroke, Henry led an expedition that was to claim Ireland and its lordship for the English crown. Three years later, victorious in a civil war fought out against his eldest son, he obtained the right to establish English garrisons at Berwick, Edinburgh and as far north as Stirling, imposing oaths of homage upon the Scots King. His military exploits, his political cunning and his courtly magnificence had already brought him and his children alliances with the rulers of Spain and Saxony and with the Capetian kings of France. In due course, the youngest of his daughters was married to the

King of Sicily. So great was Henry's reputation by the 1180s that, in the desperate days before the Battle of Hattin in 1187 (the first great defeat for the crusader kingdoms in the Holy Land), he was offered the keys to the city of Jerusalem and the prospect of ruling over the place of Christ's own crucifixion and resurrection.

Henry died in 1189, still undecided as to whether he would fulfil his crusading vows. He was succeeded by his eldest surviving son, Richard I, who almost immediately embarked for the East, conquering Sicily and Cyprus on the way and in July 1192, if not quite achieving the reconquest of Jerusalem, lost to Saladin and Islam since 1187, was said to have caught a glimpse of its glittering roofs. Richard's chief lieutenants, though not the King himself, fulfilled their vows of pilgrimage to the Holy Sepulchre under safe conduct from Saladin. In the Holy Land, Richard recaptured the port of Acre and fortified the coastal cities, ensuring the survival of Christian rule there for a further hundred years. Returning to England via Austria, he was kidnapped near Vienna, sold by the Duke of Austria to the Holy Roman Emperor, Henry VI, and ransomed for the extraordinary sum of £100,000, literally a king's ransom, raised from English taxes. The money went to pay for the German conquest of southern Italy, itself one of the greatest of European military adventures. Far from bankrupting the English, it was followed by yet further financial exactions, intended to guarantee Richard's lands in France against conquest by his one-time friend, now his most bitter rival, the French King Philip Augustus. Richard died aged only 41 in 1199, still defending his French dominions, campaigning south of Limoges. Within a few years he had already acquired his nickname as 'the Lionheart', later explained by reference to an incident said to have occurred during his captivity in Germany. Seeing his gaoler's daughter menaced by a lion, and with nothing more substantial to protect him than forty silk handkerchiefs, he is said to have reached down the creature's throat and plucked out its still beating heart, which he then proceeded calmly to salt and eat. Quite what a lion, or forty silk handkerchiefs, were doing in the vicinity was never satisfactorily explained, although legend stated that the lion was sent by the German emperor specifically to eat Richard. The legend, however, and the speed with which it developed, supplies clear proof of Richard's European-wide reputation.

Henry II had established a new 'Plantagenet' dynasty on the English throne, destined to last for a further seven generations through to 1399. By his accumulation of an estate in France greater than that held by any ruler since Charlemagne, by his conquests in Britain, and his encouragement of law, administration and learning on a scale that could not have been imagined in the days of his ineffective predecessor, King Stephen, Henry II fundamentally altered the course of English, of French and indeed of European history. His legacy was immense and in many cases enduring. English rule over Gascony, a product of Henry's marriage to Eleanor of Aquitaine, was to last for three centuries. The English crown claimed sovereignty over Ireland as recently as the 1940s, and indeed, though vigorously contested, continues to rule a part of the north of Ireland even today. The palace which Henry refurbished at Westminster, and the new courts and administrative procedures that he established there lie, even now, at the very foundations of British government and English law. More than this, in purely personal terms, Henry's reign witnessed drama on a remarkable scale. His relations with the Church, and with his own wife and sons, formed the stuff of legend even in his own lifetime and continue to be reflected in the work of poets, playwrights and screenwriters, from the sublime to the ridiculous, from Tennyson and T.S. Eliot through to the histrionics of Katherine Hepburn in *The Lion in Winter*.

Henry's enemies in France called him 'the red-headed one' and 'the little fox', perhaps by reference to the Bible (Song of Solomon 2:15), 'Catch for us the little foxes that ruin our vineyards', in medieval commentary, not least in the commentary by Bernard of Clairvaux, believed to be synonymous with heretics and those who threatened the Christian faith. When asked his opinion of Henry, then still a boy, St Bernard is said to have proclaimed 'From the Devil he came and to the Devil he will surely go.' A legend, by no means discouraged by Henry and his sons, claimed that the counts of Anjou were descended from a she-Devil, Melusine, who was part woman, part dragon, and who vanished one day in a puff of smoke when forced to attend Mass. Other stories in circulation at his court identified him with King Herla, kidnapped by underground pygmies, by whom he was doomed to gallop about the world at the head of a wild hunt of hounds and horsemen. An ever blacker legend suggested that Henry's father, angered with the bishop of Sées in Normandy, had commanded that the bishop be castrated and then forced to process through his cathedral city with his severed manhood carried before him in a basin. As this suggests, the early Plantagenets rather revelled in their sulphurous reputation. Told by his court confessor to calm his temper by imitating the lambs and doves of scripture, Henry replied that even lambs used their horns and doves their feathers to attack their fellow creatures: 'By nature I am a son of wrath', he declared. 'And why not, when God himself is capable of such anger?' On one occasion, at Caen in 1166, Henry is said to have grown so furious with his constable, Richard du Hommet, that

aflame with his usual rage, he tore his hat from his head, undid his belt, hurled his cloak and the clothes he was wearing far away from him, tore the silken covering from the bed with his own hand, and began to eat the straw on the floor, as if he were sitting in a ditch.

The Biblical sentence 'The wrath of kings is as the roaring of a lion' (Proverbs 19:12) was one which Henry II took very much to heart, and the lion, Richard the Lionheart's mascot, was in the Middle Ages regarded as a bloodthirsty and unpredictable creature, very far from the cuddly make-believe of Disney's *Lion King*.

We know a great deal about the life and personal relations of Henry and his sons, chiefly because their courts generated a quite phenomenal quantity of literature and historical writing. As this suggests, the Plantagenet court was a highly self-conscious phenomenon, perhaps as a result of its own sense of insecurity. Like many of the most outwardly confident of men, Henry was, beneath the surface, a king by no means certain of his entitlement to rule. Like each of the English, Danish or Norman kings who had ruled England since the year 1000, Henry was by no means the undisputed claimant. He had younger brothers who for a time sought a share of the spoils. He had rivals, at least to begin with, in the surviving daughter and younger son of the late king, Stephen of Blois. He was mistrusted and despised at the court of the kings of France, not least for making off with Eleanor of Aquitaine, herself freed to marry Henry only after an acrimonious divorce from the French King, Louis VII. Whilst she had still been married to Louis, wild accusations had flown, not only of Eleanor's incest with her uncle, the ruler of Antioch in the Holy Land, but of her sleeping with Henry II's father, Geoffrey, Count of Anjou, before ever she bedded the son. Sexual tensions were even more rampant at the Plantagenet than at the Capetian court, and once again seem to reflect the image of a king whose outward behaviour masked a very different inner reality. Henry maintained a whole harem of mistresses, not only after 1173, when Eleanor was locked away at Sarum as a potential rebel, but from long before this. He fathered a large number of illegitimate children by these mistresses, and like Henry I he did not scruple at cuckolding members of his own court. Recent research suggests that he enjoyed sexual liaisons not only with Rosamund Clifford, the most famous of his lady friends, later buried in the aristocratic nunnery at Godstow in Oxfordshire, but with Rosamund's aunt, Ida of Hainault, and with Ida of Hainault's own daughter, Ida de Tosny. By these last two women, mother and daughter, he fathered not only a future royal chancellor and Archbishop of York, but William Longespée, future Earl of Salisbury. This was a career of debauchery that contemporaries could only marvel at and which, in terms of rakishness, outbid even the late lamented Alan Clark.

Like most founders of dynasties, Henry was determined to proclaim the legitimacy of his rule and to silence any detractors who might point out that, far from being the son of a king, he had been born the son of a mere count of Anjou. His model here was almost certainly Charlemagne, the greatest of all French kings yet himself sprung from a dynasty that, at the time of his coronation, was widely regarded as having usurped the French throne. In the 1160s, hurling abuse at a visitor whom he accused of being the son of a priest (priests being forbidden marriage or children), Henry was more than a little disconcerted when this visitor replied that he was no more the son of a priest than Henry himself was the son of a king. A sense of insecurity, and the desire to broadcast his own legitimacy explains both the magnificence of his court and his deliberate patronage of writers, ethnographers, historians, theologians and literary figures capable of praising his achievements. For historians, the praise offered by such men has to be carefully handled. It is shot through with irony which, now that the actors themselves are long dead, can all too easily be overlooked. Gerald of Wales, for example, one of the leading writers of the time tells us that Henry II was a lover of the humble and the poor, 'filling the hungry with good things and sending the rich empty away'. By praising the King's humility, yet doing so in the words of the *Magnificat*, a hymn of praise addressed to God himself, Gerald was surely stating one thing but implying quite another. The birth of irony, 'that English virtue which purifies our rowdy passion', may itself have been encouraged by the Plantagenet court, with its insistence that the King be accorded a degree of deference which courtiers themselves on occasion found unjustified or absurd. Writers such as Gerald of Wales or Walter Map who praised Henry II for his easy manners and his ability to control his temper were surely writing, tongue in cheek, of a King who everyone knew was given to rages so violent that he chewed the straw on his own palace floors.

Far from being a place of easy manners, the Plantagenet court was a theatrical stage. Like most such stages, it was thronged by posers subject to very strict rules. Henry's mother, Empress Matilda, had been criticized in the 1140s for her insistence that she remain seated when her barons and courtiers stood before her. After 1154, a similar deference and formality came to govern such matters as the serving of the King's meals, the arrangements by which some people were invited to speak or dine with the King in private whilst others were merely permitted to admire him from a distance, or the system by which English earls now witnessed the King's charters by something approaching strict order of precedence and political favour. This was a period during which access to the King's own person became increasingly restricted. In his palaces, such as Clarendon and Woodstock, private apartments for the King were set aside from the more public buildings. At the new hunting park in Woodstock, the garden complex known as Rosamund's Bower may or may not have been associated with the historical Rosamund Clifford, Henry II's mistress, but its very existence speaks of an environment in which privacy was something demanded by kings, even in a semi-public palace garden. Formalization now extended to the rough manners of the hunt. The saintly Bishop Hugh of Lincoln, in deep disgrace with the King, once approached Henry II while out hunting, seated under a tree and using needle and thread to sew up an injured finger. 'How closely you resemble your ancestor from Falaise!' was the bishop's joke, intended to remind Henry of William the Conqueror's mother and her humble origins as daughter of a tanner or tailor. The King laughed, which meant that his courtiers could laugh too. Yet even here, not only was laughter carefully policed but, to greet the King, Hugh had to force his way through a great gaggle of attendants, arranged, so we are told, in a deferential circle or 'crown' around the royal person.

Hunting itself was increasingly ritualized. Anglo-Saxon huntsmen had driven their deer towards a 'hay' or enclosure, where they could be killed in relatively large numbers. By the late twelfth century, the hunt had instead become a mounted affair, the 'chasse par force', in which a single deer would be hunted across open country until eventually brought down by the hounds. The deer would then be ritually butchered or 'unmade', a procedure described in a number of the English hunting manuals. If a stag, its testicles and penis would be removed and hung on a forked stick, used to collect together all of the most prized tit-bits and later carried at the head of the homeward procession. The beast was then skinned, split from the chin down to the groin, the legs flayed and the feet cut off, with the skin itself now used as a blanket for the subsequent division of the trunk and as a convenient bag in which to carry home the antlers and the meat. That this was indeed the bloody ritual of the twelfth-century hunt is suggested by the fact that deer bones, when found by archaeologists, almost invariably come from the less-prized hind legs distributed amongst the huntsmen, very rarely from the shoulders or front parts which were reserved for the lord and his guests. Henry II's eldest son was thus making a particularly bold statement when he appeared before the Pope's representatives at Domfront in 1169, with the gruesome hunt trophies still dripping blood, and his huntsmen sounding their horns in a very secular and testosterone-charged declaration of Plantagenet machismo. Henry II was equally devoted to hawking, yet even the world of falcons and falconry was governed by a new formality, with particular birds being assigned to particular levels of society, an eagle for an emperor or a king (leading Richard I of England into trouble in Sicily, in the 1190s, when he observed peasants hunting with an eagle and assumed it must be stolen), a peregrine falcon for an earl, a kestrel (fairly useless in hunting terms) for a servant, and so forth.

Henry's own insecurities and the novelty of his claim, as son of the Count of Anjou, to the throne of England, contributed to a new cosmopolitan formality that penetrated far down the English social order. So much so, indeed, that it has been suggested that it was during Henry's reign, or at least in the second half of the twelfth century, that the clearly divided orders or castes of society transmitted from earlier centuries – earls and knights, freemen and villeins – began to yield place to a more variegated and potentially fluid system of social class. Before the BBC abolished such things, accent used to be one of the principal badges of social class. There are signs at Henry II's court that there was already a distinctive court or upper class accent. The court comprehended a great babble of languages, which would have rearranged themselves with giddy haste as the King shuttled between the far north of England and the most southerly of his dominions in Aquitaine and Poitou. Walter Map tells us that the King understood 'all the languages used from the French Sea [i.e. the Channel] to the river Jordan', but spoke only Latin and French. Even so, the King could apparently distinguish between a peasant and a nobleman on the grounds of accent alone, and on one occasion is said to have treated with deliberate contempt the ravings of a petitioner who addressed him in Welsh. Wace, in his history of the early dukes of Normandy, written at Henry II's request, took it for granted that a duke wishing to masquerade as a peasant would need to disguise not only his appearance but his speech. Contemporaries remarked on the Burgundian accent of Bishop Hugh of Lincoln, and the court, at the prompting of the cruel but witty Walter Map, openly laughed at the attempts made by the King's English-born illegitimate son, Geoffrey Plantagenet, to speak 'Marlborough' French.

Henry II and Thomas Becket

Part of Henry II's insecurity derived from the circumstances of his accession and birth. Another part, however, was due to four men whose names have been written out of English history but who deserve to be better known. The first, Reginald fitz Urse, was a Northamptonshire baron whose father had served at the court of King Stephen, being taken prisoner with the King at Lincoln in 1141. Despite this connection with the old regime, after the death of Stephen and the accession of Henry II, Reginald had been allowed to retain his family's recent gains, including the manor of Williton in north Somerset. The second of our quartet, Hugh de Moreville, was the son of another Hugh de Moreville, richly rewarded for his service to David, King of Scots, and after 1135 and the Scots invasion of northern England granted the town of Appleby and the lordship of Westmorland, still in the possession of the younger Hugh in the 1160s. The third, Richard Brito or Richard 'the Breton', was a West Country knight from Sampford Brett, close to Reginald fitz Urse's manor of Williton. Richard entered the service of Henry II's younger brother, William, lord of Dieppe, from whom he received a grant of land in Suffolk. Thereafter he may have gravitated to the service of the fourth of our men, William de Tracy, lord of Bradninch in Devon. William's family, from Tracy near Vire in Normandy, had prospered in the Norman conquest of Maine and thereafter had attached themselves to the cause of King Stephen, serving as constables in Devon and acquiring the great barony of Barnstaple. Although after the accession of Henry II in 1154, Barnstaple had been restored to its rightful pre-1135 claimants, William himself was permitted to hold on to Bradninch, a subsidiary lordship, acquired at much the same time as Barnstaple, for service in Stephen's reign.

So far then we have a group of four knights, three of them barons, most with connections to north Devon or Somerset, three of them with histories of service to King Stephen, perhaps all of them, after the accession of Henry II, men who had good reason to curry favour with the new king. Stephen's reign left a bitter legacy. Like many in England, after 1154, these were four men with a past, anxious to purge themselves of their too close connection to the previous regime. In December 1170, all four attended Henry II's Christmas court in Normandy where the King is said to have thundered against the treachery and spinelessness of his courtiers ('What miserable drones and traitors have I nourished and promoted in my realm, who fail to serve their lord treated with such shameful contempt by a low-born clerk!'). Taking these words to heart, our four men formed a conspiracy. Despite the winter weather and the potential difficulty of finding a ship, they crossed swiftly to England, before news of their departure could spread and a royal order go out for their detention.

After an angry interview, around sunset on 29 December, almost certainly fortified with drink, determined to prove their loyalty to the King and in most cases aware that they themselves had connections with the regime of the late King Stephen which made them suspect at Henry II's court, they burst into the precincts of Canterbury Cathedral, intending to arrest the archbishop, Thomas Becket, and to force him to stand trial at Henry's court. The archbishop's clerks insisted that Becket flee and, when he resisted, forced him bodily through the monastic cloister towards the cathedral, then in through a side door which Becket insisted be left unlocked behind him. The four knights ran after, bursting into the cathedral where the monks had just begun to sing their evening offices. 'Where is Thomas Becket', they demanded, 'Traitor to King and Realm?' deliberately employing the archbishop's low-born nickname, 'Beaky' or 'Big nose', hinting at an entire world of social disdain that divided these four knights, would-be noblemen, from the low-born Becket.

The archbishop replied in kind, calling Reginald fitz Urse a pimp, and physically resisting attempts to bundle him out of the church. Reginald was the first to lose control, striking the archbishop with his sword. William de Tracy struck next, then Richard Brito whose sword shattered as it passed through the archbishop's skull and smashed into the paving stones below. Hugh de Moreville was busy holding back the press of onlookers in the cathedral nave. It was the time of evening prayer, and a large number of townspeople had gathered to listen to the singing of the monks, wafted to them from across the stone screen that divided the congregation in the nave from the monks in the choir. A clerk attached to Hugh's household then delivered the *coup de grâce*, scattering the archbishop's brains with the point of his sword, crying out as he did so, 'This one won't get up again. Let's get out of here!' By this stage, the altar where Becket had been kneeling was literally spattered with brains, bone and fragments of bone. Bellowing '*Reaux, Reaux!*' ('King's Men, King's Men!'), the four knights then fled back through the monastic cloister, as one of them later confessed, expecting at any moment that the ground would open before them and swallow them alive.

So ended one of the most extraordinary days in English history: a story told again and again over the following centuries and in the process robbed of many of its original meanings. The dispute between Henry II and Thomas Becket has sometimes been presented as a question of liberty versus tyranny, Church versus state. There were certainly wider issues at stake here, but in essence this was a story of a royal friendship gone poisonously wrong. Becket had begun as a virtual nobody, son of a London merchant, boasting of knightly ancestors in Normandy, but in essence an upstart, rising by the 1150s to become the enforcer and archdeacon of Theobald, Archbishop of Canterbury. In 1154, hoping in this as in so much else to emulate the success of his grandfather, Henry I, the newly crowned Henry II promoted Becket as his chancellor, controller of the royal writing office, clearly in the model of Roger of Salisbury, another upstart clerk who half a century earlier had risen to become chancellor, bishop and ultimately vice-regent under Henry I. Becket delighted in his new intimacy with the great. Like many upstarts, he became notorious for his dressiness and his attention to proper form. The King poked fun at his pride and luxury, forcing him to give up a costly robe to a beggar. No matter. In the late 1150s, in full pomp and with no less than twenty-four complete changes of wardrobe (yet another reminder of the theatrical quality of court life), Becket was allowed to represent Henry on an embassy to the French King in Paris, intended to advertise England's wealth, riding at the head of a great procession that included tame monkeys and two vast wagons loaded with English beer, one of the earliest appearances of what would become a common refrain in Anglo-French rivalry: French wine versus good English beer.

Becket was a worldly man and no great scholar. Nonetheless, when the King wanted to organize an army, to besiege Toulouse, to force the English bishops to pay their taxes, or to garrison a castle, Becket was the right man for the job. In 1162, this placed him in an ideal position to be promoted as successor to the late archbishop, Theobald. The monks of Canterbury could see that Becket was a friend of the King. The other English bishops might despise him as a low-born court syco-phant, but the King gave his support. Becket was duly elected as archbishop of Canterbury. Then things went suddenly and disastrously wrong. Like St Paul after his sudden conversion on the road to Damascus, Becket underwent a crisis of conscience. He gave up his office as chancellor. He began, in secret, to wear a hair-shirt. He demanded the restoration to his Church of lands previously farmed to laymen, including laymen with close connections at court. Despite never previ-ously having shown much interest in either scholarship or the liturgy, he designated the Sunday of his consecration, the Sunday after Pentecost, as the principal feast of the Holy Trinity, the most disputed of all concepts in twelfth-century theology. At a conference at Clarendon in January 1164, the King made Becket agree, and forced him to make the other English bishops agree, to a draconian set of 'Constitutions', in effect recognizing the King's right to discipline the clergy via the secular courts, to limit the English Church's access to the Pope, to place the secular authority above the spiritual.

This was precisely the sort of thing that Becket, as chan-cellor before 1162, had been notorious for advocating. Having played out the role of a royal chancellor, however, Becket was now determined to act the role of archbishop. He had to be compelled by threats into agreeing to the Constitutions. In the process, Henry II was forced into a dangerously explicit statement of rights which the kings of England had previously exercised more or less unchallenged but which had never before been written down or granted public endorsement by the Church. Becket himself, having been compelled to agree the Constitutions, could immediately repudiate them as something extracted only under compulsion. A forced marriage is no true marriage, just as an oath extracted under threat is no true oath. The English bishops, already deeply suspicious of Becket's sincerity, told by him at Clarendon to set their seals to the Constitutions, now found themselves deserted by the very leader who had persuaded them to bow to royal tyranny. Not surprisingly, most of them now abandoned Becket. One of them, Gilbert Foliot, bishop of London, a man of considerable learning who believed that he rather than Becket should have succeeded Theobald as archbishop, now emerged as Becket's most bitter critic. Becket, he declared, was a fraud and a hypocrite. These thoughts were set down in a great manifesto of which Foliot was so proud that years later, even after Becket had been recognized as a saint and Foliot himself had received blessings from his shrine, he insisted be preserved: a most remarkable instance of authorial pride leading to the preservation of historical evidence that in any other circumstances would have been deliberately destroyed.

At Northampton, in October 1164, in what amounted to one of the first state trials in English history, Becket was ritually humiliated and, over the course of four days, ordered to render accounts for his previous service to the crown. The intention was perhaps to intimidate him into resigning his archbishopric. Instead, in a scene so melodramatic that even his fellow bishops suspected him of ham acting, Becket appeared before the King carrying his cross before him in his own hands, thereby declaring himself to be a new Christ bound for crucifixion. Rather than face the consequences, he then fled from court, in secret and by night. For the next seven years, in exile with the French king, with the papal court itself in exile at Sens, south-east of Paris, or at the great Cistercian abbey of Pontigny, Becket proceeded to make the most appalling nuisance of himself, firing off letter after letter in which he rehearsed his grievances in the most exalted of language (in many cases written for him by John of Salisbury, another of the former clerks of Archbishop Theobald, although a much better Latinist than Becket would ever be). By 1169, he had exhausted the patience not only of Henry II but of the Pope. He himself seems to have believed that Henry was still his friend, albeit a friend whose affection had been temporarily withdrawn. This was not at all Henry II's view of the matter.

When a reconciliation was at last effected, Henry was reluctant even to grant Becket the kiss of peace, the outward sign that his anger had calmed. When Becket returned to England and then proceeded to reopen exactly the same wounds that it had been agreed should be left to heal, refusing to lift the anathema he had pronounced against the English bishops who in his absence had dared crown Henry II's eldest son, excommunicating the royal bailiffs who since 1163 had administered the Canterbury estates and who, even after Becket's return, continued to impound his wine and cut off the tails of his pack horses, Henry's patience snapped. Hence the outburst at his Christmas court, when the King, far from demanding that he be 'rid of this troublesome priest' (a phrase that appears in no contemporary account), seems to have directed his fury chiefly against his own courtiers, striking a response from the four knights who now hurried to Canterbury, men who felt themselves particularly compromised by their service to the regime of King Stephen.

The ensuing murder in the cathedral transformed far more than the image of Thomas Becket, now revealed as a saint and martyr rather than as a troubled and troublesome hysteric. The monks of Canterbury who had elected Becket because he was the King's friend and who had therefore been all the more horrified to see him transformed into the King's worst enemy, found their own bitter dislike of Becket melt into veneration. Through the miracles worked at his shrine, through the droplets of his blood mixed with water and sold as wonder-working relics, through the flocks of pilgrims who now began to visit Canterbury from as far afield as France or Italy, the monks grew immensely rich. Other churches cashed in on the pilgrimage boom, translating or inventing their own saintly relics, many of them reviving memories of the Anglo-Saxon past, in an attempt to advertise their merits, if not as rivals then as sharers in Canterbury's good fortune. A great dossier of Becket's letters was collected. A dozen or more lives were written, celebrating his sanctity within five years of his death, in some cases by writers as far away as France or Iceland.

At Canterbury, a great liturgy was composed for the celebration of Becket's feast day with hymns and music, including some of the most beautiful of Latin poetry in honour of 'The shepherd slain in the midst of his flock', the greatest blessing both of England (the 'Happy land' of Thomas's birth), and of France (which had cherished him in exile). In 1179, for the first and only time before the Revolution of 1789, a reigning French king, Louis VII, came voluntarily to England, to make pilgrimage to Canterbury and there to pray for the health of his son and heir recently recovered from sickness. In gratitude, Louis made a grant to the Canterbury monks of 100 measures of wine each year, perhaps as much as 1,600 gallons, to be received from vineyards just to the south of Paris. The redness of the wine was intended to complement the martyr's blood. The gift itself marked a fit repayment for the English beer which Becket had carried to Paris in the 1150s, a triumph of French over English magnanimity. The son for whose life Louis prayed, the future King Philip Augustus, was within thirty years to prove the Plantagenets' nemesis, sweeping away the last vestiges of Plantagenet rule in northern France.

Meanwhile, Becket and his symbols, the image of the four knights and their swords, the leaden ampoules in which the bloody water of St Thomas was collected, became perhaps the most easily recognized of all English images abroad, better known even than *Opus Anglicanum* or English wool. These were images which by their very nature proclaimed the wickedness of Becket's murderers and hence the culpability of Henry II. In 1173–4, within four years of Becket's death and in the same year as his canonization, there emerged the greatest baronial coalition ever raised against an English king, comprising Henry II's own wife and sons, a dozen or more of the most powerful earls and barons of England and Normandy, the Count of Flanders and the kings of Scotland and France. All the frustrations of the previous twenty years spilled out. Men whose grievances stretched back to the reign of Stephen, or who felt themselves slighted by the Plantagenets after 1154 now made common cause with the King's wife and sons to drive Henry II from the throne. At this moment of crisis, Henry at last sought to make his peace with Thomas Becket. Arriving in Canterbury, he walked barefoot to the cathedral where he spent the night in tears and supplication before Becket's tomb, not even leaving the building (so we are told) for the normal bodily functions. The following morning, he had himself scourged, beaten on the back, by every member of the cathedral convent of perhaps a hundred monks. He then rode off for London. A few nights later, as Henry lay dozing on his couch at Westminster, a minstrel strumming a harp for his amusement and another servant massaging his feet, news arrived from the north that the King of Scots had been taken prisoner at Alnwick, this great event occurring at almost precisely the same moment that Henry had been praying before Becket's tomb in Canterbury. The omens were clear, Henry was forgiven, Becket had triumphed, and the king might again reign in harmony with his Church and his barons. Within only a few months, the great rebellion collapsed.

This at least was the official version of Henry II's penance. In reality, as is often the case, things were rather more complicated. After 1174, Henry did his best to associate himself with the tomb of Becket, visiting Canterbury on a regular basis, posing as chief sponsor of Becket's cult, even punishing the four knights who had committed the murder and who were exiled to the Holy Land where they are said to have died as Templars or as hermits, their own sons and offspring disinherited at the King's command, leaving only widows and daughters to succeed them. In 1172, under the so-called 'Compromise of Avranches', Henry had already made his peace with the Pope, promising the service of 200 knights for the Holy Land and himself to take vows as a crusader, later commuted to a promise to found four new monasteries in England, in return for reconciliation with the Church. Even so there were many who still doubted the King's sincerity. The large sums of money that Henry sent to recruit his 200 knights served merely to poison relations amongst the Christian leadership in the East, leading the King of Jerusalem into a rash campaign that culminated in 1187 with the Battle of Hattin and the fall of Jerusalem to Saladin. To this extent, Henry was indirectly to blame for one of the greatest disasters in the history of medieval Christendom. The monasteries which Henry founded in penance for Becket's murder were in at least two cases established not from his own resources but from land seized back from the Queen, Eleanor of Aquitaine, as a result of her own rebellion against the King in 1173.

Meanwhile, it is surely no coincidence that from the reign of Henry II onwards, the rash of royal biographies that commemorated earlier twelfth-century kings dried up. No contemporary wrote a life of Henry II or of any of his sons or grandsons. Ever afterwards, the Plantagenets were known in Europe as a dynasty that had murdered its archbishop, a family that trampled upon the rights of the Church. As for the Church itself, although in theory Becket's death brought 'liberty' through the 'victory' of his cause, in practice Henry II very soon resumed precisely that tight control over the English Church against which Becket had protested. The difference after 1170 was that the King no longer advertised his supremacy in writing. He continued to control appointments to bishoprics. He continued to intervene in cases before the church courts. Criminous clerks were to be judged in church courts but their chattels were confiscated for the King, and a papal legate, no less, agreed that, in respect to the royal forests and forest law, no exceptions should be made to the King's arbitrary justice, even for clerical offenders.

Twelfth-century renaissance?

The sheer number of accounts, and the sheer immediacy of the human reaction to Becket's martyrdom allows us to view the story of Henry and Becket in a detail and with an insight that are impossible for virtually any other incident in English medieval history. Even so, this should not be allowed to distract us from the broader flow of events or to overshadow the wider changes brought about during Henry II's reign. Viewing England in the 1170s, an observer would have found a very different society, and a very different elite from that of a century before. Some of these differences were the result of European-wide phenomena. The emergence of chivalry and the increasing distribution of wealth and ideas of social stratification amongst an aristocratic elite determined to display its good fortune were features of German, Spanish or even Hungarian society, not confined to England. Learning, across Europe, was on the upsurge, with the rediscovery of the works of the classical past and the opening of new secular schools, freed from the discipline of monastic orders, leading to the flowering of what historians refer to as a 'Twelfth-Century Renaissance'. Even so, in both of these fields, chivalry and learning, England had unique contributions to make.

Heraldry, originally intended to identify particular groups within the *melée* or mock battle which at this date was the tournament's climax, emerges into the light of day in England as early as the 1150s. The serjeants and household knights of King Stephen already used distinctive shields and saddles, perhaps emblazoned with heraldic symbols. Henry II's younger brother William, lord of Dieppe, is the first member of the English royal family known to have used a coat of arms, an image of three leopards displayed on his seal, perhaps modelled on the three rampant leopards or scraggy lions which had already appeared on the funeral monument of Henry and William's father, Geoffrey Plantagenet. The Plantagenet leopards of gold on red thereafter became standard symbols of a family at war, joining the dragon standard carried before the King into his battles, itself mentioned both on crusade in the 1190s and raised against the French invaders of England in 1216. Leopards appear on the seal of Richard I only a few years after the fleur-de-lys, in silver on a blue background, was adopted as a badge by the Capetian kings in Paris, symbolizing the lilies held at the Annunciation by Mary, Notre-Dame, the particular protector of France.

In England, meanwhile, chivalry and its code of honour was held, even as early as the 1130s, to exclude certain subject peoples. The Welsh and later the Irish, though not the lowland Scots (led by a king and an aristocracy of largely Norman or French descent), were placed beyond the chivalric 'pale', itself a term derived from Henry II's conquests in Ireland and the establishment of the 'pale' of Dublin as a civilized colony amidst native barbarity. As enemies who raped women, murdered children and took no hostages, they were to be treated in their turn with savage and summary violence.

We know of this barbarization of the Welsh and Irish thanks largely to English historians such as William of Malmesbury, still active in the 1140s, a Benedictine monk and one of the leading figures in England's cultural renaissance. Rather like those antiquaries of the sixteenth and seventeenth centuries who salvaged the vestiges of the medieval and monastic past at the very moment that such evidence was about to pass away, William of Malmesbury collected stories of the kings and bishops of Anglo-Saxon England, just as the Anglo-Saxon past was on the point of crumbling into dust. His findings were set down in two great books of history, *The Deeds of the Pontiffs*, and *The Deeds of the Kings*. William was a magpie collector of interesting facts, with a magnificent library of research books and an omnivorous desire to dig out the most neglected and significant relics of the past. Writing to some extent for a secular rather than a monastic audience, Geoffrey Gaimar, as early as the 1130s, had composed a *History of the English* in French verse, translating a large part of the *Anglo-Saxon Chronicle* and celebrating the Norman kings as worthy successors to the heroes of the Anglo-Saxon past. Gaimar's verses to some extent supplied a model for the poet-historians patronized at the court of Henry II. In particular Master Wace, born in the Channel Islands, later canon of Bayeux, was commissioned by Henry to write his *Tale of Rollo* (the *Roman de Rou*), a retelling in verse of the whole of Norman history from the time of the first arrival of the Vikings in Normandy through to the Conquest of England and the reigns of Rufus and Henry I. It was Wace, with his long lists of those who had fought at Hastings, who supplied the materials for many later, spurious genealogies, drawn up a century or more after 1066. For the barons of the 1160s, securing a mention in Wace's history seems to have been roughly equivalent to the kudos to be obtained for today's parvenus from an entry in *Who's Who* or Debrett's *Peerage*.

Besides his 'Roman de Rou' written for the King, Wace also wrote a 'Roman de Brut', perhaps at the prompting of Queen Eleanor. Here the emphasis shifted from Norman to old English history, with an account of how Britain itself was first conquered from a race of giants by Brutus, the great-grandson of Aeneas, himself the subject of Virgil's epic *Aeneid* which had told the story of Aeneas' exile from Troy and his foundation of the city and empire of Rome. From Brutus, according to Wace, descended a line of English kings that could be traced via Arthur to Alfred and thence to the Conquest of 1066 and beyond.

Henry II, of course, was the first King of England who could claim to share in the blood not only of Rollo but of both Brutus and Arthur. Like Brutus, he also happened to be the great-grandson of another conqueror, William of Normandy. Like Brutus, exiled from Italy for accidentally killing his father in a hunting accident, Henry was a famous huntsman.

Gerald of Monmouth

Wace acquired his extraordinary notions of Brutus as Britain's first king from one of the greatest bestsellers of the Middle Ages, Geoffrey of Monmouth's *History of the King of Britain*. If there was any book of history other than the Bible that all kings, all monks, and all literate Englishmen can be assumed to have read, then Geoffrey's was that book. As is appropriate for a bestseller, Geoffrey's was not only the most popular but probably the least accurate history of Britain ever written. Indeed, to describe it as a history rather than an outright fiction is to credit it with too great an intention to tell the truth. Geoffrey himself claimed that he had obtained his stories from a very ancient Welsh book, lent to him by Walter, the arch-deacon of Oxford. This was a claim that deserves no more credit that that afforded to the memoirs of Bilbo Baggins and his nephew Frodo. Geoffrey set out to produce a narrative of early British history that could not be recovered from the Roman classical historians and that Bede himself had been unable to supply. In explaining what had happened during this great blank on the historical map, he relied in part upon a ninth-century *History of the Britons* attributed to a Welsh historian, 'Nennius', from which he derived his basic cast of characters including the Trojan Brutus. The rest he simply made up, or at least adapted out of all recognition, in the process entirely remodelling or inventing such figures as Vortigern, Hengest and Horsa, Lear and Cymbeline, Arthur, Merlin and Old King Cole.

To a modern readership, persuaded that there ought to be a clear and uncrossable divide between history and make-believe,

Geoffrey's romancing may seem unpardonable. His motives are by no means clear, perhaps to flatter the Angevin party led by Robert, earl of Gloucester, to whom his history was dedicated, shortly before 1139, perhaps to demonstrate to an English or Anglo-Norman audience, inclined to view the Welsh as barbarians, that Wales and its ancient people could boast a history of great sophistication, as the builders of cities and the rulers of nations long before the crude Angles and Saxons had forced the Welsh into nomadic pastoralism in the far west. In the context of Plantagenet history, Geoffrey's motives are less important than his extraordinary popularity. Henceforth there was no doubt that Brutus was to be accounted the founder of Britain. Arthur and Merlin were accepted as real historical characters. Henry II's grandson, born to a marriage between Geoffrey, the King's third son, and Constance, the heiress to Brittany, was named Arthur as a badge of Breton pride. Henry II's empire, stretching from the Cheviots to the Pyrenees, could be interpreted as the rebirth of the empire of Arthur, which, according to Geoffrey's *History*, had included Poitou and most of western France, and in building which Arthur had himself defeated all other powers including Rome and the armies of the treacherous perjurer Mordred (for whom perhaps read King Stephen) before vanishing into the Isle of Avalon for his wounds to be healed. From there Arthur would himself emerge, like Henry II as proclaimed by his coinage of the 1150s, as a '*rex futurus*', a once and future king.

The so-called 'Prophecies of Merlin', which Geoffrey included in his book, spread even more widely than his *History*, being as eagerly consulted in France or Italy as in England. To people desperate for knowledge of the future, in many cases convinced that it would not be long before Christ came again, any such foreknowledge demanded careful scrutiny. Henry II himself had horoscopes cast for him in the late 1140s, in the hope that this might enable him to predict the movements of King Stephen. The astrolabe, sometimes said to have been introduced to England by Adelard of Bath, himself attached to the Angevin party and with credentials to be regarded as England's first experimental scientist, was itself used not merely to map the movement of the stars and planets, but so that such movements could lead to the more accurate prediction of future events.

In much the same tradition as other prophetic writings, from the Roman Sybil via Nostradamus to the modern horoscope, Merlin-Geoffrey's prophecies succeeded in being portentous whilst avoiding all inconvenient detail. Thus 'The feet of those that bark shall be cut off' could be interpreted as an echo of William I's treatment of those who had mocked him at Alençon in the 1050s, or as a prediction of Norman forest law, with its insistence that the front claws of any dogs within the forest be excised so as to prevent them worrying the game. 'The eagle of the broken covenant', supposed to paint Albany with gold and to rejoice in her third nesting, was widely identified as Eleanor of Aquitaine, Henry II's queen, whose favourite son, Richard, was her third-born, and whose wealth and treachery were notorious. Henry II even commissioned a painting in his apartments at Winchester, after the great family rebellion of 1173–4, showing himself as an eagle torn apart by its rebellious and sharp-taloned brood. As for such fancies as the three-branched tree sprouting from the Tower of London, built, according to Geoffrey, long before the arrival of the Normans, or the hedgehog loaded with apples that would hide in Winchester's underground passages, the deeper the mystery the more profound and significant its meaning. Just as irony can be said to have been invented at Henry II's court, so perhaps was the later English delight in nonsense.

The idea of Arthur as the once and future King, resting in Avalon until summoned back into history, was to a large extent an embellishment of Geoffrey's account, first found in the work of poets and fabulists towards the end of the twelfth century, most notably Chrétien de Troyes and the various Grail romances. Such figures as Joseph of Arimathea were now stirred into the already rich soup of British myth. Even so, before 1200, there were Bretons and Welshmen who claimed that Arthur would come again, to rescue them from English subjection. By the 1240s, cashing in on such mythologies and on much else besides, the monks of Glastonbury in Somerset began advertising themselves as custodians not only of the remains of Arthur (a large skeleton with a head wound being produced as evidence of his identity), but of the relics of St Patrick, apostle of the Irish, the tomb of Joseph of Arimathaea, and even of the Holy Grail itself, now increasingly although by no means exclusively identified as a cup from which Christ had drunk at the last supper. Like Geoffrey of Monmouth, the Glastonbury monks were the most appalling mythomaniacs. Even so, their claim that Arthur had been buried in their cemetery and that his body had been rediscovered as the result of a real, historical fire in the late 1180s, was not without political significance. If Arthur lay dead and buried at Glastonbury, then the last hopes of the Welsh for political independence were surely dashed.

Not everyone believed Geoffrey of Monmouth. William of Malmesbury was mystified by Geoffrey's claim to have discovered previously unknown sources. Forty years later, the Yorkshire monk William of Newburgh declared openly and indignantly that Geoffrey was a liar toadying to the cowardly Welsh. Even so, in the twelfth century as today, the legends of national identity do not necessarily have to be believed in order to work their spell. It is perhaps not surprising that many of the most potent myths of Englishness and English imperialism have emerged from the fringes of England itself and from artists themselves on the edges of England or the English establishment, from Bede writing at Jarrow on the far fringes of the north, via Geoffrey of Monmouth or the Channel Islander Master Wace, to the Anglo-Indian Rudyard Kipling or Edward Elgar, that Catholic, petit-bourgeois son of the Welsh Marches. For present purposes, what is significant is that writers such as Geoffrey of Monmouth had already tinted England's twelfth-century Renaissance with distinctively English pigments. It was upon this basis that the writers in and around the court of Henry II built their reputations.

Some of the greatest of these writers were themselves either Welsh or connected with the Welsh Marches. Gerald de Barri, generally known as 'Gerald of Wales' or 'Gerald the Welshman', dedicated one of his histories to the future King Richard, and undoubtedly accompanied another of Henry II's sons, John, on his 1185 expedition to Ireland. Gerald played a somewhat shady role in the public presentation of Henry II's entire Irish venture, since it was Gerald who was chiefly responsible for the transmission of a papal letter, known as '*Laudabiliter*' ('Praiseworthily') from its opening word, supposedly issued by Pope Adrian IV, himself a native of St Albans and the only Englishman ever to have sat on the papal throne. According to Gerald's version, '*Laudabiliter*', issued in 1155, only a year after Henry II's accession as King, granted Henry papal approval for an invasion of Ireland. The invasion itself was delayed until 1172 when, in the aftermath of the murder of Thomas Becket, and perhaps in an attempt to gain favour with the Church, Henry II landed at Waterford and spent nearly six months in Ireland, claiming to act for the good of the Irish and in particular for the reform and regulation of the unruly Irish Church. It was during this expedition that the King in all of his outgoing letters and charters for the first time began to use the title *Henricus Dei Gratia rex* ('Henry King By God's Grace'): a clear sign that Henry and his advisers were aware that the alteration of a couple of words might have considerable consequences for the King's reputation.

'*Laudabiliter*' supplied justification for Henry's conquest of Ireland, presenting it as a papally approved venture, for the benefit of religion. But the text as we have it was almost certainly tampered with, or even written by Gerald of Wales. It is not set out in the standard rhyming prose of other papal letters, a sort of 'Rupert Bear said take a care or we may think your letters stink' sort of language, intended to advertise the Pope's learning and magnificence. Furthermore, we have another papal letter from the late 1150s, undoubtedly genuine, beginning '*Satis Laudabiliter*' ('Praiseworthily enough'), addressed to the King of France, congratulating him on his proposal for a joint expedition with Henry II against the Islamic powers of Spain, but just as politely refusing papal support. It seems that the Irish '*Laudabiliter*' was originally a similar sort of letter to '*Satis Laudabiliter*', praising the intention behind Henry's proposals to invade Ireland but nonetheless cautioning against them. Gerald of Wales thus acted as a sort of semi-official court forger, tampering with the Pope's correspondence and in the process supplying one of the chief justifications for the English invasion of Ireland, an event with major historic consequences still very much with us today.

Gerald was a complicated character, his grandmother a Welsh princess, his father an Anglo-Norman baron. He was brought up as a younger son in Wales, where his earliest memories were of building castles on the sandy beaches, painfully aware that he himself was destined not for a military but for an ecclesiastical career. From the twelfth century onwards, denied the possibility of marriage by papal 'reforms', the clergy had to find other outlets for their sense of masculine pride. Learning and writing were undoubtedly one such outlet. Even so, mistrusted as a Norman in Wales, as a Welshman in Normandy and as a Paris-trained intellectual at the English court, Gerald never achieved the status or rewards that he believed were his due. His writings include some of the earliest and most fascinating ethnographical portraits of the Welsh and the Irish, spiced with reflections on tribal identity, on the way in which barnacles hatch into geese, and the other natural wonders of the west, not least the Welsh skill in singing, 'not in unison like the inhabitants of other countries, but in many different parts'. In later life, denied promotion to the bishopric of St David's, Gerald grew bitterly critical of Plantagenet rule, greeting a French invasion of England in 1216 as the dawn of liberty after an iron age of tyranny. As this suggests, although to some extent patronized at court, like many others of the Plantagenet 'court' writers, Gerald was a far from conventional courtier.

Walter Map, for example, although his witticisms and tall tales were appreciated at court, joked not only about Frenchmen and effeminate monks but about Henry II's resemblance to the demonic King Herla. John of Salisbury, a Parisian intellectual and theologian, at one time employed as a diplomatic agent in Henry II's negotiations over Ireland, published the first full-scale treatise on secular government to have been written since the fall of Rome, yet remained profoundly critical of kings, not least for their addiction to the idiot bloodshed of the hunt. The sense of technical mastery conveyed in John's writings, and his delight in using the rediscovered classical past to explore more modern facets of humanity is also to be found in the 'Dialogue of the Exchequer', composed by Richard fitz Nigel, Henry II's treasurer and son of the former royal treasurer, Nigel, bishop of Ely, arrested at the court of King Stephen in 1139. The 'Dialogue' (so-called because it takes the form of a debate between a master and his student) was intended to explain the technical workings of the King's Exchequer, how the money was received and accounted, how the chequered cloth was used, and how the many tens of thousands of silver pennies were assayed for their silver content. In an age of flat silver pennies, without the milled edges later introduced by Isaac Newton, the clipping of coin was both a common and a viciously prohibited phenomenon, punished as early as the 1130s by blinding and castration. In the Channel Islands, where French customs applied, false moneyers were boiled in a pot, thereby re-enacting the horrors that they themselves had committed in melting down the King's coin. There is a record of just such a brew-up on the Island of Jersey in 1304.

Technology in peace and war

The processes of the Exchequer and the royal mint should remind us that this was an age of technological as well as of literary innovation. A charter issued by Henry II towards the end of his reign is one of the earliest English documents to refer to windmills, a new means of harnessing the power of nature, now added to the more traditional technology of water mills. Fulling mills, driven by water, in which paddles replaced the agency of human feet in pounding, scouring and thickening cloth, had appeared in England within only a few decades of the Norman Conquest. Wooden machinery – hoists, tread-wheels, windlasses and cranes – was essential not only for the building of the great cathedrals but for England's trade, with cranes essential to the loading and unloading of ships in ports such as London or Southampton. At Canterbury, even in Becket's lifetime, the Cathedral's monks invested in a system of hydraulic pipes and aqueducts, intended to bring in a supply of clean fresh water from a spring more than a thousand yards away. What is remarkable here is not only that this plumbing was completed, and was still in working order three centuries later, but that two plans of it were drawn up before 1170 and inserted in an illustrated book of the Psalms (a 'Psalter'). Celebrating the most recent technological advances as works of God, these constitute two of the very earliest maps to survive from medieval England. Their survival in a Psalter suggests a closer proximity than we might suppose between science and monastic prayer.

In the King's wars his soldiers now used crossbows, which by the 1220s were being imported for the royal household from one particular Genoese merchant, himself in regular contact with the workshops of Saracen Damascus. Worked by ratchets and cogs, and capable of firing a bolt with great force, the crossbow was so effective a weapon, and seemed to offer its users so unfair an advantage, that there were attempts by church councils entirely to ban it. King Richard I died from wounds inflicted by a crossbow bolt that pierced his armour as he was reconnoitring a siege. Ratchets and cogs were also crucial to the development of the first mechanical clocks which appear in England rather later, by the 1280s. A particularly massive early example, unique for the fact that it is still in working order, is preserved in Salisbury Cathedral.

With the clock, in the twelfth century worked by water, later by mechanical means, came the possibility of accurately measuring the hours and hence of man achieving mastery over time itself. Machines, from the astrolabe to the crossbow, were now integral to royal government. Their very expense invested them with the sort of awe that today is reserved for such wonders of the modern state as the stealth bomber or satellite intelligence. Furthermore these were innovations which, with few exceptions, the Church and church leaders were happy to endorse. One of the earliest treatises on optics and the properties of the rainbow was written by Robert Grosseteste, former master in the schools of Oxford, bishop of Lincoln after 1235. Grosseteste was also responsible, as editor rather than translator, for the transmission into western Europe of much of the work of Aristotle, previously preserved in the Arab world but unexplored by western Europeans unable to read Greek. Before the fourteenth century, Greek in England was used chiefly for the consecration of churches, when the consecrating bishop was expected to trace out the Greek alphabet on the church floor. The bluffing that must have taken place on such occasions, by clerics entirely ignorant of Greek, poses intriguing questions about the honesty of England's bishops.

Once again we are back here in the laborious classification of language and the mastery of letters, words and grammar as the first steps towards enlightenment. Grosseteste's work on optics was itself concerned with the properties of light. Like God himself, light was invisible yet everywhere, essential to man's illumination. Without it there could be no understanding. One of the greatest surviving works of English medieval art, the Gloucester Candle Stick, made for Gloucester Abbey before 1113 and now in the Victoria & Albert Museum, consists of an elaborate intertwining of men, beasts and foliage, all of them struggling upwards towards the illumination cast by the candle that once stood at its centre: the light of God

embodied in bronze and beeswax. It was these same meta-
physics of light that underlay a great revolution in architecture,
from the 1120s onwards, first pioneered in northern France but
rapidly adopted in England, by which building itself was raised
to ever greater heights and flooded with an even greater
quantity of light. Through the use of flying buttresses, the
outer stone-skeleton of a building, previously massively
thickened in order to support the weight of the roof, could
now be pierced with many dozens of windows, themselves
filled with stained glass, using light itself to expound the
mysteries of God.

These new buildings – one thinks in England of the choir of
Canterbury Cathedral, rebuilt following a disastrous fire in
1174, and pre-eminently of Salisbury Cathedral, first planned
in the 1190s but not begun until after 1217 – are grouped
together by art historians under the catch-all term 'Gothic',
intended to distinguish them from the earlier style known as
'Romanesque', derived ultimately from the building practices
of Rome. Such buildings could be made to seem almost to
dissolve in light, their solid forms carved and traced into such a
refined series of pinnacles and points, none more impressive
than the great spire of Salisbury, that the border between light
and stone was itself rendered almost invisible. Even in celebrating God's mysteries, however, builders also celebrated the
achievements of mankind. The raising of such vast stone monuments speaks of an age still committed to epic ventures.

Salisbury Cathedral is a massive statement of the power of
the Church, now, in the aftermath of Becket's martyrdom,
claiming independence from royal authority, released from its
former captivity within the shadow of the royal castle at Sarum
and physically brought down the hill to the valley of the river
Avon. Canterbury Cathedral, rebuilt after the fire of 1174,
which was caused by the furnaces of the royal mint at
Canterbury becoming overheated, represented a massive rein-
vestment of the resources now made available from the profits
of Becket's shrine and was itself intended as a celebration in

stone of the cult of St Thomas, England's newest and most popular saint. The rude Norman past was not entirely to be swept away. Its most precious relics, such as the crypt of Lanfranc's cathedral at Canterbury, were to be preserved beneath a modern superstructure. Rebuilding Westminster Abbey after the 1240s, King Henry III and his architects seem deliberately to have preserved an ancient wooden door, once an internal fixture, now reused for a stairway, as a reminder of the old church built by Edward the Confessor that they were in the very process of demolishing. Even so, this was an age in which kings and bishops still believed in man's ability to conquer both time and space.

Grosseteste's work on optics emerged from the same world which produced the angel choir in his own great cathedral at Lincoln: a gallery of many hundreds of statues in which the angels, God's invisible ministers, were embodied in stone. Nature and the supernatural marched hand in hand. An interest in optics and the properties of light led not just to angels but to the grinding of glass and the manufacture of lenses such as the first primitive magnifiers used as early as the 1260s by Roger Bacon, like Grosseteste a master of the schools of Oxford. From magnifying glasses came spectacles, recorded by the 1290s, which in turn carry us back to writing and languages comprehended through the eyes as the chief agents of understanding. Books themselves could come to resemble machines, as in the 'volvelles' or revolving parchment discs with which Matthew Paris, monk of St Albans and chief chronicler of the court of Henry III, adorned his manuscripts. One of Paris' manuscripts, a book of prophecies, itself seems to have been supplied with a series of cog-wheels inset within its wooden covers. By spinning the cogs, the reader could learn his fate, being directed to a series of names and numbers, each with its own particular meaning: a mechanical device for the exploration of time, six centuries in advance of H.G. Wells' *Time Machine*.

Like the most luxurious of modern 'pop-up' books, Matthew's manuscripts were not only adorned with gadgets but lavishly illustrated, and, in the case of his 'Great Chronicle' (the '*Chronica Majora*'), supplied with an entire volume of appendices and supporting documents itself cross-referenced in what amounts to one of the earliest uses of footnotes. At much the same time, a team of Englishmen working in the schools of Paris, including Richard of Stainsby, brother of the bishop of Coventry, compiled the fullest index to scripture ever yet accomplished: a concordance to trace the appearance of every significant word or name in the Bible. Preaching and the exposition of scripture was itself becoming more 'scientific', with another group of Englishmen, including Thomas of Chobham, canon of Salisbury, contributing practical guides on how to preach and not least on how to answer the more awkward questions posed by hecklers. Even the word of God had to be more scientifically analysed and delivered.

A lot of this 'science' is very far from what we would today regard as scientific 'truth'. Neither Robert Grosseteste nor Roger Bacon had the remotest understanding of how sight actually operates. They believed, in accordance with the learning of classical antiquity, that it in some way involved active physical processes, with the eye sucking in, or being bombarded with, rays of intelligence from outside objects that themselves were capable of transmitting both good and evil properties. Just as a man might damage his natural humoral balance (yet another concept bequeathed from classical science) by listening to unpleasant sounds, or smelling evil odours, he might also do himself harm by gazing on the ugly or the obscene. The smell of camphor could cause impotence. Women who stared at deformities risked giving birth to deformed children, just as those with evil intentions could transmit disease by a single look. To call one's neighbour 'whore', 'liar' or 'churl' was positively to harm both the speaker and the person described, since such words acted on the sentient organs like so many shards of broken glass. Particular colours had particular effects. Night-time was all the more terrifying for being both silent and black, so much so that babies were best accustomed to the dark by being given black and noiseless toys to play with. In the same way, objects such as jewels were all the more prized, not only because of their monetary value, but because they were believed to emit rays of light, just as stained glass or the cloth of gold worn by courtiers were perceived as naturally luminescent. Jewels themselves were symbols of England's wealth, extracted from the furthest corners of the earth, from India and beyond. No wonder that King John had a large collection of them, including a stone hung around his neck which he believed would preserve his empire from any threat of dismemberment. His son, Henry III, was given a similarly valuable stone, to protect against thunder (itself produced by demons in the upper atmosphere), of which Henry had a morbid fear.

The willingness to invest mankind with a sympathy for phenomena in the natural world, and to pursue God's secrets not only in nature but in the body of the human enquirer brings the medieval scientists closer to their modern equivalents than might be supposed, representing one of the first real engagements with experiment as a means to the discovery of truth. Like Isaac Newton in the seventeenth century, risking blindness by using his own eyes as a laboratory for the investigation of sunlight, Robert Grosseteste and his contemporaries were in some ways closely allied to, in other ways entirely divorced from, the tendencies of modern science. Photons and neutrons have now displaced angels and bodily humours as the agents of light or of human sensation. Even so, we still seek to protect children and the vulnerable from bullying or from obscene and violent images. Today we guard against the psychological effects of such things. In the Middle Ages, the connection between words, images and the human body was believed to operate according to a more directly physical process of cause and effect.

Bodily and spiritual health

We seem to have wandered a long way here from the Plantagenet court, and yet in many respects it is in the court and its literature that we come closest to the medieval under-standing of bodily or spiritual health. For the health of their souls, kings, from Henry I onwards, had their own personal confessors: Henry I's became the first bishop of Carlisle. For the health of their bodies they had physicians, the best of them either foreign trained or at least adopting foreign sounding names. Many centuries before the establishment of any sort of National Health Service, kings such as Henry II were making grants to monasteries specifically 'for the health and wellbeing of my realm'. The king's interventions in the treatment of particular diseases were amongst the most remarkable ways in which royal authority was articulated. Both Edward the Confessor and Henry II 'touched' for the king's evil, claiming that by the mere laying on of their hands they could cure the disfiguring skin disease later diagnosed as 'scrofula'. By the late thirteenth century, the King's touch was being marketed on an almost industrial basis, with as many as 1,000 individual sufferers being brought before King Edward I each year for healing.

This connection between skin diseases and royalty was itself perhaps derived from the particular obsession displayed in the Biblical book of Leviticus (Chapter 13) which required the identification and exclusion of those suffering from what in the Latin Bible was described under a catch-all term definition as 'leprosy'. Leprosy in the Middle Ages was a term applied to a wide variety of pathologies, from severe psoriasis to full-blown Hansen's disease, the bacterial infection that afflicts today's clinically diagnosed lepers. Since it was believed to be a highly contagious punishment for sin, particularly for sexual misconduct, and since it was disfiguring, with the loss of fingers and toes, destruction of the nasal cartilage, hoarsening of the voice and progressive deformity, leprosy was feared. What is more surprising is the degree of specialist care devoted to its sufferers. In the twelfth century, there was an increasing tendency not only towards the segregation of those with Hansen's disease, revealed from the skeletons of large numbers of those buried in leper hospitals, but to the regulation and, in so far as was possible, amelioration of their affliction. Where lepers in Anglo-Saxon England seem to have received no specialist care, at least 320 leper hospitals were established in England between the Norman Conquest and 1250, many of them founded by the King. The gathering of alms for such houses became a regular social obligation, again frequently supported by the King. When collecting alms, lepers were permitted to carry a wooden clapper or rattle. This was not done in the Hollywood sense, in order to frighten away the public from the possibility of contagion or the 'unclean'. Rather, the leper's wooden rattle distinguished this particular group of alms-seekers from the clergy ringing bells to summon the faithful to Mass or to announce that the consecrated host was being carried through the streets.

Dress and uniform

This was a society increasingly obsessed with categories and their definitions, be it in language or health or in social distinctions. Certain types of people should be permitted to dress in certain types of clothes. The clergy should not be mistaken for laymen and should therefore avoid wearing gaudy or luxurious cloaks. Jews should dress differently from Christians. After 1215 and the rulings of the greatest of the medieval Church Councils, the so-called Fourth Lateran Council summoned Pope Innocent III, Jews and Saracens were obliged to wear distinctive badges. In England, the Jewish badge was modelled on the 'tabula', the image of the stone tablets of the Ten Commandments with which Moses returned from Mount Sinai. Jews themselves were prepared to pay heavy fines to avoid wearing it, since it clearly became a mark of shame or ridicule, but this was not the original intention. Rather, the badge was intended to implement the Jews' own regulations on the wearing of distinctive dress and the Biblical prohibitions against the mingling of cloth or seed. A king might hunt with an eagle, but a bishop should not. Men should not dress as

women or behave in an 'unmanly' way. A priest might ring a
bell, but a leper should make quite another sort of sound. All of
this suggests a society in turmoil, to which the authorities, both
royal and ecclesiastical, responded with attempts at definition,
regulation and segregation. From such regulation came some
of the earliest expressions of state control, from the charitable
provision of leper houses for those now expected to live
beyond the edges of towns, to the enforcement, or more often
the relaxation, of the obligation that Jews and prostitutes wear
distinguishing signs.

The regulation of those beyond the confines of the 'normal' –
the sick, the criminal, the unbeliever – has always been one of the
particular responsibilities and advertisements of power. It is no
coincidence that Henry II, besides being a generous founder of
leper hospitals, is the first English king known to have legislated
against heresy. A group of foreign weavers, denounced at
Oxford in the 1160s and declared heretical by the church authorities, was handed over to the King's officers for punishment.
They were branded on the face, their houses and all their
property were ritually purified by burning, and they themselves
were expelled from the town, to face starvation in the winter
cold. By such gestures against outsiders was the realm itself
defined and the King's royal authority expressed. After 1200,
burning was to become the standard punishment for heresy,
perhaps first implemented at London in 1210. Previously it had
been used to punish petty treason, the murder of a husband by
his wife, and it is possible that an association between betrayal of
one's lord and betrayal of the Lord God explains the future close
connection between heretics and burning. Even so, through to
the late fourteenth century when things began to change,
England as a whole was not a land either of heresy or of holy
bonfires. Isolated instances, and even, in the 1230s, a brief
attempt to introduce the papal Inquisition to Yorkshire, tend to
suggest the rarity rather than the spread of heresy. England, in
European terms, was so over-governed and over-regulated a
nation that heresy had little chance to take root.

To write of such a society as primitive or superstitious is to assume a false superiority for modern ideas of the complex or the rational. The response to Aids and its sufferers in the 1980s was not markedly more rational or more charitable than the medieval response to leprosy. Child molesters today inspire a similarly horrified reaction to that, in the 1160s, which greeted heretics. The way in which medieval fashions were worn as badges of rank or social function was often a great deal more sophisticated than the modern aesthetics of jeans and trainers. The King himself said special prayers before embarking on the cross-Channel voyages that were so necessary for the maintenance of communications between his lands. On occasion he called for particular holy relics, the hand of St James for example, normally stored at Reading Abbey, to be brought to bless his sailings. Yet he also travelled with a trained physician. One such royal doctor, Ralph de Beaumont, physician to Henry II, was drowned crossing from Normandy to Portsmouth in March 1170, during a violent storm that carried off as many as four hundred other courtiers. No wonder that the King regularly confessed his sins before boarding ship. The crossing between England and France was an extremely dangerous one, against whose perils even medical expertise could prove futile. Despite the jokes of William Rufus, that no king had ever been lost at sea, the wreck of the White Ship had proved that royal blood was no guarantee against shipwreck. In seeking divine protection for his crossings, the King thus acted in an entirely rational way.

English territories in France

Henry II's relations with the sea brings us back to one of the principal characteristics of Plantagenet kingship: the continuing involvement of England in French politics, as part of that vast assembly of lands that Henry II acquired as duke of Normandy, duke of Aquitaine and count of Anjou. Accounts of this cross-Channel 'empire' have generally taken one of two forms. They have either become bogged down in the question of the extent to which Henry's 'empire' was truly 'imperial', or dissolved into an equally trivial discussion of personalities and in particular of the volcanic relations between Henry and his wife, Eleanor of Aquitaine: a marriage generally portrayed as one long saga of infidelity, harsh words and broken crockery. In terms of empire, it is clear that what Henry II ruled was not the equivalent to an empire such as that of Rome. Each province within his dominion was governed according to its own laws and traditions. Henry and his sons, in so far as they had a home, were natives of the Loire valley, raised in the castle-strewn hills between Le Mans and Chinon, with the river Loire, the wide brown Mississippi of western France, as the dominant feature of a landscape much of which was still unploughed ancient woodland. Although their lives were passed elsewhere, with Anjou itself serving as no more than a corridor for communications between Normandy and the south, it was to the great nunnery of Fontevraud, in the forests south of the Loire, that Henry II and Richard I, together with the wives of both Henry II and King John, looked for burial.

In England the Plantagenets were kings but in Normandy, Aquitaine or Anjou they remained merely dukes or counts, in theory subject to the kings of France. Even so, there is no doubt that it was rulers such as Charlemagne or the imperial Arthur that Henry II sought to emulate. It was by comparison with the Roman emperors of antiquity that contemporaries sought to describe his reign. In so far as a system of government could be imperial in the twelfth century, with orders transmitted from a central intelligence at the wandering royal court to the furthest flung proconsuls of the Scots or Spanish frontiers, then Henry II's was an 'imperial' system, capable of functioning in the king's absence, lacking the focus or mythology that the Romans had invested in the city of Rome, yet with an empire-wide system for the levying of taxation and troops, and with at least some sense that London, and the royal palace just down the river at Westminster, were now the hub of a much mightier cross-Channel enterprise.

It was in the royal palace at Westminster that Richard fitz Nigel imagined himself sitting at the start of his *Dialogue of the Exchequer*, itself celebrating an office of government, the Exchequer, now permanently resident at Westminster, in regular communication with the other Exchequers established at Caen in Normandy and, after the 1170s, in colonial Dublin. It was in Westminster Abbey that the King was crowned, and it was there too that Henry II presided over the translation and reburial of the relics of his sainted ancestor, Edward the Confessor. London, according to Geoffrey of Monmouth, had first been founded by Brutus and christened 'New Troy' only a few years after the foundation of Rome. It was renamed in honour of King Lud, an entirely mythical descendant of Brutus, said to have surrounded the city with walls and innumerable towers in the time of Julius Caesar. With fewer legendary elements than Geoffrey of Monmouth, a remarkable 'Description' of the city by William fitz Stephen, from the reign of Henry II, also celebrated London as a city superior, not just a rival, to Paris or Rome. As described by William, London's teeming market places, public cook-shops, bear-baitings, water-sports, jewels brought from the Nile, gold from Arabia, great houses for the rich and philosophical debates for poor scholars, excelled even the commerce, games and learning of imperial Rome. By the 1160s, England was already developing not so much as a confederation of equally significant provinces but as a Londonland, its subordinate localities radiating outwards from one over-mighty hub. In some senses, these subordinate localities spanned the Channel, with the port and the markets of London as significant to the merchants of such regional capitals as La Rochelle or Rouen as they were to the herring fishermen of Yarmouth or the wool farmers of Herefordshire. By the 1170s, the merchants both of Rouen and of Cologne already maintained private harbours and halls for themselves within the city of London: the first, but by no means the last of the great multinational corporations to have set up business there.

Eleanor of Aquitaine

As for the King's personal relations, and in particular his relations with his wife, although biographies of Eleanor continue to be published on a near annual basis, full of the most detailed and lurid of imaginings, we actually know remarkably little about Eleanor the woman. In popular mythology she is presented as the patron of poets and troubadours, presiding over a court of love in which damsels swooned and knights performed their chivalric errands. As for known facts, Eleanor certainly rebelled against her husband in 1173, and as a result spent most of the next sixteen years, through to Henry's death, under house arrest at Sarum. However, to judge from the surviving Pipe Rolls of the Exchequer, her captivity was a comfortable one. Far from her household being packed with troubadours and poets, her own charters and their witness-lists suggest that she was surrounded by a polyglot household of Poitevins and Anglo-Normans, above all by chaplains and clerks, with liturgical celebrations and prayer being perhaps her keenest concerns. It was with a psalter in her hands, not a harp or a sword, that she is shown in her remarkable tomb effigy at Fontevraud.

Meanwhile, liturgy and Eleanor's 'prison' at Sarum sat very nicely together, since it was in the compact square mile of Sarum, with its castle and cathedral jostling for superiority on their chalk hill, that there grew up one of the greatest of liturgical inventions, the Sarum Rite: an elaborate series of services, prayers and ritual processions, mapped out according to the dimensions and physical arrangements of Sarum's old cathedral, adopted, after 1200, as the standard non-monastic liturgy for most of southern England, even after the canons of Sarum had decamped from their white hill to the valley of the Avon at Salisbury. Eleanor was already using Sarum as a residence and its cathedral archives as a place to deposit her own private deeds as early as the 1150s, long before she was sent into 'captivity' there.

As for her more personal tastes, she may have had a fondness for chestnuts – there is an entry in the 1159 Pipe Roll recording three shillings' worth of chestnuts brought to her from Warwickshire – and she certainly spent a small fortune on clothes. But the only literature that she is known to have commissioned was in Latin or Norman-French, not in the southern French or Provencal language of the troubadours, and it was devoted to works of piety or history rather than to courtly love. After the death of Henry II in 1189, when Eleanor was free to do as she liked, and when for a period she acted as one of the great powers behind the throne of her favourite son, the absentee King Richard, she seems to have devoted particular attention to endowing prayers for the commemoration of Henry, referring to her late husband in affectionate and respectful terms that call into question the received opinion of their marriage.

In so far as personal relations were crucial to public policy, and given that the King's wars were precisely that – his own private affairs albeit backed by the full majesty and clout of a nation in arms – Henry II's dealings with his wife and children are of more than merely trivial concern. Contemporaries wrote of the Plantagenets as a particularly dysfunctional family, suffering from something approaching sick-dynasty syndrome. From 1170, it was a family rarely at peace with itself. Henry's refusal to make a permanent division of his estates, or to entrust his four surviving sons with any real authority led to the great civil war of 1173–4. Thereafter, it was rebellions, by the eldest of these sons, Henry the 'Young King', and later, after the Young King's death, by Richard, that marked the chief political turning points of the 1180s. Even so, in the longer term, of far greater significance than these personal vendettas was the wider question of England's place in France. Under Henry II, the question was not so much whether the French King, Louis VII, would threaten the Plantagenet lands, but whether the Plantagenets themselves might swallow up the whole of France. The Seine valley as far east as Mantes, within forty kilometres and almost within sight of the modern Eiffel Tower, was now in Plantagenet hands. Paris itself was increasingly a frontier city, encircled to the north, west and south by Henry II and his allies. After 1189, all of this changed. First, and as a result of his detention in Germany, King Richard lost the easternmost parts of Normandy. Then, in the five years after his accession in 1199 through to the final collapse in 1204, Richard's brother, King John, lost all but a small part of the former Angevin 'empire'. By 1204, Normandy, Anjou, Maine, Touraine and the northern parts of Poitou were under Capetian rather than Plantagenet rule. The modern kingdom of France was built upon King John's failures and defeat. From 1204 onwards, only Gascony and the far south, those regions least governed and least visited by previous Plantagenet kings, were to remain under Plantagenet control. Like a bright meteor, briefer even than the imperial system established by Charlemagne, Henry II's 'empire' returned to the darkness whence it came.

5

FROM RICHARD I TO HENRY III, 1189–1272

Richard I and John

A younger son, spoiled by his mother, intimidated by his father, King John had shown signs of unpleasantness from early youth. In 1185, aged just eighteen, he been sent to rule Ireland, where he outraged the Irish kings by laughing at them and pulling their long red beards. In the 1190s, whilst Richard was abroad, John stirred up rebellion in England. For this he was pardoned: 'Forgive him, he is merely a boy', had been Richard's verdict. At the time, John was already twenty-seven years old. After 1199, a chain of violence and treachery led directly from his coronation to the loss of his continental estate. Shortly after being crowned, John divorced his first wife in order to marry a southern French heiress, Isabella of Angoulême. Despite the fact that Isabella was perhaps only eight years old, John seems immediately to have consummated the marriage. A local baron, to whom Isabella had previously been betrothed, was so outraged that he rebelled. He was joined in rebellion by the King's fifteen-year-old nephew, Arthur of Brittany, the son of John's elder brother Geoffrey, who had died in 1186. Many had argued, even in 1199, that as the son of an elder brother, Arthur, the nephew, had a better claim to the English throne than John, the wicked uncle. In 1202, John decisively crushed Arthur's rebellion, following a lightening raid on the fortress of Mirebeau just south of the Loire. Arthur himself was taken prisoner together with a large number of his supporters.

The prisoners were in most cases later ransomed or released, with John apparently taking great delight in the formulation of passwords and secret codes by which he could communicate with their gaolers. Arthur, by contrast, simply vanished. The most likely explanation is that he was murdered, either by John in person or by a subordinate, perhaps by the King's French captain Peter de Maulay, following a drunken dinner. His body, it was alleged, was thrown into the Seine but later dredged up in the nets of fishermen and buried in secret 'for fear of the tyrant'. Be that as it may, Arthur's disappearance supplied a pretext for appeals by the barons of northern France to their feudal overlord, the Capetian King Philip Augustus. The combination in Arthur's story of youth, abduction, murder and a body thrown into water neatly encapsulated themes familiar from the cults of other child martyrs and must have heightened the sense of outrage against King John. Kings in the past, such as Henry I with Curthose or Henry II with Eleanor of Aquitaine, had incarcerated their brothers or wives. They did not, however, stoop to murder within the royal family.

In 1203, Philip invaded Normandy. Rather than stay and fight, John took ship from Barfleur to Portsmouth, landing on 6 December 1203. After him came whatever could be salvaged from the Plantagenet treasure trove, including a portion, but from the historian's point of view sadly only a small portion, of the archive previously used for the government of northern France. One hundred and thirty-seven years after Duke William had landed at Pevensey to do battle at Hastings, and forty-nine years (almost to the day) since Henry II had crossed to be crowned as the first of England's Plantagenet kings, John's landing only a few miles up the English coast threatened to sever the last of England's ties to Normandy. Within sight of Normandy and a day's sailing from the nearest English port, only the Channel Islands remained under English rule, pearls dropped from the necklace of the Norman empire, havens for wreckers and pirates: England's medieval, and rather chilly, Tortuga.

The loss of Normandy was not entirely the fault of King John. A large burden of guilt might be attached to his elder brother. Lionhearted though he may have been, even in the East Richard had experienced almost as much military failure as success. His captivity in Germany, itself the product of his recklessness and refusal to placate the ego of the Duke of Austria, placed him in the same tradition as the feeble King Stephen, captured and ransomed fifty years before. Henry II had been absent from England for several years at a stretch, without this leading to civil unrest. Richard, by contrast, through his promotion of his former chancellor, William Longchamps and his failure to take decisive action against his brother John, left his realm in the care of regents who were quite incapable of working with one another, let alone of containing the threat of civil war. Money was Richard's sole concern on the eve of his departure, to such an extent that he was prepared to sell off valuable rights over the King of Scots that his father had won, boasting that he would sell London itself if the price were right, leaving the Jews to carry the blame for the financial hardships to which his policies contributed, leading in turn to the most notorious pogrom in English history.

Within a few weeks of Richard's departure, a gang of local thugs forced the Jewish population of York first to seek refuge within the royal castle, and then, when the tower where they were sheltering seemed doomed to fall, to commit suicide, as Christian witnesses saw it, in deliberate and gruesome re-enactment of the suicide pact of the Zealots at Massada in 71 AD. The period of a crusade was always a time of danger for the Jews, as with the allegations involving St William at Norwich in 1144, in the midst of another crusade, when once again those unable to make the journey to the East in person may have turned against a local 'eastern' population as a means of sating an unsatisfied craving for military glory. Even so, never before had royal administration shown itself so powerless to protect the Jews. When order was eventually restored in England, it was at the hands of ministers such as Walter of Coutances, Hubert Walter and William Marshal, all of whom owed their first promotion at court not to Richard but to his father, a far better judge of character and a far better manager of men. William Longchamps, Richard's own favourite, was meanwhile forced to flee from England dressed as a washerwoman, pursued across Dover beach by a local sailor outraged to learn that the object of his amorous attentions was a man in drag.

As government dissolved into French farce, and as the French themselves prepared to lay siege to Normandy, Richard's only concern remained war and the means to pay for it. Even after the financing of his crusade, and even after the ransom had been raised to pay for his release from captivity, in the last two years of his reign he extorted fines from his subjects for the reissue of all royal charters previously awarded, using the entirely spurious argument that his great seal had been lost in the East, when in fact it had been mislaid for no more than a few days. Richard's taxation, his sale of justice and his debased reputation for respecting the terms of even those privileges which he himself had granted led inexorably towards that sense of common grievance against the crown which was to cause such problems for his successor, King John. Meanwhile, by failing to produce an heir, and by leaving the inheritance to the throne open to the most unscrupulous of the claimants, he sowed the seeds of hatred between his brother, John, and his nephew, Arthur of Brittany, that was to lead to John's murder of Arthur, and hence not only to John's forfeiture of his French estates but to the most notorious act of Plantagenet tyranny since the martyrdom of Thomas Becket.

Nineteenth-century historians were in no doubt that Richard was a boastful, southern French absentee, resident in England for less than three months, yet responsible for a vast wastage of English public finance. To the Victorians, Richard seemed to have the manners of a cad. His repeated public confessions of sexual misconduct, all the more terrifying because imprecisely defined, were exactly, so the Victorians thought, what one might expect of a Frenchman. In recent years there has been something of a revival in Richard's reputation, partly because the story of his reign is such a gift to narrative historians in search of exciting stories set in exotic locations, in part, bizarrely enough, because of attempts to integrate Richard within the counter-culture of the 1960s by proposing that his sexual appetites, so publicly confessed, were homosexual. In every sense a man's man, he could join Alexander of Macedon or Frederick of Prussia as a model of that particular queer aesthetic in which beards, battles and army boots remain the order of the day.

In 1187, Richard is said to have shared the same bed as King Philip of France. At Messina in 1190, on his way to crusade, he stripped naked to do public penance for his unspecified sins and, on his return in 1195, having been warned by a hermit to amend his lifestyle and thus to avoid the fate of the city of Sodom, he once again did penance, so we are told, returning to the bed of his wife from which he is assumed to have strayed. Even so, none of Richard's enemies accused him of deviant sexual practices, as they surely would have done had his homosexuality been widely known. In 1182, it was for his kidnap and alleged rape of the women of Aquitaine that he was criticized by the Yorkshire chronicler, Roger of Howden, and he undoubtedly fathered at least one child in southern France: Philip, later lord of Cognac. Sharing a bed was a political, rather than a sexual gesture, and it may have been the punishment, not the crimes, of the city of Sodom which inspired the hermit's outburst in 1195. For all of these reasons, the case for Richard's homosexuality has never been satisfactorily proved. By contrast, his part in the collapse of Plantagenet authority in France seems both well documented and undeniable.

Such a highly personal narrative of the loss of empire has to be supplemented with other factors, political, social and economic. Ever since Henry II's accession in 1154, indeed for much of the period since the death of William the Conqueror in 1087, it had been unclear whether Normandy and England were to be treated as two distinct entities or as an inseparable Anglo-Norman whole. Like William the Conqueror, Henry II had several times proposed to partition his continental lands amongst his sons. Purely by accident, the tensions between father and sons and the military successes of Richard had prevented such partitions from taking effect. At a more profound level, the cross-Channel entity brought into being in 1066 had been breaking apart almost from the moment of its creation. As early as the 1080s, individual Anglo-Norman families had been inclined to divide their estates in each new generation, between one branch established chiefly in Normandy, another branch in England. English and Norman national identities, far from merging, had tended towards an ever sharper divide, with myths of nationhood emerging on either side. The English, even those of Norman or Anglo-Norman descent, were said by the French to have tails. A decade after 1204, the Norman-born soldiers in the King of England's army were claiming that their 'Normannitas' entitled them to occupy the front row of the King's cavalry in battle, just as the men of Kent claimed that it was they who should take precedence over all others in the English infantry.

Many of the families which by 1200 could claim Norman descent no longer possessed much by way of Norman land. Those marooned in England after 1204, like the Welsh in nineteenth-century Patagonia, wore their Normannitas as a proud badge of nobility, but in France itself they would have been laughed at as the most Anglicized of country cousins. Only at very top of society, chiefly amongst the royal family and in the case of half a dozen of the twenty or so earls, were there individuals with significant holdings on both sides of the Channel, still uncertain by 1200 as to whether their principal interests lay in Normandy or in England. The earls of Chester, taking their title from their vast estate in the east Midlands, yet also major landholders in the Avranchin and the Bessin regions of Normandy, might hesitate after 1204 as to where their best interests lay. Families such as the Bohons or the Chesneys, with only small inherited estates in Normandy but vast resources in England, could have few doubts as to whether they should stay in France or accompany King John into 'exile'.

As for the Plantagenet dominions further south, from La Rochelle to the Pyrenees, still in King John's hands after 1204, Henry II had never attempted to create Anglo-Poitevin or Anglo-Angevin baronies, to bring his southern subjects into direct contact with England or to bind together his empire in the way that William the Conqueror had bound England to the lords of Normandy, by granting them significant English estates. As a result, the southern French never thought of themselves as in any way of mixed English descent. On the contrary, England to them represented a major source of wealth and, at least through to the 1240s, of administration that was effective without being excessively predatory. The south had been spared the worst excesses of warfare or oppressive government after 1154. By contrast, ever since the 1080s, Normandy had served as a battlefield, disputed first between the sons of the Conqueror, thereafter between King Stephen and the Plantagenets, finally between the Plantagenets and the Kings of France. War weariness, and an active hatred for the King's mercenary soldiers, especially for the Flemings, perhaps helps to explain the growing Norman disaffection with King John. As early as 1174, during the civil war against Henry II, Flemish mercenaries had been singled out as particular objects of hatred, being massacred in their hundreds by the population of East Anglia in what amounted to an anti-Flemish race riot.

Unfortunately for the men of Poitou and Gascony, after 1204 prepared to remain loyal to King John, a similar xenophobia marked their reception in England. After 1204, it was the French exiles introduced to court, in particular the former mercenary captains from southern Anjou, compromised by their previous service to the Plantagenets, granted refuge in England, used by King John and later by Henry III as a means of maintaining contacts with the lost Plantagenet domain, who bore the brunt of a backlash in England against 'aliens'. The greatest of these exiles was Peter des Roches, a clerk native to the Touraine (the region of the city of Tours), in 1205 elected bishop of Winchester, one of the richest sees in Europe, thereafter chief patron both of Frenchmen at the English court and of dreams of continental reconquest. By his enemies, Peter was branded a 'Poitevin', not because he or the majority of his friends were natives of Poitou but because Poitou's fissile baronial politics had become a byword for treachery and double-dealing for at least the past fifty years. As one of the King's chief ministers, from 1214 onwards, Peter was dogged by rhetoric in England against the 'aliens'. Ironically enough, this was rhetoric itself first stirred up in the 1190s by the French-born King John, in an attempt to discredit William Longchamps, the French-born minister of Richard I, left in charge of England whilst Richard himself was absent on crusade. Many of those who afterwards were responsible for spreading anti-alien rhetoric were themselves either of French birth or closely linked to France. There is no one so good at deriding the faults of others as one who fears that these are faults shared between critic and criticized.

Finally, as in all modern debates from which statistics and the spirit of Karl Marx are never far distant, it has been argued that, by 1200, Philip of France was far richer than the King of England and therefore ideally placed to seize the Plantagenet lands. The argument here depends upon comparison between the English and Norman Pipe Rolls and the one surviving budget that we have for French royal income and expenditure. The debate has proved interminable and hotly contested, since not only is it impossible to arrive at agreed totals for these accounts, but it will never be possible to establish how great a proportion of royal income was audited in writing. More significant than these statistical wranglings is the fact that, from the 1160s onwards, England underwent a significant period of inflation. The cost of paying a knight's wages more than doubled. The causes here are uncertain: perhaps monetary inflation brought about by the release into the economy of significant new supplies of silver, from the mines of Cumbria perhaps, and above all from the Harz mountains of Germany.

Most English landlords could respond fairly effectively to the crisis. Their estates, previously leased for a fixed annual 'farm', were brought back into direct demesne management, with the lord now taking the full profit of his lands. The King could not respond so easily. His estates in the English counties were traditionally managed by local sheriffs, for a fixed county farm payable at the Exchequer. As the real value of these farms began to dwindle through the effects of inflation, and as the sheriffs therefore pocketed an ever greater sum in profits over and above the fixed rent that they were obliged to pay at the Exchequer, the King could try to increase the county farms or to charge the sheriffs additional annual rents, known as increments. King John even attempted an experiment in direct management, by which sheriffs no longer paid a farm, keeping all excess profits for themselves, but were paid an annual allowance by the Exchequer, in return being expected to account for all profits, not merely for their traditional fixed farms. Neither measure succeeded. Courtiers and the great men necessary for the effective government of England baulked at serving merely as paid bailiffs, or at abandoning so large a proportion of the profits that they now received from local government. In the meantime, inflation bore down upon the

King's revenues, placing John in an ever weaker financial position, both in respect to the King of France and to his own English barons.

The events of 1204, culminating in Philip Augustus' acceptance of the surrender of Rouen, the ducal capital, had an enormous impact not upon the future history of Normandy, now united to the French crown, but on England. One consequence, pregnant with future significance, was the construction of an English fleet of royal galleys, at least fifty ships, powered by oarsmen rather than sail, built for speed, to overtake and seize ships dependent upon the wind, to police the shipping lanes, to impound contraband and to take prize from enemy merchantmen. Some of the technology here may have been devised in the 1190s to assist Richard's warfare on the Seine, including the importation of shipbuilding techniques from Bayonne, in the far south of Plantagenet Aquitaine, and the construction of a major new naval base at Portsmouth. Even so, King John has some qualifications to be accounted the true founder of the Royal Navy, created in direct response to the loss of Normandy and the transformation of the Channel from a vector of communication into a bulwark against the threat of French invasion.

Another, even more significant consequence of the loss of Normandy was the arrival in England of a King now determined to amass the sort of treasure necessary to launch a reconquest of his lost continental estate. At the time, no one was aware that the breach between England and Normandy would prove permanent. King John, like the French friends whom he brought with him into exile, was determined to regain his lost lands. By the very nature of things, most barons owed money, often very considerable sums of money, to the King. What mattered was not how much was owed but the terms for its repayment. Just as today, men and women are happy to negotiate mortgages for vast sums of money that they would be quite incapable of financing if the entire sum had to be repaid over a matter of months or a few years, so in the Middle Ages debts to the crown could be repaid over decades or even centuries without the debtor being forced into bankruptcy. John not only increased the levels of debt that burdened his barons, but in certain cases, and in a deliberate attempt to ruin the debtors, demanded summary payment of the money owed. It was in this way, for example, that he turned against William de Braose, at one time amongst his closest cronies, ruined, perhaps for disclosing the true fate of Arthur of Brittany. William was forced into exile in Ireland. His wife and children were supposedly starved to death in Windsor Castle.

The King's 'Fine Roll', the list of payments negotiated with the King, was on occasion transformed into a clubland wagers book, with men offering bizarre payments for favour or grace: 'the wife of Hugh de Neville offers 200 chickens to lie one night with her husband', 'Robert de Vaux offers five of the best riding horses so that the King might stop talking about the wife of Henry Pinel', and so forth. England, previously governed at a distance by absentee kings who passed much of their lives across the Channel, now had a King in permanent residence, travelling the country, eyeing up the profits and, if the chroniclers are to be believed, the daughters and wives of his barons. The experience was not a happy one. Debauchery and adultery had been characteristics of English kingship since at least the time of Henry I. Where Henry I or Henry II had managed to bed the wives and daughters of their barons with a minimum of complaint, however, John once again merely stirred up ill feeling. Where Henry II's reputation had been salvaged despite the murder of a sainted archbishop, John was incapable of living down even the disappearance of Arthur, his unloved Breton nephew.

Archbishop Langton

After 1206, what another king might have handled more lightly, an attempt to intrude a royal candidate into the archbishopric of Canterbury developed into a full-scale standoff between the King and the Church, with the Pope seizing the opportunity to discipline a Christian ruler he had long had in his sights, insisting not only that John's candidate for the archbishopric withdraw but that the monks of Canterbury accept a complete outsider, Stephen Langton, as leader of the English Church. Langton was an Englishman, born to a minor family of Lincolnshire knights. At one time he had been associated with the household of Geoffrey Plantagenet, Henry II's illegitimate son. He had gained his reputation, however, and had passed most of his life since the 1180s not in England but in Paris, as a commentator on the Bible and as one of the most famous masters of the Paris schools, the first and the greatest of all universities established north of the Alps.

Reading Langton's Bible commentaries today, one is struck, first and foremost, by their vast, still unpublished and probably unpublishable length, secondly, by their determination to interpret absolutely everything in scripture, from Hebrew names, to the significance of the creatures in Noah's ark, through to the hyacinth fringes with which the Jews were enjoined to trim their clothes, according to Langton, as a symbol of the blue of the heavenly kingdom. Langton was clearly a great teacher. Like many great teachers, he was also something of a bore, fond of the sound of his own voice, hammering home sentence after sentence of his own opinions into the unformed but perhaps rather over-stuffed minds of his students. Langton's Bible commentaries are also shot through with a deep distrust of monarchy in general, and of Plantagenet monarchy in particular.

Inheriting an entire programme of ecclesiastical prejudice, Langton believed that kingship was an unpleasant compromise, imposed upon the Jews of the Old Testament in punishment rather than reward: 'I gave you a King in my wrath', as God is said to have threatened (Hosea 13:11). Unlike the kings of France, who tempered privilege with justice and who took their counsels from the Church – a sensible exception for Langton to make, given his own residence in Paris – the kings of England, murderers of the sainted Archbishop Becket, ruled by the sword and according to the arbitrary traditions of the Exchequer, failing to heed the injunctions of scripture or to accept a written code of laws equivalent to the Old Testament book of Leviticus for the guidance and instruction of kings. The English themselves, in Langton's writings and sermons, are presented as a nation of drunks, hardly deserving a better king or the liberty which was the privilege of the French.

Drink had already been mentioned in William fitz Stephen's description of London as the greatest of English vices and, together with fire, the most severe of threats to London itself. In July 1212, as the result of a rowdy drinking contest or 'scotale', at the height of Langton's dispute with the King, drink and fire did indeed combine with horrendous ferocity to burn the suburbs south of the Thames, from Lambeth to Bermondsey. One contemporary, noting that the flames had spared London Bridge and hence had allowed many people to escape, concluded that God was in the process of testing the English. Conventional sin had been purified by the waters of Noah's Flood. Only the unnatural vices of Sodom, or now of London, he concluded, could have persuaded God to attempt purification by fire. Even in the twelfth and thirteenth centuries, English 'binge drinking' exacted a heavy toll. Modern politicians who hold forth against the demon drink might care to remember that drunkenness, and the expression of moral outrage against it, is an English tradition even older than Parliament.

Papal Interdict
Neither Langton's opinions nor his long residence in the capital city of Philip Augustus, the new conqueror of Normandy, endeared him to the Plantagenet King John who did his best to exclude Langton from England. The result was a standoff between Church and King in which England was placed under papal interdict from 1209 onwards, effectively prohibiting the population from receiving the sacraments of the Church or burial in consecrated ground. Interdict was a

blunt weapon, and there is plenty of evidence that, in England, it was implemented in ways more subtle than such bluntness ideally required. Ceremonies were still held in churches. The King himself maintained some sort of liturgical observance at court, taking baths, for example, before each of the major festivals of the Church, distributing lavish alms and perhaps instituting, at Knaresborough in 1210, the very first distribution of royal Maundy money: a tradition maintained to the present day.

With the majority of the English bishops fled into exile, John was able to confiscate a vast quantity of ecclesiastical property and wealth. If we add to this the taxes and exactions which John received from the barons, the proceeds of lands confiscated from Normans who after 1204 had remained behind in Normandy, perhaps the greatest influx of lands to the crown between the Conquest of 1066 and the Dissolution of the monasteries in the 1530s, and the savings made now that English silver was no longer required to pay for the defence of Normandy itself, then John emerges as easily the richest king in English history, master of a vast war chest, intended to pay for armies and alliances in France.

Peace with the Church, War with France

Throughout the period of interdict, although in theory an excommunicate, John was in regular contact with other European powers – the counts of Flanders and Toulouse, the kings of Aragon and Navarre, even the Almohad rulers of North Africa – bent upon launching a multi-pronged attack against Philip Augustus for the reconquest of the Plantagenet lands north of the Loire. In 1213, in what deserves to be remembered as the first great naval victory in English history, John's galleys launched a lightening raid on the French fleet stationed off Damme, the port of the city of Bruges, putting paid to what were said to have been plans by Philip for an invasion of England. In the same year, John made his peace with the Church, recognizing Langton as archbishop, allowing the return of the exiled bishops and sending for a papal legate to assist in the settlement of differences. Financial compensation and a lifting of the Interdict were not forthcoming even then, and, in the final analysis, John repaid only a fraction of the money that he had milked from the Church. Nonetheless, with a papal legate to support him in England, John was now able to embark upon his long-anticipated campaign of reconquest in France. Two great armies were launched against Philip, one commanded by John moving northwards from Poitou, the other commanded by the German emperor and John's illegitimate half-brother, William Longespée, Earl of Salisbury, moving southwards from Flanders. The result was a catastrophe for King John. On Sunday, 27 July 1214, the northern army was destroyed by Philip at the Battle of Bouvines, as significant a date in the history of France as the day of Hastings had proved in England. John himself was brought to a standstill in Poitou, from where he was forced to slink back ignominiously into England.

John already had an evil reputation as an adulterer, a murderer, a liar and a malicious persecutor of his foes. His murder of Arthur of Brittany and his supposed condemnation of women and children to death by starvation were now matched by failure in war as the very gravest of his crimes. In an age in which people believed that God's support alone could secure military victory, failure in war could only be accounted a sign that a king had been abandoned by God. If God had abandoned him, then might not King John's barons make common cause with the Almighty?

Rebellion

It was in these circumstances that a baronial coalition began to emerge. Calling themselves 'The Army of God', although by others described as the 'northerners' from the attachment of several of them to estates in Yorkshire and the north, this was a closely knit conspiracy, many of its members cousins or brother-in-laws, with particularly close associations to the

great baronial house of Clare. Their hope was either to persuade
the King to reform his government or, in the ultimate extreme,
to force him from his throne.

Similar coalitions had been formed against Plantagenet kings
in the past. The greatest such rebellion, mustered in 1173–4, in
the aftermath of Becket's murder, had threatened to deprive
John's father, Henry II, of his lands and authority. In the end
Henry had made his peace with Becket's shrine and thereby
been restored to God's favour, capturing the King of Scots in
battle and decisively defeating his enemies. It was in the aftermath
of this great rebellion that the full extent of Plantagenet predatory kingship had been displayed. The King had confiscated
large numbers of baronial castles, for the first time since 1066
holding a balance of power in terms of the number of castles in
royal rather than baronial hands. There had been a massive
extension of the authority of the King's courts both in respect to
civil and criminal law. The King's Assize of Northampton of
1176 required that all suspected criminals and wrongdoers be
denounced by their local communities to the King's justices to
be sent to the ordeal, either forced to carry hot irons or plunged
in water. Should they fail this test of God's judgment, they were
to have a foot cut off and then to be banished as outlaws. Lists of
such criminals, county by county, suggest that the assize was
enforced with brutal efficiency.

The King's laws, like the Assize of Northampton, have been
only haphazardly preserved. This itself speaks of a society in
which not even a written statement of law could be relied upon:
a society that, if not exactly lawless, was accustomed to kings
who made or broke laws as they saw fit. Kings claimed to rule
in the interest of their people, and yet kingship itself was so
predatory, and the King so dependent upon arbitrary taxes and
exactions for the financing of his wars and his courtly magnificence, that public and private interest were never fully distinguishable. Royal justice itself was as often about the profits
that could be extracted for the King as ever it was about the
delivery of abstract ideas of what was 'just'. The delaying of

justice, in order that both parties might attempt to buy the King's favour at the highest price, was a favoured technique of Plantagenet government, according to one chronicler specifically recommended to Henry II by his mother, Empress Matilda, as the best means of emphasizing royal power.

Perhaps the most obvious contrast between medieval and modern approaches to the public good comes in the virtual absence of policing, at least in the sense that we would understand it as a public duty for which the state takes responsibility. Policing today can sometimes be seen as an infringement of 'civil liberties'. Only by the surrender to the state of individual freedom of action, however, has the state been raised to a position from which it is capable of defending or impinging upon the liberties of individual citizens. In the thirteenth century this surrender of liberties was so embryonic and unregulated that the whole idea of a 'state' in twelfth- or thirteenth-century England is best avoided as an anachronism. 'Liberty' itself was a word more often understood to mean the right to independence from state control, as in the great 'liberties' held by barons such as the archbishop's 'liberty' of Canterbury, or the 'liberty' of the earls of Chester, rather than some abstract freedom possessed by the individual confronted with the demands of the many. To this extent, the machinery of government in the twelfth and thirteenth centuries depended upon a delicate and frequently disputed balance between the local and the central, between communal responsibility and anything approaching state control.

Crime and the Frankpledge

The prosecution of crime in medieval England worked according to the so-called 'frankpledge system', according to which every freeman belonged to a tithing responsible for reporting crimes or suspicious deaths to the local court of the hundred or the vill. It was within the tithing that the 'hue and cry' would be raised to arrest criminals suspected of malfeasance. Rather as today, when those who exercise a restaurant franchise are supposed to deliver up a standard meal but are themselves ultimately responsible for the profits and complaints that their franchise may generate, so, in the Middle Ages, large parts of England were 'franchised' out to lords and barons who themselves took the profits of justice and bore responsibility for trial and punishment, up to and including the erection of gallows for the execution of felons. Certain pleas, the pleas of the crown such as homicide, rape or arson, were in theory tried only in the King's courts. Nonetheless, cases in which the criminal was caught red-handed might be tried and punished by any local franchise-holder with right of gallows.

From 1194, local coroners appointed within each county were responsible for the investigation of sudden or suspicious deaths, and the county community of the knights also discharged public duties, serving on juries within the county court, and turning out, supposedly in large numbers, when the county 'posse', a term later exported from England to the United States, was required for national defence or to arrest and apprehend particularly notorious felons. Offences that directly concerned the King could be transferred to the royal courts of the county or of the crown itself, these latter 'crown courts' at this stage including the infrequent visitations of the country by the King's justices (the 'eyre'), the more regular sessions held before royal justices at Westminster (the Court of Common Pleas, or the 'Bench') and special sessions held before the King in person, the so-called court 'Coram Rege'. At virtually every stage in criminal prosecution, it was nonetheless the local community which bore chief responsibility for defence against crime. Since large numbers of tithings answered not to the King's jurisdiction but to hundred courts in the hands of barons, or to town courts with their own oligarchic system of communal government, the King's court processed only a small part of the criminal justice system.

Even gaols, which were maintained by the King and his officers in royal castles and the great county towns, were else-

where often in baronial rather than royal custody, albeit with
the King claiming the right to fine lords who permitted prisoners to escape. The greater private liberties, such as the bishopric of Ely, maintained their own prisons and their own
courts for the exercise of jurisdiction, even over criminal cases
detected within their private liberties. The bishop of Ely's
prison survived until 1836. The privately controlled soke of
Peterborough, relic of the liberty of Peterborough Abbey
dissolved in the 1530s, maintained its own prison until 1877
and had the theoretical right, last exercised in 1812, to impose
capital punishment as late as 1971. Instead of a nationwide
police force, the King's capacity to maintain the law depended
upon local officers, often no more than the gangs of serjeants
who gathered around his sheriffs and constables and who just
as often caused as quelled disorder.

When the courtier William Brewer attempted to transfer
large quantities of silver coin from Cumberland southwards in
1204, for example, to pay a fine owed at the royal Exchequer, it
was the men of the local sheriff who ambushed and robbed the
baggage train, stealing more than £60 in silver pennies as well as
the helmets, hauberks and horses with which Brewer's servants
had been travelling. The depredations caused by King John's
sheriff of Nottingham are still a byword for royal tyranny. A
man named Baldwin Tyrel was heard in 1212 spreading
rumours in Cornwall about the supposed murder of King
John. His words were reported to the local sheriff, but Baldwin
himself would have walked free had it not been for two of the
King's household knights who, claiming that they were sworn
to report all such rumours, took it upon themselves to arrest
Baldwin so that he might be brought before the King for trial
and sentencing. Most notoriously, it was the rallying cry of the
royal household, 'Reaux, Reaux!', that had rung out at
Canterbury in December 1170, bellowed by the four murderers
of Thomas Becket as they fled from the scene of their crime.

As this implies, whatever kings themselves might claim
about their public responsibilities as the chosen instruments of

God's justice, it was force, or the threat of force, that under-pinned all royal authority. No king could rule, however velvet his gloves, unless there was a fist of iron to back up his claims to authority. By 1200, indeed almost certainly by the 1130s, there was already a major force of knights and sergeants attached to the King's household, augmented in time of war by mercenaries and paid muscle, the forerunners of the sergeants-at-arms, by the fourteenth century the chief enforcers of royal authority in the English localities. In ordinary circumstances, the King held so great a balance of military power within the realm that no one could resist his will for long. Even in the reigns of Stephen or King John, when relations between King and barons dissolved into acrimony and civil war, the sheer military might of the royal household and its attendant army of Flemish, Welsh or southern French mercenaries, was sufficient to maintain an unpopular ruler on his throne, in the case of Stephen for a decade or more. Set against the King, however, was a tradition of local baronial or municipal rights to the exercise of power, of knights accustomed to public service, and of communities scattered from one end of England to another, already conscious of their own responsibilities not just in the preservation of public peace but in the interests of a public good often easily distinguishable from the interests of a pred-atory royal administration.

Rule by Custom and the Law?

How could the public good best be served? How could a bad king be made to reform his administration? The first possi-bility was that the King himself might be persuaded that it was in his own best interest to govern in accordance with custom and the law. Some such idea was already present in the oaths sworn by Aethelred in 1016, or by Edward the Confessor in 1042, to uphold the good laws of the past. A similar idea emerges from the written promises of Henry I and Stephen, their so-called coronation charters, promising better government than that offered by their predecessors, as a means of buying baronial support in the midst of the succession crises of 1100 and 1135. On several occasions, force or rebellion was employed in the hope that this might compel the King to observe his promises of good government, from the great rebellion of 1075 against William the Conqueror onwards. However, since the Church was convinced that anything extorted under duress was invalid, just as a woman compelled into marriage might seek annulment from her marriage vows, so a king forced into concessions by his barons could always seek to wriggle free from his promises once circumstances changed. The chief risk with rebellion, as shown in 1075 or again in the 1170s, was that the King would simply defeat the rebels and in the aftermath behave with even greater disregard for law. From the great crisis of 1173–4, Henry II had emerged with his authority not weakened but greatly strengthened.

An alternative possibility, far more drastic even than rebellion, was simply to kill the King. The killing of tyrants, 'tyrannicide', had a great deal to recommend it. It had been common in Roman antiquity and had served to justify the killing of Harold at Hastings. The surprise is that it was so rarely attempted in the twelfth or thirteenth centuries. Readers of the classics or indeed of the Bible, most famously John of Salisbury in his treatise on government, the *Policraticus*, were fully aware of the possibilities of assassination. John of Salisbury, indeed, was prepared to allow that, in certain circumstances, where God had agreed that it might be done, a bad king not only could be but *should* be killed: 'it is right to kill a tyrant'. The problem lay in deciding whether a king was or was not truly tyrannical, and thereafter in determining what God's wishes in the matter might be. Here, like all other medieval commentators, John of Salisbury urged caution. The mind of God was unfathomable, and in the end God himself would make all things straight. Better therefore to be patient, to endure bad government, like Job in the Old Testament, who had endured far worse, and to await events. There were assassinations in the twelfth century, most famously of Charles,

Count of Flanders in 1127, and later, during Richard I's crusade, of Conrad of Montferrat, claimant to the throne of Jerusalem, murdered, so it was whispered, with Richard's tacit approval. As we have seen, the fear of assassination explains the number of occasions when the death of the powerful, of Rufus or of Eustace, the son of King Stephen, was blamed upon poisoning rather than natural causes. In a notorious dispute, King Stephen's candidate for the archbishopric of York, William fitz Herbert, was reputed to have been murdered in the very act of taking communion, by a priest who had placed poison in the chalice. Yet the severity of the punishments meted out to assassins, and the posthumous elevation of their victims to the status of martyrs – Charles of Flanders and William of York were both recognized as saints, and even the unloved Harold Godwinson was promoted in some quarters as a martyr – was itself a deterrent against the killing of kings.

In 1212, rumours circulated that King John had been murdered, his wife raped and his youngest son dashed to pieces at Marlborough, yet these remained precisely that, rumours which were very swiftly quashed. Even in the 1230s, when a plot against the life of Henry III was unearthed, masterminded by an exiled gang of criminals working from Lundy Island in the Bristol Channel, the reaction was universal revulsion. It was to take a full 250 years after the Conquest of 1066 for the English to dare actually to kill a king, and even then the killing was to be a hole in the corner affair, hushed up, spoken of only in whispers and so concealed that many remained uncertain whether the King, Edward II, King John's great-grandson, was dead or alive.

Rebellion and Magna Carta

It is against this background that we need to view the outbreak of rebellion against King John in the spring of 1215. A sworn coalition of barons, commanding the sympathy if not the active support of leading figures within the Church, seized London in May 1215 with the cooperation of the city's men, forcing the

King into negotiations at Runnymede, a location halfway between London and the royal castle at Windsor. On 15 June, John agreed the issue of a document, under negotiation for at least the previous six months, which was intended to impose restrictions upon the future exercise of arbitrary royal rule. The document itself is known as Magna Carta ('The Big Charter') and, broken down into its individual chapters, runs to more than sixty clauses. It is undoubtedly the most famous document in English history. Yet what did it signify?

It was most certainly not the first written statement intended to limit the King's authority or freedom of action, an accolade that perhaps belongs to the coronation charter of Henry I issued more than a century earlier. It was not even the first such written statement issued by King John. Throughout his reign, John had offered charters of liberties to individual franchise-holders, to the men of London, for example, to many of the great cities and towns of England or Aquitaine, or to communities, such as the royal charters awarding privileges within the King's forests to the men of Devon or the tenantry of the honour of Lancaster. An assize for the men of the Channel Islands, supposedly issued by King John after 1204, attempted to regulate several aspects of Channel Islands law from the appointment of twelve 'jurats' to hear the pleas of the crown, a system still in operation today, to the restriction of the period during which conger eels might be salted. In April 1215, before the issue of Magna Carta, John issued a charter establishing communal self-government for the men of Bayonne, guaranteeing widespread liberties and privileges to the most important city of Aquitaine south of Bordeaux including detailed provisions for the city's governance by a mayor and a council of 100 citizens, the city already having acquired its own naval council set to monitor such matters as the price of freight between Spain and Flanders or the whaling fleets of the Bay of Biscay. Such documents can be linked not only to the discipline of law, and to the demands by churchmen, by Stephen Langton for example, that kings be

bound by a Leviticus just as the kings of the Old Testament
were bound. They also reveal the twelfth century's growing
fascination with categories and definitions. The sixty or more
clauses of Magna Carta not only imposed definitions and categories of this sort but resembled the division into clauses of
the Old Testament books of law, a system attributed to
Stephen Langton, or the law codes of the pre-Conquest
Anglo-Saxon kings.

Many of the clauses of Magna Carta are concerned with the
King's financial regime: the limitation of the fines that he
could charge his barons when they inherited their father's
estates, the protection of wards and widows, the restriction of
the King's ability to charge arbitrary taxes, known as 'aids',
without the consent of his barons and the Church. At the
same time, a surprising number of clauses were targeted at
particular interest groups whose demands the King sought to
satisfy. The Church was to have its ancient liberties. The
barons were to be free from arbitrary royal demands. The
merchants of London might trade without unreasonable
hindrance. Certain clauses might seem especially ephemeral:
clause 33, for example, demanding the removal of all fish
weirs on the rivers Thames or Medway. Why these two rivers
in particular? To the men of London and the Archbishop of
Canterbury, with his estate at Maidstone, it was essential that
these rivers remain navigable, and the building of mills or
weirs threatened such navigation. Special interests were at
stake. Clause 50 of the 1215 charter included a long list of
names of foreigners, Girard d'Athée and his associates, who
were to be dismissed from office, and under clause 51 banished
from England. These were in fact the most important of the
King's French constables, recruited from the region of the
Loire valley, essential to John's military control over England
and as links to his lost continental domain. One of them,
Philip Mark, is still a familiar figure in English history, albeit
known by his title rather than his name, as King John's sheriff
of Nottingham, adversary of the mythical Robin Hood.

Only a very few of the charter's clauses can be read as general statements of principle, the most important being clause 39:

> No free man shall be taken or imprisoned or disseised or outlawed or exiled or in any way ruined, nor will we go or send against him except by the lawful judgment of his peers or by the law of the land.

Of more pressing concern to both barons and King was the question of how to bind the King to the future observance of the charter's promises. Here, the charter included a 'sanctions' clause, clause 61, according to which a committee of twenty-five barons was to be appointed to oversee the charter's implementation. Should the King in any way infringe the charter's terms or fail to heed baronial warnings, then the twenty-five might rise against him and seize his resources, short of causing him or his family physical injury. A charter issued by the King as God's supposed vicar on earth was thus made to impose a baronial committee of twenty-five extremely angry and selfishly motivated barons between God and the King.

With this sanctions clause at its climax, there could be no question that the charter itself would survive. The King almost immediately repudiated it. Pope Innocent III, confronted by a document that threatened to institute rebellion as a constitutional instrument and to place limitations upon the God-given authority exercised by all sovereigns, from popes to kings, not only annulled Magna Carta but ordered the suspension of the Archbishop of Canterbury, Stephen Langton. If not exactly responsible for encouraging the barons in their claims, or for writing any particular clauses of the charter, Langton had failed to lend the King the unconditional support that the papacy believed was John's due. Like the very idea of reducing English custom to writing, as a sort of Plantagenet Leviticus or code of laws, some of the statements of principle expressed in Magna Carta, such as the insistence under clause 60 that customs and liberties granted by the King to his barons be extended by the barons to their own men, have an ecclesiastical stamp to them. To this extent, Langton's Parisian background was crucial in the formulation of the most detailed statement of English 'liberties' yet attempted. Meanwhile, born in June 1215, Magna Carta died ignominiously and ignored, within only three months of its issue. So at least the King believed.

Henry III

There followed a year of civil war, in which John's military household and a loyalist party headed by the veteran William Marshal, Earl of Pembroke, was pitted against the baronial coalition, itself now prepared to invite the son of the King of France to join them in London. Louis, Philip's son, was a grandson of Henry II of England and therefore a suitable foreign claimant to be groomed for the English throne. John himself died at Newark on Trent, in October 1216, with England in disarray, leaving a nine-year-old boy named Henry as his eldest son and heir. A rerun of the events of the 1130s seemed imminent, with the unsuitability of the legitimate heir to the throne – Henry III in 1216, compared with Empress Matilda and her three-year-old son, the future Henry II, in 1135 – opening the way to an opportunistic rival to seize the throne. The Plantagenet dynasty itself seemed destined for extinction. In other parts of Europe where boys had been recognized as kings, most notably in the kingdom of Sicily and the German empire where the young Frederick II had been only two years old at the time of his father's death in 1197, attempts to govern via minority councils until the boy came of age had been marked by bloodshed and internecine strife.

In England, a dynastic revolution was prevented by two chief factors. Firstly there was the memory of the disastrous reign of Stephen and the determination never again to deprive a young heir of his throne merely because he was not of age. This was clearly in the mind of the King's councillors in 1216. It was still there in the 1370s, and again in the 1420s, when the future

Kings Richard II and Henry VI were both crowned in boyhood, with disastrous consequences as we shall see. Secondly, in 1216 not only did John himself decree that his son Henry should succeed him, but he enlisted the assistance of the Pope to ensure that this was done.

Ever since 1213, John had technically been a subject of the Pope, having delivered up England to Pope Innocent III as a papal fiefdom owing an annual 'census' or tribute of 1,000 marks (700 for England, 300 for Ireland) as part of his settlement with the English Church. Regarded by monastic chroniclers at the time as a dangerous invitation to papal imperialism, and derided by later Protestant historians as perhaps the very worst of King John's crimes, the homage rendered by John to the papacy was in reality a clever political device, like John's subsequent taking of vows as a crusader, intended to place England under papal protection, and above all to ensure that the Pope was now intruded as John's overlord at a time when the French King's claim to overlordship had already led to the confiscation of Normandy and now threatened a French invasion of England. In 1216, it was the Pope's representative, the papal legate, Guala of Vercelli, who crowned the boy king at Gloucester Abbey. The ceremony was conducted with extreme haste, clearly to prevent Louis and the barons organizing a coronation of their own in Westminster where Louis might 'officially' be received as King. Because the coronation regalia, the crown and so forth, were in baronial hands in London, the legate had to employ a chaplet or crown of flowers as a makeshift alternative. Ever afterwards, Henry III looked to the Pope as his chief guardian and guide, keenly remembering that it was a papal legate who had 'recalled the realm to our peace and subjection, consecrated and crowned us King, and raised us to our throne'.

The influence of the Pope and his legates was not always regarded by the English as so benign. It led, after 1215, to the importation of large numbers of Italians into England, promoted to churches and benefices previously held by clergy attached to the rebel barons, these churches thereafter transformed into the object of regular papal 'provision', a system whereby the Pope claimed the right to override the claims of local patrons and to intrude his own candidates into parishes and cathedral prebends. As early as the 1220s, provision led to complaints in England culminating in a full-scale riot against Italians and provisors. Through to the 1350s, it remained a major source of tension in dealings between England and Rome.

It is therefore all the more ironic that it should have been the papal legate, the representative of Pope Innocent III (who himself had done most to annul and anathematize the 1215 Magna Carta), who now sought to rescue the charter, presented at Bristol in November 1216 as a manifesto of future good government, reissued by the boy King and his counsellors, sealed by the legate Guala, in very similar terms to the 1215 document, save for the omission of the controversial sanctions clause which in 1215 had placed a baronial committee above the King. Magna Carta was reissued again in November 1217, again under the legate's seal. It was these reissues of the charter that rescued it from oblivion and set it on its course to fame and semi-scriptural status as the foundation stone of English constitutional law. Without Paris-trained theologians such as Stephen Langton, and without Italian papal legates, Magna Carta might never have been written, and would most certainly never have survived. The emergence of English liberties was a truly European affair, embodied in the universalities of the Latin language, not an isolated 'island story' to be narrated in Anglo-Saxon or Eurosceptic grunts.

Parliament

With the reissue of Magna Carta came the idea of the King as a member, albeit as the most senior member, of the council by which England was governed. Kingship was not divested of its sacral elements. Indeed, King John's son and successor was to attempt to portray himself as direct heir to Edward the

Confessor, the most sacral King in English history. Even so, with the adoption of Magna Carta as a manifesto of good government, and with the insistence at each successive political crisis that it be reissued as a totemic summary of English 'liberties', we do indeed find ourselves on the broad highway that led via Magna Carta to the recognition that the King could not act without council or consent, to Parliament and to the idea of a 'community of the realm' in whose interests the King must govern and with which he must work in harmony.

The word 'Parliament', in the sense of a 'talking shop' or meeting of the King's great council, was first used in 1236. Parliament itself first met in 1254, whilst Henry III was in Gascony. The King's brother, who presided over this meeting, required each of the counties of England to send two elected representatives to discuss the matters of the realm, which in practice meant to discuss the possibility of assisting the King with taxes. In 1265, these county members were joined by nominated representatives of up to sixty English boroughs and towns. The county and borough members, the 'Commons', thereafter were summoned only intermittently during the reign of Edward I and did not become a regular feature of Parliament's meetings until the reign of Edward II, when it became accepted that they alone had the right to grant or withhold 'subsidy' (the grant of taxation) to the crown.

Parliament itself, meanwhile, in the sense of the seventy or so earls, barons and bannerets and the twenty bishops and fifty abbots entitled to individual summonses, met on a near annual basis during the reign of Edward I, through to the 1290s. By the 1320s, when the practicalities begin to become clear, the nominated county and borough members were meeting as a House of Commons, for the most part distinct from the 150 or so 'lords' spiritual and temporal who claimed the right, by precedence and status, to sit in a 'House of Peers'. Within the next twenty years, the lower clergy (parish priests and so forth), who through to the 1320s had sent representatives to the Commons, were meeting separately in their own assembly known as 'Convocation', alone judged capable of granting or withholding taxes payable by the Church.

To constitutional historians of the seventeenth and eighteenth centuries, the road from Magna Carta to Parliament appeared both swift and straight. In fact, this sort of 'Whig interpretation' of the emergence of constitutional liberty is a gross oversimplification of more complicated and less linear processes. To understand this, we need to engage with the events of a reign longer than those of Henry II and King John combined, longer indeed than any reign in English history save for those of George III, Victoria and Elizabeth II.

Henry the 'Preoccupied'

Henry III, King of England from 1216 to 1272, is one of those unfortunate kings famed neither for great wickedness nor for outstanding worth. Dante, writing less than fifty years after Henry's death, considered him worthy of inclusion in the *Divine Comedy*, but placed him in Purgatory, amidst the third class of the late-repentant, the 'preoccupied': 'There, alone, sits Henry of England, King of the simple life', more blessed in his posterity than by his own deeds. Shakespeare, three hundred years later, had no use for Henry III save as a walk-on part in his tragedy of *King John*, where the infant Henry attends the final agonies of his father, but spends more time in weeping than in speech. The one point of agreement between Dante and Shakespeare, shared by most historians who have since written on the subject is that Henry III pales into insignificance when compared either with his father, the 'wicked' King John, or with his eldest son, the 'good' King Edward I.

Even in his own lifetime, Henry never caught the imagination of his contemporaries in the same way as his father or his son. Although ruling at the same time as two of the most vividly reported kings of the Middle Ages – the German Emperor Frederick II, and King Louis IX of France – Henry was commemorated by no contemporary biographer. Instead, his life, his 'policy' (if he ever had one) and his personality have to be reconstructed using a less than satisfactory combination of chronicle and administrative sources that tends to emphasize 'policy' at the expense of 'personality'. Matthew Paris, the great chronicler of St Albans Abbey, who several times met the King and on occasion seems to have been treated almost as an official royal historiographer, tells us that Henry, despite a less than prepossessing appearance (one of his eyelids drooped), was no fool. He could recite the names of 250 English baronies, of all of the electors who had the right to choose the Holy Roman Emperor, and, here demonstrating his extraordinary personal piety, of all of the sainted kings of the Anglo-Saxon past. Such lists, however, like the extraordinary detail that emerges from the records of the King's commands for paintings, statuary and decoration in his palaces, speak less of great intelligence than of a rote-like determination to demonstrate the King's expertise.

Henry was not autistic. The record of his genuine affection for his wife and children, and even his remarkable petulance and bursts of rage, speak of a rich emotional engagement with those around him. Even so, he was perhaps the least 'clever' king to have ruled England since Edward the Confessor. Hence the incredible events at Lincoln in 1255, when Henry effectively sponsored a pogrom, moved by the complaints of a local woman that her son ('Little Saint Hugh') had been abducted and murdered by the city's Jews. Previously, whenever such stories of Jewish ritual murder had reached the ears of kings or royal justices, they had been rejected with a healthy degree of scepticism. Henry's emotional engagement and his deep identification with the cult of a child martyr, led to tragedy and appalling injustice. Hence too the story told by the Italian chronicler, Salimbene. Henry III, so this story went, was insulted at his court by a jester or minstrel. In a variation of remarks already passed against William the Conqueror, the jester announced that Henry resembled Jesus Christ. When questioned, he explained that just as Christ had possessed the wisdom of a man of thirty from the time that he was conceived, so Henry, though an adult, could claim to possess the wisdom of a baby boy. Henry demanded that the man be taken away and hanged. His courtiers pretended to comply, but as soon as they were out of earshot, let the jester go free. The story was intended to illustrate Henry's simplicity and petulance, his lack of authority, of guile and even of common sense.

To some extent, the dearth of direct biographical reporting on Henry III is characteristic of a wider phenomenon that affects historical writing on all of the early Plantagenet kings: the sudden explosion in record sources after the year 1200. The twelfth-century kings of England may or may not have kept copies of their outgoing correspondence. If they did, virtually all such copies have been lost. From 1199, however, and with ever mounting volume thereafter, the royal chancery began not only to draw up but to preserve 'rolls' of its outgoing letters, divided between various classes of business and by the 1230s preserving, for any one year of the King's reign, a quite phenomenal number of individual royal letters, several thousand for each year. Where for the twelfth century we depend upon chroniclers, rumour and the King's financial accounts (the 'Pipe Rolls') for our knowledge of events and government, from 1200 onwards there is a risk that the historian becomes overwhelmed by a mountain of detail. Later Plantagenet history can all too easily dissolve into an encyclo- pedic recital of thousands of individual 'facts': the narrative excitement of a train timetable is joined to the intellectual profundity of the London telephone directory, letters A to B. As a result, Henry III remains one of the least appreciated of England's medieval kings. As Sellar and Yeatman put it in their comic masterpiece *1066 and All That*, parodying the cruder political narrative taught in England's schools, Henry III was neither a good nor a bad but 'A Confused Sort of King'.

As a mere boy for his first ten years on the throne, Henry could not be permitted either to fight or to govern. Instead, a self-appointed minority council stepped in to rule on the

King's behalf. At Lincoln, in May 1217, the ageing regent, William Marshal, triumphed in battle against the rebels. Louis of France remained in occupation of London, but was starved of further supplies when his ships were ambushed and sunk off the coast of Sandwich by a fleet commanded by the royalist constable of Dover, Hubert de Burgh. Louis sued for peace and did public penance outside Kingston upon Thames, dressed only in his woollen underwear, promising to pay 10,000 marks in damages for his assault upon a realm in theory placed under papal protection as a result of its status both as a papal fief and at a time when the Pope wished men's attention to be focussed upon crusading for the recovery of Jerusalem, not upon selfish squabbling nearer home. Louis's clerical supporters were to attend Mass, shoeless and wearing only their shirts, and to be ritually beaten seven times within the coming year. Magna Carta was reissued for the second time since 1215, as a pledge of good government from royalists to rebels. In May 1220, at Westminster Abbey – since 1066 the traditional place of coronation – Henry was crowned for a second time, by the newly returned Archbishop Langton, in a ceremony intended to wipe clean all memory of the chaos of 1216. But still he was not permitted to rule. Within the governing minority council, bitter rivalries developed, most notably between Peter des Roches, the French-born bishop of Winchester, and Hubert de Burgh, for all his French-sounding name a native of Burgh in Norfolk and one of the first native-born Englishmen since 1066 to achieve a leading role in English government. Both Peter des Roches and Hubert de Burgh were former servants of King John, so that their hatred of one another was fuelled not only by issues of nationality or policy but by tensions stretching back twenty years or more.

In 1223, des Roches attempted to persuade the Pope to end the King's minority. The scheme misfired, and instead it was de Burgh who edged des Roches from power. The King was declared of age and began to issue charters in his own name. Magna Carta was reissued in 1225, in its final and definitive form and in return for a grant of taxation by Church and barons, intended to pay for the defence of Henry's remaining dominion in France. Superficially, this can be read as a sign of reconciliation and recovery after the civil war of John's reign. In reality, not only did it paper over deep divisions within the court, but it marked the first occasion since 1066, indeed perhaps the first time in English history, that a reigning king had been forced into concessions by a simple lack of funds. In 1225, 1232, 1234, and almost continually from the late 1230s onwards, the King's lack of financial resources was to become a predominant theme in politics, forcing Henry and his successors into negotiations with their realm that were entirely to reshape the face of English kingship.

In 1230, with Hubert de Burgh's assistance, Henry mounted an ineffective expedition to Brittany in the hope of recruiting allies for the reconquest of the Plantagenet lands north of the Loire. Hubert himself had little interest in France: his family had hardly possessed any land there before the French conquest of 1204. As a result, the King was perhaps right to suspect Hubert of only lukewarm support for his continental ventures. The expedition led to financial crisis. In addition, Hubert and his household were implicated in nationwide riots against the absentee Italian clergy intruded to English churches since 1215. In the midst of these wranglings, provoked by a new sense of English national identity, the King's former guardian, Peter des Roches, returned to court.

Since 1224, des Roches had earned both admiration and a European-wide reputation as a crusader and as a power broker between the papacy and the Holy Roman Emperor, Frederick II, himself a king who sought to rule in magnificent style, independent of any cloying council or restraint. Exploiting the King's frustration with the government of de Burgh – who continued to treat Henry as if he were still a child and on one notorious occasion had even threatened to box the young King's ears – des Roches stage-managed the arrest of his rival. From 1232 to 1234 he presided over a regime that threatened to restore many of the worst practices of King John. Estates, in theory guaranteed by royal charter, were arbitrarily seized and handed over to des Roches's friends. A hugely expensive operation was mounted to support the King's allies in France. The outcome was baronial rebellion, led on this occasion by Richard Marshal, younger son and heir to the King's first regent, William Marshal, Earl of Pembroke. Richard was killed in the subsequent fighting, the most serious outbreak of public violence since 1217, a civil war in all but name in which the Marshal affinity, one of the greatest of the military households of medieval England and previously the gamekeepers of royal policy in Ireland and the Welsh Marches, turned poacher, raiding the King's manors, burning barns and, in dramatic circumstances late in 1233, springing Hubert de Burgh from his fog-bound prison at Devizes to carry him off to safety in Wales. In 1234, des Roches was toppled. For the first time since his accession, Henry was free to wield undisputed sovereignty.

His response to this new-found freedom is proof both of his own weakness, and of the extent to which his character had been moulded by his former tutors. In 1236, the King took a wife, Eleanor, daughter of the Count of Provence, and related, via her mother, to the ruling house of Savoy, a county controlling the rich valleys and trade routes of western Switzerland and north-west Italy, of pivotal significance in relations within Europe, north and south of the Alps. Having shaken off one group of over-powerful ministers, the King merely replaced them with another. From 1236, it was the Queen's Savoyard uncles, William, Thomas and Peter of Savoy, builder of London's first Savoy hotel, created Earl of Richmond, and Bartholomew of Savoy, elected Archbishop of Canterbury, who stepped into the breach left by des Roches and de Burgh. From 1236 to 1258, Henry was to become notorious for the way in which he allowed policy to be dictated by whichever faction at court he was momentarily inclined to trust. To begin with, this trust resided with the Savoyards, and to some extent with his younger brother, Richard, Earl of Cornwall. After 1247, however, Henry began showering favours upon his Poitevin half-brothers, the sons of his mother, Isabella of Angoulême, who had retired to France after the death of King John, and there married Hugh de Lusignan, lord of La Marche. The King's Lusignan half-brothers – most notably William de Valence, eventually created Earl of Pembroke when the last of the Marshal line died without male heirs, and Aymer de Lusignan, elected bishop of Winchester – swiftly came into competition with the Savoyards and with other factions at court, over patronage and perhaps above all over the degree to which they commanded the affections of the King's son Edward, already by the mid-1250s eager to rule his own estate. The unpopularity of the Lusignans was in part personal, the consequence of their own notorious arrogance, and in part the result of deeper-seated problems in royal finance.

England was a wealthy country, and Henry III had the potential to raise revenues far greater than those of neighbouring rulers. However, he was also committed to reconquering his father's lands in Normandy, Anjou and especially Poitou. From the 1220s, a pattern had emerged in which the King obtained taxation from the English barons and the Church, in return for his undertaking to uphold the terms of Magna Carta, promising government by consent rather than by arbitrary royal will. The money so raised was then squandered on military expeditions to France, themselves undermined by the King's own military incompetence and the fickleness of his French allies. For twenty years after 1237, and claiming the right recognized in Magna Carta to withhold consent to extraordinary taxation, the English barons refused to accede to the King's repeated demands that they grant new taxes. By wringing as much as he could from his own demesne and from feudal aids not subject to baronial veto, Henry succeeded in launching two further expeditions to Gascony and Poitou. Both were costly fiascos. Indeed, the expedition of 1242 very nearly resulted in Henry being taken prisoner by the

French King Louis IX. In the process, the King was forced to mismanage his own resources, sending sheriffs and judges into the counties with the chief purpose of raising money rather than doing justice. The Jews were so severely taxed that, by the 1250s, the once rich resources of their community were running dry. Complaints against misgovernment mounted.

The King's talent at spending more than he possessed merely increased the competition between the factions at court to grab whatever favours remained at the King's disposal. Added to this, the Savoyards and the Lusignans were all of them aliens, Frenchmen or Franco-Italians. Alien favourites had long been a target for the hatred of the politically discontented barons of England. The King found it impossible to lay such hatred to rest. Nonetheless, from the mid-1230s onwards, and no doubt learning from the experiment in arbitrary rule attempted under Peter des Roches, he came increasingly to adopt King Edward the Confessor as his patron and role model. Edward appealed to Henry III, in part because of his perceived Englishness, wisdom and sanctity, in part because, like Henry, he was a King who had been raised as an orphan, a mere boy at the time of his father's death, abandoned thereafter by his strong-willed French mother. Under Henry's patronage, the history of Edward's reign was rewritten to supply a model of harmonious and pious rule. In token of this, from 1245 Henry set about rebuilding the Confessor's great church at Westminster.

For his work on Westminster Abbey, as for his many other building projects, Henry deserves to rank as one of the most artistically inclined of England's kings, the greatest royal patron of the arts before Charles I. His patronage was no mere aesthetic self-indulgence, but emerged from a keen sense of religious duty. At a time when Europe's kings outbid one another to advertise their Christian piety, Henry stood out as a man of almost fanatical religious sentiment. A keen family man, who appears to have lavished genuine affection on his wife and children, he is more or less unique amongst the medieval kings of England in having fathered not a single bastard. Fidelity was just one amongst his many Christian virtues. At Westminster and his other palaces, Henry instituted a quite extraordinary programme of alms for the poor, at the feast of All Souls in 1234, for example, demanding that his servants find and feed 10,000 paupers, a figure regarded as absurd. The King, so it was said, attended Mass as many as three times a day. At the altar, he would hold and kiss the priest's hand as the sacraments were consecrated. At Westminster and elsewhere, he built up a vast collection of Christian relics. In one six-month period in 1235, for example, he is recorded taking possession of bones and other mementoes of saints George, Theodore, Panteleon, Jerome and Augustine, besides relics of the golden gate at Jerusalem, of the Holy Sepulchre, of the burning bush from which God had spoken to Moses, and a stone 'to protect the King against thunder', a reminder that Henry III had a morbid fear of thunderstorms. A few years later, in 1247, he obtained a relic of the blood shed by Christ at the crucifixion, deposited amidst elaborate ceremonial at Westminster Abbey.

It is symptomatic of Henry's wider failure that his blood relic, in theory one of the greatest treasures that could be boasted by any Church in Christendom, was scoffed at almost from the moment of its arrival in England. How could Christ, it was asked, who had ascended into heaven perfect in every part, have left behind such relics as blood (or elsewhere milk teeth, hair, his umbilicus and most notoriously his foreskin)? An answer was devised for the King by Robert Grosseteste, bishop of Lincoln and one of England's greatest scientists, but it was not widely read and even less believed. Only one miracle is known to have been worked by Henry's blood relic and, unlike the dozens of miraculous healings worked at such 'anti-royal' centres as the shrine of Becket at Canterbury, this Westminster miracle was an entirely local affair, involving a boy drowned in a pond at Hyde, the park belonging to the Westminster monks just to the north of the abbey precinct, revived when a candle measured to the boy's height was burned

before the Westminster relic. In thanksgiving, Henry processed to the abbey from Tothill (now in the modern St James'
Park), ordering that the abbey's bells be rung and promising
the monks a gold cup decorated with precious stones, in
commemoration.

Such ceremonies served political as well as religious ends,
helping to advertise Henry's self-image as a benevolent
Christian prince. The cup in which the Westminster relic was
stored seems deliberately to have echoed the image of the Holy
Grail, itself now entering English mythology as a precious
treasure hidden somewhere on the estates of Glastonbury
Abbey. Ceremonial and processions through the London
parks, jewels and an appeal to antiquity are still amongst the
most potent symbols of English monarchy. The King's celebration of the feasts of St Edward the Confessor at Westminster,
in January and October each year, became the high points of
the royal calendar, intended to draw together King, barons and
people to both worship and take counsel together.
Unfortunately, such majestic gestures were extremely costly to
mount and, set against a background of factionalism and
personal incompetence on behalf of the King, only emphasized
the disparity between Henry's ambitions and his achievements. The jewelled path that Henry laid towards his own
salvation was the same path that led to baronial rebellion and
civil war.

All might still have been well had Henry restricted his
territorial ambitions to England. In the early 1250s, there
were signs that this would indeed be the case. Negotiations
were opened with King Louis IX, in which Henry offered to
abandon his by now empty titles to Normandy and Anjou, in
return for French recognition of his rights in Gascony. At
this point, however, Henry became embroiled in one of the
greatest acts of folly ever perpetrated by an English king. For
some years the Pope had been seeking a buyer for the realm
of Sicily, in theory confiscated from the German Emperor
Frederick II, in practice still ruled by Frederick's sons. The

price that the Pope demanded was wholly absurd: not only would his candidate for the Sicilian throne have to mount a campaign of conquest, but he would be required to repay the expenses that the Pope himself claimed to have incurred over Sicily, a sum eventually calculated as 135,000 silver marks (£90,000), well in excess of Henry III's annual income. Henry was nonetheless persuaded to accept the offer, in part through his own folly and his desire to provide a kingdom for his younger son, Edmund, in part through the diplomatic skills of the Savoyard party at court. The febrile but absurd antici-pation that these arrangements generated at court can be gauged from a list of the Sicilian crown jewels now released into English custody: the great crown of Emperor Frederick II, a golden apple and so forth, all of the baubles with which monarchy was advertised, yet entirely meaningless in terms of land or power. Sicily had still to be conquered, even if the King could raise the vast sums promised to the Pope. Into this spiralling flood of debt and disappointed expectations vanished the Sicilian regalia, pawned to pay for a venture that lacked the slightest prospect of success.

The outcome was predictable. Despite an ever harsher exploitation of the King's resources, and hence an ever growing sense of baronial discontent, the money that had been pledged to the Pope could not be raised. The English barons opposed all calls for their assistance, either military or financial. Anger at the favours showered upon Henry's foreign kinsmen mounted, and in 1258, following a series of violent encounters sparked off by the Lusignans, a deputation of barons, headed by the Earl of Norfolk, came before the King in Westminster Hall, armed and demanding reform. The Lusignans were to be banished. The King's finances were to be thoroughly over-hauled. All bad customs were to be abolished, and the King's personal government itself to be put into commission. A council representing barons and royalists would be appointed to exercise what had previously been considered the prerog-ative and patronage powers of the King. There followed a complicated process of manoeuvre, marked by the issue of a series of constitutional settlements, the so-called Provisions of Oxford (1258) and Westminster (1259) concerned with the regulation both of central and of local government. From this, one man, the King's brother-in-law, Simon de Montfort, emerged as a somewhat improbable champion of English and baronial interests. Simon was not only a courtier, married in controversial circumstances to the King's sister Eleanor, but undeniably a Frenchman, born and raised in France. He had no great respect for the King's intelligence. During Henry's expedition to Poitou in 1242, he is said to have declared that the King was a fool who should be locked away for his own and other people's safety. Like Henry, Simon was something of a religious fanatic, with a hatred of Jews and a strong sense of his own religious duty. Unlike Henry, he was a competent commander of troops.

When, in 1263, Henry attempted to reassert his personal authority, Simon insisted that the disputes between King and barons be put to arbitration before Louis IX. When Louis passed a judgment entirely in favour of the King, Simon summoned his supporters to arms. On 14 May 1264, at Lewes on the Sussex downs, not far from the site of Battle of Hastings. with the London mob and a rag-tag army of baronial supporters behind him, Simon defeated Henry III in battle. The King, his eldest son Edward, and the King's brother Richard were all taken prisoner. For the next twelve months Simon ruled, in reality if not in name, as protector of England. Mistrusted by even his closest allies, and faced with the threat that the King's friends overseas were preparing a counterattack, Simon summoned a Parliament attended by representatives of the English boroughs and shires. Kings had often summoned great councils, and on occasion such councils had not only been described using the French word 'parliament', but had been attended by representatives from the shires. The Parliament summoned in 1265 did little to alter the course of civil war. It marked, nonetheless, the first occasion when the borough and county franchise served as the basis of a parliamentary summons to the third estate. From this, by many twists and turns, was to emerge the idea of a House of Commons meeting in council with King and lords.

From his Parliament, Simon rode out to defeat and death at Evesham. The King's son Edward escaped from imprisonment at Hereford and mustered an army. On 4 August 1265, he and his royalist allies caught up with Simon de Montfort and the King at Evesham. Confused by the banners which Edward's army carried (yet another proof of the significance of heraldry), Montfort and his men at first thought that allies were approaching. When their mistake became clear, Montfort commented on the discipline of Edward's army:

> By the arm of St James [one of England's most precious relics, long prized by Henry II] they are advancing well. They have not learned that for themselves but were taught it by me!

In the ensuing blood bath, fought out in a loop of the river Avon, in the meadows and gardens in front of the town of Evesham itself, Montfort and a large number of his knights were slain, at least thirty of them, compared with only half a dozen royalist knights killed in the previous year's battle at Lewes and perhaps only one or two killed at Lincoln in 1217. Evesham marked a sudden and alarming escalation in political violence, ratcheting up the scale of upper-class vendetta. Not until the 1680s, or perhaps the 1720s, it might be argued, were the tensions created here fully dissipated. In token of the hatred that had driven on his enemies, Montfort's feet and hands were cut off. His testicles were hung either side of his nose on his severed head, which was then sent as a trophy by Roger de Mortimer to his wife at Wigmore Castle. Henry III, who had been kitted out in Montfortian armour and had been forced to cry out at the height of the battle 'I am Henry of Winchester your King. Do not kill me!', was released from captivity.

Over the next few months, in an orgy of revenge, the King's men occupied and pillaged the lands of anyone suspected of supporting de Montfort's regime. Those Montfortians who survived had little choice but to persist in their rebellion. Henry III spent 19 October 1266, the fiftieth anniversary of his accession to the throne, at Kenilworth in Warwickshire, encamped before the walls of the great castle which for the past four months had resisted siege. As a boy, Henry had attended the jubilee of St Thomas at Canterbury Cathedral, marked by the translation of Becket's remains to a magnificent new shrine on 7 July 1220, a date calculated in precise accordance with the Jubilee recorded in the Old Testament book of Leviticus, ten days into the seventh month after seven-times-seven years from the date of Becket's martyrdom. By contrast, in 1266, so far as we can tell, no crowds of well-wishers gathered, and no anthems were raised in thanksgiving for the King's long reign – the longest yet recorded for an English sovereign. Instead, men awaited in trepidation the proclamation of peace terms intended to save England from civil war.

Under the terms eventually agreed, former rebels might buy back their lands. Until his death, on 16 November 1272, the King continued to rule and to conduct his customary religious devotions. The last few years of the reign were spent in resolving the disputes of the late civil war and in raising the money needed to dispatch Henry's son Edward at the head of a English crusade to the Holy Land. Henry himself had taken vows as a crusader many year before, but characteristically it was the King's son rather than Henry himself who was to discharge Henry's promises. England meanwhile remained in a state of disturbance and high tension, its castles garrisoned, gangs of outlaws on the loose. Virtually the last act of Henry's life, in the autumn of 1272, was to ride over to Norwich to view the ruins of the cathedral, burned when tensions between the Norwich monks and the surrounding townsmen boiled over into riot and arson. Winchester Cathedral only narrowly escaped a similar fate in January 1274. Two of the greatest

Norman cathedrals in England, monuments to the Conquest of 1066, untouched by the feeble English rebellions of the eleventh or twelfth centuries, were very nearly destroyed by a resurgent England of burgesses and townsmen convinced of their own rights and determined to guard against the predations of either monks or kings.

Buried in pomp at Westminster, in a magnificent tomb adorned with relics, part of his massively expensive rebuilding of the abbey which had involved the importation of craftsmen from as far away as Rome, Henry was to enjoy a brief period of fame from beyond the grave. Shortly after his burial, a local beggar claimed to have been cured of blindness by praying at Henry's tomb. Henry's widow, Queen Eleanor, was inclined to believe the story. For a while, it seemed that Henry's tomb might become venerated as a wonder-working shrine. It was Henry's own son, Edward I, who put a stop to all this. The man who claimed to have been cured, so Edward reportedly exclaimed, was a fraudster whom Henry would rather have hanged than helped. By Edward, as by posterity, Henry was to be judged a good man, yet never a saint: a King of extraordinary personal piety, who nonetheless failed in his chief aim of ruling in peace and harmony. From that failure, however, and from Henry's very personal and very Christian misrule, were to emerge some of the more significant constitutional developments of English history.

Between 1204 and 1259 when the terms of the Treaty of Paris allowed Henry III to surrender his rights in Normandy and Anjou in exchange for French recognition of English lordship over Gascony, the Plantagenet empire in France was effectively dismembered. Partly through the cruelty of King John, partly through the feckless affability of his son, the Plantagenets lost a large part of their landed dominion. In England, a sense of political identity emerged so that by the 1260s the *Song of Lewes* could declare that through Henry's defeat in battle

The proud people are fallen, the faithful are glad.
Now England breathes again, hoping for liberty,
To whom may God's grace grant prosperity.

The baronial wars of the 1260s were fought out for the most part between English barons and an English-born King, with both sides claiming the support and interest of 'the community of the realm', an entity whose very existence might have been doubted fifty years before. Even if we allow that Simon de Montfort, the rebels' leader, was a Frenchman, almost all of his followers were English by birth. The rebellion of 1264, therefore, stands in stark contrast to the previous rebellions of 1173–4 or 1215–17, in which the English or Anglo-Norman baronage had looked to foreign alliances, chiefly with the Capetian kings of France, and in which the barons of Henry II and John had actively encouraged French or Flemish armies to cross the Channel. In 1215, the idea of placing restraints upon the King by written statute must have seemed to many as doomed to fail. Yet by 1272 no King of England could go against the terms of Magna Carta without risking heavy and immediate retribution. England was set on the path to constitutional monarchy and the limitation of the King's sovereign powers. France, by contrast, was fast developing a Parlement that was little more than a royal law court, its kings rich enough and surrounded by such an aura of omniscience that absolutism rather than constitutionalism became increasingly the national norm.

In Henry III, Protestant historians of the seventeenth century could point to a King whose subservience to Rome and to foreign favourites led to national English resistance to the financial and superstitious excesses of the Roman Catholic Church. In even broader terms, Henry's reign could be written as a story of the struggle between King and the barons represented in Parliament, prophetic of the greater Civil War that was to engulf England in the 1640s, and similarly brought to pass through the King's financial extravagance and the consequent 'national' resistance to taxation. From this derives the view still commonly held: that Henry III was essentially an incompetent absolutist; a believer in the divine right of kings some four hundred years in advance of the Stuart monarchs; a spendthrift patron of wicked foreign favourites, opposed by the stern will of the English barons, themselves acting as little more than 'Whigs in armour'.

Roger of Wendover and Matthew Paris Chroniclers

In reality, although by the 1260s the Plantagenet family had lost a large part of their European 'empire', their role in European affairs remained undiminished. For a more balanced, less anachronistic view of the situation here, we might turn to the chief contemporary chroniclers of Henry III's reign, both of them monks of St Albans in Hertfordshire, both of them with contacts at the royal court and with the many courtiers who visited St Albans in travelling to and from London. Neither Roger of Wendover, whose chronicle ends in 1234, nor Matthew Paris, who continued Wendover's chronicle from 1234 until his own death in 1259, was an admirer of Henry III or of royal administration in general. It is through their writing that we gain our keenest insights into both the King's particular incompetence and the failings of his administration as a whole. Yet no reader of their chronicles could fail to notice that Henry III, like his Plantagenet predecessors, was a truly European figure, whose interventions in European politics were significant for the histories of France, Sicily, Spain, the papacy and the German empire. Even such distant events as the Albigensian crusade against heresy in southern France, from which the reputation of Simon de Montfort and his ancestors was chiefly derived, or the fate of the Norwegian King Haakon IV, an almost exact contemporary of Henry III, dependent upon England for the engraving of his seal, and a patron at one time of the chronicler Matthew Paris who himself visited Norway, fell within Henry's sphere of influence as recorded by the St Albans' chroniclers.

The menagerie which Henry installed in the grounds of the Tower of London to some extent symbolized this world-wide reach, including three leopards sent by the German emperor (to commemorate the three leopards of Henry's heraldic shield), a polar bear sent from Norway (kept chained, but allowed to catch fish in the Thames), and an elephant acquired by Louis IX of France whilst on crusade in Egypt. When the elephant died, after only three years at the Tower, its bones were gifted by Henry to the monks of Westminster. According to the *Bestiary*, the standard medieval encyclopedia of animal lore, burnt elephant bone could drive out snakes. It seems improbable that this was a useful function so far as the monks of Westminster were concerned. More likely, the King's elephant, like the Holy Blood, and the rest of Henry III's vast relic collection, joined that jumble of objects that had already been gifted to Westminster Abbey, in effect the first British Museum, with the King as its principal benefactor and the monks as curators in chief: part time-capsule, part monument to the sacral authority conferred by coronation, part cabinet of curiosities, in all respects testifying to the historical and international significance of England's kings.

Meanwhile, England had moved from the periphery to the centre of European affairs. The marriages of successive members of the ruling dynasty, culminating in Henry III's marriage to Eleanor of Provence, and the marriage of his sister to the German Emperor Frederick II, entangled the Plantagenets and their English subjects with the politics of Italy, Germany and southern France. It was the English dowry paid to the German Emperor Henry V in 1120, and the ransom payments made on behalf of Richard I of England to Henry VI in the 1190s that had helped the twelfth-century German emperors in their campaigns in Italy, enabling Henry V to re-enter the Italian scene and greatly assisting Henry VI in his conquest of Sicily. In the same way, by the late 1230s, it was the wealth of England that Emperor Frederick II milked in support of his own Italian campaigns. Perhaps more significantly still, in the late 1250s, following Frederick's death, it was to Henry III's brother, Richard of Cornwall, that the German electors were to turn in their search for a successor to Frederick as King of Germany. Richard, a forgotten figure in the mainstream of popular history, is the only Englishman ever to have aspired to rule over the Holy Roman Empire. His aspirations proved fruitless, but for a decade, from the late 1250s, it was Richard, buoyed up by the vast resources that he obtained as Earl of Cornwall from the stannaries (the tin mines) of western England, who ruled a Rhineland kingdom stretching from the North Sea to the Alps.

It was from the Rhineland that Richard's son returned in the 1260s, bringing with him yet another blood relic, this time said to have been collected from the Crucifixion by the apostle Nicodemus and to have been hung around the neck of all emperors from the time of Charlemagne onwards. Gifted to the Cistercian Abbey of Hailes in Gloucestershire, this was destined to become the focal point of one of the most popular (and controversial) shrines in England, its merits still being debated in the 1530s when the Holy Blood of Hailes was 'exposed' by Protestant reformers as a holy fraud, rumoured to be topped up each week with the blood of a freshly slaughtered duck. Meanwhile, and calling upon yet another rich vein of mythology, it was Richard of Cornwall who rebuilt the cliff-top castle of Tintagel, intending it, as early as the 1230s, as a sort of theme-park re-creation of the castle of King Arthur, described by Geoffrey of Monmouth, now made visible to any mariner tacking up the north Cornish coast. At precisely the same time that the legends of Arthur, Parsifal and the Grail Castle were scaling the heights of popularity in Europe, Richard of Cornwall, with his relics and his castles, his wealth and his claim to stand as imperial successor to Charlemagne, should remind us of the close and significant cultural ties that now bound England not just to France but to the mainstream of European history.

For all of the xenophobic rhetoric of its barons, thirteenth-century England was very much a part of European affairs, wealthy and confident enough to launch the career of a Richard of Cornwall or an aspiring King of Sicily. Perhaps the clearest indication of this confidence comes not just from Matthew Paris' recital of the details of Anglo-European diplomacy, but from the maps with which Paris decorated his chronicles. Here, not only did Paris seek to place Britain within a wider context, but produced what are in effect the first recognizable images of the British Isles. Paris' world map – a 'Mappa Mundi', like the far more elaborate late thirteenth-century example still preserved at Hereford Cathedral – shows Britain as a small detached fragment of northern Europe, clinging on at the very bottom margin, clenched between channels facing Normandy and Spain, with Africa closer even than Flanders. Far more realistic are Paris' attempts to plot, through a series of strip maps, the journey to be followed between London and Jerusalem, noting the more important landmarks en route, the greater churches, the terrible Alps and even such features as the storks roosting on the towers of Turin. In this telling, Britain was very much a part of the Christian or European mainstream.

As for Britain itself, what is perhaps most striking about Matthew Paris' various attempts to map these islands is not just his attention to detail but his willingness to imagine England as merely part, albeit by far the largest part, of a North Sea archipelago that included Wales, Scotland and the Isle of Man (though not Ireland). In these maps, the Severn divides England from Wales, and Hadrian's wall together with a whole series of rivers, from the Tyne northwards, snake across the borders between England and Scotland. At the bridge of Stirling, Matthew shows Scotland tightening to a narrow causeway, rather like the waist to an hourglass. Even so, it is clear from these drawings that a man, might travel, should he so wish, from Dover to the furthest reaches of Caithness without ever quitting dry land. In the decades to come, one particular man was to attempt just such a journey, seeking through warfare and diplomacy at last to unite the various parts of Britain and to bring both Wales and Scotland under English rule. His name was Edward, the son of King Henry III, and it was at Stirling Bridge, Matthew Paris' narrow causeway between England and the north, that his plans first came unstuck.

6

EDWARD I TO EDWARD III,
1272–1377

In the 1080s, Robert Curthose, son of William the Conqueror, had declared that he would become King of England even if he were in Alexandria when his father died. It was an empty boast. In the entire period between 1066 and 1272, only one King had followed his father on to the English throne as his father's eldest son, and the circumstances here, with the accession in 1216 of the nine-year-old Henry III, at the height of civil war, with most of southern England under rebel or French control, were hardly an advertisement of the stability of English kingship. By contrast, in 1272, not only was Henry III's eldest son accepted unquestioningly as England's King but, in bizarre fulfilment of Curthose's boast, he happened at the time to be, if not in Alexandria, then returning across the Mediterranean from crusade in the Holy Land. Edward's very name, chosen in honour of Edward the Confessor, the last of the Anglo-Saxon kings, promised stability and a return to good order.

In the century after 1272, England was to be ruled in turn by three kings, all named Edward, each of them of very different character. The heroic, crusading Edward I is generally ranked amongst the premier league of great English kings, responsible for the conquest of Wales, for the first attempted English conquest of Scotland and for the restoration of royal authority after the chaos and confusion of his father's reign. By contrast, Edward I's son and heir, Edward II, ranks if not as the worst, then as perhaps the most feckless of England's medieval rulers, utterly unsuited to his position, a sexually ambiguous wastrel, literally a layabout who had difficulty even in getting up each morning, persuaded after fifteen years of weak rule and disasters both in foreign and domestic policy into a final period of tyranny and extortion which plunged England into yet further baronial rebellion and led eventually to his deposition and murder.

Whatever qualities Edward I had possessed skipped a generation, being reborn in Edward III, albeit that the character of the new King, like that of Edward I before him, was moulded in quite deliberate determination to avoid the failings of his father. Edward III it was who built up the great war machine of England, reviving the military glories of his grandfather's reign, setting England on course to become a state organized for war. As the son of the King of England and of a daughter of the King of France, Edward III inherited a claim to the French throne, leading after 1337 to the outbreak of the Hundred Years War, that great slogging match in which the national and political identities of both countries were reforged. It is already symptomatic of the emergence of English identity, that, even in 1340, when Edward III came to devise a new style for himself, as King of both nations, he chose to place England above France in the list of his titles: 'Edward King of England and France', positioning (in his letters to the English, though not on his seal or his letters to the French where he styled himself 'King of France and England') what in the twelfth century would have been regarded as the cart of French plenty very much behind the proud and no longer supine English horse.

Europe's Oldest Dynasty

Through to the thirteenth century, the Plantagenet kings of England could still be dismissed as callow new bugs in the playground of European dynastic politics, overshadowed by the sixth-formers and prefects of other nations. Four generations on, by the end of the reign of Edward III, all this had changed. The Plantagenets, first crowned in 1154, were by the 1370s well on the way to becoming the longest established dynasty in Europe. The Hohenstaufen emperors of Germany had vanished from the imperial scene as early as 1250. The royal houses of France, Sicily, Navarre, Castile, Scotland, Norway, Denmark, Sweden, Poland, Bohemia, Hungary, Armenia, Byzantium, Jerusalem and even Bulgaria had all suffered deposition or dynastic disruption. By the time of the death of Edward III in 1377, only the rulers of Aragon and Portugal could claim that their crowns had passed from King to King in unbroken succession to match the succession of the Plantagenet rulers of England, and even then not without slips and skips along the way. As the crowned representative of a sixth generation of Plantagenet kings, Edward III could claim that he and his ancestors had ruled England for as many generations and for an even longer period of time (six generations, and 233 years as opposed to 195) than that which separated Alfred, true founder of the house of Wessex, from the Norman Conquest. The Plantagenet house had become a venerable and time-honoured institution, just as hallowed by antiquity as the house of Alfred had been in 1066.

As befitted their rank, the Plantagenets had also acquired a family mausoleum, Westminster Abbey, and patron saints: King Edward the Confessor, whose presence there determined the emergence of Westminster as the principal royal family mausoleum from Henry III onwards, and St Thomas Becket who, for all the anti-royal and potentially subversive qualities of his original legend, had been recruited as a supporter of kingship as early as 1174, with Henry II's reconciliation at his shrine. By 1318, Becket was believed to have endowed the kings of England with a miraculous gift, the 'Oil of St Thomas', supposedly granted to him by the Virgin Mary and intended for use in the English coronation. Edward II asked that he might be anointed with this oil, although it was not actually employed in royal ceremonial until 1399. Its purpose was clearly to rival the oil held in the 'Sainte Ampoule' at Rheims, supposedly brought down to earth in the mouth of a dove and used at the inauguration of all kings of France from Clovis in 496 through to its destruction by the French revolutionaries in 1794. Even in terms of its sacral stage properties, the Plantagenet dynasty was beginning to rival the greatest royal actors in Christendom.

St George: New English Saint

To this list of his family's heavenly protectors, Edward III added the Cappadocian warrior St George, already commemorated as the particular patron of crusaders, now granted his own chapel and cult centre within the precincts of Edward III's castle at Windsor. England itself had previously been a flagless nation, or at best one that marched under the Plantagenet leopards or the dragon standard of Kings Richard and John, itself perhaps a 'Draco Normannicus' (a 'Norman Dragon'), adopted after 1066 from the dragon banner which Harold's standard-bearer is shown as holding in the climactic scene of the Bayeux Tapestry, and related to the triumphs of St Michael over the dragon-beasts of Mont-St-Michel or to the dragon tamed by St Romain, semi-mythical patron saint of Rouen, the capital of ducal Normandy. The King's dragon standard was still being carried into battle by Edward III at Crécy in 1346, albeit by now quartered with the heraldic symbols of Edward III, with leopards and with the French fleur-de-lys. These French, Norman or Plantagenet devices were now replaced by something distinctively royal, martial and chivalric: St George's banner, the red cross on a white background, first adopted for Edward's new order of chivalry, the Order of the Garter, in the aftermath of the battle of Crécy. England's new flag is first recorded as being carried into battle a decade later, by Edward, the Black Prince, during his great victory at Poitiers in 1356. St George was henceforth intended to triumph, in heraldic flag-waving as in legend, over all dragons, Saxon, French or Norman as the case might be. This device, formerly worn by crusaders fighting God's wars, would lend a new patriotic dynamic to English warfare, no longer viewed as a polite chivalric encounter between cousins in arms but as a stark confrontation between Englishmen and the forces of evil.

The English Language

If English nationhood and English kingship triumphed in the reigns of the three Edwards, then so too did the English language. There were still those in the thirteenth century who looked to France as the true cradle of civilization. Multilingualism remained a feature of upper-class society into the fourteenth century, as indeed into the twenty-first. English pronunciation of French might be mocked in France, never more effectively than in the thirteenth-century fable *The Two Englishmen and the Donkey*, in which the inability of a pair of English merchants to distinguish between the words 'agnel' ('lamb') and 'anel' ('donkey') leads to one of them being fed donkey-meat rather than lamb. The mistake is only discovered when the men resort to animal noises ('This isn't baa-baa, but hee-haw, hee-haw'). As the donkey story illustrates, nonetheless, England was already a land of merchants who had a need to communicate, however inadequate their linguistic means. Moreover, after 1300, the English language itself began to penetrate elite society in a way not encountered since 1066.

In the county courts, as early as the 1250s, Magna Carta and the documents associated with Henry III's reforms were being recited and occasionally even written in English as well as in Latin and French. Parliament's business was from the start discussed and from 1331 recorded in French. From the fourteenth century through to the present day, the clerk pronounced the royal assent in French rather than English: '*Le Roi le veut*' ('The King wishes it', with direct and no doubt deliberate echoes of the crusader cry '*Deus le volt*', 'God wishes it'). Nonetheless, by royal command from 1362, all pleas in the law courts and, from 1363, the majority of discussions in the Commons had to be conducted in English: one might speculate here on a bilingual Parliament in which, for a time at least, the Commons spoke mostly in English, the Lords mostly in French. Between the two choices, it was clear that English was already beginning to win out. As early as the 1290s, Edward I, himself a French-speaker, had already threatened that a French invasion might wipe not just England but 'the English language' from the face of the earth. The *Cursor Mundi*, a massive poetic description of world history written in English, suggested 'That we give each country its own language', explicitly identifying English nationhood with the English language.

By the time of the death of Edward III in 1377, Geoffrey Chaucer was already retained as a royal pensioner, a veteran of Edward III's wars in France. Chaucer's *Canterbury Tales* of the 1390s commemorated not just the birth of the new Middle English language, smoothed out from the diversity and barbarity of regional accents into something courtly and polite, but the very saint, Thomas of Canterbury, identified by many as the chief patron of English nationhood. Chaucer's English, like the vernacular of Anglo-Saxon royal government before 1066, was in many ways an artificial, literary language, far removed from the realities of day-to-day speech. Three of the individual stories that go to make up his *Canterbury Tales* are set in Italy, two in Flanders and one each in France, Athens or Tartary. Nonetheless, the posterity of Chaucer's 'Middle English' was to prove even more remarkable than that of the now moribund 'Old English' or 'Anglo-Saxon' of *Beowulf* or the *Anglo-Saxon Chronicle*. By 1400, English students of Latin, a no less artificial literary language, were being taught their basic grammar directly from the English vernacular rather than via the medium of French.

The English Nation

From the disasters and defeats of the 1060s, and from their Babylonian captivity under the Normans, the English themselves had re-emerged as a nation no longer ashamed of Englishness be it in dress, laws, sainthood, symbols or speech. In the process, they had also acquired an empire. In Ireland, Wales and Scotland, by the death of Edward I, England's kings boasted an authority that stretched from Galway to Norfolk and from Land's End as far north as the Firth of Forth. By 1350, at Ramsey Abbey in Cambridgeshire, a map attached to Ranulph Higden's *Polychronicon*, the most popular of fourteenth-century chronicles, itself intended to demonstrate a peculiarly English role in world history, showed Britain as an island on the margins of Europe, now coloured red from north to south, the same colour as the Red Sea and as Jerusalem, itself the very epicentre of the Christian world.

To present the history of England in the century after 1270 as one long upward curve of achievement would be significantly to warp reality. The reigns of the three Edwards witnessed a significant shift in the zeitgeist, but it was for the most part a shift from major to minor, from heroic optimism to pessimistic fatalism. Like ghosts in general, zeitgeists ('spirits of the age') tend to have as many people passionately convinced of their existence as there are those who just as passionately deny it. Even so, there seems little doubt that there was a significant shift in both political and cultural norms from around the year 1300.

The two centuries from 1066 had seen violence certainly, but also expansion, discovery and the pursuit of dreams, sometimes on an epic scale. The fall of England to the Normans, the capture of Jerusalem by the First Crusade, the great cathedrals and churches that new wealth now bought, the pushing back of woodland and fen, the increase in the human population, the rediscovery of ancient knowledge and the development of new technologies, all of these suggest an upward curve in human expectation. London's population is estimated to have increased from 25,000 in 1100 to more than 100,000 by 1300, the population of England as a whole from something like two or three million to five or six million. After 1300, the wheel of fortune turned once more, from fair to increasingly foul. Famine, warfare, endemic disease and ultimately plague brought a significant population decline. God's vengeance seemed to lie heavy upon the land. The climate itself rebelled against mankind.

Edward I

Ironically, some of these disasters could trace their origins to the reign of Edward I, generally regarded as one of the greatest of English kings. It was under Edward I that the seeds were sown of English domination over Wales and Scotland. It was under Edward that Parliament was nurtured and that English law reached maturity. It was Edward's diplomacy and foreign marriages that laid the foundations of England's later claims in France and in particular those claims to the French throne which were to emerge from the 1330s onwards in the Hundred Years War. As if to emphasize his own greatness, Edward I lived to the age of 68, longer than any other king in the 500 years after the Norman Conquest. Henry I had reached 67. Henry III, despite the great length of his reign, was a mere 65 at the time of his death, Edward III only 64. For the rest, the vast majority (eleven of the eighteen kings between William I and Richard III) died before reaching 50. Yet his very longevity was to ensure that Edward I outlived the triumphs of his early years, to witness the catalogue of failures and setbacks that marred the second part of his reign. All political careers are said to end in failure. The failures of Edward I were to have consequences that overshadowed the lives of many millions of English men and women as yet unborn.

Young Edward

To appreciate this, we need to begin in the sunnier uplands of the 1260s and 70s. Here, Edward had already shown himself gifted with the sort of military and administrative skills necessary for successful kingship, but which his father, Henry III, had so signally lacked. A wild youth (aged only twenty-one, he and his cronies had smashed all of the windows of the bishop of Winchester's palace at Southwark, in one of the earliest recorded examples of upper-class, Bullingdon Club-like love of the sound of broken glass), the future King Edward I had proved himself both brave and ruthlessly competent. His escape from imprisonment at Hereford in 1265, having pretended to test a number of horses whilst out riding and then making off on the swiftest of them, and his subsequent defeat of Simon de Montfort, his former military tutor, at Evesham, were merely the springboards from which Edward launched himself upon crusade in the East. He thereby fulfilled crusading vows that had been left unfulfilled by every previous Plantagenet king save for his now legendary ancestor, Richard I.

Not only did Edward acquire kudos merely by embarking on crusade, but his expedition, although marked by no dramatic improvement in the fortunes of the Latin East, garnered legends of its own. Within a century, it was being claimed that Edward's wife, Eleanor of Castile, had sucked the venom from his wounds when a Moslem assassin stabbed him with a poisoned dagger. Other versions attributed his salvation to one of his household knights, or to a magic stone given by the Master of the Temple, perhaps ground up and used as a purgative. Edward's career as a successful crusader, the Olympic gold, or Oxbridge blue, of medieval warrior prestige, was in no small part responsible for his later fearsome reputation as king. In one person he seemed to combine the heroism of Richard the Lionheart with the administrative efficiency of Henry II.

Three problems above all had dogged the fortunes of Edward's father: the lack of financial resources by which the crown could pursue its ambitions beyond the frontiers of England; the longstanding rivalries with England's neighbours, above all the kings of France, focussed upon the continuing demand that the former Plantagenet lands be restored to English rule; and the difficulty of controlling an English political elite unprepared to meet the costs of the King's own household or military ambitions. Edward was not slow to master all three problems, employing the lessons that he had learned from his uncle, Simon de Montfort, the kudos that he had secured from his victory over Montfort at Evesham, and his newly won status as a veteran of the crusades to advertise a kingly panache very different from the feckless piety of his father. Success in battle would henceforth be matched to reform of government. Reform in turn would be rewarded with financial subsidies from the English elite sufficient to pay for yet further success in war.

The King's Finances and Laws

Before the 1270s, England's kings had relied for their income upon the profits of their own royal estates, worth perhaps £10,000 a year, combined with the profits of royal lordship, justice and the law courts, in a good year worth considerably more. This in itself was just about sufficient to pay for the needs of the royal court and household and for the machinery of royal government, the sheriffs and justices who themselves reaped rich profits from their offices. For anything more ambitious, for campaigns beyond the frontiers of the realm, even for successful warfare against the Welsh or the Scots, the King required subsidies from his subjects. Since no such subsidies were awarded to Henry III after the 1230s, Henry's administration had lurched from one financial crisis to another, with never enough funds to pay for its schemes. Edward I determined from the outset to avoid these difficulties.

He did so by imposing a tax on wool exports, the principal overseas trade of England and the source, perhaps for several centuries before this, of much of England's wealth. The tax itself would be paid by the merchants responsible for exporting wool, but they in turn would recoup their losses by reducing the prices they paid to wool growers in England and by increasing the prices they charged to wool buyers overseas. In turn, these new customs duties, of 6s 8d per sack of exported wool, amounting to perhaps £10,000 a year, were linked to the offer of good government for the realm, first broadcast via a county by county investigation of the King's resources and of abuses of royal authority, instituted almost from the moment of the King's return to England in 1274 and known as the 'Hundred Rolls' enquiry.

In its way as ambitious as the Domesday survey of the 1080s, the 'Hundred Rolls' enquiry set the pattern for two subsequent investigations of resources and encroachments upon the King's rights: an inquest known as Kirby's Quest, headed by John de Kirkby commissioned in the 1280s to investigate debts to the crown and the King's local income, and a wholescale impeachment of royal justices and investigation of their crimes that followed the King's return to England from Gascony in 1289. In each instance, the offer of reform was linked to the crown's financial needs, with the King demonstrating his willingness to sacrifice his own ministers in order both to buy public support and to advertise his credentials as a virtuous prince. This had been very much the policy of Louis IX, who himself had exercised a significant influence over the methods of Simon de Montfort, King Edward's own tutor turned bitterest foe.

The virtue of King Edward was itself chiefly broadcast via Parliament, now summoned on a near annual basis as a forum for the display of royal authority, through to the 1290s largely supine in its approach to royalty, yet broad enough as a representative assembly of national opinion to negotiate grants of taxation to the crown. The first such tax, negotiated in 1275, yielded upwards of £80,000, more than enough to repay the King's outstanding debts. Parliament both granted subsidy and heard petitions from the King's subjects, once again acting as a safety valve to the grievances of those previously denied access to the King's grace.

In turn, petitioning and parliamentary debate went hand in hand with the issue of new laws. Between the First Statute of

Westminster in 1275 and the first real crisis to engulf his regime, after 1290, Edward's administration enacted an impressive array of legislation, much of it directly modelled on or indeed simply copied from the reformist legislation of the 1250s and 60s. It was intended to clarify relations between lords and tenants, to prevent the wholescale alienation of property to the Church, to ensure that lords were not deprived of the services that land had formerly rendered, and to regulate such processes as the pursuit of debt or the indictment of crime.

In 1290, this very public advertisement of the King as law-maker and father of his people was crowned by Edward's expulsion of the Jewish community from England. Already bled dry after decades of punitive royal taxation, the Jews were in effect used as yet another sacrificial victim to broadcast a carefully controlled image of the King as virtuous Christian prince. Their property and houses supplied Edward with a timely pool of patronage from which to reward his friends and followers. The Jews themselves were shipped across the Channel to France, not officially to return to England until the time of Oliver Cromwell, after 1656. Like various rather more notorious rulers of the twentieth century, Edward was in effect employing the persecution of a minority as a means to advertise his leadership and benevolence to a grateful majority.

Ironically, none of this would have been possible without the assistance of precisely those 'aliens' – Frenchmen and foreign merchants – who had previously served as the chief targets of English xenophobia. With his new customs duties, Edward widened the circle of virtue by farming receipts from the wool tax to Italian merchants, most notably the Riccardi family of Lucca, the centre of the Italian silk trade, borrowing large sums of money in the short term, repayable from future customs revenues. The capital from the Mediterranean silk trade was thus invested in English armies financed on the security of future profits from wool. With the resources now at his disposal, and with the immediate situation in France governed by the peace that had been put in place since 1259,

Edward could turn his attentions first and foremost to the Welsh, using attacks upon yet another minority group to advertise his glory and invincibility.

The Welsh

Ever since the 1050s, when Harold Godwinson had earned his military reputation as a slayer of Welshmen, the English had sought to expand their authority westwards across the Wye and the Dee into territories ruled by Welsh-speaking princes. The Normans after 1066 had continued this process, seizing most of southern Wales as far west as Pembroke and extending the frontiers of the county of Cheshire in the north. Henry II's conquest of Ireland in the 1170s had further embedded this English 'Drang nach westen' ('push to the west'), ensuring English control over one side of that Welsh–Irish axis around which had been focussed a great deal of the native Welsh economy and with it the tribute, in silver and cattle, paid to the native Welsh princes.

Llywelyn ap Gruffydd

As early as the 1180s, Henry II was being advised how to defeat the native Welsh by the Anglo-Norman-Welshman, Gerald of Wales, author of two great books on Welsh affairs. Gerald advised that in their mountain fastnesses, above all in Snowdonia, the Welsh were impregnable. As with the Vietnamese of the 1960s or the Afghans of the early twenty-first century, no amount of head-on confrontation would bring the Welsh to decisive engagement. Threatened by the shock and awe of an English expeditionary force, they would merely retreat to the hills, avoid pitched battle, emerging to raid and pillage once more when the threat had passed. What was needed, Gerald suggested, was a chain of castles and centres of Englishry running along the Welsh coastline, to contain Welsh access to their Irish sea-borne trade and to confine the rebellious Welsh to the uplands from which few resources for future rebellion could be obtained. The problem here was that the means for such an undertaking were lacking to Henry II's successors. Both King John, after 1215, and Henry III, in the 1250s and 60s, had been forced to stand mutely by as the Welsh capitalized upon English political weakness to extend their authority, raiding the Welsh Marches and burning castles. The princes of Gwynedd – Llywelyn ap Iorweth (d.1240) and his grandson, Llywelyn ap Gruffydd (d.1282) – without any settled capital 'city' but ruling from the enclave of Garth Celyn overlooking the Menai straights, between Bangor and Conway, had exploited English political turmoil to obtain recognition of their special status as rulers over the native Welsh, entitled to the homage of the other Welsh princes and to a degree of legal autonomy from England and its kings.

It was this situation which Edward I now sought to reverse. In the summer of 1277, an English army, more than 15,000 strong, advanced from Chester along the north Welsh coast. Ships transported further troops to Anglesey to harvest the grain and hence deprive Llywelyn ap Gruffydd of the means with which to wage further war. The outcome was a negotiated settlement in which Llywelyn abandoned various gains he had made in the 1260s and was forced to promise a war indemnity of £50,000, a figure which in itself suggests a booming Welsh economy, based upon Irish sea-born trade. At this rate, Edward's wars could be made almost to pay for themselves.

Open hostilities with the Welsh erupted again in 1282, when Llywelyn's disgruntled younger brother, Dafydd, believing himself to have been insufficiently rewarded for his part in Edward's success of 1277, broke with the English and on Palm Sunday attacked Hawarden Castle in Flintshire (future residence of a very different sort of English statesman and a far more assiduous observer of the Sabbath, W.E. Gladstone). Once again, a concerted land and sea force, including levies from Edward's dominions in Gascony, and the construction of a great pontoon bridge between Anglesey and the mainland, forced the Welsh into surrender. This time, however, Llywelyn himself was lured into an ambush at Irfon Bridge, near Builth Wells, and killed. Dafydd's resistance continued for a further six months until he too was betrayed, handed over to the English and, at Shrewsbury in September 1283, hanged, disembowelled for his breach of the Sabbath at Hawarden and his body then cut into quarters to mark his treason. The heads of both Llywelyn and Dafydd were exhibited on spikes outside the Tower of London. Llywelyn and Dafydd's children were imprisoned and, in the case of the daughters, forced into English nunneries where the last of them died half a century later.

In less than a year, the last effectively independent Welsh princes had been removed from the scene. Only fifteen years separated the official 'English' recognition of Wales as an independent principality in 1267 and the brutal suppression of that independence in 1282. So feeble was the image of these Welsh princes conveyed to posterity that, in the 1890s, when it was proposed to raise a monument to Llywelyn at Irfon Bridge, so little money was subscribed in Wales that a neighbouring English squire, an Eton-educated disciple of Sigmund Freud, was obliged to step in to supply the funds.

The extinction of Llywelyn's family did not in itself bring an end to Welsh resistance. Despite (or rather, precisely because of) the building of that chain of castles which Gerald of Wales had proposed, stretching from Harlech to Conway and from Caernarvon to Beaumaris in Anglesey, despite the wholesale importation of English settlers to a series of new towns, at Flint, Rhuddlan and elsewhere, and despite the division of Wales itself, including Snowdonia, into a series of administrative units modelled on the English shires where major felonies were now to be tried according to English rather than native Welsh law, the Welsh themselves rose in rebellion in 1287 and even more seriously in 1294. This second uprising required the efforts of nearly 30,000 men and subsidies of more than £50,000 to suppress.

Wales, the First English Colony

Nevertheless, by 1295, Wales was effectively conquered. The Welsh princely regalia, Llywelyn's treasures, were fashioned into plate off which the English king might dine. Edward I had achieved something which no predecessor on the throne of England could claim: the complete conquest of a neighbouring principality and the obliteration of its future independence. Not even Ireland, only partially conquered or settled after 1172, had suffered such a fate. Wales thus became the first and greatest of Edward I's military conquests, and England's first imperial colony. These imperial connotations were deliberately emphasized at Caernarvon, where the walls of Edward's new castle were banded in layers of light and dark masonry, in imitation of the land walls of the Roman imperial city of Constantinople and in conscious reflection of the Welsh legend that the father of Constantine, the first Christian emperor of Rome and the founder of Constantinople, had been buried at Caernarvon, his tomb supposedly discovered there earlier in the thirteenth century.

Further south, across the Bristol Channel, as early as 1278, Edward had presided over the reburial, at Glastonbury Abbey, of the supposed bodies of two other figures prominent in Welsh legend: King Arthur and his wife, Guinevere. The intention here was simple: to demonstrate to the Welsh, once and for all, that Arthur was dead and buried, not waiting to rise again as champion of an independent Wales. It was at Caernarvon, in April 1284, once again almost certainly a carefully stage-managed event, that Edward's queen, Eleanor of Castile, gave birth to a son destined to be the future King of England, Edward II. If the intention here was that the new Edward emulate the imperial glories of Constantine, then these arrangements were entirely in vain, the absurdity of Edward I's expectations presaged as early as 1294 when the unfinished fortress at Caernarvon was the only one of Edward I's new castles to be captured in the Welsh rebellion. Meanwhile, Edward's English empire was itself constructed on foundations that were very far from firm. Italian merchants had financed Edward's Welsh wars and his Welsh castles were built not by an English architect but according to the instructions of Master James of St-George, from the Franco-Swiss-Italian frontier duchy of Savoy.

The Scots

By the mid-1290s, other shadows had begun to fall across Edward's imperial horizons. If his ultimate goal was the consolidation of the British Isles under English imperial authority, then he needed to look not just westwards to Ireland and Wales but northwards to the kingdom of the Scots. Here, since the late eleventh century, a dynasty of kings, as much Anglo-Norman as Scoto-Gaelic, had been established in the lowland regions with their own network of earls and barons, in many cases themselves of Anglo-Norman descent, stretching out into the still essentially native-ruled highlands and islands. The last of this Scots royal line, King Alexander III, died after a fall from his horse in March 1286 while attempting a late-night crossing of the Firth of Forth, having ignored the advice of those with whom he had feasted in Edinburgh Castle, in order to visit his young new queen. As with many a highland motoring accident, neither lust nor strong drink was ever publicly alleged as a factor contributing to this tragedy. Alexander's son, born to a first marriage to a daughter of King Henry III of England, had died only two years before, in his early twenties. No doubt, Alexander's anxiety to visit his new wife had something to do with his desire to replenish the royal quiver.

His untimely death ensured that his only surviving heir was a granddaughter, Margaret, known as the 'Maid of Norway', herself born in 1283 to a marriage between Alexander's daughter and King Eric II of Norway. After 1286, Margaret was in theory Queen of Scotland. In practice, the Scots themselves chose a committee of guardians, who eventually, after negotiations between Scots, English and Norwegian ambassadors, agreed that Margaret should be dispatched from Norway to Scotland, leaving open the possibility that she might in due course marry Edward, the eldest son of King Edward I of England and thereby bring about a union in which the future Edward II would become *de facto* ruler of England, Ireland, Wales and Scotland. In the event, Margaret died in October 1290, in the Orkney Islands (not sold by Norway to the Scots crown until the 1470s), without ever having set foot on the Scottish mainland. Edward I's plans for an easy imperial succession were brought to nothing. The Scots themselves were left with neither king nor queen. The union of the Scots and English thrones was postponed by three hundred years.

It was into this situation that Edward I now stepped, claiming to act as arbiter in the 'Great Cause', to nominate a successor to the Scots crown. Two candidates emerged, both of them members of Normanno-Scots families with landed interests both in Scotland and in England: Robert de Bruce, lord of Annandale in the central lowlands, and John de Balliol, lord of Galloway. The Bruces were of Norman descent, from Brix near Cherbourg. Robert himself held extensive lands in Essex and had fought in Edward's army during the English conquest of Wales. The Balliols were ultimately from Picardy, from Bailleul, near Abbeville. Established in northern England under the early Norman kings, like other northern French families, they had risen to greater prominence during the rule of King Stephen, himself Count of Boulogne. One of John de Balliol's ancestors had been captured alongside King Stephen at the Battle of Lincoln in 1141. Another had fought for Henry II, playing a leading role in the campaign which culminated, in 1174, with the capture of the Scots King, William I, near Alnwick.

Neither the Balliols nor the Bruces, therefore, were exactly unfamiliar to the English court. From the Great Cause, in 1292, Edward chose the claims of John de Balliol over those of Robert de Bruce of Annandale. It was a fateful choice. Balliol, favoured precisely because of his pliancy (he had already named his eldest son and heir Edward, which supplies a rather heavy-handed clue as to his loyalties), proved incapable of bringing order to Scotland. Bruce's son, the rather more famous Robert Bruce, rebelled, almost certainly with his father's sanction. A council of a dozen Scots barons now claimed to have wrested authority from Balliol. Early in 1296, this council negotiated a treaty with the King of France, the origins of the so-called 'Auld Alliance', by which the Scots and the French sought mutual support against their common enemy, the King of England.

Techniques which Edward had employed against the Welsh, by using English law and his status as overlord to undermine Welsh independence, had been applied with equal success by the French to Edward's own subjects in Gascony who were encouraged by the French King, Philip IV, to present their cases for arbitration not before Parliament in England but before the French Parlement in Paris. War with France broke out in 1294. Edward's response was rapid and apparently overwhelming. In a campaign lasting barely twenty-one weeks, he brought the Scots to heel, seizing the border fortress of Berwick and defeating the Scots army at Dunbar. Having suppressed the Welsh rebellion of 1294, he negotiated a series of alliances in Germany and the Low Countries to launch a two-pronged attack on the French timed for 1297. Here, however, his luck ran out.

The costs of war in Wales, Scotland and France were too high for royal finance to bear. Additional charges of 40s per sack of wool exported from England merely brought outcry against this 'maltote' or 'bad tax', not least from English land-owners and wool growers who feared that the price that they received for their produce would be lowered so that wool merchants could recoup the tax. Edward's allies in the Rhineland, like the earlier allies recruited by King John of England for his campaign of 1214, demanded extortionate subsidies, in excess of £250,000. Meanwhile, the clergy of England, spurred on by the Archbishop of Canterbury, and backed by papal letters intended to starve both the English and the French war machines of finance, resisted attempts to impose subsidies on the Church. The Riccardi bankers upon whom Edward had relied for credit were bankrupted, probably already overstretched by the costs of the Welsh campaign and owed nearly £400,000 by the crown, in theory repayable from future proceeds of the customs, in practice just as useless a security as the junk bonds of modern Wall Street.

This was in effect the first and in some ways still the most serious sovereign debt crisis in the history of England. Into this perfect storm of financial catastrophe, strode two further heralds of apocalypse. The earls of Gloucester and Hereford, long resentful of the King's extension of authority over the Welsh Marches, refused to serve in France unless with the King in person. In other words, they would sail with the King to Flanders but they would not take up independent command of the King's army in Gascony. By the time that this crisis was resolved and Edward was ready to sail for Flanders, his allies had already been defeated by the French. The only real hostilities left for Edward to witness took place amongst his own sailors, between the men of the Cinque Ports of Kent and Sussex and the fishermen of Yarmouth. Worse still, the King left England at the precise moment that events in Scotland reached climax.

William Wallace

In May 1297, a freeholder from Ayrshire, William Wallace, apparently already outlawed as a robber and brigand, murdered the newly imposed English sheriff of Lanark. Perhaps with the tacit approval of the bishop of Glasgow, perhaps as an independent agent claiming to act on behalf of King John de Balliol, Wallace now launched himself on a campaign of terror. He attempted the assassination of the English justiciar, William Ormsby. At Stirling Bridge, in September 1297, he lured an incompetently led English cavalry into slaughter by his own Scots spearmen. The army's commander was so determined to observe the chivalric conventions that he effectively required the battle to be started twice, recalling more than 5,000 troops who had already crossed over to the Scots side of the bridge, in order that he might publicly confer knighthood on various of those about to fight. Edward I's treasurer of Scotland, Hugh of Cressingham, was killed in the ensuing bloodbath. His body was flayed and his skin reputedly used to make a sword belt for Wallace's waist.

A great deal of myth-making obscures our image of the true William Wallace. Much of what is recorded of him depends upon the testimony of a fifteenth-century Scots bard, 'Blind Harry', whose writings are as wildly romantic as his name and who seems to have made up most of what he wrote. Blind Harry's lead here has been followed by any number of later bards, romantics and Hollywood film producers. What is clear is that Wallace's rebellion could not have come at a worse time for Edward and the English. Stirling Bridge was followed by a wholescale invasion of Scotland by Edward I, for the first time making use of Welsh archers and infantry as a major contingent in his army, culminating in the defeat of Wallace's spearmen at Falkirk in July 1298. In English eyes, one set of defeated barbarians was to be used to bring order to another.

Wallace melted away in the confusion and was not captured for a further seven years. Tried in Westminster Hall, he was eventually hung, disembowelled and quartered, like Dafydd of Wales before him, and his head displayed on London Bridge.

Robert Bruce

Meanwhile, the Scots, emboldened by Wallace's victory at Stirling, and not subsequently cowed even by expeditions which Edward I launched against them in 1300, 1301 and 1303, found both a cause and a leader, the younger Robert Bruce. Robert Bruce had toyed with rebellion at least twice before, on each occasion making his peace with King Edward. In February 1306, however, during a meeting with John Comyn, another major player on the Scots political scene, at the church of the Greyfriars in Dumfries, Bruce murdered Comyn before the high altar. A month later, on the feast of the Annunciation, 25 March, at Scone near Perth, Bruce was crowned as King Robert I of Scotland by the patriot bishop Robert Wishart of Glasgow.

Scots Independence and Welsh Subjection

The Stone of Scone, an oblong block of red sandstone on which Scottish kings were traditionally inaugurated, had been removed to Westminster Abbey in 1296, after the opening campaign of the Anglo-Scots war, and incorporated into a wooden chair used at the coronation of subsequent kings of England. It was not officially restored to Scotland until 1996, 700 years after its removal, and even now is due to be returned to Westminster whenever required for a British coronation.

Meanwhile, and although few at the time might have guessed it, the coronation of Robert I of Scotland, the first ever conducted without the Stone, ensured a renewal of Scots independence and a further three hundred years of Scots kingship. Far from the English absorbing the Scots, in 1603 the Scots King, James VI, was crowned in England as King James I. Where the Welsh princes had fallen before the might of Edward's armies, fading into an impotent nostalgia for a vanished Welsh past, Scotland recovered both its independence and its own line of kings.

The reasons for this disparity in the fates of Scotland and Wales were both geographic and economic. Scotland was not only wealthier than native Wales but a far more extensive landmass. The network of castles which Edward constructed around the Welsh coast, to contain the princes of Snowdonia, was unfeasible in the case of Scotland. Even though in 1296 Edward had pursued his enemies as far north as Aberdeen, and in 1303 English troops were garrisoned in Inverness, there were always points further north or west to which the Scots could retire, from where they could sally forth once the threat had passed. Scotland was ideal bandit territory, and Wallace's victory at Stirling Bridge was a classic example of the way in which a poorly equipped, pastoral people could nonetheless inflict total defeat upon an army accustomed to more chivalric usages.

Within only a few years of Stirling Bridge, at Courtrai in 1302 where the Flemish town militias of Bruges, Ghent and Ypres inflicted a crushing defeat upon a mounted French army, and at Morgarten in 1315, when a small army of Swiss infantry inflicted total defeat upon the cavalry of Duke Leopold of Austria, the powerlessness of cavalry in the face of spearmen and archers, and the essential futility of much that passed for chivalric valour, were more than amply demonstrated. Scotland, Flanders and Switzerland were each born from the actions of small 'primitive' armies faced with what should have been overwhelmingly more 'sophisticated' opponents. Brawn triumphed over boasted birth and courtesy just as surely as the peasants of Indochina or the tribesmen of Afghanistan have triumphed over the helicopter or the smart bombs of our own ever more sophisticated and murderous age.

Christendom in Crisis

It is ironic that those things which Edward I himself might have supposed to be the crowning achievements of his reign – the expulsion of the Jews, the recognition of Edward's client John Balliol as King of Scots and the crushing of Welsh independence came at almost precisely the same moment that the wheel of fortune elsewhere in Christendom began to revolve from hubris towards nemesis. On 18 May 1291 the great sea port of Acre, last bastion of the crusader states, fell to a siege by an Egyptian army. From here onwards, Christendom itself was placed on the defensive, with Saracens ruling in Jerusalem, a Mongol hoard threatening the outposts of Christian Russia and, within a century, Turkish armies on the loose in Serbia, threatening to lay siege to Prague.

Less than a year after the fall of Acre, in April 1292, the death of Pope Nicholas IV ushered in a period of crisis for the western Church, from which emerged an Italian pope, Boniface VIII, so at odds with the kings of the West that in

1303, at much the same time that Edward I was garrisoning Inverness, a French army surprised the Pope at Anagni, just south of Rome, and beat him so badly that within a month he was dead of injury and shame. The outcome was the election of a French pope, Clement V, and the removal of the papacy from Rome to Avignon in southern France. For seventy years or more the Avignon popes were more concerned with taxation and meeting the costs of their own bureaucracy than ever they were with the right order of Christendom. Finally, to add to this catalogue of man-made disasters, nature itself began to rebel.

Climate Change and Famine

The European peasant economy depended upon agricultural surpluses to supply a population that had more than doubled over the previous century and a half. A series of hot, wet summers now left crops rotting in the fields. Earthquakes and volcanic eruptions in Iceland, sun spots, some other great yet mysterious terrestrial or solar cataclysm, or simply the slow revolution of the climate from a 'medieval warm period' to a 'little ice age', have all been proposed as ecological explanations for the impending catastrophe. Radiocarbon data suggests a sudden increase in the size and spread of the Alpine glaciers at Aletsch after 1230, at Grindelwald from 1280. Pastures where trees had grown and the local inhabitants grazed their cattle, were now, for the first time since the eighth century, covered in ice. None of the explanations for these phenomena is entirely convincing, though, like modern dogmas on climate change, each tends to attract its own small band of fanatics. Although after 1066 vines were cultivated as far north as Gloucester or Norwich, implying a climate in the twelfth century warmer than we might expect, winters were sufficiently cold in London in the 1150s for William fitz Stephen to describe skating on the Essex marshes, and the Thames is reported regularly to have frozen throughout the Middle Ages.

Whatever the underlying climatic changes, by 1300 the demographic expansion that had characterized the period since 1066 had reached what seems to have marked a natural ceiling. The food supply was the key factor here. The yield of cereal crops such as wheat or barley remained pathetically low, promising even on prime agricultural land and in years of relative abundance no more than ten times the weight of seed-corn sown, and in years of famine less than a doubling of the seed. As a modern comparison, and even before the introduction of techniques of seed selection and fertilization, nineteenth-century farmers expected a yield nearer to thirty times the quantity of seed sown. The clearance and cultivation of new acreage, although conducted on a massive scale throughout the thirteenth century, tended to bring land under the plough that was at best marginal, such as the Cotswold uplands or the Norfolk Breckland, and often of little use for anything save the poorest of sheep or livestock farming.

By 1300 there were perhaps ten million acres of land laid to arable in England, a figure not achieved again before the early nineteenth century. Cattle murrain and sheep disease, which accompanied the poor harvests after 1290, reduced the value of marginal land yet further. The expanding human population was vulnerable even to relatively brief periods of dearth since, rather as in nineteenth-century Ireland, an over-abundant population was dependent upon what, even in good years, was a barely sufficient supply of food. Hoarding or long-term food storage, as in the modern Third World, was a luxury that only the wealthier could afford. For the peasantry, the inability to store agricultural produce ensured not only that people starved as a result of poor harvests, but that, when the harvest produced too much rather than too little, goods had to be sent to market at prices unprofitably low. Add to this the ravaging of much of the north of England and lowland Scotland as a result of the Anglo-Scots war after the 1290s, and rural England was already poised on the cusp of disaster even by the final years of the reign of Edward I.

Violence

With famine and disease came despair and ultimately violence. There had been only a light death toll amongst the leaders of baronial rebellion throughout the twelfth and thirteenth centuries. Richard Marshal, Earl of Pembroke, had been killed in the midst of his rebellion in 1234, but in Ireland and as a result of treachery rather than publicly stage-managed brutality. The slaying and subsequent mutilation of Simon de Montfort at Evesham in 1265 ushered in a new period of unease in dealings between rebels and kings. Above all, perhaps, Montfort's brutal end demonstrated that, short of killing a king, there was no way to bind a king to his promises, even if he were as weak and changeable as Henry III. In the meantime, the families of those slain at Evesham continued to dream of vengeance. In 1271, Henry of Almain, Edward I's cousin and the eldest son and heir of Richard, Earl of Cornwall, King of Germany, stopped at Viterbo in Italy on his way to join Edward I's crusade. There, hearing Mass at the cathedral's high altar, he was set upon by two of Simon de Montfort's sons and brutally murdered in revenge for the killing of their father at Evesham. The deed was so notorious that it earned a place in the seventh circle of Dante's *Inferno*. Blood still called to blood, and the royal family found itself now part of a revenge tragedy.

Judicial Violence

This was a violent age, even though 'popular' historians are inclined to slaver rather too much over the details and to forget that judicial violence remained a feature of English society for several thousand years. The last woman to be publicly burned in England for petty treason (in this instance for counterfeiting) was executed in 1789. Women were still being publicly hanged as late as 1868, and there was a working gallows at Wandsworth Prison until 1994, tested every six months and still displayed as a museum piece. The death penalty was mandated in the Middle Ages with a frequency that we today might regard as barbaric, even though juries showed a marked reluctance to condemn to the gallows anyone not convicted of homicide. Until increased by a statute of Edward I to a minimum of one shilling, the theft of goods worth no more than four pence was deemed a capital offence, and children as young as fourteen were considered old enough for the rope. In certain localities, local punishments still operated. Thieves in the Scilly Islands were left on a rock to be swept away by the tide. At Dover, they were thrown from the cliffs.

Elsewhere, the general rule was that felons should be hung, though, as early as 1076, the public beheading of Earl Waltheof had suggested that noblemen might expect distinction, in death as in life. The lord's private gallows was as significant a symbol of his lordship as the deer park or the seigneurial mill or dovecote. Hanging itself could prove a messy affair. The gallows might collapse, the rope break or the prisoner make a run for sanctuary. At a time of only poor understanding of the distinction between death and life, the person hanged might be cut down too early, or even recover from the hanging. Like other 'miraculous' escapes either from danger or from death, this occurs as a regular theme in miracle stories of the saints. In 1335, the vicar of Cowley in Oxfordshire was charged with burying alive a thief, hanged nearby but not yet dead. In an age without doctors to certify death, the vicar's offence was perhaps not manslaughter but lack of due professional diligence.

Into the 1290s, the death penalty in itself had been deemed sufficient punishment for all save a handful of crimes. The very worst of traitors might be humiliated as well as hung, dragged by horses through the public streets on a hurdle or an animal skin, as was the fate of William de Marisco, the Lundy pirate, who in the 1230s had plotted the death of King Henry III, or Peter of Wakefield, a Yorkshire prophet who preached that King John was about to be toppled from his throne and who was drawn and then hung in 1213 when his prophecy failed to come true, his body torn apart between the horses before ever it reached the gallows. But such cases were extraordinary. Only from the 1290s, as Edward I began to grow impatient with the speed of progress in Wales and Scotland, was the full array of judicial violence brought to bear upon his enemies. Thomas de Turberville, convicted in 1295 of treasonable conspiracy with the French, the Scots and the Welsh, was dragged on an ox-hide from Westminster to Cheapside and hung at Smithfield, with six tormentors dressed as devils to attend his final moments. His body was left to rot on the gallows 'so long as anything of him should remain'.

The punishments meted out by Edward to the leaders of Welsh and Scottish resistance, above all perhaps the deliberate dismemberment of Dafydd of Wales, of the Lord Rhys (leader of the 1287 Welsh rising) and of William Wallace, signalled a new brutality in English dealings with reluctant colonials. None of these 'traitors' was of Anglo-French noble birth, even though Dafydd and the Lord Rhys might claim that the blood of King Arthur flowed in their veins. In 1306, however, and in response to Robert Bruce's final defection, Edward for the first time turned his anger not just against noble prisoners but against women, ordering the execution of John, Earl of Atholl (the first earl to have been executed, rather than killed in battle, since the beheading of Waltheof in 1076) and the imprisonment of Isobel, Countess of Buchan and of Mary, Robert Bruce's sister, deliberately displayed in cages of wood and iron in the castles of Berwick and Roxburgh. Judicial violence had jumped the species barrier, from foreign enemies to the Anglo-Norman aristocracy. From this to the execution of English earls, the deposition and murder of kings and the killing fields of the civil wars of the fifteenth-century was only a short chronological step.

Edward's Last Years

The young heir to the throne whose youthful escapades had led to broken glass at Southwark had grown into an elderly king filled with bitterness and cold hatred. We can almost hear King Edward's foul temper seeping out of a letter to the Earl of

Dunbar written in 1304, accusing the earl of excessive caution. The King's original choice of metaphor ('Whilst the dog shits, the wolf runs off') has been scratched out and something superficially more polite but no less sarcastic written in its place ('Once the war was over, Audigier drew his sword', Audigier being the hero of a particularly scatological parody of French chivalry). We can sense the mood at court from an account book of 1297, recording the cost of repairing a coronet belonging to the King's daughter Elizabeth, hurled by Edward into the fire. By the same token, royal kindness (the shilling paid by Edward to a poor Welshman who showed him to his lodgings, his clearly genuine expressions of care for his wife and children), appetite (Edward's box of stem ginger) and sickness (the cordial of amber, jacinth, musk, pearls, gold and silver, or the sugar rosettes made with pearls and coral, fed to him in his final months), emerge from the records with a vividness that makes our knowledge of modern royalty seem paltry by comparison.

The king's personality remained a fundamental element, for good or bad, in all late medieval English government. Edward I died in 1307, wracked with dysentery, on his way to what was already proving yet another doomed attempt to impose English authority upon the Scots. Edward was a harsh man. His anger is said, as late as 1304, to have killed the Archbishop of York stone dead.

Edward II

Unlike his bitterness, which he bequeathed to his son and heir, Edward II, the old King's heroism and competence were not transmitted via the royal DNA. Edward II, although raised for glory, born in imperial Caernarvon, proposed as husband for the Queen of Scots, and crowned as Prince of Wales in 1301 as a symbol of his father's conquest of the furthest west, proved to be perhaps the medieval King least-well qualified for kingship. A nature-lover, a keen swimmer (as early as 1303, one of his jesters was compensated for an injury sustained 'through the prince in the water'), a digger of ditches and holes in the road, Edward was a pleasant enough young man, albeit over-passionately attached to his friends.

Head of the Regency Council

It is nonetheless symptomatic that his first proper taste of government came in 1297, aged only thirteen, when he was appointed head of the regency council whilst his father campaigned in Flanders. The result was turmoil, the transformation of Parliament from a supine display of royal authority into a forum for anti-royal polemic, and the forced issue of a series of decrees, including a reissue of Magna Carta, as tokens of the regime's desire to establish harmony with barons and the community of the realm. The 1297 reissue was in effect Magna Carta's swan song. Although recited at the head of endless collections of statutes thereafter, and granted one final outing in 1300 (reissued under Edward I's great seal this time, rather than the seal of absence which had been employed in 1297), it was not again officially issued by an English king. Its principles, of binding the King to some sense of right and wrong government, had become deeply ingrained in the English political subconscious. Its precise terms were now superseded by other needs and other quarrels, most notably from the 1290s onwards by disputes over taxation, over the King's right to take subsidy without the consent of Parliament or his leading subjects, his rights to purveyance (the forced sale of goods to the court, often at well below market values) and prises (his right to seize supplies, most notably wool or foodstuffs for the needs of his armies, repayable at low and often long-delayed terms).

The Ordinances and Piers Gaveston

The first major crisis over these issues came in 1310, when Edward II, less than three years into his reign, was forced to agree to the appointment of a committee of twenty-one 'ordainers' to draw up detailed proposals for reform, the so-called 'Ordinances', eventually issued in 1311. Behind these disputes lay one fundamental issue: the King's powers of patronage. Edward II had developed a passionate and, so far as his critics were concerned, unhealthy affection for a Gascon courtier named Piers Gaveston, son of a minor captain in the royal armies. Introduced to Edward's household as early as 1300, Gaveston was already the subject of controversy before the death of the old King. After his coronation, Edward II's very first act had been to create Gaveston Earl of Cornwall, previously a royal dignity held by successive members of the ruling royal family. Shortly thereafter, Gaveston was married to Edward's niece, herself a very considerable heiress. When Edward himself was married, in January 1308, to Isabella, daughter of the King of France, his betrothed bride for the past ten years as part of the guarantees of Anglo-French peace, he is said to have sent his marriage bed to Piers as a love token.

Twentieth-century writers had little doubt what was at stake here, and even in less sexually liberated times, the Victorians were happy to portray Edward and Piers mincing and simpering at one another in a fully Oscar Wildean way. Yet both Edward and Piers fathered children, both in and outside wedlock. Edward, on those occasions when he could be persuaded to rise early enough in the morning, was a not inconsiderable commander of men. Piers met his end with grim stoicism bordering on bravery. If their love was illicit (and there is no doubt that by this date, whatever might have been the case a few centuries earlier, sodomy was considered one of the very worst of sins, close cousin to heresy and the denial of God), then it was probably a very long way from the sort of effeminacy against which the bearded Victorians were inclined to pronounce anathema. It may even have been not sexual love but a sworn blood brotherhood.

The problem here was that it was a pact between two very unequal partners. Only in romantic fiction could princes and paupers be friends. Moreover, like a lot of upstarts, Piers was possessed of a particularly wicked tongue. He had nicknames for all of his rivals at court, none of them polite, including 'Bust-Belly' for the Earl of Lincoln and 'The Black Dog of Arden' for the Earl of Warwick. The King's cousin, Thomas of Lancaster, himself a grandson of King Henry III, would not have relished being described as 'Ham actor' by a man half his age and without a tenth of his noble ancestry. As early as April 1308, there were demands that Piers be exiled and his earldom confiscated. But, although Piers was sent to Ireland as the King's lieutenant, and although the Ordinances of 1311 included specific clauses against 'evil' or 'deceptive' counsellors, Edward was not prepared to dispense with his favourite.

Patronage, the choice of who to promote and who to keep out, has always been one of the most jealously guarded of royal powers, least susceptible to limitation. It had been the attempts by the rebels of 1215 to force King John into recognizing the authority of a committee of twenty-five barons in the final clauses of Magna Carta, and by the barons of the 1260s to control appointments to household offices at court, that had proved, from the King's perspective, amongst the most objectionable clauses in earlier 'reforming' legislation. As late as the 1840s, one of the very last constitutional crises for the English monarchy turned on just this issue of appointment to household offices at the court of the young Queen Victoria, and it could be argued that the most recent such crisis, came in the Abdication of 1936, itself provoked by outcry against a particularly feckless King and his choice of royal favourite. A direct line can be traced between the sharp-tongued and all-too heterosexual Wallace Simpson and the sexually ambiguous though no less sharp-tongued Piers Gaveston.

Arrest and Murder of Piers Gaveston

If a king could not choose his own friends and bedfellows from his own court, then he risked becoming a mere cypher of his enemies. Just as Edward II was determined that Piers Gaveston remain, so his enemies were determined that Piers must go, by violent means if necessary. With the approval of the Archbishop of Canterbury, the earls of Pembroke and Surrey were appointed early in 1312 to pursue and arrest Piers. In May, at Scarborough, Piers surrendered to his pursuers who took him south. At Deddington in Oxfordshire, the party was ambushed by the Earl of Warwick. Piers was carried off to Warwick itself and there executed, on Blacklow Hill, with the approval of the earls of Lancaster, Hereford and Arundel. The effect was to create an undying enmity between the King and his critics, in particular between Edward and his cousin, Thomas of Lancaster.

Thomas was himself the beneficiary of one of the great achievements of royal government in the 1260s and 70s. To supply a portion for his younger brother, Thomas of Lancaster's father, Edward I had ensured the transfer not only of the estates in Lancashire and the north once held by King Stephen, but the honour and earldom of Leicester confiscated from the heirs of Simon de Montfort, and the earldom of Derby whose holder, Robert Ferrers, a rebel of the 1260s, was in effect cheated of his inheritance, confronted with impossible terms for the payment of a ransom. The result was an assembly of lands greater than any other honour in England, with estates in most of the English counties and an income with which to recruit a substantial body of followers. From the death of Piers Gaveston until the deposition of King Richard II in 1399, Thomas of Lancaster and his successors as earls and dukes of Lancaster were inevitably to play a significant role in English history.

Battle of Bannockburn

In the immediate aftermath of Gaveston's execution, the infighting at court was obscured by events in Scotland. Ever since the coronation of Robert Bruce in 1306, English armies had struggled to impose terms on the Scots. Early in 1314, news arrived at the English court of the fall of both Roxburgh and Edinburgh castles. Unless relieved by midsummer, the

English constable of Stirling was also pledged to surrender to the Scots. To forestall this, Edward advanced into Scotland with the greatest English army mustered since his accession, albeit an army from which the earls of Lancaster and Warwick were signally absent. At Bannockburn, near Stirling, on 24 June, in an even more catastrophic rerun of the Battle of Stirling Bridge fought twenty years before, Edward's cavalry was cut to pieces by the Scots spearmen. The Earl of Gloucester, accused by the King of cowardice on the day before the battle, was killed leading a courageous but entirely futile charge. The Earl of Hereford was taken prisoner. Edward himself had a horse killed beneath him before being led to safety.

Bannockburn was one of the most crushing defeats in English history. It secured Robert Bruce his throne in Scotland and ushered in a period during which the Scots overran or taxed large parts of northern England, perhaps as much as one-fifth of the English realm. Amidst the recriminations that followed, Edward was forced to reissue the Ordinances and to allow Thomas of Lancaster a new supervisory role at the centre of English government. More catastrophically still, Bannockburn was followed by pillage, poor harvests and extended periods of famine in the English countryside, a great famine from 1315 to 1317 (with rumours of cannibalism), exceptionally poor harvests in 1320 and 1321, and outbreaks of cattle and sheep murrain in 1319 and 1321: perhaps the worst agrarian crisis in English history since the Viking invasions of the ninth and tenth centuries. Teeth recovered from plague pits or other burial sites of the 1340s often reveal patterns of decay and deformity (in technical terms 'hypoplasia', tell-tale ridges in the enamel of developing teeth) which suggest severe malnutrition for at least a generation before the arrival of plague in 1348. Scurvy and rickets, caused by deficiency in vitamins C and D, and iron-based anaemia, revealed through a characteristic honeycomb pattern in the bone of the eye-socket, occur in a remarkable proportion of such medieval skeletal remains. In other words, it was the children of the famines of Edward II's reign who grew up, already malnourished and lacking resistance, to become the adult victims of the great pestilence, twenty years later.

The Despensers

Meanwhile, having been deprived of one favourite, Piers Gaveston, Edward II merely turned to others, and in particular to the two men, Hugh Despenser the elder and Hugh his son, whose rise at court began shortly after Bannockburn. Once again there were probably unfounded rumours here of a sexual infatuation, but above all a pattern of over-lavish patronage and dependence which speaks of a King unable to keep either his emotions or his public actions under proper restraint. Most of the English earls had hated Piers Gaveston. Pretty much everybody hated the Despensers. The irony is that, although fiercely loyal both to Edward II and to his father, the Despensers were descended, as son and grandson, from another Hugh Despenser, baronial justiciar during the 1260s, who had died as a rebel fighting alongside Simon de Montfort at Evesham. From traitors to royal favourites over three generations, the Despensers were held in check only by the power still exercised by Thomas of Lancaster.

In 1321, in an attempted repeat of the coup against Gaveston, Thomas and a group of northern magnates entered into a pact with the Earl of Hereford and other barons from the Welsh Marches, intended to force the Despensers into exile. Within a year, the King was openly at war with his barons. In March 1322, outflanking the army of Thomas of Lancaster and the Earl of Hereford, Edward forced the earls to flee. They had got only so far as Boroughbridge in Yorkshire when they were intercepted by the King's captain, Andrew Harclay. The Earl of Hereford was killed in the fight that followed. Thomas of Lancaster was taken prisoner, tried before the King at Pontefract and beheaded as a traitor. At least a hundred of his baronial and knightly followers lost either their lands or their lives. Harclay, who had been created

Earl of Carlisle in the immediate aftermath of Boroughbridge, was himself executed, drawn and quartered within less than a year, following allegations of defeatism and treason in his dealings with the Scots. Mistrust and the fear of conspiracy were (and remain) contagious commodities.

King Edward, with the Despensers at his side and with the hated Ordinances of 1311 now officially revoked, embarked on a policy of terror and extortion unprecedented since the reign of King John. Like John, Edward became immensely rich, amassing a fortune of at least £60,000 to set against the debts of nearly £200,000 that his father had bequeathed. Also like John, he became the object of dark rumours, not only of sexual deviancy but of sorcery and plots, leading to the arrest of twenty-eight conspirators in Coventry, accused of employing a necromancer, John of Nottingham, to make wax images and cast spells so as to harm Edward, the Despensers and the prior of Coventry, one of the principal local land-holders. This, the first public accusation to combine witch-craft with treason, was an ill omen of many such accusations still to come, not least against those in the sixteenth and seventeenth centuries accused of 'maleficium' against the Tudor and Stuart kings. An attempt by Edward to follow up his success against the rebels of 1322, with a campaign in Scotland, ended in failure with his army forced southwards by starvation and disease. Even so, in Scotland, and from 1323 in France, Edward now had the resources, thanks in large part to the confiscations made after 1322, to wage war on a scale unseen since Bannockburn.

In the longer term, none of this was of any account. Thomas of Lancaster had been a self-seeking and uninspiring politician. Despite his great wealth, his finances, like those of the King, were permanently overstretched so that, like the other earls, he found it difficult to operate outside the court, whilst his pursuit of royal patronage brought even him, the richest baron in England, into competition with Edward II's low-born favourites. His had been a futile career. He was nonetheless the grandson of a king. His death, by many regarded as a martyrdom, was followed by a popular outcry for his recognition as a saint. In much the same way, the monks of Evesham, after Simon de Montfort's death in 1265, had encouraged the veneration of Montfort and his relics as a focus of miracles and political opposition to the crown.

Queen Isabella and Roger Mortimer

The rise of the Despensers and the King's inability to curb either their greed or their cruelty led to the defection even of Edward's queen, Isabella of France, who in 1325 ensured that neither herself nor her twelve-year-old son, the future Edward III, returned from France to which they had been sent as mediators with the French King. In France, Isabella entered into a liaison with her fellow exile, Roger Mortimer, a leading baron from the Welsh Marches who now became the Queen's lover and the principal focus of opposition to the Despenser regime.

In September 1326, in league with Mortimer and the Count of Hainault, whose daughter had hastily been married to the future Edward III, Isabella took ship from Holland to Orwell in Suffolk, leading the first but by no means the last invasion of England to have been mounted from the Low Countries. Like a much more famous invasion, by William and Mary of Orange in 1688, this was one in theory led by a woman, resulting almost immediately in the collapse of a hated royal authority, the flight and the arrest of the King. In November, Edward II and the younger Despenser were captured at Llantrisant, between Neath and Caerphilly, the irony here being that it was the Welsh, conquered by Edward's father only forty years before, who proved Edward's staunchest supporters in adversity. For the third time in less than fifty years, a ruling Prince of Wales was taken captive in the principality and handed over to English enemies.

The Despensers, father and son, were executed. The King was held prisoner at Kenilworth whilst desperate measures were taken to arrange a succession. Once again, the problem lay in bridling a sovereign above whom stood no authority save for God. As the rebellions of the thirteenth century had clearly demonstrated, short of killing the King, there was little that an opposition could do to prevent him from revoking whatever promises he might be induced to make under compulsion. As a result, in the first weeks of 1327, in a Parliament carefully managed by Isabella and her supporters, Edward II was declared a tyrant, incapable of rule, governed by others rather than by his own will. Even his favourite pastimes, swimming and digging, were now held against him as activities unbefitting a king. On 20 January, the bishop of Hereford met the King in person and demanded that he abdicate. With great reluctance, Edward agreed. In a series of premeditated and theatrical gestures, William Trussell, acting in the name of Parliament, formally renounced his homage to Edward. The steward of the royal household broke his ceremonial staff of office. Edward III officially acceded to the throne on 25 January and on 1 February was crowned in Westminster Abbey.

Death of Edward II

None of this theatre was sufficient to calm the violence that was now becoming an ingrained part of English high politics. Edward II remained in captivity, first at Kenilworth, later at Berkeley Castle on the Bristol Channel, from where various attempts were made to rescue him. In September 1327, as it was later announced, Edward died at Berkeley, either as a result of illness or, so it was rumoured, killed in a botched rescue attempt. In all probability he was suffocated by his gaolers; the later claim that the murder was committed secretly, using a red hot poker to burn out his entrails, appears only in accounts written twenty or so years later. Even more extravagant rumours, that Edward had survived as a wandering hermit in Italy or southern France, seem to derive from romance and the tradition of the disguised and undying king; similar stories, equally groundless, had been told of

King Harold after 1066. In 1327, Edward II became the first English King since Stephen to have been deposed, and the first since Harold to have been, in all probability, killed in his rivals' scramble for power. Having killed a king's nephew at Viterbo in 1271 (with the murder of Henry of Almain), and a king's grandson in 1322 (with the execution of Thomas of Lancaster), English politics had now encompassed the murder of the King himself. Edward II's fate was all the more horrific for having been arranged by his own wife, Isabella of France. Nor did the killing end here.

Edward III

Isabella and her lover, Roger Mortimer, now attempted to employ the fifteen-year-old Edward III as a pawn in their own schemes. In March 1330, they arranged the execution of Edward II's half-brother, Edmund of Woodstock, Earl of Kent (son of Edward I and grandson of a king of France), accused of plotting to restore the late Edward II to the throne. Shortly afterwards, in November 1330, only a week after his eighteenth birthday, Edward III, attended by a small band of friends, entered Nottingham castle via an underground passage and arrested Roger Mortimer. Once again, Parliament was used as a stage for the condemnation of treachery. Mortimer, the Queen's lover, was executed. Queen Isabella was deprived of rule, spending the remainder of her long life in comfortable but enforced retirement. By the time of her death in 1358 she had, either in remorse or hypocrisy, endowed a chantry at Eltham in Kent for the soul of her late husband, Edward II. She was buried in London in her wedding mantle, with Edward II's embalmed heart placed over her breast. Meanwhile, a pattern of bloodshed and murder had been established, up to and including the person of the King, unparalleled in English history at least since the blood feuds of tenth- and eleventh-century Northumbria.

Kings who failed to heed political opposition henceforth went in fear not merely of correction but their lives.

Parliament, devised as a showcase of royal clemency and conciliation, had been transformed, in a crisis, into the chief mouthpiece of criticism directed against the crown. The popular French belief, widely circulating after 1400, that 'the English kill their kings' had already been proved true. Even so, king killing remained a secretive affair. The King himself was God's anointed. Even his authority to abdicate, let alone the authority of barons or Parliament to depose him, remained uncertain. Not for a further 320 years, until 1649 and the trial of Charles I, did Parliament dare to put a king openly on trial. In the meantime, what is perhaps most remarkable about the aftermath of all the killings that resulted from Edward II's misrule, at Boroughbridge in 1322, at Berkeley in 1327 and at Nottingham in 1330, is that the new King, Edward III, managed, albeit without altering the underlying impulses of society, to curb the violence between crown and aristocracy, between Englishmen and their rulers. It was almost as if the bloodshed had been forgotten.

Increasing Bureaucracy
The reasons for this lull can in part be sought with Edward himself, determined to avoid the character faults of his father. Edward's personality, however, remains shadowy and uncertain. For all of the vast heaps of parchment piled up by the great offices of the crown, still stored in the Public Record Office at Kew, the wellsprings of power become more rather than less difficult to fathom the greater the quantity of our evidence. By the 1330s, each single term of the Exchequer or the chief law courts produced a vast slab of parchment sheets, closely written, containing hundreds of thousands of words, only a tiny number of which have ever been or are ever likely to be published. Somewhere amidst this routine, in the anonymity of the chancery and Exchequer's scribes who now vied with one another to adopt identical handwriting and standard bureaucratic language, the leaves and branches of the modern state had already begun to sprout. Yet the very wealth

of the detail here tends to render our view of policy that much more opaque.

We know the names of the King's hawks (under Edward I 'Clynton', 'Strathbogie', 'Droxford', suggesting that these at least were gifts from particular courtiers). Under Edward III we have the crazy logic of horse lists, recording the condition of horses in the royal stables, and the colour and value of particular war horses lost on campaign, now to be repaid from royal funds. By the fifteenth century, besides an officially appointed 'Keeper of the King's Swans', we even have illustrated rolls of swan marks, paintings that show the ownership symbols notched into the beaks of swans belonging to the King, his dukes, earls and bishops. In the meantime, our insight into the human processes of politics, into the formulation of policy and the interaction between King, councillors and Parliament tends to recede. The lists of earls and bishops witnessing the King's charters, previously our most important glimpse into the attendance and ranking of courtiers, tend to decline into mere formality, even as early as 1300. The burning question of who was 'in' and who was 'out' at the royal court is rendered difficult or impossible to probe.

The rolls and the petitions of Parliament survive in considerable quantity from the 1280s onwards, but we learn from them virtually nothing about debates nor about how or by whom Parliament was controlled, nor indeed about such basic matters, before the 1320s, as whether the Lords and the Commons met together or as two distinct chambers. For any single year in the 1250s, the careful historian could hope to read all of the evidences generated by royal government, for the most part using printed editions. The whole process might take a day or two of careful research. By Edward III's reign, the task has become virtually impossible. Too much remains unpublished. Too many details cloud the overall picture. The wood cannot be seen for the sheer number of its individual trees. The historian risks producing a mere chronicle of departmental or bureaucratic initiatives rather than a portrait of political society or of royal government in the round. The history of the reign of Edward III becomes a history in two parts: one part chivalry and derring-do reconstructed from the exaggerated reports of chroniclers, the other part generating all of the excitement of a history of income tax, reassembled from the dullest and driest of archival materials.

Edward's Personality

Edward III's personality mattered. Indeed, Edward's is perhaps the first English royal face whose appearance has been preserved to us in a real portrait rather than via some generic image of kingship. His wooden funeral effigy, perhaps carved from a death mask, suggests a twisted expression and hence, perhaps, that it was a stroke that killed this King, the first even remotely plausible diagnosis that we have for the cause of death of any medieval English king save for those, like Harold, killed in battle. Before he declined into senility or chronic ill health, Edward stamped his authority on most government initiatives: the arrest of Mortimer in 1330, the equally dramatic coup in which, almost exactly a decade later, the King returned secretly to England from war in France, to arrest and impeach those ministers he blamed for the shortage of funds for his troops. It was Edward in person who commanded the English forces against the Scots at Halidon Hill in 1333, against the French at the Battle of Crécy in 1346, and against French, Genoese and Castilian forces in the maritime encounters known as the battles of Sluys in 1340 and Les Espagnols ten years later. It was Edward's personal claims, as son of a King of England and grandson of a King of France, that provoked the Hundred Years War. It was Edward's own devotion to chivalric and knightly pursuits, his love of tournaments and round tables, his determination to outdo the mythical King Arthur and to supply England with an order of knighthood fit to rival the greatest knights in France that led, after Crécy, to his establishment of the Order of the Garter, in many ways his most personal creation, established with its own chapel dedicated to

St George at the heart of Windsor Castle, the King's birthplace, itself redesigned as a pleasure palace and public display of royal splendour, very much at Edward's own command.

At Windsor and in the royal residences at Westminster and King's Langley in Hertfordshire, hot water was for the first time piped into the King's baths, and mechanical clocks make their earliest appearance as royal rather than as exclusively ecclesiastical luxuries. Devotion to chivalric principles explains a number of Edward's political actions: his horseback dash, forty miles in a single day, to Lochindorb, south of Inverness, in 1336, to relieve the widowed Countess of Atholl besieged in the castle; the mercy he showed to the burghers of Calais in 1347 whom he had intended to hang but instead pardoned after intercessions on their behalf by his Queen, Philippa of Hainault; his determination in the 1350s to prosecute the bishop of Ely, Thomas Lisle, in the face of concerted opposition from Lisle's fellow bishops, for attacks said to have been made by Lisle's men upon the King's cousin, Lady Wake, sister of the Duke of Lancaster. Like a lot of gallant gentlemen, Edward perhaps behaved less politely in private than the perfection of manners that he affected in public might lead us to suppose. Accusations that he raped the Countess of Salisbury were almost certainly untrue – French propaganda copied from the ancient Roman legend of the rape of Lucretia. Even so, there was certainly a seamier side to his relationship, late in life, with Alice Perrers, royal mistress, accused of corruption and scandal in the handling of government finance.

Edward's Administration

As this dependence on his mistress suggests, Edward was a ruler, perhaps the first since Richard I in the 1190s, whose ministers enjoyed a higher profile in day-to-day government than the King himself. It was upon officers such as his chancellor, Robert Stratford, bishop of Chichester, and his treasurer, Roger Northburgh, bishop of Coventry, that Edward pinned both the credit and blame for the financial exactions of 1340. Later, it was another chancellor, William of Wykeham, bishop of Winchester, overseer and presiding genius of Edward's work at Windsor, who headed the King's administration. Removed from office after clashing with the King's son, John of Gaunt, Wykeham was nonetheless still sufficiently powerful to play a leading role in the constitutional crisis at the end of the reign and to survive as a major political force into the reigns of Edward's grandsons, Richard II and Henry IV. Many of the King's ministers were clerks, subsequently promoted as bishops. They can appear on occasion a self-serving but monotone bunch. The worst of the fourteenth-century bishops could barely begin to match the crimes attributed to their eleventh-century predecessors such as Stigand or Ranulf Flambard. Even so, there had been an undoubted shift after 1250 or so, from the saints and scholars of the twelfth century to the competent 'all-rounders' of the later Middle Ages. The Franciscan friar, John Pecham (archbishop 1279–92) was the last intellectual of truly European stature to serve as archbishop of Canterbury before the Reformation of the 1530s, though the mathematician and theologian Thomas Bradwardine might have revived this tradition had he not died only thirty-eight days after obtaining the archbishopric in 1349.

Saints and Sinners

The period from 1170 to the 1260s had witnessed a remarkable flourishing of saints' cults in England, associated principally with English bishops famed for their devotion to the liberty and reform of the Church: Thomas Becket (d.1170, canonized 1173), St Wulfstan of Worcester (d.1095, canonized 1203), St Hugh of Lincoln (d.1200, canonized 1220), St Edmund of Canterbury (d.1240, canonized 1246), St Richard Wyche of Chichester (d.1253, canonized 1262) fell within this category, as did the bids, unsuccessful though they proved, to obtain the canonizations of Stephen Langton (Archbishop of Canterbury d.1228), Robert Grosseteste of Lincoln (d.1253) and even,

most improbably, King Henry III's half-brother Aymer de
Valence of Winchester (d.1260), and Henry's uncle Boniface of
Savoy (Archbishop of Canterbury, d.1270). Boniface was
rumoured to have worn chain mail under his clerical habit and
to have once delivered a distinctly un-archiepiscopal punch to
the jaw of the prior of St Bartholomew's Smithfield. He was
nonetheless a conscientious visitor of monasteries, an issuer of
reformist legislation for the English Church and even, in the
1250s and 60s, an upholder of the rights of the community of
the realm to better government than had previously been
supplied by his royal nephew's incompetent favouritism. In
Italy and southern Europe, saints in the thirteenth century
were almost exclusively holy men set apart from the mainstream of ecclesiastical administration or secular politics. In
England, with its well-regulated Church matching the state's
increasing obsession with law-making and legality, it was
bishops who achieved sainthood and a role as intercessors for
their local communities from beyond the grave.

The last of these saint bishops, Thomas Cantiloupe of
Hereford (d.1282), was canonized in 1320 having been so at
odds with his archbishop, John Pecham, that he spent the final
months of his life as an excommunicate exile in the court of
Rome. Thereafter, the electrical matter of sanctity seems to
have passed underground, no longer channelled through an
episcopal hierarchy increasingly reserved for civil servants and
royal diplomats. Virtually every archbishop of Canterbury
after 1300 had seen previous service as King's clerk or ambas-
sador, and several of them continued, even after their promotion
as archbishop, to hold office as chancellor or treasurer to the
crown. It was not that Pecham's successors lacked either
courage or competence. Even the supine civil servant
Archbishop Walter Reynolds had broken with Edward II in
the 1320s and assisted the court coup which brought Edward
III to the throne, preaching on the ancient proverb 'The voice
of the people is the voice of God.' Most of these men were well
schooled. Archbishop Reynolds owned an impressive library,

although he was perhaps more familiar with the covers than the contents of his books.

With the exception of William Courtenay, son of the Earl of Devon and great-grandson of Edward I (the first archbishop of Canterbury to have been of direct royal lineage, succeeded by Archbishop Thomas Arundel, a great-great-grandson of King Henry III), most of these men emerged from precisely that stratum of the lower gentry or upper levels of freeholder that had produced the Thomas Beckets or Stephen Langtons of the past. William of Wykeham's father was a man with the far from aristocratic name John Long, a yeoman freeholder, married above his station to the granddaughter of a minor local knight. Compared with their predecessors, nonetheless, the bishops of the fourteenth century can only be regarded as second-raters. They included the first English bishop ever to be tried for incitement to homicide (Thomas Lisle of Ely, a Dominican friar, accused of leading a gang of fenland brigands) and the only two bishops ever to have been beheaded by the London mob: Walter Stapeldon, bishop of Exeter, treasurer of the deposed Edward II, decapitated in Cheapside with a bread-knife in 1326, and Simon Sudbury, Archbishop of Canterbury, killed during the Peasants' Revolt of 1381, his head displayed on London Bridge with an episcopal cap nailed to the skull. Both Stapledon and Sudbury were 'building' bishops, Sudbury as principal benefactor of the new nave at Canterbury Cathedral, Stapeldon as the second founder of the cathedral church of Exeter. Yet in neither case was there even a token suggestion that these agents of royal government be acknowledged as martyrs or workers of miracles.

Many but not all of these bishops were learned men. Louis de Beaumont, a cousin of Edward I's Queen, was accused in 1318 of floundering through the Latin of his consecration service and of muttering, after one particularly troublesome polysyllable, 'By St Louis, he was no gentleman who wrote that word!' Beaumont was amongst the first of the English bishops to plaster his episcopal seal with his own heraldic arms.

From the time of his successor, Thomas Hatfield, the bishops of Durham, as 'palatinate' lords of their county, employed a double-sided seal, on one side showing them enthroned, on the other as a mounted warrior, with sword and crested helmet barely concealed beneath their episcopal mitre. Not since Odo of Bayeux in the eleventh century had an English bishop been portrayed in this way on his seal, riding into battle. Meanwhile, rather like star conductors or musicians of the twentieth century, the bishops of fourteenth-century England were capable of a virtuoso performance using the materials already at their disposal, but were not themselves able to rewrite the music, let alone to compose new tunes.

Monks

This lack of charisma was all the more significant because the Church, as an undying institution, its lands guaranteed against division or alienation, in theory growing richer year by year, was perhaps the only force in England that might have held in check the violence that was increasingly the hallmark both of relations within the English political elite and of England's dealings with its neighbours. In the past, it had been English monks who had supplied the intellectual and moral example of good government. By the fourteenth century, however, even the more ascetic orders of the twelfth century had become ossified, sometimes almost literally so, under a weight of tradition and oligarchic self-interest. In the richer Benedictine communities, such as Westminster Abbey, the monks are estimated to have been served, on a daily basis, at least a pound's weight of fish or two pounds of meat, a loaf of bread weighing a further two pounds, half a dozen eggs, large quantities of cheese and milk and at least eight pints of beer. No wonder that the Benedictines were depicted in contemporary satire as overweight gluttons, or that modern archaeological investigation has suggested that, in the richer of their communities, they suffered from a variety of bone diseases associated with excessive eating.

The monastic cloister was not a prison but a place in which to open the mind to spiritual enquiry, to the heavenly as opposed to the earthly Jerusalem. Hence the richness of the decoration assigned to the cloister itself, as an aid to meditation and not least to the meditation of the careers and spiritual well-being of the monastery's donors, whose arms were emblazoned on heraldic shields, as in the cloisters at Westminster or Canterbury or Norwich, placed directly over the heads of the monks as they contemplated the kingdom of heaven. As this juxtaposition of the secular and the sacred should suggest, rather like today's public school headmasters, or the more superior sort of tradesmen, there were few greater snobs than England's medieval monks, themselves often of humble background yet thrown into almost daily contact with the noble dead. As the existence of monastic deer parks, none more famous than Westminster's Hyde Park, should remind us, although monks themselves were not supposed to hunt or engage in blood sports, they did not baulk at associating themselves with the most aristocratic of sports, with venison as a further supplement to the monastic diet. Even the Cistercians on occasion maintained deer parks. As long ago as 1215, the Cistercian abbot of Beaulieu, one-time diplomatic envoy of King John, was accused before the Cistercian General Chapter not only of engaging in public drinking contests, in a game known as 'garsacil', but of keeping a greyhound tethered to his bed on a silver chain. These were not the sort of thinkers or moral leaders capable of resisting the trend either towards war or disorder.

Oxford and Cambridge

After the 1220s, the friars, followers of St Francis and St Dominic, in theory pledged to lives of poverty like the original disciples of Christ, had settled in many English towns and had brought new insights to their preaching, in particular in their condemnation of materialism and the pleasures which money could buy. Jesus, so they argued, had sent his followers penniless into the world, and it was by abandoning money rather than by fleeing the world that the religious could best pursue their vocation.

Because of their emphasis upon preaching, generally regarded as a learned pursuit, the friars had established particular connections with the schools, settling in both Oxford and Cambridge almost immediately after their arrival in England. Already by the time of Gerald of Wales in the 1180s, Oxford was emerging as England's pre-eminent seat of learning. Even earlier, Geoffrey of Monmouth, weaving his fabulous account of English history, claimed to have relied upon a book belonging to the archdeacon of Oxford, just as today's fantasists and conspiracy theorists might cite anything that lent the approval of Oxford University Press to their own fantastical ideas. Walter Map, court chronicler and wit under Henry II, was himself archdeacon of Oxford.

Why Oxford? In part because the town was a regular meeting place for ecclesiastical courts, one of the most convenient points close to London in a diocese, the see of Lincoln, which stretched from the Thames as far north as the Humber. It was also, perhaps, a place of cheap rents. With Oxford today boasting some of the highest property prices in England, it is hard to imagine that the city was once awash with tenements, plots and halls where students could be lodged at little expense. In the twelfth century, however, the silting up of the Thames reduced navigation and ensured a glut of cheap property into which teachers and students now moved. It was precisely to guard against the further congestion of the Thames and the Medway navigations that Magna Carta, in 1215, forbade the construction of fish weirs on either of these rivers.

The self-government of the University of Oxford dates from this same period, with the removal of authority over students and schools from the bishop of Lincoln and their investment in a new officer, the University's Chancellor. The dominance of the University over the city of Oxford, gown over town, was not finally cemented until the reign of Edward III, following a full-blown riot, provoked by an argument in the Swindlestock

Tavern on St Scholastica's Day 1355 (10 February). In penance for the slaying of a considerable number of students, the mayor and corporation were condemned to pay an annual fine to the University (last paid in the 1820s), and the University henceforth obtained wide-ranging authority over the city's markets and commerce.

Cambridge, likewise a port town with a declining trade and navigation, emerged as the location for a much smaller and, during the Middle Ages, less-distinguished university only a few years after Oxford. The precise circumstances here remain unclear, but perhaps, where the presence of the bishop and archdeacon's courts had been crucial to the emergence of the schools of Oxford, the freedom of Cambridge from supervision by the local bishop, and the fact that, in the 1220s, the archdeacon of Ely was an absentee Italian, more often to be found acting as papal agent in Croatia or Hungary than on the wind-swept banks of the Cam, encouraged the emergence, by 1225, of a university Chancellor apparently ruling the scholars and their schools.

To begin with, both at Oxford and at Cambridge, scholars and masters were lodged in halls and dormitories, bought and sold as private enterprises, with no permanent endowment to ensure their long-term survival. The first of the endowed Cambridge colleges, Peterhouse, was founded in 1284 by a Benedictine monk, Hugh of Balsham, bishop of Ely, whose statutes grafted elements of the Benedictine rule on to decrees already awarded, twenty years earlier, to one of the first of the Oxford colleges, founded by Walter de Merton, chancellor to King Henry III. Another of the early Oxford colleges, Balliol, was founded in the 1260s by the father and mother of the future King of Scotland, John de Balliol. New College at Oxford, was the work of William of Wykeham, chancellor to Edward III, established in 1379 as the Oxford end of an educational network that was intended to channel boys from school at Wykeham's foundation at Winchester to higher learning at Oxford. All told, of the surviving Oxford and Cambridge colleges, fourteen were founded before 1370, a further eight between 1370 and 1480.

Extending beyond the immediate needs of education, the idea of the college, served by a body of clergy celebrating the liturgy in honour of their founder, often with elaborate choir schools or professional musicians attached, itself became one of the most characteristic phenomena of the late medieval English Church, inspiring the actions of Edward III himself in his foundation of the colleges of St George at Windsor and St Stephen's at Westminster, within the shadow of the monastic abbey and royal palace. Music, that great accomplishment and delight of the English, appears as an especially royal art from the 1350s onwards, associated with the collegiate foundations of Edward III, as later of William of Wykeham or King Henry VI. Those who tune in to the service of nine lessons and carols from King's College Cambridge at Christmas each year are probably aware that this particular service is a Victorian pastiche. The basic idea, however, of a college, with a royal or distinguished founder and with religious songs to accompany the good and godly learning of its fellows is at least seven centuries old.

Like Walter de Merton and other college founders, Wykeham, both at Winchester and New College, laid particular stress upon the obligation of his foundations to support and educate his own kinsmen. Even now, the names Balliol or Wykeham have a resonance, thanks to their educational foundations, that others, just as famous in their day now lack. Wykeham was in some ways a less competent or significant administrator than his predecessor as bishop of Winchester, William Eddington, yet, thanks to his school and his college, it is Wykeham not Eddington whose memory has survived. Founders' kin were still being admitted to Oxford, on preferential terms, as late as the 1850s, resulting in a lucrative though shadowy trade in false pedigrees intended to demonstrate kinship to long dead bishops. In particular, kinship to Henry Chichele, Archbishop of Canterbury, founder of All Souls

College Oxford, could guarantee a handsome lifelong stipend in a college which had no undergraduates but only fellows whose original purpose had been to pray for the dead of the Hundred Years War. It is sometimes asserted that medieval monasticism was swept away in England by the Reformation of the sixteenth century. In practice, a large number of the Oxford and Cambridge colleges retain identities that are essentially medieval and monastic, the arrangement of their buildings, and the election, dining and self-government of their 'fellows' (or teachers) being conducted according to procedures remarkably similar to those practised by medieval monks. Even monastic celibacy persisted long after the Reformation. The majority of the fellows of the Oxford colleges were not permitted to marry until as recently as 1881.

The fourteenth century marked a high point for the universities, especially for Oxford where a rich tradition of theological speculation emerged, associated with such names as Duns Scotus (perhaps trained at Oxford, though owing his fame to his teachings at Paris), William of Ockham (trained at Oxford, but for most of his life an exile from England), and John Wycliffe (one time master of Balliol College, who we will encounter again in due course, and who throughout the 1360s and 70s was the most distinguished theologian permanently resident in Oxford, albeit later denounced as a heretic). Even these representatives of the highest of high learning nonetheless had their feet firmly on the ground of politics and the day-to-day management of the Church.

Ockham wrote in support of the legitimacy of royal or imperial authority judged against that of the Pope. Wycliffe stood on the fringes of the circle around Edward III's son, John of Gaunt, employed as a tame intellectual to bait the advocates of the Avignon papacy and to deny the Church's claims to temporal as well as spiritual rule. All of these scholars, and in particular Scotus, played with the Latin language and invented their own terms of reference in ways that, on occasion, rival the most baffling of the statements of Wittgenstein or the modern philosophers of language. Nonetheless, grammar and the correct apprehension of terms and meanings remained at the heart of academic discourse. The outcome in the late medieval schools was perhaps a growing divorce between the worlds of thought and action, the relegation of much academic discourse to that bickering over abstractions that later critics would decry as 'mere scholasticism'. Even so, the most famous question said to have been debated in the late medieval schools – 'How many angels can dance on the head of a pin?', probably invented by critics – was nothing like so absurd as it might appear. Behind it lay debates over mathematical infinity, the nature of corporeal bodies and abstract entities, the mechanics of space, time and movement that would still engage university students in the lecture rooms of Oxford or Harvard today.

As in nineteenth-century England, where an intense grounding in the ancient languages of Latin and Greek was assumed to be the best training for those who would go on to rule nation and empire, so in medieval Oxford, there was an intensely practical side to a lot of tuition. 'Business' or 'Management' studies were already a feature of the Oxford curriculum in the fourteenth century, long before the twentieth-century mania for capitalist efficiency led to the endowment of some of the most hideous structures in a city famed for the ugliness of much of its modern building. Students were taught about angels, but also how to draft a letter, how to read a budget, how to conceal or disclose meanings from linguistic statements. From the debates of Ockham to the running of a diocese or service as a King's clerk was only a short step. It was civil servants, not philosophers, that the universities were chiefly intended to produce.

The Civil Service
The civil service of Edward III was awash with such men. Government itself grew at a pace unparalleled since the twelfth century. By the 1350s, the royal chancery was issuing at least a hundred, and sometimes as many as two or three hundred

routine legal writs on any day of its business, besides the longer or more significant of chancery letters that were then copied and enrolled in the chancery archives. The chancery was just one small part of government, and already stood apart from the business conducted under the King's privy seal, itself now the focus of a bureaucracy of its own, or subsequently of the King's signet with which the most personal of royal letters were sealed. All of this work, to which we must add that of the law courts and the massive efforts of the Exchequer to extract the revenues with which to fuel this bureaucracy, required the labours of several hundred clerks.

Westminster Hall was the focus of these activities, partitioned into a series of spaces rather like those of the vaster 'open plan' offices of the twentieth-first century, with various other parts of the old palace of Westminster given over to the Exchequer or the annual three- or four-week-long meetings of Parliament, all of these institutions and occasions crammed in almost as afterthoughts to the domestic needs of the King, his household and family. The construction of houses, many of them on a lavish scale, up Whitehall and along the banks of the Thames, was intended to accommodate the greater men in attendance on the court. Long before Downing Street became the home of a prime minister, the surrounding properties were given over to courtiers and counsellors, direct antecedents to the ministers and chief secretaries of the modern departments of state.

This state building was itself the product of pressures placed upon English government by the needs of war. Through the reigns of the first two Edwards, credit arrangements had been put in place to employ the future revenues of customs on wool and baronial taxation to raise loans from Italian bankers. Into the footsteps of the Riccardi of Lucca, bankrupted in the 1290s, stepped firms such as the Frescobaldi, the Bardi and the Peruzzi of Florence, who had continued to prop up royal finance into the 1330s. Quite why such firms were willing to undertake this work remains unclear, since all of them were eventually bankrupted when the crown, as was inevitable, defaulted on its debts. Perhaps they found themselves only slowly sucked into an arrangement from which it was then impossible to extricate themselves. Perhaps, like modern bankers, they had their eyes too firmly on future profits to remark the more imminent signals of apocalypse. From the 1330s, however, the King had somehow to raise cash himself, without mortgaging future revenues in return for injections of foreign capital. Far from this reducing Edward III's appetite for war, the 1330s were to prove the decade in which, after fifty years of being a regular though by no means annual business, warfare and the taxes to pay for it became a more or less permanent feature of royal government.

Military Campaigns

To distance himself from the catastrophes of his father's reign, to divert the violent impulses of the aristocracy into foreign rather than domestic strife, to satisfy his love of chivalry and daring deeds, to associate himself with the glories of his family's past (Henry II, Richard I and Edward I), Edward III embarked on a series of military campaigns that involved English armies in warfare in Scotland, France, the Low Countries and Spain, and at sea from the Firth of Forth to the Bay of Biscay. Intense military activity, against Scotland in the 1330s, immediately after Edward's seizure of personal power, and against France from 1337 onwards, with the outbreak of the Hundred Years War, was punctuated by periods of truce, both with the Scots and the French. Even here, however, there was no permanent peace but a series of near annual raids and 'chevauchées' (mounted ravagings of the French or Scottish countryside).

Scotland

In Scotland, Edward III to some extent rebuilt the position that Edward I had enjoyed in the first decade of the fourteenth century, before the disaster of Bannockburn had led to the Scots overrunning of northern England. Edward Balliol, son of the humiliated King John de Balliol, was supported as an English pretender to the Scots throne, against the claims of King David II, son of Robert Bruce. At Dupplin Moor, in 1332, Balliol's army inflicted a significant defeat upon the Scots, which was followed by a full-scale English invasion that was to last for most of the 1330s, leading to the transfer of Edward's Parliament, Exchequer and chancery to York, to the successful siege and recapture of Berwick upon Tweed and, at Halidon Hill in July 1333, to a major English victory in battle. The English army won the day by mimicking precisely those techniques that the Scots had previously used to defeat English cavalry charges at Stirling Bridge and Bannockburn, adopting a defensive position and using mixed formations of archers and dismounted men-at-arms to see off the Scots' attack. Henceforth, archers, many of them recruited from Wales or the Welsh borders, and the mounted infantry, riding to the battlefield but fighting on foot, were to become the hallmarks of English warfare.

Military Techniques

Just as after Hastings in 1066 the Normans had adopted the Anglo-Saxon technique of riding to war but fighting on foot, so, after a brief flirtation in the thirteenth century with mounted warfare and the magnificence of the cavalry charge, Edward III and his successors put aside such chivalric but potentially disastrous techniques in order to win their battles by patient defence and endurance. It was by precisely these means that Edward III won the Battle of Crécy in 1346, Henry V the Battle of Agincourt in 1415, or indeed the Duke of Wellington the Battle of Waterloo a full 400 years later. The English 'square' was first introduced to the King's army at Halidon Hill, in direct and deliberate imitation of the Scots 'schiltroms' that William Wallace had commanded at Stirling. The techniques of Welsh archers and Scots spearmen, regarded in chivalric circles as mere barbarians, were now deliberately copied by what was intended to be the most chivalric fighting force in Christendom.

France and the Hundred Years War

Edward III's Scottish campaign was arguably already grinding to a stalemate by 1337 when a far more ambitious prospect of war presented itself. Ever since 1328 and the death of King Charles IV of France without an heir, there had been a prospect that Edward III, son of Isabella of France and therefore the eldest living grandson of Philip IV of France, might be regarded as right claimant to the French throne, in preference to Philip of Valois, Charles IV's cousin, who in 1328 had stepped in as King Philip VI, the first of the Valois kings. Edward's claims had passed through the female line, but the so-called 'Salic' law, forbidding inheritance by women, was not cited in Valois propaganda until 1413, as part of a later attempt to revive defunct early-medieval law codes to justify the exclusion of Isabella and Edward from the French royal line. Even so, the English claim to the throne of France was not nearly so strong as might be supposed. Women claimants, even those themselves the daughters of kings, had been excluded both in 1316, following the death of the six-day-old King Jean I 'the posthumous' (the first time that the Capetian bloodline had failed in more than 300 years), and again on at least three occasions, following the deaths of the last of the Capetian kings in 1322 and 1328. Both in 1325 and in 1329 to Philip VI, Edward had performed homage for his lands in France, which by this stage included not only Gascony and the southernmost remnant of the old Angevin empire of Henry II, but the county of Ponthieu, on the mouth of the river Somme, acquired as part of the dower of Edward I's wife, Eleanor of Castile.

It had been as a result of his landing in Ponthieu, in 1066, that Harold had been taken captive and handed over to the Normans, a scene famously illustrated in the Bayeux Tapestry. It was from the port of St-Valery, within sight of Ponthieu, that the Norman fleet had embarked for England in 1066. Now, in 1337, it was because of Ponthieu and his own connections, by blood to the Capetian throne of France, and by marriage to Philippa, daughter of the Count of Hainault (in modern-day Belgium), that an English king for the first time contemplated a reverse restaging of the Norman Conquest, leading an English army across the Channel for what was intended as a full-scale 'conquest' of France. Like William I in 1066, Edward possessed a claim to the French throne that was very far from secure. Like William, he had to rely on propagandists to boost his cause, upon foreign allies to sustain him in hostile territory, and ultimately upon the fortunes of war controlled by God to determine the justice of his claim.

Confiscation of Aquitaine and Ponthieu

The catalyst to this English invasion was Philip VI's formal confiscation of Aquitaine and Ponthieu in 1337, on the pretext that Edward III was harbouring Philip's cousin and arch-enemy, Robert, Count of Artois. Like Edward I in the 1290s, Edward III now looked for allies in the Rhineland and the Low Countries, at vast expense (at least £124,000 in 1337 alone). Edward's ultimate intention, perhaps, was to rebuild the empire of his predecessor Henry II, and at last to repair the humiliation of 1204 when Normandy and the Plantagenet lands north of the Loire had been seized by the French. Not for the first time in English history, nor the last, nostalgia for a lost epoch played a significant role in controlling 'modern' events. Edward himself set sail in July 1338, from the estuary of the Orwell in Suffolk, which itself had first entered English history in 1326. It was via the Orwell river that Isabella, Edward's mother, had disembarked at the start of her campaign against Edward's father. Just up the Suffolk coast lay the fairy-tale castle of Orford, built by Henry II, founder of Edward III's Plantagenet dynasty, the only royal residence in this part of East Anglia, left virtually unaltered and unvisited since Henry had built it in the 1160s. Edward's choice of embarkation point in 1338 was thus highly symbolic, governed by the practical logistics of shipping an army across to Antwerp, but evocative of the triumphs of Henry II and of Isabella of

France, of the greatest of Edward III's Plantagenet ancestors and the source of his claims in France.

Opening Campaigns

Like the world wars of the twentieth century, the Anglo-French conflict generated so vast an archival footprint, in chronicles, contracts for military service, letters and tax returns, that an entire lifetime could be spent in reading the evidence let alone in making sense of it. To summarize, very briefly: from 1338 to 1340, the opening campaign in northern France witnessed Edward himself assume the title 'King of France' (in January 1340, largely at the insistence of his Flemish allies who feared that, unless they fought for a titular King of France, they might be accused of breaching their obligations as subjects of the French crown), a major naval victory over the French at Sluys on 24 June 1340 (the exact anniversary of Edward II's great defeat at Bannockburn in 1314), but also the breakdown of his alliances with the German and Flemish princes and above all the inadequacy of ordinary tax receipts to meet the costs of war. By 1340, for all of his boasted titles, the King was more than £400,000 in debt. In 1341, the threat of concerted action between the French and the Scots nonetheless forced the resumption of war, this time focussed upon the King's support of the claims of John de Montfort to the succession to the duchy of Brittany, itself poised like a great reef in the Atlantic approaches, between the English Channel and Edward's colonies in Gascony. The Breton succession dispute shifted the focus of war from northern to western France. An expedition, planned to take place via Flanders in 1345, was itself diverted by the murder of one of Edward's remaining Flemish allies; the King set sail from Portsmouth instead, in July 1346, apparently intending to make for Gascony and the south.

Caen

Only when his fleet was blown off course was it decided to make a landing in Normandy, at St-Vaast-la-Hougue, south-east of

Cherbourg. From there, Edward marched to the ancient ducal seat at Caen, the enclave from which William of Normandy had planned his invasion of England, 300 years before. Caen was taken on 27 July amidst scenes of slaughter and pillage every bit as terrible as those witnessed in England after William the Conqueror's victory at Hastings. The bishop of Bayeux, custodian of one of the chief monuments to the Norman Conquest of England in 1066, the Bayeux Tapestry, was besieged within the castle of Caen. From Caen, Edward's army moved eastwards, seeking a way back to the coast and thence to England. A campaign of conquest was fast degenerating into yet another raid on the French countryside: a '*chevauchée*', in which the land itself would be wasted to feed and reward Edward's troops. Such '*chevauchées*', grim though they were, had one distinct advantage over French methods of war: they ensured that English armies received regular and invaluable practice in concerted troop movements. They were also, in a sense, one of Scotland's greatest contributions to European history, since it was surely in imitation of the Scots raids south of the border and the reprisals taken by the families such as the Percys and Nevilles now set to guard the northern Marches, that these murderous affairs were first adopted. Once again, techniques of warfare normally associated with 'barbarian' peoples were adopted by the supposed flower of chivalry.

The Battle of Crécy

It was Philip VI who now changed the pace of war. Pursuing Edward and his army across the Somme, on 26 August 1346, Philip forced the English to take up a defensive position on high ground, on the right bank of the river Maie, just outside the village of Crécy. Here an undisciplined charge by the French cavalry broke upon the ranks of dismounted English infantry supported by archers, a formation that had become classic English style. The dukes of Alençon and Lorraine were killed in the attack, as was the blind King of Bohemia, who had insisted on being led into battle. Although he had fought against the English, his emblem of an ostrich feather was now appropriated by Prince Edward (later known as the 'Black Prince'), son of Edward III, destined, in a design of three ostrich feathers with the Flemish motto '*Ich dene*' ('I serve'), to become the symbol of all future princes of Wales: African wildlife, Bohemian chivalry, Dutch courage and Welsh pride combined in a most improbable way.

Another of the badges of modern monarchy, the motto '*Honi soit qui mal y pense*' ('Shame upon him who thinks ill of it') was first adopted for Edward's new Order of the Garter, intended to honour the chief captains who had fought alongside the King at Crécy. Like the order's blue robes, themselves borrowed from the colours of the Capetian kings of France and ultimately from the blue mantle of the Virgin Mary, France's chief protector, Edward's motto was a deliberately Francophile gesture, intended both to justify and symbolize his claims to the French throne. Chivalry, as such incidents reveal, was a matter of conduct and appearances, not at all of the sort of patriotic or nationalistic anti-French sentiment that was to become a feature of later Anglo-French wars. War itself was a means by which the King could display himself to the maximum number of his subjects, no longer locked away in the semi-seclusion of his palaces or Parliaments, but parading through the streets or at the head of his armies, dressed in the most gaudy colours, with Edward himself the proudest peacock in the flock.

Siege of Calais

Victorious, with God's verdict now cast decisively in his favour and with the heraldic surcoats of 2,200 French knights captured in the battle piled up as booty in his pavilion, Edward III now lay siege to Calais. It fell after nearly a year, in September 1347. Thereafter, it was to remain as the chief port of access to England on the continent, its merchant company recognized after 1363 as the only 'staple' (from 'stapler', the trade of sorting wool according to its quality) at which English wool merchants could sell their products overseas. Calais, administered from the 1370s in ecclesiastical terms as part of the archdiocese of Canterbury, was destined to return members to the English parliament throughout the 1530s and 40s. In contrast, Manchester had no member of Parliament until the 1650s, Birmingham until 1832. Throughout the Middle Ages, as 'palatinate' jurisdictions standing apart from the ordinary counties of England, neither Chester nor Durham sent representatives to the Commons.

Meanwhile, in October 1346, within three months of Crécy, the Scots were defeated at Nevilles Cross near Durham and their King, David II, taken prisoner. Not since 1174 and the crushing defeats inflicted upon the enemies of King Henry II in Scotland and France had an English King enjoyed such extraordinary fortune in war.

Capture of the French King

Despite the vast cost of these campaigns, Edward III's winning streak was to be continued into the 1350s. From 1349 to 1360, Edward fought off a threat to Calais, obtained yet another naval victory at the Battle of Les Espagnols, and in 1355 launched a two pronged attack via Calais and Gascony culminating when Prince Edward once again inflicted a crushing defeat on the French at Nouaillé five miles south of Poitiers. This Battle of Poitiers, of September 1356, led not only to the destruction of yet another French army, in circumstances similar to those at Crécy, but to the capture, in the midst of the fighting, of the French King, Jean II. When the Black Prince returned with his prisoners in the following year, the gutters of London ran with wine as part of the victory celebrations, something not reported since 1220 when a similar display, to mark the translation of the relics of St Thomas Becket at Canterbury, had plunged the monks of Canterbury into fifty years of financial hardship.

Kings' Ransoms and Recovered Lands in France

With both the Scots and the French Kings in English custody, and following a final expedition to France in 1359 in which his

plans to have himself crowned in Rheims Cathedral, the traditional coronation church of the French, devolved into yet
another '*chevauchée*', this time through Burgundy, Edward III
was able to negotiate treaties, allowing for the ransom of David
II of Scotland for 100,000 marks, and, under the terms of the
Treaty of Brétigny, eventually ratified in 1361, the ransom of
Jean II for £500,000. Edward renounced his claims to be recognized as King of France and, in return, the French abandoned
any claim to sovereignty over Aquitaine and the English
possessions in France. Edward III now held a position across
the Channel stronger than that enjoyed by any previous ruler
of England up to and including the legendary King Arthur.
This triumph seemed to be cemented in the early 1360s by a
series of marriages arranged for Edward's sons and daughters,
by which the earldoms of Pembroke, March, Lancaster, the
duchy of Brittany and the counties of Flanders and Burgundy
seemed all to have been brought within the royal family's orbit.

Economic Costs

Superficially at least, Edward's combination of warfare and
diplomacy rode high. Beneath the surface, however, lurked
deep gulfs of economic and strategic miscalculation. The cost
of maintaining garrisons at Calais, in Gascony and on the
borders with Scotland were themselves crippling, let alone
the costs of mounting expeditions from these redoubts.
Edward had perhaps already spent even more on his naval
forces than on his land army. On the one hand, this suggests a
new bid for sovereignty of the seas, the first occasion since
the reign of King John when the English had effectively
sought mastery of the Channel: an important contribution
towards the pride and reputation of the later royal navy.
Edward had new gold coins minted, including the 'noble',
worth 6s 8d (half a 'mark'), intended for high value payments
in trade and diplomacy: precisely the sort of coin that was
needed in an era of massive taxation and no less massive
ransom payments. They were stamped with a portrait of the

King standing crowned and armed on board a great vessel of war, emblazoned with the heraldic symbols of England and France, the reverse bearing an inscription comparing Edward III with Christ himself passing through the midst of his enemies ('Jesus passing through the midst of them, went his way', Luke 4:30). Yet such empty boasting was small recompense for the costs of Edward's naval operations. Far from the English gaining supremacy over the seas, the Channel itself became a vector of warfare, with French, Genoese and Spanish ships raiding along the southern English coast. Portsmouth was burned in 1338 and 1342, Plymouth was attacked in 1340, Winchelsea in 1356. For the first time in recorded history, English merchant shipping had to travel in convoy. The trade which such shipping carried and the English political classes who profited from it were taxed and taxed again. Meanwhile, the strategy behind Edward's continental campaigns remained simplistic to the point of idiocy.

The more defeats inflicted upon the French, the more noblemen captured, the more territory ravaged, the greater the proof of God's favour and the higher the potential profit to the English King. Yet no manner of victory, not even such victories as Crécy or Poitiers, could alter the fact that the English lands in France remained open to counterattack and to essentially French cultural and economic influences, that the ransoms demanded from noble prisoners were often impossible to enforce, and that, even after the Treaty of Brétigny, the French subjects of Aquitaine and the south continued to look to French royal justice and to the French Parlement in much the same way that Capetian influence had been intruded into Plantagenet Gascony in the years after 1259. The basic problems of English rule in France remained unresolved.

Whether Edward or his advisers had any real idea of the broader strategy of their war, as opposed to the potential glory of its individual episodes, remains unclear. Perhaps they pursued a conscious policy of inviting the French to pitched battle which the English believed they could win. Perhaps like one of the war's chief chroniclers, the French poet Jean Froissart, they were inclined to confound romance with history and to mingle fiction with fact. In the long winter evenings, Froissart had alternated writing his *Chronicle* with reciting long passages from his epic romance *Meliador*, in which damsels in distress, wild bears and shipwrecks on an Isle of Man implausibly peopled by the ancient Hebrews rubbed shoulders with more 'realistic' events. The Treaty of Brétigny was stored by the English in a special box, the 'Calais Chest' (still in the Public Record Office), an exquisite symbol of chivalry and diplomacy, emblazoned with the arms of the Kings and their ministers who had negotiated peace. Its terms, meanwhile, were a dead letter almost from the moment that it was consigned to its magnificent casket.

King Jean of France died in English captivity with the bulk of his ransom still unpaid. The costs of maintaining peace as of waging war mounted beyond all control. The Black Prince's expedition into northern Spain in 1367, intended merely (and in the final resort unsuccessfully) to ensure a continued alliance with the King of Castile, inflicted a great victory at Nájera but nonetheless cost nearly 3 million gold florins for no tangible economic or strategic return. Strategy was sacrificed to chivalry and common sense to the pursuit of glory, in a way more reminiscent of the posturings of a Napoleon than of the caution and parsimony normally associated with English warfare. The Spanish Armada of 1588 was, in this reading, merely Spain's belated response to an even more pointless and vindictive English aggression. Long before the Peninsular War of the early nineteenth century, the armies of the Black Prince had trudged through the future battlefields of Vitoria and Burgos in pursuit of their own small measure of fame.

The Black Death
The Great Pestilence or 'Black Death' of the 1340s has traditionally been identified with the disease today known as Bubonic Plague or 'Yersinia pestis', named after the Swiss

bacteriologist, Alexandre Yersin, who in 1894 first isolated the plague bacillus during an outbreak in Hong Kong. The disease itself travels via animal hosts, especially rats, the ultimate agent (or 'vector') of transmission being fleas whose digestive tracts become congested with plague bacilli, exciting the fleas into a frenzy of biting and repeated vomiting in their attempts to ingest blood, thereby spreading infected blood, and hence the disease itself, all the more speedily from one flea-bitten victim to another. The fleas themselves travel in the fur of rats, and can on occasion survive, even without an animal host, in the grain or grain debris which is the rat's preferred environment. Symptoms of infection amongst humans include painfully sensitive 'buboes' or swellings, varying from the size of a pea to that of an egg, generally located in the lymph nodes nearest to the point of infection, most often in the groin or armpits, although sometimes in the neck or behind the ears. Infection occurs as, or more, easily in villages and the countryside than it does in towns, perhaps because the ratio of rats to humans in a village is higher than would be the case in urban areas with a denser population of humans.

There are problems in identifying the Black Death as *Yersinia pestis*. Diseases, like people, change over time. The pathology of bubonic plague as experienced in China or India in the nineteenth and twentieth centuries will not necessarily assist us towards an understanding of plague in the 1340s. Although fourteenth-century writers describe symptoms, including the painful buboes, that seem consistent with plague, there are other features to the disease – its apparent failure to observe the seasonal life-cycle of the plague flea, the speed both of its distribution and the resulting mortality – which suggest that some other cause should be sought, a pneumonic form of plague perhaps, anthrax, influenza or some other pestilence that may itself have died out or mutated to such a degree that it can no longer be identified with any particular modern virus or bacterium. None of this should be allowed to detract either from the terror of the Black Death or the human suffering that it caused.

To a human population already weakened by the famine and disease that had characterized the period after 1315, living on the thin edge between starvation and survival, the pestilence of 1348–9 brought disaster on a unprecedented scale. From Weymouth the pestilence spread to the West Country, reaching Bristol by August 1348. Probably via multiple points of entry, it infected East Anglia and by the autumn was threatening London. Its causes – a great rain of worms and serpents in China? A foul miasma spread through the air? God's vengeance? – were as poorly understood as the precautions that might be taken against it. The English had never liked foreigners. In an essentially rural society of villages and villagers, in which everyone knew everyone else's business, Christ's injunctions to feed the hungry and shelter the stranger (Matthew 25:35) were answered as much in the breach as the observance. There had always been a tension between the urge to charity towards groups such as lepers, and the law's insistence that other outcast communities be hunted down and destroyed. Now, in the 1340s, townsfolk in places such as Gloucester tried vainly to stem the progress of pestilence by closing their gates to outsiders. The attempt, needless to say, proved merely that death knows no bounds.

The actual rate of mortality from the plague will never be known. The evidence upon which we rely here, chiefly manorial court records and bishops' registers, tells us only about the death rates amongst certain sorts of priests and peasants. But did all priests seek to bring comfort to the sick, in which case we might extrapolate statistics from the number of priests recorded as dying, or did they instead send auxiliaries, in which case the records will supply no reliable gauge? Three archbishops of Canterbury in succession died during the course of 1348–9, two of them certainly from the pestilence. Of the forty-two monks and seven lay brothers at Meaux Abbey in Yorkshire, thirty-two are said to have died. Plague killed all of the friars living in the house of Our Lady at Norwich, and only three of the twenty-six monks of Newenham in Devon survived. Yet at Canterbury Cathedral, out of a community of more than a hundred monks, there were only four deaths. How are we to extrapolate national trends from such figures?

Modern estimates suggest that anything between a third and two-thirds of the population died as a result of the outbreak of 1348–9, but there is an enormous difference here between the upper and lower ends of this range, and it would be unsafe merely to opt for a median figure of fifty per cent. The poor, infants, the old and those least likely to find a place in the surviving records will clearly have died in greater numbers than the rich and the well-fed, or those able to run for their lives, as appears to have been the case for the King, who throughout the winter of 1349–50 assiduously avoided London, spending Christmas at Otford in Kent, and then moving by easy stages to Woodstock. Any attempt to convene Parliament was abandoned. Even then, the King did not entirely escape the disease which seems to have caused the death of his fifteen-year-old daughter, Joan, at Bordeaux in September 1348. Another of the King's children, William of Windsor, apparently born in 1348, seems to have died in infancy, perhaps again as a result of pestilence. Even so, no earls died of the plague, and in 1348 the death rate amongst the peerage seems to have run at less than one in twenty, lower than in an average year, rising only to one in eight in 1349.

So great are the possibilities here for statistical analysis, number-crunching and the reduction of human history to a series of graphs and diagrams, that social and economic historians have gone wild in their pursuit of plague as a factor in England's history. The Black Death has been presented as the wellspring of virtually everything that happened thereafter: social unrest provoked by a labour shortage, followed by rising wages, followed by a transformation in rural society; increased legal regulation and the rise of the modern 'state', as kings, from Edward III onwards, issued legislation intended to freeze social relations in their pre-plague state, to guarantee deference to the great and servility amongst the many, coercing every group within society, from bishops to blacksmiths, to stand by their obligations one to another; an upsurge in piety, as humanity petitioned God to remove the scourge of plague, or alternatively a rise in anticlericalism, as men cursed God and his ministers for their failure to prevent the pestilence; the encouragement of such phenomena as prostitution previously regarded as sins, as young men were encouraged to procreate to relieve the population shortage; a recourse to increasing extremes in war and pleasure, as life was counted cheap and to be lived to the full before the inevitable snuffing out; growing fatalism and a fascination with death and decay, seen, for example, in the 'transi' tombs of fifteenth-century England, in which bishops such as Richard Fleming at Lincoln or Henry Chichele at Canterbury were shown both robed and magnificent in life, and rotted and cadaverous in death; or a rising tide of optimism and a determination to master nature via medicine and science, leading not just to the rediscovery but to the surpassing of classical knowledge, and hence to the origins of the European Renaissance. Virtually everything, black or white, positive or negative, can and has been traced back from the fifteenth century to the pestilence of the 1340s.

Plus ça change

In the meantime, significantly, little changed, even at the King's court. Far from the pestilence putting an end to the more ambitious schemes of King and nobles, between 1349 and 1357 Henry of Grosmont, Duke of Lancaster and the King's cousin, spent nearly £35,000 rebuilding and decorating his Savoy Palace in the Strand. In July 1349, glaziers moved in to complete the windows in Edward III's own chapel of St Stephen at Westminster, more than twenty of them working there, with glass brought from Shropshire, London and the Kentish Weald, at a total cost of nearly £4,000 on glass, painting, altars and statuary. Death and disease did nothing to curb the King's or the court's appetite for luxury and display, particularly in costume: the £500 spent on a single dress for the Queen to

attend Edward's great annual celebrations on St George's Day,
for example, or the £200 paid by the Black Prince in 1362 for
jewelled buttons for his wife, a price equivalent to more than
ten years of the wages of a master craftsman or esquire. The
war with France dragged on throughout the 1350s, with sufficient money raised and armies recruited to produce the great
victory at Poitiers in 1356. What we see here perhaps is the
extraordinary resilience of mankind. Amidst the plague pits of
the 1340s, as 600 years later amidst the horrors of man-made
genocide, humanity has proved itself more resilient even than
the bacteria that threaten its continued existence.

The Plague Becomes Endemic

The real effects of the pestilence were not felt in its immediate
aftermath. Instead, the Black Death of 1348–9 (a term invented
much later) was merely the harbinger of a more insidious,
endemic pestilence that was to hover on the nightmare edge of
society for centuries to come. The high mortality rate of the
1340s could fairly easily be repaired. Where the young and the
old had died, the survivors, many of them in the prime of life,
could marry and produce children. It was only when plague
returned to claim this next crop of humanity that the real
demographic effects began to be felt. A falling birth rate, rather
than a rising rate of adult mortality, is most likely to lead to a
real decline in population.

Plague was reported across Europe again in 1361–2, and this
time hit lords as well as commoners: nearly one in four of the
English parliamentary peerage died in the course of a single
year. A third epidemic erupted in 1369. Both outbreaks resulted
in a mortality rate in England perhaps as high as one in ten of
the population. Thereafter, its return became cyclical, in 1375,
in 1379 to northern England, to the Midlands in 1381–2, to
East Anglia and Kent in 1383 and 1387, on a national scale
again in 1390, 1399–1400 and 1405–6, and so on throughout the
fifteenth century. The effects upon a population already
stricken by the initial great mortality were beyond doubt to

reduce the human population of England to a level perhaps half of that at which it had stood in 1348, possibly 6 or 7 million, reduced by 1450 to nearer 3 million.

Economic and Social Consequences
The yield of mankind itself fell below even the pathetic levels recorded for sown wheat. Large amounts of land went out of cultivation. The cost of labour and wages rocketed. Food, by contrast, became if not cheaper then more readily obtainable. Green vegetables, fruit and above all meat, beyond the dreams of those who had eked out an existence before the Black Death, were now within the reach of peasant families themselves now able to break free from the restrictions and forced labour services that had previously defined them as 'villeins' or unfree. From the 1350s onwards, bondsmen broke their bonds and the age-old shadow of villeinage melted away from the land. The farm labourers of the nineteenth century portrayed by Thomas Hardy might have lived in squalor or ignorance, but they were free to come and go as they pleased. This would not have been the case for the peasants of the generation before 1340. As in Ireland before and after the famine of the 1840s, a human tragedy left behind survivors whose own living standards and expectations were far greater than those that had gone before.

Edward III's Last Years
It was against this background that the political history of the final years of Edward III was played out: the reopening of Anglo-French hostilities after 1369, the King's decline into ill health and senility, his virtual retirement from all state affairs save for his attendance, at Windsor each year, at the great junketings associated with the Order of the Garter and the feast of St George. In 1375, after a series of military humiliations and following vast expenditure on diplomatic display, a year-long truce was agreed by which, in farcical circumstances and without any thought for the consequences, the English negotiators forced the abandonment of recent gains

in Brittany. The death of the Black Prince in June 1376, after a prolonged period of infirmity, not only deprived government of its most dashing military leader but opened up the question of the succession to the throne. The King's younger son, John of Gaunt, Duke of Lancaster as a result of his marriage to the heiress to Thomas of Lancaster's once vast estate, now emerged as a potential rival to his nephew Richard of Bordeaux, born in 1367, son of the Black Prince, grandson of Edward III. Unflattering comparisons were drawn between the position of John of Gaunt in the 1370s and that of a previous King John of England, younger son of King Henry II, who in 1199 had seized the throne and accomplished the murder of his nephew, Arthur of Brittany. In 1376, John of Gaunt as effective vice-regent was forced to stand by as the so-called 'Good Parliament' took action against the more corrupt ministers of the King, including Edward III's own mistress, Alice Perrers.

Good and Bad Parliaments

For the first time on its own initiative rather than merely as a tool in power struggles within the royal family, Parliament emerged as a political force acting in the common interest against the King's own government. A 'Speaker' was for the first time appointed to represent the Commons. The man chosen for this task, Peter de la Mare, was a member of the affinity of the Earl of March and probably owed his promotion to magnate influence. Even so, the very fact that the Commons elected a spokesman represents their claim to new privileges, independent of the authority of the King or the King's representative in Parliament, John of Gaunt. Ministers henceforth had to work not just to please the King but under the threat of impeachment by Parliament acting as a high court to discipline the executive. As under Henry III or Edward II, the community of the realm, now voiced through Parliament, threatened to subvert the patronage powers of the crown and hence to attack royal authority at its most vulnerable point.

The experiment was short-lived, so short-lived indeed that, had it not served as a precedent for far more radical measures in the seventeenth century, this brief experiment might well have been forgotten. The Good Parliament closed its business in July 1376. By October, the disgraced courtiers had all been pardoned. Peter de la Mare, the Commons' Speaker, was imprisoned at Nottingham Castle. Within six months, John of Gaunt's 'Bad Parliament' of 1377 had revoked virtually all of the measures of 1376. William Langland, in the late 1370s revising his great English prose poem *Piers Plowman*, itself intended as a howl of protest against the iniquities of society, introduced a fable to his new preface in which a parliament of rats advised by mice debates but then fails to implement a scheme to place a bell upon the neighbourhood cat; the cat (for which perhaps read the King or more likely John of Gaunt and aristocratic privilege) is needed, so the mice suggest (themselves perhaps symbolizing the 'Bad Parliament' of 1377), because the community itself can only cohere and survive under the threat of oppression.

Social, Political and Economic Context
Set in a broader context, the reign of Edward III can be seen not, as Langland might have viewed it, as a slow decline into tyranny and corruption despite all attempts at reform, but as yet a further stage on the road levelling the playing field not just between King and aristocracy but between aristocracy, gentry and peasantry. In the Black Death or the wars with France and Scotland, knight and ploughman died alike, whatever the trappings of their funerals or tombs. Death did not discriminate between palace and mud hut, and there is nothing so effective as death to emphasize that rich and poor share a common destiny, however much the rich may wish otherwise. Even without the great pestilence of the 1340s, Edward's ambitions in France far overreached the capacity of his Exchequer to finance his campaigns. Just as in the 1290s Edward I had proceeded from hubris in Wales to nemesis in

Scotland, so now, once again, the greed for glory and dominion threatened thrombosis to a royal administration starved of the blood supply of tax.

Demands for ever higher subsidies to pay for the King's wars merely excited the Commons, the aristocracy and such new phenomena as the self-governing oligarchies of towns or trades to combine in developing means to defy the King. Rhetoric, the writings of John Wycliffe, in which such institutions as the established Church were brought into contempt, was matched to a new willingness by Parliament to take practical steps to control the executive, and it is highly significant that the chief voices calling for restraint both in Church and state, however much they have been orchestrated by courtiers such as John of Gaunt, now came from the lower clergy and from simple laymen. Where we learn most of the evils of the early Plantagenets from monastic chroniclers, from the letters of great churchmen such as Thomas Becket, or from the Bible commentaries of Archbishop Stephen Langton, all of them written in Latin and therefore veiled behind the polite conventions of a learned tongue, by the late fourteenth century we can turn to an entire literature of protest, now expressed in the English vernacular itself distinct from the French of the King's court.

Moreover, the subversion of royal authority continued to gather pace, as the King's dependence upon subsidy and customs duties became habitual. The introduction of customs on wool exports in the 1270s, their raising to unprecedented levels in the 1330s (when the 'maltote' of 40s a sack which Edward I had tried but failed to impose in 1297 became not only accepted but standard), the recognition after the 1290s of Parliament's authority to grant or withhold tax, and the demand, from the 1340s onwards, and again as a result of the French wars, that such taxes be bestowed on a near-annual basis rather than as occasional subsidies to a King in theory expected to live off his own resources in land and the profits of lordship, served initially to gorge the King's executive with cash. But the cash itself was then squandered on foreign adventures whose essential futility merely excited resistance to further taxation.

Warfare was to some extent a joint-stock enterprise between King and aristocracy, with large profits for those who supplied the armies, ransomed the more valuable hostages or seized the most valuable prizes. Even so, the costs of fourteenth-century taxation fell ultimately upon the land and upon that class of peasant farmer or labourer whose silver was demanded by their lords in increasing quantities but who themselves gained least from either taxation or warfare. This was an age before old age pensions, before a 'health service', before the recognition of any public duty to alleviate the effects of poverty or unemployment. The tax 'take' was miniscule compared to that of the modern state, but the profits of taxation were almost exclusively targeted towards the pride, glamour and honour of a King whose subjects gained very little from their sovereign's glory. As in late Soviet Russia, public display and a massive 'defence' budget took priority over all other economic considerations. The 'state' in medieval England, save at times of particular crisis or royal incompetence, remained very much the servant of the King.

By the time of Edward III's death in 1377, the Plantagenets had precious little profit to show for the past forty years of warfare and profligate expenditure in France. The heavier customs duties charged on wool, the decision (motivated in part by a desire to make the garrisoning of Calais a self-financing operation, in part by the selfish interests of those wool merchants working in close cooperation with the court) to establish the Company of the Staple at Calais to tax English exports of wool but to allow foreign merchants to buy wool at English markets and to export it in their own ships untaxed, had already begun insidiously to undermine the taxable profits of an industry which had traditionally defined England as a land of wool and hence of wealth. The Chancellor of England now sat on a woolsack, yet another new symbol of Englishness and of English pre-eminence destined for a long posterity. Meanwhile, in part as a result of demography and the falling population, in part as a result of economic incompetence, the woollen industry itself went into decline.

Rather than export wool at the rates now offered by the Staple in Calais, wool growers turned from foreign markets to the domestic production of cloth. The great trading entrepôts of Flanders and northern France themselves faced economic catastrophe as the cloth industry was transformed from a long-distance into an increasingly localized trade. In the process, the King's profits, both from tax and from customs duties, began themselves to decline. Wool exports fell from an annual average of 32,000 sacks in the decade after 1350 (each sack being measured as twenty-six stones of wool, so comprising a total export of over eleven million pounds of raw wool by weight), to under 24,000 sacks in the 1380s, 14,000 by 1420, sinking thereafter to 9,000 sacks for the thirty years from 1430 to 1460 (just over three million pounds of wool by weight).

By the 1440s, cloth exports had overtaken the export trade in wool. All told, the King's revenues from customs and tax declined from an average £70,000 in the 1360s, to £45,000 by 1400 and less than £30,000 in the decades after 1430. As with the lack of strategic thinking devoted to the wars in France, the central failure to grasp economic realities, or to address the declining revenues of the crown, was to have fateful consequences in the longer term. A government which attacks the basis of its own tax revenues, which fails to protect the industry upon which it relies for its financial survival, which mortgages its future revenues on the international money markets, and which spends the money thus borrowed on futile wars or a display of the state's largesse is heading very rapidly for economic and social disaster. Aquitaine or the kingdom of Castile, the objects upon which were lavished the proceeds of the Edwardian fiscal state of the 1360s and 70s, were as remote from the interests and perceptions of most Englishmen of the fourteenth century as the Falkland Islands or the mud and dust of the Euphrates or the Oxus from those of English taxpayers of a mere recent era.

7

LATE MEDIEVAL ENGLAND

Having sped so far and so fast along the highway of English kingship, it is time to take pause, to switch off the engine for a while and to attend to the new scenery in which we find ourselves. The century from the accession of Edward I to the death of Edward III had witnessed only a brief minority (the period when a king, in this case Edward III, fifteen years old in 1327, was deemed too young to rule), and the death by violence of only one English ruler (Edward II). The century which followed, by contrast, witnessed three minorities (one of them, involving Henry VI, only nine months old at the time of his accession, lasting for nearly sixteen years) and no less than four murdered kings. It is perhaps no coincidence that it is during this period that charges of madness first begin to be levelled against the English royal family. King John had been bad and King Edward II incompetent without any suggestion that either of them was clinically insane. By contrast, after 1377, five of the six immediate successors to Edward III have, at one time or another, been described as mad: Richard II as manically paranoid, Henry IV as a paranoid depressive, Henry V as a religious fanatic, Richard III as a well-educated psychopath and Henry VI (the only one of these kings definitely to have suffered mental breakdown) as the craziest and most catastrophic of them all.

Historians, rather like poachers or policemen, spend a lot of time in stake outs, watching for signs of change at the front doors of history, whilst the real changes are taking place around the back. Traditionally, an explanation for the disasters of the fourteenth and fifteenth centuries has been sought at the top end of society, with the kings, with their 'madness' or incompetence, with the balancing out of resources of king, aristocracy and gentry, and with the effects of endemic warfare, first in France and then, as part of a general breakdown in civil order, in England. Medieval intellectuals had been inclined, from a time long before 1066, to divide society between three orders: those who fought, those who toiled and those who prayed (warriors, peasants and clerks). At the head of these three orders stood the King, God's representative on earth. Lacking any more sophisticated metaphors by which to characterize society, the tendency was always to imagine the various parts of the body politic as representative of the parts of the human body, with the King as the head, the organ of rationality and direction, the warriors and churchmen as the active members discharging the head's commands, and the peasantry as the more brutish bodily parts, the guts and muscle of society. After 1370 or so, the head part of society is generally supposed to have lost its reason, sending the rest of the body politic into near-fatal convulsions.

Those who played chess – a game introduced to England from the more distant regions of Persia and India, highly popular amongst aristocrats of both sexes – might imagine a similarly simplified social structure, in which the qualities and the lifestyles of the 'higher' pieces, knights and bishops amongst them, were played out in quite another dimension from that of the stolid and ultimately dispensable pawns.

Edward III, although he almost certainly did not rape the Countess of Salisbury, quite possibly played chess with her. For those with eyes to see, and no doubt helping to explain why chess itself was so popular amongst an aristocracy never inclined to subservience in its dealings with royalty, the chess King himself was not only outmanoeuvred but frequently outwitted by a much more agile queen. Knights and sometimes even pawns could topple royalty. Like the real kings of late medieval England, the chess-piece king is obliged to move slowly, cautiously and, if he wishes to survive, no longer at the head of his troops but as a venerable figurehead, weighed down by the baggage of administration and tradition.

At least in part in response to the emergence of Parliament as an institutional framework for the display of privilege, by the 1350s the heads of about seventy families in England claimed the right to be individually summoned to Parliament, as earls, barons or bannerets. Such 'lords' increasingly insisted that they constituted an 'estate' with rights, for example to trial by their fellow peers. The peerage itself included the twenty-one English bishops and the fifty or so abbots attending Parliament, these lords 'spiritual' being ranged in Parliament on the King's right-hand side, the lords 'temporal' on the left. Precedence disputes within this group, as to who should sit or dine first, were increasingly common. By 1405, the King's council was required to pronounce on at least three such disputes, between the earls of Warwick and Norfolk, Kent and Arundel, and the lords Beaumont and Grey.

As early as 1337 Edward III had appointed his eldest son 'duke' of Cornwall, introducing to an England previously only familiar with earls, a title perhaps intended to rival the chivalric trappings of France and the empire (and incidentally to distinguish between Edward's son and a former and notorious figure, Piers Gaveston, himself a mere 'earl' of Cornwall). The first non-royal duke, Robert de Vere, duke of Ireland, was created in 1386. There were also promotions as marquess (in 1385) and viscount (in 1440), so that by the late 1440s there were five dukes, two marquesses, nine earls and two viscounts amongst the English peerage.

At the same time, amongst the knighthood, sobriquets emerged to distinguish the full-blown 'knight' from the 'esquire' or the mere 'gentleman'. From 1413, it became a statutory requirement for personal status to be specified in actions at law. There was as much social distinction amongst the pilgrims of Chaucer's *Canterbury Tales* as there would be today in the royal enclosure at Ascot, and the rise in social dignity of a figure such as Chaucer's Franklin, a one-time sheriff and MP, with his baked meats and his house that 'snowed' with food and drink, his diet changing to fit the seasons in accordance with the latest medical advice, straddling the line that divided the lowest grade of gentility from the yeoman farmer below, suggests a society constantly in flux, with merchants, lawyers and minor estate officials all struggling upwards towards social respectability, and with marriage to a rich widow (young heiresses being reserved, save in romantic fiction, for husbands of their own class) being the means by which to rise most quickly.

Amongst that level of the 'lower upper class' where thinking and strategic snobbery cohabit most easily, a world of difference distinguished the gentleman with his hall, his communal dining arrangements and his retinue of servants (a bare minimum of twenty-four, however decrepit or ill-dressed, for the 'greater knighthood, according to the *Liber Niger* of 1471) from the mere yeoman farmer, even though the yeoman might command a far higher annual income and be in the process of buying up what remained of the gentleman's estate. From the fifteenth-century gentry to the world of Jane Austen can seem only a minor imaginative leap, if we swap armour for top boots and allow for a rather less blunt approach to bodily functions. As if to symbolize this continuity, in hundreds of the parish churches of England, the effigies of fourteenth-century knights rub shoulders with the urns and monuments raised to their eighteenth- and nineteenth-century successors. Yet the squirearchy of the fourteenth and fifteenth centuries would itself have found equivalents in the eleventh or twelfth centuries if only we possessed the sources and the sensitivity to probe such continuity. The interests of this 'gentry' class – horses, hunting, games of hazard, command of troops, food and drink, competition with those higher up the pecking order and contempt for those beneath, not least via the deliberate and competitive display of houses and furnishings, almsgiving and charity – have remained constants in English as of human society from the Anglo-Saxons through to very recent times. From the audience of *Beowulf* or the *Chanson de Roland* to the modern readership of *Country Life* or the novels of Jilly Cooper there stretch connections rather stronger than might be supposed.

Without for a moment imaging that the social structures of the fourteenth and fifteenth centuries were any more 'complicated' or 'sophisticated' than the phenomenally rich social fabric of the tenth or the eleventh centuries, it is nonetheless clear, not least as the result of the survival of far more records and documentary evidence, that late medieval society was subject to evolution and change. New and greater fears were articulated against the danger that one class, the aristocracy, might seize power that historically was supposed to be vested in a king working for the common interest of all. There was a diversification of titles and marks of social distinction, last witnessed in the twelfth century, that itself suggests a society in which claims to privilege and deference were being staked with greater vehemence, perhaps precisely because such privilege was coming increasingly under attack. The aristocracy remained a privileged kleptocracy, collecting land, money and the loyalty of men as and where the opportunity arose. But those immediately below the aristocracy – the gentry and knighthood – had acquired a new voice, complaining that the aristocracy were abusing their position to gain undue influence within the localities and to place a stranglehold of 'magnate' influence over English provincial society.

Even here, however, we must beware exaggerating the extent of change. Local government, and the failure of the king and his court to bring good lordship to provincial society already lay behind a lot of the political manifestoes of the thirteenth century, not least behind the baronial 'reform' movement of the 1260s, led by an aristocracy which claimed a controlling interest within the King's affairs precisely because it was capable of articulating the complaints and concerns of the knights and those lower down the social scale. By the 1320s, this aristocratic monopoly over politics, if not broken, had been openly called into question. The *Modus Tenendi Parliamentum*, composed as protest against the regime of Edward II, suggested that the lower clergy and the communal representatives of the shires should rank above the baronage and aristocracy in Parliamentary proceedings. As yet this was an aspiration rather than a reality. The *Modus* itself was composed within the circle of Thomas of Lancaster, to bolster rather than to undermine Thomas' own highly aristocratic cause. Nonetheless, aristocratic privilege was increasingly called into question by a 'gentry' class unconvinced that aristocratic self-interest and the good order of society were compatible goals.

At the same time, the aristocracy was itself challenged not just from below but from above. A great magnate such as Thomas of Lancaster in the north Midlands or Hugh Despenser in the West Country, remained very much a power to himself, able to pack juries and to subvert the King's writ more or less whenever it suited. Yet the lure of the court, and the riches that royal patronage alone could confer, the very fact that, for all his financial difficulties, it was the king who remained sovereign, not merely first amongst equals, with far more wealth and patronage at his disposal than any other magnate, ensured that even the richest of the rich and the most powerful of the local super-magnates continued to focus their attention upon the court and upon the national as opposed to the purely local political scene. There thus developed a significant divide between centre, focussed upon the pursuit of favour and glory at the king's court, and locality, with its essentially provincial concerns.

Ties between the gentry and the court, between periphery and centre, were in theory strengthened by attempts to ensure gentry participation in local government: the emergence of the office of magistrate, associated with the enforcement of royal legislation such as the Statute of Labourers (1351) intended to control wages, or local inquests into crime or public works, against 'trailbastons' or armed gangs, via special commissions 'to hear and complete' ('*oyer et terminer*'). In practice, there was nothing especially novel about such measures. The participation in government of local knights as jurymen and coroners had been a central feature of the legal reforms of the twelfth century, and had been stressed again in Edward I's legislation of the 1280s, commanding the appointment of two constables within each hundred of the shire, to ensure that the locality maintained a proper watch against wrongdoers. As long ago as 1181, Henry II's Assize of Arms, itself merely reiterating Anglo-Saxon, pre-Conquest traditions of defence and watch, had required all freemen with property worth £7 (which would have included the upper levels of the yeomanry, not merely the knights) and all burgesses living within towns to equip themselves with a bare minimum of weaponry – mail coat, iron helmet, spear. Such requirements were regularly repeated thereafter, albeit with archery practice now replacing the skills of the spearman.

Law and disorder

This was a society organized not merely for war but for self-defence, in which the carrying or ownership of lethal weapons was a legal obligation rather than a controversial privilege. Despite the insistence after 1285 that local constables be appointed, and despite Edward III's use of sergeants-at-arms as enforcers of his authority within the counties, there was still nothing remotely like a professional police force to maintain law and order. Nor was lawlessness a new development of the fifteenth century. As early as the 1230s, the pass of Alton in Hampshire had been a notorious haunt of criminal gangs preying upon the trade passing between London, Winchester and the Channel ports. They were still there in the 1260s when they were joined by Adam Gurdun, a local forester and landowner who had sided with Simon de Montfort against the King and thereafter turned outlaw. Gurdun's hideout was stormed by the future King Edward I, with later accounts claiming not only that Edward had met Gurdun in single combat, but that Gurdun's bravery won him Edward's respect and friendship. The story itself is myth (Gurdun was in fact imprisoned and released only after the payment of a stiff ransom), but a myth suggestive of the ambiguous reaction that outlaws could inspire. On the one hand they were a menace to public order. On the other they appeared to cock a snook at laws and law-makers judged harsh and unreasonable.

Criminality had been rife even in the reign of a 'strong' king such as Edward I. Over a five-day period in May 1303, a criminal gang headed by Richard Pudlicott had broken into the vaults under the royal palace at Westminster and made off with treasure initially valued at £100,000 (approaching £1 billion in modern values). The abbot of Westminster and forty-eight of his monks were imprisoned in the Tower of London on suspicion of being accessories to the crime and, although they were subsequently released and Pudlicott himself was hung, this was perhaps the most daring robbery of any king until 1671 when Captain Thomas Blood managed, albeit only for a few minutes, to take possession of the Crown Jewels in the Tower of London, crushing the crown inside his cloak and stuffing the orb into the breeches of an accomplice.

Other more successful gangs flourished in the fourteenth century. One at Ashby Folville in Leicestershire, for example, was led by the local lord, Eustace de Folville, responsible in 1326 for robbing and murdering one of the barons of the

King's Exchequer and six years later for the kidnap and
ransom of a notoriously corrupt royal justice. Another was
the associated gang led by James Coterel, a Derbyshire knight
involved in murder, kidnapping and extortion throughout
the Peak District, yet, despite the outlawry of his associates
and his own attachment for murder in 1331, he was sufficiently well-protected to die officially pardoned in 1351. As
late as the 1370s, Langland's *Piers Plowman*, was insisting
that 'Folville's laws' might be the only means by which the
poor could recover those things wrongfully plundered from
them by the rich.

In the meantime, the establishment of the office of magistrate and the measures taken to involve local lords and knights
in the enforcement of law and order merely entrenched
oligarchic interests, ensuring that, at a local level, within each
region of a twenty-mile radius, political society was dominated
by the half a dozen or so gentry families capable of imposing
deference and obedience upon their inferiors. Such gentry
families might themselves owe allegiance to whichever aristocratic affinity held sway in that particular region or county.

Religion

Across England, meanwhile, in thousands of parish churches
the gentry advertised their own status and privilege through
the building of elaborate tombs for their ancestors, and the
establishment of chantry chapels to pray without cease that
the souls of such ancestors might be released from purgatory
into the eternal rejoicing of heaven. At least 900 such chantries
were established in the fifty years to 1350, and a further 660 in
the fifty years afterwards. Cheaper than the foundation of a
monastery, chantries both emphasized the Church's
monopoly over the rituals and industry of death and helped
to establish private spaces within what in theory was the most
'public' building of each village community, creating walled-
off and physically segregated symbols of gentry or aristocratic privilege. Like today's stretch limo or heavily built

bodyguards, they served as very public advertisements of the desire and ability of the rich to use privacy as a means of achieving exclusivity.

Added to the sense that society was controlled by powerful interests not necessarily devoted to the common good, warfare itself had begun to warp the social fabric. New defences, thicker and more effective town walls, the rash of castles scattered across the landscape, the fact that from the 1280s the kings of England were no longer merely at war within or on the fringes of their own realm but carrying a campaign of outright conquest, first to Wales, then to Scotland and ultimately to France, all of this ensured that war became prolonged and a great deal costlier.

The effect here, above all after Edward I's failure to subdue the Scots, was to instil viciousness and a mentality of revenge amongst the English political elite, whilst at the same time levelling the playing field between King and aristocracy. Where Henry II took a mere eighteen months to suppress rebellion in the 1170s, Edward II struggled for most of his twenty-year reign to establish his own authority over that of his earls. Where William the Conqueror had the resources to engage in near-permanent probing of the Norman frontier with Maine or Brittany, Edward III had to resort to extraordinary measures, and in particular to prolonged negotiations with Parliament and the wool merchants to finance his own far more extensive military operations in France. As a result of their obeisance to the cult of chivalry, itself an organized hypocrisy in which outward splendour and civility masked a reality that was violent and squalid, after 1340, like two rams in the same field, the kings of England and France were obliged, in the name of honour, to pursue aggression to the point of mutual exhaustion or death. At the Battle of Poitiers in 1356, according to the chronicler Geoffrey Baker, men

trampled in their own guts whilst others spat out their teeth...The blood of serfs and princes ran down in one stream to stain the nearby river purple, and with this delicate nectar to frighten the fish.

Chivalry itself was called into question, not merely because of the increasing costs or futility of war, but because new technology threatened to render knighthood itself an obsolete phenomenon.

Technological advances in warfare and professional armies

The great wonder weapon of the twelfth-century, the crossbow, was now outclassed by the English longbow, with its superior range and firing rate. The Italian crossbowmen who fought for the French at Crécy, their weapons already damaged in a thunderstorm, deprived of the coverings of hide (or '*pavisses*') behind which they would normally have sheltered between volleys, were simply cut to pieces by the English archers. But at Crécy too there appeared another weapon, cannon fired with gunpowder, itself an import from China and the Far East. To begin with, these cannon created more noise than destruction. In the longer term, as the technical capacities of cannon improved, no manner of horse or knightly armour could withstand their effects. By the 1430s, hand-held firearms or 'culverins' had joined the armoury of the Hundred Years War, and were already only half as expensive as the larger steel crossbows with their costly cranking mechanisms. John Payntour, an esquire killed by a culverin shot at La Réole in 1442 was perhaps the first Englishman shot dead with a handgun. Already, four years earlier, cannon had claimed their first royal victim when Don Pedro, brother of the King of Castile, was decapitated during the siege of Capuana near Naples. With warfare an increasingly brutal and deadly business and with new technology rendering old methods absurdly ineffective, it has been suggested that even the 'very perfect gentle knight' of Geoffrey Chaucer's *Canterbury Tales* was intended as satire: the battles in which Chaucer lists his particular knight as having engaged included some of the more notorious of fourteenth-century massacres. The age-old certainties of muscle, iron and horse-flesh inherited from the Roman and classical past were being consigned to redundancy. The five centuries from Crécy in the 1340s to the Crimea in the 1850s marked the slow but inevitable death agony of the principles of aristocratic leadership in war.

New professional armies required new professional means of recruitment. The King's armies were no longer raised on the basis of feudal service, of knights' fees owed to a 'feudal' lord, but became fully monetarized and professionalized, even amongst the cavalry where the old 'feudal' levies were now replaced with knights serving for wages rather than personal obligation to their lords. With this came the introduction of indentures, a new instrument, in essence a two-part contract, one half kept by the recruiter, the other by the recruited, by which the captains of an army or greater lords raised retinues of knights or sergeants serving for a fixed number of months or years for fixed financial reward, in the ultimate extreme, in peace or war and for an entire lifetime of service. 'Feudalism' itself became a redundant concept, at best a shadowy series of tax obligations that themselves now spoke of an increasingly monetarized economy.

As a halfway house between feudalism and capitalism, historians of a Marxist tendency have striven to imagine a society of 'bastard feudalism', introduced from the 1280s onwards, in which chivalry and knighthood rubbed shoulders uneasily with mercenary warfare and the cash nexus. Like a lot of Marxist imaginings, this one too has proved a chimera. Money had always been fundamental to the feudal contract: there were mercenaries in the army of William the Conqueror, and in the twelfth century probably more knights served the King for cash than were ever rewarded with land. William Marshal, himself the embodiment of the feudal ideal, complained vociferously in the 1180s that his wages were insufficient, and was supported in his conquests in Leinster and on the battlefield of Lincoln by a military following (fifteenth-century historians, using a new term for an old concept, would call it an 'affinity' or 'retinue') only a couple of dozen of whom were recruited because they held land from the Marshal estates, most of them serving for hard cash and in effect for life, not just as knights but as administrators, counsellors and friends in all of the later functions that are attributed to the affinities of 'bastard feudalism'.

In the thirteenth century, it is true, grants of land were increasingly restricted and policed, in part because of the fear that knights rewarded with land, like other servants granted land rather than money, became possessed of the means of freeing themselves from the very obligations of service which such land was intended to reward. The tendency was towards contracts for shorter terms and for pay or other material rewards, away from grants of land in theory made in perpetuity to bind not just the grantees but their heirs and successors. Nonetheless, warfare, or at least the claim to command men in battle, remained both an obligation and a badge of pride amongst the upper classes. Chaucer's knight may have been intended as a figure of satire, or perhaps merely as a gentle mockery of the crusading warrior in an age of failed crusades. In either case, he continues to rank at the very head of Chaucer's band of pilgrims. Amongst the 'rising' families of the fifteenth century, knighthood remained an essential first step on the social ladder upwards.

Snakes and ladders: social mobility

A very few examples must suffice. William de la Pole began his career after 1310 as a wine merchant of entirely unknown parentage, trading out of Hull. At a time when the royal household was consuming the annual equivalent of 600,000 bottles of wine, for the most part imported from Gascony, through Bordeaux, William's connection with the court wine trade led to his rise within the government of Hull, then at court as chief butler from 1327. A wealthy man at a court starved of credit, William began to advance loans to the crown, at high rates of interest. This in turn encouraged other merchants, in both wool and wine, to channel their own lending activities via the de la Pole firm, so that by the 1350s William was in effect acting as chief middle man between the English mercantile community and the crown, lending sums of over £100,000 in the opening years of the war with France. Through dealings that were distinctly shady, and despite two attempts by Edward III to rein in his profiteering under the threat of impeachment, William became an indispensable agent of crown finance. His brother was knighted in 1340, and William himself was summoned as a baronet to Parliament in 1339. Having wriggled free from charges of forgery and embezzlement that might have made a Robert Maxwell blush, and having bought up a great collection of manors, especially associated with the wool trade of the North Riding of Yorkshire, he lived just long enough to see his son, Michael de la Pole, summoned as a peer to the Parliament of 1366.

Michael de la Pole, knighted in 1353, married a Suffolk heiress and, via the affinity of Edward III's son John of Gaunt Duke of Lancaster, entered the service of Richard II, assisting in the negotiation of the King's marriage. Chancellor in 1383, created Earl of Suffolk two years later, he was impeached on charges of mishandling public funds and eventually forced to flee abroad, attempting to enter Calais with his head and beard shaved, disguised as a Flemish poulterer with a basket of capons under one arm. He died in Paris in 1389, but his lands and his earldom were restored to his eldest son, Michael, the second earl who, perhaps not surprisingly, kept out of the orbit of the court, concentrating instead upon the creation of a regional power network based around Hull and his father's estate at Wingfield in Suffolk, where a moated castle and a chantry college were built as symbols of family power. The second earl died of dysentery during the siege of Harfleur in 1415, followed shortly by his eldest son, another Michael, who was killed fighting at Agincourt. The earldom thus passed to a younger son, William de la Pole, admitted as a Knight of the Garter in 1421 (the Nobel prize of late-medieval social climbing) and in

1448 created first Duke of Suffolk, amongst the greatest and most controversial figures in the politics of Henry VI's reign, eventually beheaded in 1450. By a marriage between the first duke's son and a sister of the Duke of York, the de la Poles were brought, in six generations and only 160 years from the obscurity of a wine merchant's business, to within grasping distance of the crown. John de la Pole, grandson of the first duke, was recognized in the 1480s, informally, as heir to King Richard III. If King Richard had not been killed at the Battle of Bosworth, it is at least conceivable that the great-great-grandson of a Hull wine merchant might have ascended the English throne.

The de la Poles were the most spectacularly successful of all the nouveaux-riches of late medieval England. Nonetheless, albeit on a more modest scale, there were plenty of other families that could claim to have risen from invisibility to riches within only two or three generations. Like the de la Poles at Wingfield, Sir Edward Dallyngrigge, scion of a minor dynasty of knights from Dalling Ridge, near East Grinstead, sank the profits of his service in the French wars into a moated manor house that had come to him by marriage to a local widow. There, at Bodiam in Sussex in the 1380s, he built one of the greatest fairytale castles in England, complete with moat and drawbridge, with all of the requisite battlements and turrets. Ostensibly, Bodiam was intended to assist the county's defence against the threat of a French invasion. In reality, it lay more than ten miles inland, a mere shell with no keep and little prospect of defence in wartime. This was knighthood and chivalry displayed after the manner of Walt Disney, still as gorgeous and as utterly impractical today as it must have seemed to Sir Edward Dallyngrigge's successor who, in 1641, at the height of the English Civil War, preferred to sell the castle as building stone rather than take any steps for its fortification.

On the opposite side of the Kentish Weald to Bodiam, John Pulteney, of obscure Leicestershire parentage, rose via the trade in wine and wool to become one of the King's principal suppliers of the equipment of war. Knighted in 1337, mayor of London on four occasions during the same decade, he built a manor house at Penshurst, whose great hall still forms the nucleus of Penshurst Place, later home to Sir Philip Sidney, the author in 1580 of the *Arcadia*, one of the greatest celebrations of English pastoral, in which the fluting of shepherds and shepherdesses mingles with the clash of knights in tournament. Much that is most beautiful and apparently timeless in the English countryside is in fact the creation of men like Pulteney, tied to the counting house: profiteers, arms dealers and worse. A contemporary of John Pulteney, from a family that had imported wine via Ipswich, had established himself by the 1330s as a vintner or wine seller in Thames Street, in London's Vintry ward. His name was John Chaucer, and his son, Geoffrey, was destined to become a poet even more famous than Sir Philip Sidney.

Pulteney himself died during the Black Death of 1349. At about the same time, in Gloucestershire, the wife of William Whittington of Pauntley gave birth to a third son, christened Richard who took to the mercer's trade, dealing in silk, linen and luxury small goods. By the 1380s, Richard was one of the principal suppliers to the royal court, with an annual turnover of more than £1,000 and with the wealth and contacts, like William de la Pole before him, to begin advancing loans to courtiers and ultimately to the King. Like John Pulteney in the 1330s, Richard Whittington rose to become three-times mayor of London, ducking and weaving his way around the political turmoil of the 1390s. Having no children, Whittington became one of the greatest sponsors of the charities of fifteenth-century London, transforming the church St Michael Paternoster into a college and almshouse. He also contributed to the building of libraries at Greyfriars and Guildhall, to the costs of installing fountains in the City (by this stage already a place of piped water, with strict regulations against the pollution of what remained of the city's rivers by such noxious trades as tanning or butchery), and at St

Martin Vintry to the construction of a longhouse combining a public lavatory and almshouse, which today might be accounted a rather peculiar arrangement, but which once again was intended to reduce the health hazards associated with a teaming and still expanding urban population.

With almost Victorian foresight, Whittington's philanthropy neglected neither books nor sewage. Again, like the Victorians, he liked to see a prison decently kept. Newgate Gaol was rebuilt with part of the £7,000 that he bequeathed by his will.

Bells, bullets and cannons

Whether or not he owned a cat, and although his social origins were rather grander than the pantomime legend allows, the real Dick Whittington undoubtedly spent a large part of his life within earshot of the bells of St-Mary-le-Bow off Cheapside, the glorious thunder of brass bells being yet another of those means by which the late medieval Church sought to advertise its services and its authority. The oldest certainly dated church bell in England, from 1254, is preserved at Lissett near Bridlington, although the bell at St Botolph at Hardham in Sussex perhaps dates from only a few years after the Norman Conquest. The London bell-maker, Richard of Wimbish, at work in the reign of Edward II, and whose products would have sounded out across the city of Richard Whittington, was so well regarded that at least seven of his bells still survive to be rung today in parish churches from Devon to Kent and from Oxfordshire to Suffolk. We know this because, like some glass-painters and a few of the more exceptional masons and skilled artisans, Wimbish 'signed' his work. From the ranks of anonymous labour, the artist had been born.

It was the technical skills of English bell-makers, with their ability to cast large quantities of bronze, that lay behind subsequent improvement to the cannon employed by English armies in the Hundred Years War. These new heavy bells had to be hung in a wooden 'belfry', itself a word first employed in English in the thirteenth century, derived from the French '*berfroi*', a moveable wooden siege tower. The Chinese had invented gunpowder, but it was left to European bell-makers to combine the skills of the chemist with those of the metalworker and in the process almost literally to sound the death knoll of medieval knighthood. The 'brasses' with which fourteenth- and fifteenth-century gentry families chose to memorialize themselves in the parish churches of England were yet another by-product of the ascendancy of English metalwork.

The Pastons

The De la Poles, John Pulteney, Richard Whittington, even Richard of Wimbish the bell-maker, all grew wealthy through trade. The professions were another means by which men might rise. The Paston family, ultimately (from the 1670s) earls of Yarmouth, first emerges into the light of day in the opening decades of the fifteenth century, when William, son and heir to Clement Paston, a 'good plain husbondman' of Paston in Norfolk, obtained education at the local grammar school and then at the London Inns of Court, in effect England's third university after Oxford and Cambridge. A successful career in the law culminated with his appointment as a justice of common pleas, and led to prestigious marriages, for himself and for his eldest son, John Paston, betrothed to the heiress to nine Norfolk and Suffolk manors. Via his wife's family, John Paston, himself educated at Cambridge, entered the circle of Sir John Fastolf of Caister, a former member of the affinity of Michael de la Pole, Earl of Suffolk and a veteran of the wars with France in which Fastolf, like Sir Edward Dallyngrigge of Bodiam, had greatly prospered.

We know so much of the Pastons, of their rise, of the attempts by John Paston, after 1459, to dispute the will of John Fastolf, of the consequent scattering of the Fastolf fortune (a lot of it to Bishop Waynflete of Winchester, and thence to Waynflete's foundation at Magdalen College Oxford) and of the ultimate success of John Paston's sons who took up arms against Edward IV but who nonetheless made their peace with the Yorkist regime, because the family archive has survived: more than 800 letters to and from the Pastons, covering the years between 1420 and 1500. These 'Paston Letters' supply extraordinary insight into fifteenth-century attitudes. They are generally described as a 'unique' resource. In reality, an almost equally large and informative collection of letters, with an even broader coverage of the attitudes and alliances of the great, already survives from the early thirteenth century, from the correspondence of Bishop Ralph Neville of Chichester, chancellor under Henry III. What distinguishes the Paston letters from the Neville archive, apart from fact that the Neville letters have never been treated or published as a unified collection, is not so much their contents as their language. Both sets of correspondence describe local and national goings on, gossip, the gathering of intelligence for the furtherance of schemes to acquire or dispose of land. Neville's exclusively male correspondents wrote in Latin, in elegant clichés that read awkwardly and impersonally when translated into modern English. The Pastons, by contrast, both men and women, wrote in a bold demotic English that can shock by its intimacy and its almost contemporary ring.

A mere accident of language has rendered one set of letters dull and apparently archaic, another vivid and seemingly 'modern'. It is questionable whether anything much more profound than this divides the fifteenth century from earlier periods. Between the gangs of warriors established around the great men of eleventh-century Normandy or the affinity of Sir John Fastolf in the wars of fifteenth-century France, there are as many points of similarity as of distinction. The fortune-hunting crusaders of the twelfth and thirteenth centuries, or the alien constables seeking service under King John were in many ways forerunners of the mercenary captains and 'routiers' of the Black Prince, or the great privateers such as Sir John Hawkwood, leading their *chevauchées* of pillage and terror across fourteenth-century France or Italy.

Maintenance and Livery Badges

'Maintenance', the buying up of a locality, its gentry and its agencies of law-enforcement by one particular magnate or courtier became a major source of complaint from the fourteenth-century onwards, with petitions regularly addressed to Parliament against such practices. With maintenance came the bestowal of livery badges – symbols of lordship worn by those retained by a particular lord – which themselves provoked outrage and came to symbolize the worst abuses of maintenance. Yet maintenance and badge-wearing were hardly radical innovations. Magnates, as early as the thirteenth century in the case of a William Marshal in Wiltshire or Berkshire, or a Richard of Cornwall in the south-west, had been very much powers unto themselves able, when it suited them, to subvert the King's writ. In extremes, such men had to go into exile, as was the case for William Marshal after 1208, to avoid the full consequences of royal wrath. But even in the darkest decades of the fifteenth century, when royal authority was supposedly at its lowest ebb, political dissidents such as Richard of York did not consider themselves immune from the vengeful attentions of the crown. Richard of York in the 1450s, like William Marshal long before him, instead used Ireland as a base from which to relaunch himself into English affairs. Some 200 years before Marshal and 400 years before Richard of York, in the political crisis of the 1050s, Harold Godwinson had done precisely the same thing.

Heraldry and the wearing of devices were a great deal more ancient than the introduction of livery badges to the houses of Lancaster or York. Metal badges had been worn by pilgrims, marked with the signs and symbols of St Thomas of Canterbury or St James of Compostela, long before they were appropriated as props of secular power. Tradesmen and artisans were already organizing themselves into guilds by the 1150s. By 1350, in London alone there were at least twenty such craft guilds or livery companies, some of them such as the Merchant Taylors or Goldsmiths already in possession of their own guildhalls, each with its distinctive badges, symbols and 'livery' of membership and its attachment to the cult of one or two particular saints: Joseph (and Noah) for the carpenters, St Peter (that great fisher of men) for the fishmongers, and so forth.

Moreover, it would be folly to suppose that attachment to the affinity of one particular lord was the only means by which the identity of lesser men was expressed: in reality, society was onion-layered. The historians who have written on bastard feudalism have for the most part been academics, surrounded by their own coteries of pupils and admirers, convinced that patronage and deference are closed systems which, once established, abide for life. Retaining, according to this model, reduced those retained to the status of worshippers, unthinking acolytes of the Communist party, or house-elves in the following of Lucius Malfoy. In reality, as the disobedience or disgruntlement of many house-elves (or pupils) surely indicates, affinities are more volatile than this.

At any particular crisis, attachment to nation, to locality, to trade, to lord, to religious sentiment, to family, to fraternity or caste, or even the desire to 'go it alone', might take precedence over other considerations. The tendency to suppose that because a man was retained for life, in peace and in war, in the household of a particular lord he necessarily became a mere automaton obedient to that lord's will in all things is a tendency to be resisted. Just as the uncertain loyalties of the Anglo-Norman baronage after 1066 had been keenly sought, with knights rendering homage to a variety of lords even though their principal allegiance might lie elsewhere, so, four centuries later, the loyalty of one's inferiors had not only to be purchased but maintained, often in the face of stiff competition from other equally attractive poles of influence or reward, not least in the face of competition from the King.

If maintenance and the buying up of affinities were by no means new phenomenon, then the fifteenth century has nonetheless been presented by historians as a period of rapid social change. Social mobility is a difficult phenomenon to quantify, but recent estimates place the total acreage of land changing hands on the property market at well over 80 per cent in a county such as Warwickshire over the period 1350–1520, or two-thirds of the knights' fees in Nottinghamshire over the course of merely three generations, a volatility which reflects the fall of old men and the rise of new on a scale normally associated with such supposed periods of social 'crisis' as the 1560s or the 1620s. Yet the thirteenth century had already seen the transfer of manors and knights' fees on a very considerable scale, the rise of new men and the fall of old. 'New men' were themselves the target of criticism as early as the 1120s, amongst chroniclers whose immediate forebears had witnessed the greatest upheaval ever recorded in English history: the Norman Conquest after 1066, and the eruption into English society of hundreds if not thousands of landowners whose ancestors could certainly have rivalled the Pastons or the de la Poles in the lowliness of their origins.

Perhaps the truth is that society is always in a state of crisis and change. Whether there was anything quantifiably different about the rise of the fourteenth- and fifteenth-century gentry, as opposed to the crisis between Normans and Englishmen after 1066, or between courtiers and county elite in the centuries either side of 1250, should not be allowed to obscure the greater evidence for continuity. In 1450, England was still an essentially rural society, with more than 90 per cent of its population established outside towns, with one or two per cent, constituting the politically active classes, relying upon agriculture and the land for the majority of their wealth. The sense that the social fabric was being entirely rewoven and that such concepts as aristocracy or deference were no longer benign necessities, was articulated in a new vernacular literature either championing or challenging the status quo, which in itself suggests unease and in particular that old patterns were being replaced by new. Similar sentiments had been voiced in the twelfth century, albeit in Latin rarely read by historians of the fifteenth century. Such sentiments are still voiced today, not least in the national newspapers, without anyone necessarily believing that society stands on the edge of a bottomless precipice of revolution and social unrest.

Liaisons dangereux

The great irony here is that the reign of Edward III witnessed not just the diversification of distinctions between the various orders of society but the first open recognition, at least since the time of Herleva, the mother of William the Conqueror, that the King himself might take a lower-status mistress and treat her as his wife. Edward III began a liaison with Alice Perrers in the mid-1360s, some years before the death of his queen, Philippa of Hainault, in whose household Alice had previously served. Alice herself was probably the daughter of a minor Hertfordshire knight, though hostile chroniclers claimed that her father was nothing more than a weaver or even a thatcher of other people's roofs. Like a later Thatcher of the 1980s, herself regarded as low-born and tarnished by too close an association with trade, Alice proved a ruthless and successful operator, loathed with irrational fury by her critics. In 1375, by which time he was perhaps going more than slightly ga-ga, Edward III held a tournament at Smithfield in which Alice was exhibited to Londoners as the Lady of the Sun, hardly the most appropriate disguise for a low-born courtesan. In Langland's *Piers Plowman*, by contrast, she appears as Lady Meed, the embodiment of avaricious worldliness.

Ironically, her downfall after the King's death in 1377 was masterminded by Edward III's son John of Gaunt, who by this time had himself entered into a liaison, subsequently a marriage, with a low-born member of his household, Katherine Swynford, daughter of a Flemish herald. Katherine bore John four children before their marriage was solemnized in 1396. These children, the Beauforts, became leading political players through to the 1450s, and it was a direct descendant, Katherine Swynford's great-granddaughter Lady Margaret Beaufort, who transmitted the royal bloodline to Henry Tudor. Tudor himself was the grandson of a secret marriage between a low-born Welshman (without even a surname to advertise his gentility) and Catherine of Valois, daughter of King Charles VI of France, widow of King Henry V of England and mother of King Henry VI.

Another member of the royal family, Joan, from 1361 the wife of Edward III's eldest son, Edward the Black Prince, and mother of the future King Richard II, herself a granddaughter of Edward I and the cousin of Edward III, had been secretly married in her youth to Thomas Holland, a minor knight of the royal household. The complications that arose here, when Joan married for a second time, potentially bigamously, to the Earl of Salisbury, when Holland became steward to Joan and her new husband, and when, using the profits of ransoms taken in the Crécy campaign, Holland launched a successful attempt to reclaim his wife by litigation at the papal court, almost beggar belief. They certainly rendered Joan, the 'Fair Maid of Kent', as scandalous a partner as any other selected by a future heir to the throne. The fact that all three of her husbands were amongst the knights of the Order of the Garter, newly appointed after 1346 (Joan's husbands making up no less than twelve per cent of the Order's original membership), is a remarkable indication of Joan's charms. At the same time, it supplies yet another hint that the chivalry of Edward III's court, and even his order of knighthood intended to be the most exclusive and chivalrous in Christendom, masked a rather seamier human reality.

Edward III might be said to have been the first king in English history successfully to have played upon the image of a royal 'family', refashioning the dysfunctional Plantagenet brood of the twelfth or thirteenth centuries into one whose members acted together in peace and love. In the 1380s, a decade after his death, miniature gilt images of twelve of his children were placed around Edward III's tomb chest at Westminster Abbey, complete with their heraldic arms, symbolizing harmony within the Plantagenet family as the embodiment of age-old national virtues. Yet, as with more recent attempts to broadcast such virtue amongst the houses of Windsor or Saxe-Coburg-Gotha, this was also a family whose liaisons, both outside marriage and outside social class, raised many an eyebrow.

Their kinship to such clans as the Beauforts, the Hollands or the Tudors, all rewarded with earldoms or dukedoms, was to bring the kings of England into potentially dangerous proximity to the English upper classes, themselves about to embark upon an unprecedented orgy of self-slaughter. It even threatened to establish cousinhood between the descendants of William the Conqueror and a mere English scribbler and composer of light verse: Geoffrey Chaucer, married to Philippa, the sister of Katherine Swynford, became uncle by marriage not only to an earl and a cardinal but to a future King of England, Katherine Swynford's step-son, Henry IV.

There is one other consequence of these liaisons. As anyone who has made sense, or indeed failed to make sense, of the horrendous catalogue of cousinhood and kinship set out above will surely realize, historians of the fifteenth century are sometimes so busy compiling family trees, recalling the details of family alliances and attempting to make sense of the relations between second or third cousins that they forget either that they have readers to entertain or that their readers are unlikely, unless deranged or highly peculiar, to enter into these questions of kinship with quite the same degree of enthusiasm that they inspire amongst the experts. The snobbery with violence that constitutes fifteenth-century history can all too easily devolve into the worst sort of genealogical train-spotting, with John of Gaunt or Edmund Somerset cast in the role of the Flying Scotsman or the LMS Stanier Class 5 4-6-0 with (or without) exterior Caprotti valve gear.

Peasants

Perhaps, in our search for the real signs of change in society after 1350 we need to look not so much to the royal family, to the aristocracy or to the politically active gentry, but to a class thus far consigned to the role of a mere chorus in history: the peasantry, who tilled the land, bore the brunt of taxation and who, throughout the fourteenth century had died from a variety of pestilences and natural or human disasters in anonymous and unquantifiable droves. Peasants in the Middle Ages have names, but rarely any more rounded identity. Peasant surnames, which develop earlier in England than elsewhere in Europe, themselves are a consequence of subservience rather than liberty, since they come to us chiefly from the rich sources recording taxation and justice imposed by kings and other lords. Collectively, peasant lives revolved around the great open fields cultivated on the edge of the village, assessed as so many plough-lands (bovates or virgates), divided into strips over which there was near permanent dispute. Some 90 per cent of peasant homicides took place in these fields or on the paths and roads that divided them, very often as a result of boundary disputes.

The peasant home, although a comparatively safe place, was very far from being a luxurious one. The old idea, favoured by historians who wished to see a dramatic and disastrous collapse in family values as a result of the rise of capitalism, was that peasants inhabited houses themselves generations old, in which large, extended families of uncles, aunts and cousins lived side by side. In reality, the house was a short-lived structure, built of wood and mud, its clay floor regularly swept and cleaned. A hole in the thatch allowed some (but one suspects never enough) of the smoke to escape. Such homes were intended to last a single generation, twenty years or so, before being razed and rebuilt.

There was a clear distinction here between peasant modes of life and the 'big houses' of urban merchants, the gentry or the aristocracy, often constructed of stone and intended to last. The gentry house revolved around its communal dining and its entourage of servants and dependents. Service, either to a great landowner, as a domestic retainer in a gentry house, as a retained labourer, or as the humblest of maids or menials in a yeoman farmhouse was one of the underlying pillars of English society. From at least the time of Beowulf through to the First World War, an extraordinary proportion of the population lived as servants in other people's houses. By contrast, the peasant hut was reserved for a nuclear family, for the most part merely parents and children, living in close proximity to their livestock.

There were hazards to such an existence. Smoke and dust inflamed eyes already weakened by a diet of cereals from which vitamin A was notably lacking. The straw used for bedding and floor-covering provided an ideal breeding ground for fleas. Zoonotic diseases (those shared with or spread by animals) were unavoidable: internal parasites, ringworm, whipworm and tapeworm were transmitted from the faecal matter of domestic animals. Sheep scattered ticks. Bovine tuberculosis was acquired through the ingestion of infected meat or milk, and in its glandular form, as 'scrofula' or the 'king's evil', was reputed to be treatable only through the touch of a king: by the reign of Edward I, as many as 1,000 sufferers, for the most part peasants, were queuing up each year at the royal court in order to be cured.

Modern health and safety officers would have been appalled by communal ovens (into which children could all too easily climb for warmth), wells and outside latrines (into which the unwary could tumble), and ponds (in which they could drown, especially at night, which was unlit save by moon and stars and, in modern terms, eerily quiet). Most collections of miracle stories of the English saints will include at least one or two instances of children who strayed too near building sites or mills. The King himself was occasionally called upon to exercise mercy by pardoning homicides accidentally committed by peasants, as for example on behalf of Katherine Passeavant, aged four, in 1249 imprisoned in the abbot of St Albans' gaol because, opening a door, she had accidentally knocked a younger child into a cauldron of hot water from which injury the child had died. To judge from coroners' records, nearly half of the fatal accidents that befell adult males involved carting or transport. Hernias (from heavy lifting) were common, and osteoarthritis, aggravated by cold and damp working conditions, has been diagnosed in as many as half of the skeletal remains of those involved in manual labour.

The medieval equivalent of the tractor, the ox-cart or handcart, essential to harvesting and to the gathering of timber for fuel, was a dangerous and lumbering piece of equipment from which it was easy to fall, and under which it was all too easy to be crushed. With ale brewed from malted barley drunk in preference to water, available in almost unlimited quantities to those working the lord's land, drunkenness was frequent and affected both men and women. Even so, and by contrast with the Russian peasantry of the nineteenth century described by Maxim Gorky, violence within such communities tended to be accidental and occasional rather than deliberate and habitual.

The disciplining of wives by husbands was advocated as a necessary duty: 'For he that fails to beat his wife, will never wear the britches the rest of his life'. Chaucer's Wife of Bath, from a class somewhere between yeomanry and gentry, married for the fifth time to a much younger husband, dared tear out a page from a book that he was reading her about the wiles and wickedness of women. The husband struck her such a blow that she was permanently deafened. She, however, responded in kind, and there can be little doubt who it was in that particular household that henceforth wore the britches. In illustrations of peasant life, most famously in the Luttrell Psalter (made c.1340 for Geoffrey Luttrell of Irnham in Lincolnshire, and intended to emphasize the exalted but benign nature of his lordship), it is more often women who are shown chastising their husbands than men who are shown beating their wives. Women undoubtedly worked as hard if not harder than men, in the home, in the fields and in such tasks as brewing or spinning which were considered specifically female occupations. The husband-beater of the Luttrell Psalter wields a large broom that is itself perhaps an ale stake, the symbol stuck from the eaves of a house to indicate beer for sale. The English 'pub', often regarded as a traditionally male enclave only recently invaded by women, began its existence as the village alehouse, recorded from at least the thirteenth century. Generally, as in rural Ireland, it was a peasant home rather than a purpose-built tavern or inn, run by a female ale wife and supplied with ale, often as thick and cloudy as fermented bread, that she herself had brewed.

Within this world, there was a vast distinction to be drawn between the poorest labourers, barely able to support them-selves, and the richer peasants, already, before the Black Death, accustomed to those habits of thrift and hard work which ensured their status as property-owners, able to save money and to lend it to their neighbours in return for favours or profit. In the Middle Ages, we are told, work was generally ineffi-cient, small-scale and task orientated rather than determined according to time. In reality, the modern work ethic is by no means as modern as might be supposed. The very fact that the Church found it necessary to insist that everyone cease work on the Sabbath and on a series of the greater Church festivals (about twenty days in all during the course of the liturgical year), suggests that it was necessary to compel medieval peasants *not* to work. Manorial by-laws suggest that there were time restrictions and curfews, by the 1450s by clock hours, imposed on labour. Our first knowledge of the existence of alehouses comes from the 1190s, precisely because certain people, above all the clergy, were prohibited from entering them. Langland's Piers Plowman was beset by 'wasters' who preferred singing songs to tilling the land, but Piers, who owned his own equipment and draft animals, was himself clearly a successful and hardworking kulak. The Luttrell Psalter is as full of illustrations of peasant hard labour as it is of peasants wrestling, setting dogs on a tinker, bear-baiting, or engaged in other 'leisure-time' activities. Even the shepherds' flutes shown in the Psalter have a utilitarian purpose, not just to wile away the time in Arcadian sloth, but to summon their sheepdogs to their work.

Throughout history, from the eleventh century to the fourteenth, a large proportion of the peasantry was regarded as human property: a brood of animals belonging to their manorial lord. Heriot (the obligation by a peasant, when his lord died, to hand over the peasant's best beast as a token that all his property belonged to the lord's successor), merchet (the obligation to pay a fine on the marriage of a daughter, in essence because such women and their progeny were now removed from the lord's labour force), legerwite (a fine payable when such girls were deflowered, with or without marriage), boon work in cultivating the lord's land without recompense as a natural consequence of the privilege of cultivating one's own few strips of field: all of these marked out the peasant as unfree, unable to leave his servitude, unprotected by a large part of the law by which the freeman's status was affirmed. The voice of the peasants themselves is first heard filtered through clerical spokesmen, through demands that the great do justice to their dependents and succour the hungry and the weak. From around 1300, a tradition of vernacular poetry emerged in which the sufferings of the poor take a particularly prominent place. This is poetry written by clergymen merely pretending to speak in the accents of the peasantry. Nonetheless, there is no reason to doubt the sincerity of the indignation that it expressed. Such protests increased beyond measure as a result of the famine and pestilence after 1315. The so-called *Song of the Husbondman* (and we might remember here that Clement Paston, ancestor of the Pastons of Caister, was himself by origin described as nothing more than a 'husbondman') laments, *c.*1320, a brutal existence, in which the peasant and his wife, her bleeding feet wrapped in rags, drive the plough whilst their baby lies in a basin at the end of the field and two other infants howl from cold and hunger.

Before the fourteenth century, peasants played little role in English politics, although King Henry I is said to have dreamed, as early as the 1120s, of three angry peasants threatening him with a spade, a pitchfork and a scythe. As illustrated in John of Worcester's *Chronicle*, for the peasants of Henry's dream already to be carrying either a tax demand or a parchment schedule of their grievances is a portent of many such manifestos of reform yet to come. Henry II was occasionally approached by peasants (in the sources generally referred to as 'rustics') offering advice or prophesying doom. On one occasion, riding with his court, he was addressed in English by such a man who warned the King to pay greater respect to the Sabbath. Rather than reply in person, the King turned to one of his knights and, in French, told him to deal with 'that rustic'. In the 1260s, during the turmoil of baronial rebellion against Henry III, peasants had become mixed up in the violence, on occasion claiming to act in the interests of the 'community of the realm', a highly significant concept that sought to join King, barons and peasantry into a single, indivisible and English political cooperative, committed to the welfare of the many rather than the few. For the most part, however, when peasant violence erupted it was incoherent, sudden and directed against particular injustices or individuals.

As early as the 1220s, all but four of the peasants of the village of Sandford in Somerset had attacked their lord, Nicholas de Arundell, chasing him through the town to the church whose chaplain slammed the door in his face. The peasants then killed Nicholas, carrying his body to his house, which was set on fire in the hope that it might be supposed he had died by accident. Fifteen men and women were drawn and hung for this offence. Six others fled and were outlawed. In 1303, Archbishop Winchelsea's local representative at the manor of Selling in Kent was set upon by villagers who

> threw him into filthy mud, and with his face turned to his horse's tail, holding the tail in his hand instead of the bridle, led him with songs and dances through the middle of the village.

They afterwards cut off the tail, ears and lips of the horse, mutilation of a lord's animals and in particular of his horses, one of the greatest symbols of lordly privilege, being a popular means by which the poor could vent their fury against the rich. In the same year, Henry Bobbe of Lower Caldecote in Bedfordshire, having hung a local felon, was set upon by peasants and stabbed in the chest with a fork. But these were unconcerted expressions of rage or contempt, of little political significance.

Only in the towns were there serious outbreaks of political violence: at London in the 1190s, when a movement gathered around William fitz Osbert, known as William Longbeard, claiming to represent the interests of the poor against the rich city oligarchy; again in London in the 1220s, when civil unrest had brutally to be suppressed; at Norwich and Winchester in the 1270s when Norwich Cathedral and one of the gates of Winchester were burned down in civic riots inspired by anti-monastic feeling; at Bury St Edmunds, in the 1320s, and at Canterbury in 1343, when the townspeople are said to have attacked the prior's house, stealing forty horses and assaulting his men and servants. After the 1340s, something of this previously urban spirit of resistance leaped the city walls into the countryside. The peasant, the labourer, the skilled artisan, gradually began to impinge upon the concerns of a royal government convinced that the poor were growing rich at the expense of their social superiors and that government itself was starved of revenue through the refusal of the new-rich to pay tax.

The labour shortage and the consequent rise in wages occasioned by the Black Death led to a rise in peasant expectations and opportunities. In a society accustomed to a shortage of land, there was suddenly a glut of empty fields waiting to be cultivated by peasants with the sense and resources to take advantage of changing circumstance. Lords who attempted to enforce old burdens, to demand boon work or unpaid labour, found themselves confronted by a peasantry keen to throw off the shackles of villeinage. Attempts by government to regulate wages and prices were as ineffective in the 1370s as in the 1970s. There had been widespread withdrawal of services from the Archbishop of Canterbury's estates in Kent within only a few years of the great pestilence of 1348. In 1377, in the immediate aftermath of the Good Parliament, a great rumour spread across forty or more manors in southern England that the King was about to declare all manors named in Domesday ('The King's Book', or 'The Book of Winchester') immune from labour services not mentioned in 'The Book'.

The Peasants' Revolt

In the early summer of 1381, these expectations burst out in the form of a 'Peasants' Revolt', most acute in Kent and Essex but with outbreaks reported as far away as Derbyshire and York, in which the peasantry rose to demand an end to villeinage, to burn manorial records and to denounce the evil counsellors by whom the King had been led astray (generally identified as John of Gaunt, the King's uncle, and the chancellor and Archbishop of Canterbury, Simon Sudbury). The immediate spur to their rebellion was the attempt by the government of the fourteen-year-old Richard II to impose a poll tax, the third in the past five years, intended to ensure that those who might otherwise escape the net of more traditional taxes would be forced to contribute to the costs of national defence. The tax of 1381 was set at a punitive rate of a shilling a head and, although hedged about with assurances that the rich should assist the poor, it was met with widespread resistance. As many as half a million contributors to earlier, lower taxes, simply disappeared from the tax roll. Attempts to redress this were met with armed resistance by three Essex villages convened at Brentwood on 30 May, and shortly afterwards a royal judge sent to reimpose order was sent packing by the mob.

What little we know of the rebels themselves (chiefly from the record of their prosecution after 1381) suggests that their leaders were drawn from the upper levels of village society, from those who had experience as reeves, or bailiffs or constables, manorial officials accustomed to being obeyed, crudely or perhaps not so crudely literate, familiar with record keeping and accounting, quite able to organize themselves in resistance to their lords' demands. Their self-appointed spokesman, Wat Tyler, himself bore a surname (from his trade as a tiler) that suggests that these were precisely the sort of artisans and skilled labourers who had most to gain from a relaxation in the burdens of villeinage.

As rebellion spread across the Thames from Essex into Kent in the first fortnight of June 1381, Tyler and his mob stormed the cathedral and the archbishop's palace at Canterbury. Where 200 years earlier the poor people of Canterbury had proved the most faithful supporters of Archbishop Thomas Becket, they now rampaged through Becket's cathedral demanding the blood of their present archbishop. By 12 June, the rebels were in sight of London, and on the following day, the feast of Corpus Christi, in other circumstances one of the most joyous festivals of the medieval Church, marked by processions and celebrations, the King himself was rowed out to Greenwich from the Tower in order to view the mob. South of the Thames, the rebels looted Southwark, attacking the chief prison of the Marshalsea and releasing the prisoners. By some means unknown, they then crossed into the city itself, sacking the prisons, looting and destroying John of Gaunt's great treasure house at the Savoy, their fires visible by the King, now sheltering in the Tower of London.

Seeking, or at least pretending to seek reconciliation, the King rode out to Mile End on the following day, where he was greeted courteously and where he promised both to grant the rebels manumission (release from the bonds of villeinage) and to deal firmly with the 'traitors' and evil counsellors blamed for their actions. Even as he was parleying, however, another group of rebels broke into the Tower, made off with weaponry and flags bearing the royal arms, sat on the beds, and even tried kissing the King's widowed mother. The Archbishop of Canterbury and the King's cousin Henry Bolingbroke, son of

John of Gaunt, were both seized by the mob. Bolingbroke narrowly avoided death. The archbishop was beheaded. The mob now began the systematic hunting down of foreigners within the city, executing at least 150 of them, for the most part Flemings involved in the wool and cloth trades.

On the following day, the King rode out once again to meet the rebels, this time at Smithfield. He was greeted by Wat Tyler with a peremptory bow, a shake of the hand and an insistence that he call the King 'brother' (*frer*, and we might note here that even Tyler is imagined by the chroniclers employing a French salute). Tyler then delivered a series of demands before drinking off a flagon of ale. At some point, either in the heat of the moment or as part of a prearranged ambush, a struggle broke out between Tyler and the mayor of London, William Walworth, a successful fishmonger who, like the Poles or the Pulteneys of an earlier generation, had prospered by advancing loans to the crown. Walworth stabbed Tyler – the dagger he is said to have used is still displayed in the Fishmongers Hall – and the King, bravely distracted the mob, shouting 'You will have no captain but me. Follow me to the fields and you will have what you wish!' In the ensuing turmoil, the mob dispersed. Walworth achieved the ambition of all successful nouveaux-riches, being knighted by the King on the field of battle. Over the course of the next month or so, order was restored and a series of trials arranged throughout the southeast to bring the rebel leaders to justice. The most prominent of them were either executed or, in a majority of cases, imprisoned. The revolt was at an end. So, despite the best efforts of the elite to reimpose its authority, was villeinage.

The end of villeinage

The exact circumstances and chronology here remain obscure. Probably the process would have occurred with or without the rebellion of 1381. Lords unable to persuade their peasants to remain on the land, faced with the flight of labour to towns or other jurisdictions, slowly and in some cases reluctantly began once again to lease out the majority of their estates, transforming themselves from high farmers into rentiers. The processes of the twelfth century, in which a predominantly leasehold economy had yielded place to the great demesne estates of the Church and aristocracy, was put into reverse. Within a generation of 1381, and in many cases even before the turn of the century, land had been leased to a new generation of farmers, in many cases themselves the beneficiaries in the rise of prospects for the yeomanry and upper peasantry. The manor, itself the principal unit of land management and legal authority since the late eleventh century, declined, like villeinage, to a mere shadow on the landscape. In its place, fully formed, loomed the parish with its church wardens and its ability to function as a unit of tax collection and poor relief. The rural society of parishes known to Jane Austen and to Thomas Hardy was born from circumstances rather more revolutionary than the readers of either of these authors might suppose.

In the meantime, the Peasants' Revolt had to a large extent proved an urban rather than a rural phenomenon, its greatest crises fought out in towns such as Canterbury or York and ultimately in London. The very speed with which the rebels captured London, as in 1215 against King John or in 1264 against Henry III, and the near total paralysis to which this reduced royal administration, is an important indication of how easy it remained to cross the gulf between order and anarchy. Much as he might claim to control dominions stretching from Scotland to Spain, the King of England did not even possess the resources to prevent a few thousand peasants armed for the most part with staves and stones from seizing the very control-centre of his administration, making free with the King's bedclothes, his private treasures and even his own mother. Those who witnessed the resulting spectacle were haunted by the memory of a world turned upside down. In his *Parlement of Foules* (c.1382), superficially an apolitical meditation on love as birds are shown gathering to choose their mates, Chaucer has the assembly suddenly interrupted by the noise of the lower orders, domestic and base birds capable only of incomprehensible cacophony: 'Kek, kek! Kokkow! Quek quek!'

Just so must the babble of the crowd have sounded to those in London a year before. John Gower, a contemporary of Chaucer, also resorted to animal metaphors, likening the peasantry to oxen or donkeys, demanding to be fed on the best hay and to be loaded with jewelled harness. In his *Canterbury Tales*, Chaucer's portrait of the ploughman is intended as satire precisely because, at a time of discontented labour, here was a peasant prepared to help his neighbours without pay, gladly taking on such detested jobs as muck-spreading and ditch-digging. More typically, Chaucer's band of pilgrims included such base figures as a carpenter and a dyer, artisans displaying their wealth in high-quality clothes, fine livery and silver knives. The assumption made by most readers, that all of these figures rode rather than walked to Canterbury, is in itself an indication of the extent to which they had risen in the world, literally as well as figuratively. The Smiths and Bakers, Carpenters and Dyers who today rule the academic or political establishments, as their surnames proclaim, are themselves the heirs to such newly risen, horse-riding folk.

Religious Radicals

Two other consequences of the rebellion are worth considering. The first is the spotlight that it threw upon religious opinion. One of the principal targets of the Kent rebels had been the release from Maidstone gaol of John Ball, a radical preacher, previously a chantry chaplain, who had been in trouble with the Church authorities for nearly twenty years before his imprisonment in 1381. To Ball's preaching is attributed what in fact was a popular English proverb: 'When Adam delved and Eve span, Who was then a gentleman?', a rejection of the deference traditionally required by gentry and aristocracy, still resonating in socialist manifestoes well into the twentieth century. Letters attributed to Ball, urging on the rebels, contain some of the earliest contemporary references to *Piers Plowman*, itself a protest poem which had preached obedience and peaceful reform rather than Ball's more radical message of social levelling. To the authorities, nonetheless, the association of rebellion with preachers, and perhaps especially of vernacular literature, was highly alarming.

Ball himself was hung, drawn and quartered in July 1381. His activities, his apparent immunity from arrest or punishment for many years before 1381, and the fact that at Smithfield Watt Tyler had apparently demanded not only an end to villeinage but the complete disendowment of the Church, stripping ecclesiastical landlords of their wealth in order that they might live like the early apostles of Christ, all contributed to a determination to root out such radicals from the Church. The most obvious target for this counterattack was the Oxford theologian John Wycliffe.

Wycliffe

Already, in 1377, as a result of his teachings on papal authority and the eucharist, Wycliffe had been condemned by the Pope, who had ordered his imprisonment. By this time Wycliffe was proclaiming that the papacy, by its corruption and pursuit of wealth, had forfeited all entitlement to lordship. Since the bread and wine of the Mass continued to have the appearance of bread and wine, and since to have accidents without substance was to contradict the natural order, Christ could only be said to be present in the bread and wine figuratively or sacramentally. Without denying that Christ was thus present, Wycliffe in effect condemned the whole rigmarole of chantry masses for the souls of the dead, the feast of Corpus Christi and much else besides, arguing that the Church needed to return to its primitive purpose and teachings, jettisoning much that was late or corrupt.

Wycliffe was a charismatic teacher. He commanded a close personal following in Oxford. However, his preaching that loyalty and obedience could only be won, as by Christ, through love, and his assertion that only through the Bible, where necessary translated into English, could mankind find truth and salvation, appeared to cut at the roots of the Church's established authority and, in the aftermath of the Peasants' Revolt, could be regarded as a dangerous incitements to the rejection of authority. In fact, there is no evidence whatsoever that Wycliffe or any of his followers were involved in the 1381 revolt. John Ball was certainly no Wycliffite, and Watt Tyler's demand for the disendowment of the Church and the seizure of its resources for the poor was part of a longer standing anti-clerical tradition with no direct links to Wycliffe. Nonetheless, in 1382, the new Archbishop of Canterbury insisted on the condemnation of ten of Wycliffe's propositions, in theory condemning Wycliffe and his followers as heretics. Wycliffe himself died two years later, still unpunished but convinced that the papacy itself had become an arm of the Antichrist.

For nearly twenty years after 1382, no decisive action was taken against Wycliffe's followers, who went on to publish a series of increasingly anti-clerical tracts and to translate the entire Bible into English as a collaborative venture. The fact that, despite condemnation and prohibitions, at least 250 manuscript copies of this translation are known to survive supplies some indication of its success. By comparison, only 21 complete copies survive of the great Latin Gutenberg Bible, printed in Mainz in 1452, and there are as many manuscripts of the Wycliffite Bible as there are copies of the First Folio of Shakespeare, printed in 1623. The intention behind the translation was that believers should return to simple scriptural truths, putting aside the theatrical props of a Church too concerned with statuary, pilgrimages and relics to correct its own corruption of Christ's teaching. As a puritan creed, in tune with much else in Catholic spirituality, this form of Wycliffism, more pietist than intellectual, exerted considerable influence even at the royal court where a group of knights close to the King was accused by the chroniclers of being secret supporters of what was already being called 'Lollardy': a term of uncertain origin, perhaps from the English 'loller', an idle wastrel, or from the Latin 'lolia', the tares or weeds to be divided from good Catholic wheat.

Here matters might have rested, with Wycliffe's supporters as covert puritans operating on the far extreme of opinions that the Church was prepared to tolerate. Philip Repyndon, initially one of Wycliffe's most enthusiastic disciples, returned like other Wycliffites to the orthodox fold, preferring to work from within the Church in order to institute reform. Repyndon died in 1424 as bishop of Lincoln. A hint as to the continuing extremity of his puritanism occurs in the terms of his will, in which he demanded that his body be left naked and unburied in a sack placed outside the church of St Margaret in Lincoln Cathedral close, there to be food for worms. Only the town crier was to announce his death, and every penny that he possessed was to be given to the poor, even the black cloth on the bier being given away as clothing. Needless to say, these conditions were ignored. Repyndon was instead buried simply but decently in the cathedral's south-east transept. In the history of the established Church, propriety has generally trumped sincerity.

'Popular' Religious Belief

Since 1066, England had never been a nation particularly troubled by heresy. Even so, there had been alarms. As long ago as the Council of Oxford in 1222, which had promulgated the most significant series of decrees for the government of the Church enacted before the 1530s, the fear of false prophets was already on the minds of those in attendance. A priest who had converted to Judaism and been circumcised was handed over to the local sheriff to be burned. A layman who had allowed himself to be crucified, so that he might bear the wounds of Christ, and his companion, a woman who claimed to be Mary the mother of Christ and who had fashioned a chalice out of wax so that she might celebrate Mass (a male prerogative), were both condemned to be walled up, either as involuntary hermits or in order that they might be starved to death. In the 1230s, a Dominican inquisition had been briefly appointed for Yorkshire with the King's support, at much the same time that the Dominicans were rooting out heresy and burning heretics in Flanders and in Languedoc, almost within sight of the King of England's bastides and fortified towns of Gascony. In the reign of Edward II, the Templars were suppressed in England just as elsewhere in Europe, albeit without quite the hysteria that attended their condemnation in France.

Throughout this period, the laity were regularly questioned and tested for the orthodoxy of their faith, if not by an inquisition then in accordance with local episcopal legislation that made confession, the examination of conscience and the rooting out of sin a model of how false belief might be segregated and destroyed. A great deal of the expression of 'popular' religious belief caused alarm to the Church authorities. May Games and mell suppers, the Feast of Fools and the play of the King and Queen were all barely tolerated by episcopal synods. The veneration of holy wells, prayers and charms for sick livestock, love potions, an alarming interest in pagan or pre-Christian sites, and even a taste for strange images, such as the 'horrid cross' (imported from Germany, that great source of the macabre) apparently showing Christ as if he were being torn apart on a gibbet, condemned by the bishop of London in 1305, suggests a community of religious belief that was not entirely at ease with itself and which the Church authorities insisted be carefully policed. In 1313, at Bexley in what is now suburban Kent, a man named Stephen le Pope (itself a name highly suggestive of megalomania) is said to have made stone and wood images of gods in his garden and to have worshipped them. On the same night, he murdered his maidservant. He was clearly mad, but his madness itself reveals the hysterical potential of much late-medieval religion.

Women in religion

The Church, then as now, was made especially uncomfortable by the religious role claimed by women. Houses of nuns continued to flourish, from the poorest anchoresses (female hermits) to Chaucer's prioress with her lapdogs and her cockney French. It was for women that a large proportion of saints' lives written in French were composed in the thirteenth century, and later in Middle English, the assumption being, even as early as the 1240s, that nuns needed to confess, to read their prayers and to conduct their devotions not in the Latin of the schools but in the vernacular. It is nonetheless a remarkable fact that, throughout the fourteenth and fifteenth centuries, the Church was reluctant officially to canonize more than a handful of female saints. Even the holiest of female hermits, Julian of Norwich, author of a series of mystic 'Shewings', again written in English, failed to achieve official canonization.

Tainted with the sin of Eve, their bodies more permeable than male bodies and therefore more open to the influence of demons and the Devil, women were mistrusted as oracles or purveyors of divine truth. Where the particular balance of the four 'humours' within the human body – black bile, yellow bile, phlegm and blood, a system inherited from classical antiquity – rendered men strong and steadfast, and adolescent males strong but inconstant, the cold and humid nature of the female humoral balance tended towards weakness and unreliability. Instead of championing the contemporary virtues of any Englishwoman, the Church emphasized the splendour and peerless sanctity of Christ's own mother. The Virgin Mary became every bit as much the protector of England as she was already of the kingdom of France. Her shrine at Walsingham in Norfolk, supposedly founded at her direct command, as a copy in England of the Holy House of Nazareth where Christ had been conceived through the virtue of the Holy Spirit, attracted the patronage of several English kings. Richard II's greatest surviving monument, the Wilton Diptych (a panel painting), shows the King kneeling before the Virgin and child, having just presented them with England symbolized by the banner of St George. Within the ferrule or stopper at the very top of the banner, only revealed in recent cleaning, is a miniature map of a green island, only a centimetre high, painted with trees and a white tower, set in a sea of silver leaf with a boat in full sail. England itself had become the Virgin's dower.

The stately magnificence of the Wilton Diptych represents one facet of English spirituality. A very different approach to the Church emerges from the life of the eccentric Norfolk woman, Margery Kempe. Born in the 1370s at King's Lynn where her father was mayor, Margery was unhappily married to a local brewer by whom she had fourteen children, even the first of these births provoking a spiritual crisis (what we might today diagnose as post-natal depression). From this, Margery was rescued when Jesus himself sat down at the end of her bed to offer her comfort. Having at last persuaded her husband that they should live chastely, after 1413 Margery embarked upon an extraordinary career as self-appointed holy woman, consulting with both Julian of Norwich and bishop Repyndon at Lincoln. Her pilgrimages were to take her from Jerusalem to Rome, where her insistence on wearing white as a symbol of her chastity, her uncontrollable tears, her 'roaring' in church and her claims to have been mystically married to the Godhead caused more than a little alarm to her fellow pilgrims. We know all this because, having failed in an earlier attempt to employ a naturalized German with illegible handwriting to record her story, Margery was eventually able to dictate her memoirs to the local priest, becoming in the process the very first author of an autobiography written in English.

Lollardy

Since pilgrimages were a display of piety discouraged by Lollards, Margery Kempe was clearly no Lollard. Nonetheless, many of her contemporaries, including other semi-educated women from the diocese of Norwich, were attracted to Lollardy, not for its intellectual content so much as for its sense of pious extremity, of belonging to a secret yet elect body of Christians, knowing more and enjoying a closer relationship to their Saviour even than the priests in church. Before 1400, only a few English bishops took measures actively to pursue Lollardy. This changed, however, following the deposition of Richard II, very much at the personal initiative of Thomas Arundel, Archbishop of Canterbury. Arundel perhaps hoped to use the pursuit of Lollardy as a negotiating tool with a court and a King, Henry IV, known to harbour knights sympathetic to the Wycliffites. The new King's father, John of Gaunt, Wycliffe's one-time patron, had broken with Lollardy after 1381, but, nonetheless, at his own deathbed had demanded that his body be left unburied and unembalmed for forty days, clearly in puritan expiation of his sins. The pursuit of heresy was also a means by which, after a distinctly uncomfortable start to his archiepiscopate in which he had been intimately involved in the deposition of King Richard, Arundel could stamp his authority both upon Church and state. Not for the first or the last time, the demand for strength and discipline was instituted by a leader who himself feared accusations of weakness.

In 1401, reinvestigating the heresy of a Norfolk chaplain, William Sawtre, first condemned by the bishop of Norwich two years earlier, Arundel found evidence that Sawtre had reverted to his condemned beliefs. As a relapsed heretic he was handed over to the King's officers for punishment, and in March 1401 burned at Smithfield 'bound, standing upright, to a post set in a barrel with blazing wood all around'. The punishment was all the more remarkable for having been carried out some weeks before the King formally promulgated the new statute by which it was justified, '*De Haeretico comburendo*' (allowing for the burning of relapsed heretics). Sawtre is generally reckoned both the first Lollard martyr and the first criminal burned at the stake in England. In reality, burning had long been a punishment meted out in England to wives who killed their husbands (the crime of 'petty treason'). A group of Cathar heretics unearthed in London in the reign of King John is said to have been summarily burned, and there were burnings again, as noticed above, at the Council of Oxford in 1222.

Even after Sawtre's execution, the statute against heresy was used only once or twice before 1407, when a temporary eclipse in the fortunes of Archbishop Arundel allowed a petition to be introduced to King and lords in Parliament, clearly Lollard inspired, calling once again for the total disendowment of the established Church. Catholic priests should henceforth live by the alms of the faithful. The money obtained from the sale of the Church's lands and treasures should be employed in part to ensure that future kings had no need to call upon extraordinary taxation, for the rest to endow fifteen new earldoms, 1,500 knights, 6,200 squires, 100 new almshouses, 15 universities and 1,500 Wycliffite priests for pastoral duties. Anticipating Henry VIII's disendowment of the Church by more than a hundred years, and even then far exceeding the Reformation settlement in its ambition (there were not to be 15 universities in England until the chartering of the University of Nottingham in 1948), this was not a proposal that had any chance of being debated let alone of success. Even so, it demonstrates that Wycliffite sentiments continued to command sympathy even within the political elite.

Its probable author, Sir John Oldcastle, a Herefordsire knight with connections to the royal household, was also to prove Lollardy's unwitting executioner. By marriage to the heiress of Lord Cobham, Oldcastle had risen to considerable wealth, with properties scattered across five counties and including Cooling Castle on the marshes north of Rochester. Archbishop Arundel sought to move against the heretics in Oldcastle's household as early as 1410. However, it was the death of Henry IV and the accession of his son, Henry V, a King determined to display his orthodoxy, that gave the Archbishop his chance to act. Oldcastle was arrested and charged with heresy. Committed to the Tower, he escaped and in January 1414 sought to raise a rebellion, planning perhaps to kidnap the King amidst the celebrations of Twelfth Night. His conspiracy was betrayed. Forty of the conspirators were executed, seven of them by burning. The chroniclers, reflecting government propaganda, allege that 20,000 rebels had been waiting for the call to arms. In reality, there were never more than a couple of hundred. Oldcastle escaped, and was not recaptured until 1417, when he was at last burned as a heretic and outlaw. His reputation as a malign companion of the young Henry V lived on to inform Shakespeare's *Henry IV*, where the character of the prince's tutor was originally named Sir John Oldcastle. Protests from the then Lord Cobham, successor to Oldcastle's barony, forced Shakespeare to think again, lighting, more or less by hazard, on the name of the Norfolk adventurer and patron of the Paston family, Sir John Fastolf. By such means was Sir John Falstaff, greatest of comic inventions, foisted upon an unsuspecting world.

Oldcastle's rebellion put an end to all flirtations between the gentry and the Wycliffite heresy. Tarred by its associations with treason and rebellion against the King, Lollardy was destined to become a low-status puritan sect, secretly maintained in the households of a few thousand devotees, for the most part semi-literate artisans, its flame kept burning by only a handful of fully committed evangelists and preachers. Before 1414, the heretics themselves had enjoyed international contacts, in particular with the Hussite movement in Bohemia (themselves protesting against the privileges of the clergy and demanding a return to a simpler 'Bible' Christianity). Oldcastle himself had corresponded with Prague. The burning of Jan Hus at the Council of Constance in 1415, and the subsequent outbreak of a Hussite rebellion threatening the rights not only of the Church but of aristocratic property, merely confirmed the assumption that Lollardy in England must be ripped out by the roots. Before 1414, there had been no systematic inquisition into its spread. After Oldcastle's rebellion, and with one eye clearly focussed on events in Europe, bishops sanctioned systematic persecution of the English Lollards. In the late 1420s, for example, whilst the bishop of Winchester, Henry Beaufort, was leading a contingent on the crusade launched against the Hussites of Bohemia, the bishop of Norwich investigated the Lollard communities of East Anglia, burning four of the Lollard leaders (one of them a former skinner, the rest former priests) and imprisoning more than sixty sympathizers. A suspected Lollard 'rising' in 1431 resulted in yet another wave of persecution, and there were further burnings in London in 1440.

Historians of the twentieth century, as always keen to imagine medieval society as if it were merely an offshoot of their own liberal concerns, have tended to argue that the persecution of heresy had both a good and a bad side. On the one hand 'medievals' were clearly at fault in denying the rights of religious minorities. At the same time, by clubbing together to burn a few heretics or massacre a few Jews, they asserted their own sense of community and greatly improved society's 'feel good factor'. This, of course, is a crude parody of the modern debate. It has nonetheless been asserted that, far from being inimical to the sense of community, inquisitorial procedures devised to counter the 'threat' of Lollardy presented 'opportunities for the individual to become more involved in public action than he, or to a lesser extent she, had been before'. In an academic vacuum, this is no doubt true. The recruitment of large numbers of parishioners to spy and report on their neighbours, and the segregation of those who failed to comply with society's norms, can no doubt be accounted a social good. In the same way, those today who report to the local council on the illegal dumping of garden waste, or the failure to sort plastic cups from tin cans in a bag of recycled refuse, can rest assured that they are securing their neighbourhood against the tentacles of the Antichrist. Whether it would be of even greater benefit to the community to burn all fly tippers, exterminate the burners of leaded petrol or arrange for the communal kicking of bigots and the illiberal, is best left to public (rather than academic) opinion to decide. In the meantime, there should be little doubt that heresy and its persecution had tragic human consequences.

Some Lollard communities survived into the sixteenth century, merging in due course with the earliest exponents of 'Protestant' reform. As a result, as 'proto-Protestants', the Lollards themselves were taken up by Tudor historians keen to demonstrate how 'primitive' Bible-based Christianity had survived all of the corrupt excrescences of the Middle Ages to re-emerge as Protestantism after 1500. Archbishop Cranmer, the first of the Protestant archbishops of Canterbury, seems deliberately to have encouraged the destruction of the tomb of his predecessor, Archbishop Arundel, precisely because of Arundel's association with the persecution of Lollards. The Lollards themselves, not least in John Foxe's *Book of Martyrs*, were represented as keepers of a sacred flame fanned back to life by Luther, Calvin and their English disciples. The irony, surely not lost on sixteenth-century readers, was that the Lollards, with their secret meetings, their need to hide from the authorities and their outward conformity to orthodox opinion, resembled nothing so much as the Catholic recusant priests in hiding in England after 1570.

Spies

Spies and spying had already played a leading role in English warfare, both in Scotland and in France. As early as 1066, the Bayeux Tapestry shows what are clearly spies reporting back to William both on Harold's landing in France and on the lie of the land before Hastings. 'Explorators' or spies were a ubiquitous feature of the Anglo-French wars after 1340, with paranoia against their activities rising to a frenzy of suspicion. Oldcastle's plot of 1414 had been exposed by spies, with the government thereafter whipping up a deliberate and exaggerated propaganda storm, intended to give the impression that heresy and traitors lurked behind every corner. Ironically it was a Welsh spy, from a nation itself undone by English spying and propaganda, who in 1417 finally betrayed Oldcastle's whereabouts to the authorities. At much the same time, in the build-up to the Agincourt campaign of 1415, Henry V had arrested the French ambassadors who came to discuss peace with him at Southampton, fearing that, having viewed his invasion fleet, they might betray his plans to his enemies. In warfare, as in his persecution of heresy, Henry V was determined to show himself an even more effective operator than the kings of France. With the instigation of a full-scale inquisition into Lollardy, spying itself joined irony, drunkenness and violence as a peculiarly English phenomenon.

The fifteenth century's persecution of minorities perhaps represented nothing new. Twelfth-century Englishmen had massacred Jews and Flemings. In the thirteenth century it had been Frenchmen and Italian clergy (set upon in the 1230s by a band of semi-outlaws led by a Yorkshire knight acting under the pseudonym 'William Wither' or William 'the Avenger'). This proud tradition of xenophobia was still alive to the revolting peasants of 1381 who massacred the foreigners of London. What was different about the persecution of Lollards was that they were not strangers but neighbours, more English than many of the churchmen and bishops who ordered their burning. Their persecution may have allowed the rest of the community to cohere, just as the modern segregation of pederasts or smokers is reckoned to allow the majority to sleep more complacently at night. Nonetheless, the fears to which inquest and persecution gave rise, that Christian society was itself infiltrated by conspirators and undermined by plots, should not be underestimated. The fifteenth century was a century in which society began to root out heretics from within. It was also a century in which the upper classes began killing one another with unprecedented regularity and enthusiasm, seeing 'treason' or 'conspiracy' behind ever turn in the political road. From the enquiries into the activities of the Lollards, via the civil wars of the 1460s and 70s, through to the seventeenth century's burning of witches (in medieval England a rare event, though known in Ireland as early as the 1320s) can be traced a direct and not necessarily very comfortable path. The sense that society was corrupted from within, that even the King's military household could become a nest of heretics, and that the upper classes were riddled with traitors determined upon self-slaughter, merely added to the existing fear that endemic plague and pestilence were signs of God's disfavour. So much for the idea that society 'coheres' around the persecution of its minorities.

Outlaws

Of course, not all secrets are necessarily guilty, nor all lawlessness necessarily a threat to the silent majority. Despite the apparent efficiency of royal and episcopal spy networks, there was a vast gulf between ambition and achievement in medieval policing. Sir John Oldcastle managed to disappear into hiding for three years, despite being the most wanted criminal in England. John Ball, the radical preacher of 1381, had been in hiding or under threat of arrest for nearly twenty years before he was eventually incarcerated in Maidstone gaol. Their contemporary, the Welsh rebel, Owen Glyn Dwr, managed to live beyond the reach of royal justice for at least fifteen years. Outlawry, the legal placing of criminals beyond the protection of the law, was as old as the Anglo-Saxons, who had offered outlawry and exile as an alternative to death to convicted felons. It could be delivered as a sentence in court. It could also be actively sought by the criminal. From even before 1066, certain great churches, most famously Durham and Westminster, claimed the right to award sanctuary to those who fled to their precincts, with entire quarters both of Westminster and the city of Durham recognized as lying within such special jurisdictions. The future King Edward V was himself born in Westminster sanctuary in 1470, during the temporary disgrace and exile of his father, King Edward IV.

Elsewhere, each of the 30,000 or more parish churches, chapels and cemeteries of England was recognized as conferring rights of sanctuary upon felons who sought refuge there. Provided that the sanctuary-seeker had not yet been tried or convicted, they were permitted a forty-day stay, fed by the parish priest and guarded by the local community both to ensure that they did not simply escape into hiding and they were not killed by their victims' families or removed from sanctuary against their will. At the end of these forty days, they might officially 'abjure' the realm, swearing an oath to travel by the King's highway as far a port of embarkation, generally Dover, and there take ship beyond the realm of England. On Dover beach, where they were to remain until a ship could be found to take them (generally to France, the Channel Islands or Scotland), they were to remain in public view, entering the sea each day up to their knees or neck in token of their willingness to depart. Such exiles were branded on the thumb with a capital 'A', to denote their status as 'abjurers'. Should they return without official pardon, or wander from the most direct route to their port of exile, they were deemed to 'carry the wolf's head', being subject to summary execution by anyone they encountered. Indeed, any community which failed to apprehend and kill such outlaws was itself, in theory, subject to the full rigors of royal law.

The evidence of coroners' records (coroners being the principal supervisors of the process of abjuration) suggest that in any year, something between two hundred and two thousand abjurations took place in England, the wide disparity in the estimated figures here being itself proof of the degree to which such people were marginalized. Quite how many abjurers melted away into hiding before exile remains equally uncertain. Even so, as early as the thirteenth century, there were already substantial communities of 'outlaws' and runaways living on the social margins: escaped prisoners, runaway serfs, monks or nuns who had jumped their convent walls, abjurers of the realm who failed to depart overseas, all of these communities being forced to live in hiding within a society generally so close-knit that strangers were by their very nature an object of suspicion.

Many of them sought the anonymity of the urban crowd. Hence, as early as the twelfth century, the evil reputation of certain parts of towns as refuges for thieves and runaways. Prostitution was merely one amongst the many trades of this medieval 'underworld', albeit the trade which has perhaps attracted the most attention from modern historians, commemorated in street-names such as the 'Grope Cunt' alleys or 'Maiden' lanes to be found from Shrewsbury to London, and in the case of the greatest of the London bordellos, the 'stews' (from the Old French *estuve* or stove associated with public bathhouses) of Bankside in the Bishop of Winchester's jurisdiction south of the Thames, certainly in existence by the 1380s, probably for a century or more before that. In 1452, the Bankside stews were the subject of a detailed written ordinance, insisting, for example, that the stew-holders be married men, warned against prostituting their own servants or girls who were sick or pregnant, and instructed not to beat or forcibly detain their workers or embroil them in debt as has been the habit of pimps and brothel-keepers throughout the ages.

The fact that these regulations specifically forbade the employment of veterans of the French wars as servants in the stews reminds us that military deserters were as ubiquitous a feature of London lowlife in the Middle Ages as they were of twentieth-century Saigon or Bangkok. The prostitutes (amongst whom the surname 'Frow', from the German *frau* was particularly common) were not to wear aprons (apparently a garment of respectability), nor were they to grab at potential customers or lure them into playing at cards, dice or other games of hazard. Having once accepted a customer's money, they were not to limit the contract to a period less than one full night. On the major feasts of the Church, they were to leave Southwark altogether save between the hours of 11am and 1pm (apparently their principal daytime hours of business) on nights when a Parliament or royal council was being held at Westminster, presumably so that Parliamentarians, then as now, could seek relaxation from the strains and stresses of political life, in this instance secure in the knowledge that trading standards would ensure them a full night-time money's worth. Once again we find ourselves here in a society where even unrespectable trades could be subjected to curfews and clock hours.

Meanwhile, the ability of those wanted by the authorities merely to melt away either into the crowd or the greenwood was a remarkable feature of medieval society and rendered outlaws such as Ball, Oldcastle or Glyn Dwr almost as famous in their day, and in certain quarters no doubt as admired, as Osama Bin Laden in his mountain cave. Celebration of the myths of the successful outlaw enabled the oppressed of medieval England to cock a snook at their oppressors. It is precisely in this period that the legends of Robin Hood first come properly into focus. Although not specifically referred to until Langland's *Piers Plowman* (*c*.1377), the legends themselves were far older than this. A variety of fugitives recorded in English courts from the 1220s onwards called themselves by some variety of the name 'Robert Hod' or 'Robehod', adopting, in places as far apart as Yorkshire and Berkshire, what must already have been a well-known pseudonym for a robber. The search for the 'real' Robin Hood is almost certainly a fruitless one. Nonetheless, by 1420, and as far away as Scotland, attempts were being made to place him within a specific historical context, originally in the reign of Edward I, moving in the 1450s to that of Edward II, only later, after 1520, claiming that he was a figure of the 1190s and the reign of Richard I. The first written stories of Robin survive from the 1450s, and have a Nottinghamshire setting. However the so-called *Gest* of Robin Hood, again from the fifteenth century, places him in Yorkshire, specifically in the bleak West Riding valley of Barnsdale, north of Doncaster. Other members of his fictitious gang joined him in the fifteenth century: Little John, Maid Marion and Friar Tuck, this latter associated with a real historical character, the murderous Robert Stafford, parson of Lindfield in Sussex, who called himself 'Friar Tuck' as leader of a criminal gang which terrorized Sussex between 1417 and 1429.

Drama, ballads and minstrels

The audience for these legends and ballads was clearly widespread, both geographically and socially. Not just the rising yeoman farmer but the great lord in his hall listened to these stories, and by the 1430s they can be found referred to by the King's judges, by a sheriff's clerk, by monks, chroniclers, juries and even in petitions to Parliament. In 1473, Sir John Paston wrote to his brother complaining that a servant was on the point of departing his household despite the fact that 'I have kept him this three years to play Saint George and Robin Hood and the sheriff of Nottingham', presumably in some sort of household entertainment. Ballads and plays circulated throughout late medieval society, not just in the mystery or miracle plays that emerged from an ecclesiastical setting, organized by parish and trade guilds.

Drama and playgoing were only a step away from the liturgical dramas of the Church, and the performance of a successful preacher was in many cases the closest approximation that a medieval village or town could achieve to the modern cinema. Chaucer's Wife of Bath, free to gad about whilst her adulterous and drunken husband visited London, was more than happy to put on her best scarlet dress and to go the rounds of vigils and processions, preachings and pilgrimages, miracle plays and marriage feasts that, even in Lent, provincial society could supply. As early as 1306, an extraordinary array of harpers and minstrels and musicians is found in attendance upon the court of Edward I when he knighted his eldest son, the future Edward II, at Caernarvon Castle, and Edward II himself is to be found in the 1320s at Whorlton Castle in Yorkshire entertained by two local ladies, Agnes the Redhaired and Alice of Whorlton, who sang him stories of Simon de Montfort and other songs. The bursar's accounts for the Cistercian monks at Fountains in the late 1450s include payments to a whole array of minstrels and players: to a blind minstrel 6d, to the boy bishop of Ripon 3s, to a story teller ('whose name was unknown') 6d, to the King's minstrels 3s 4d, to a fool named Solomon 'who came again' 4d. Even Robin Hood's livery of Lincoln green, his evident courtesy (stressed in most of the stories), and his desire to obtain not land but a position in a great man's household, all speak to a fifteenth-century context, to a world of liveries and households and to the entertainment not so much of an audience of simple yeomen in their farmsteads but of great men in their hall.

The essentially subversive message of the Robin Hood legends was intended for recital not just before the peasantry, who might have appreciated Robin's ability to outwit the rich, but before the rich themselves. Were we looking for a crisis in aristocratic self-identity, for a sense that the old order was changing, that peasants no longer wished to be protected but freed, that the paternalism of the aristocracy as a whole, like that of the Church, was more resented than welcomed, that the old ties of deference were being strained, and that chivalry and the essential futility of the medieval knight were already being challenged by those obliged to pay hard-earned silver in order to indulge the knightly taste for slaughter, then the adoption of Robin Hood by the upper classes is itself a most remarkable phenomenon. Like those modern patrons of the arts, delighted by the anti-bourgeois rantings of the avant-garde, yet supporting such patronage from expense accounts and family trust funds, the patrons of the Robin Hood ballads were perhaps aware that they were reading or watching entertainments intended to ridicule precisely the people who paid to laugh at them. Since at least the twelfth century, irony and an ability to see both sides of the picture have been distinctly English qualities.

Forests and demand for wood

There is another irony to the Robin Hood legends that makes them especially interesting. By the time that they came to be written down, after 1400, the very greenwoods whose revels they celebrated were being levelled and mapped. Today, we look upon the ancient trees of England as amongst the most venerable of historic monuments. Some yew trees are perhaps 2,000 years old. The Major Oak in Sherwood forest, with a girth of over thirty-three feet, is said have been planted at about the time of Magna Carta. The Bowthorpe Oak, at Bourne in Lincolnshire, is perhaps older still, so large that its hollow interior can seat twenty people for dinner. Even so, as early as the thirteenth century, such was the pressure on timber and forest resources that the very tallest oak trees were already in short supply. The builders of Wells Cathedral after 1220, looking for the longest and strongest beams, were already importing their oak from Ireland. Ships' masts were fashioned from conifers rather than oaks, and so were easier to grow, but there is plenty of evidence to suggest that timber in large quantities, including yew for bows and pine for ships, was imported from Spain and Norway throughout the four-teenth and fifteenth centuries. The wars with France created an enormous demand for bow-wood: 7,800 bows and 13,000 arrows were ordered for the King in 1341 alone. Arrow shafts were made from the quicker growing ash, but, even so, such was the demand that in 1416, Henry V's government had specifically to forbid the making of clogs from ash rather than from willow or alder. The 'cruck' building of peasant houses, which required massive single beams, yielded place to 'trusses' made of shorter lengths.

Our earliest proper estate or local maps date from much this same period. The forests themselves were becoming not so much a place of tall trees but of mappable coppices, harvested to supply unimaginably vast quantities of fuel for heating, for building and for charcoal, essential for the smelting of metals, the firing of glass and pottery, and incidentally for the burning of heretics. Like the royal navy, or the ships that carried English armies into France, this was a society whose very heartbeat was the thump of axe on timber. By 1400, the beat from English forests was becoming increasingly tachycardic. Meanwhile, the emergence of the coal industry as an alternative to timber, and especially of the trade in sea coal from the north-east, shipped by clinker barges to London, brought wealth to the fifteenth-century bishopric of Durham and to such great northern families as the Nevilles of Raby. The furnaces of the industrial revolution had yet to burst into flame. Black soot did not yet clog the public buildings of London. But, in various places, the chimneys had at least begun to belch a rather darker smoke. A village such as Chiddingfold, on the Surrey–Sussex border, today the very embodiment of picture-postcard charm, was in the fourteenth century a semi-industrialized settlement of charcoal burners and glass makers, supplying such great enterprises as St George's, Windsor, and St Stephen's at Westminster.

Hunting

The clearances and grubbing up of the forest settings of the Robin Hood ballads was not just an economic phenomenon. It posed a deeper conundrum for the aristocracy. Since 1066, indeed probably since Roman times, the forests of England had been a specifically aristocratic resource, with the hunting of deer as the ultimate advertisement of aristocratic privilege. To a peasant who saw his lord thundering on horseback across forest pathways and winter fields, there can have been few more obvious proofs of lordly privilege. Hunting manuals and the rituals of the hunt remained central to the concerns of the fifteenth-century gentry and aristocracy. Virtually all kings hunted, even the generally soft-sworded Richard II or Henry VI. Henry VI hunted, even though he is said to have abhorred the actual slaughter of game. His courtiers brought their hawks with them into church. Of Richard II's favourites, Simon Burley was keeper of the King's falcons, and Robert de Vere is said to have been killed whilst hunting wild boar. The greatest of the medieval hunting manuals, the *Livre de Chasse* composed in the 1380s by the southern French nobleman Gaston Phoebus, Count of Foix, not only formed an essential item in

every gentleman's library but was translated into English by
no less a figure than Edward, Duke of York, grandson of
Edward III, killed at Agincourt in 1415. The hunting of deer
was still regarded as the ultimate aristocratic pastime, even as
late as the reign of Charles I. But the fox was already regarded
as a beast of the chase, with fox hunting itself favouring a landscape cleared of timber. From a clear run across plough and the
excitement of fences came the racing of horses, steeple-chasing
and all those other pursuits that, in the seventeenth and eighteenth centuries, were to replace the deer of old England as the
true sport of kings. In the fourteenth and fifteenth centuries,
kings favoured Windsor in order to be close to their deer and
their forests. By 1700, they had transferred their affections
from the greenwood to the heath-lands of Newmarket or
Ascot. Kingship had come out from the trees.

Social change

Nostalgia, a desire to return to a vanished Eden, a collapse in
aristocratic self-confidence masked by ever greater demands
for deference and ever greater emphasis upon aristocratic privilege, these are significant features of late medieval society to
set against the impression that social change must always be
equated with progress. The aristocrats of the fifteenth century
no doubt seemed on occasion almost as futile to their contemporaries and dependents as they have tended to appear to
modern historians. Nostalgia is perhaps the key emotion of the
period. It can be found at all levels and in all social classes. In
law, the Statute of Labourers or the Sumptuary laws of 1363
were attempts by the elite to legislate a return to former wages
and to former modes of dress, allowing some but not all social
classes to use family coats of arms, limiting the use of fur (itself
one of the great industries of the forest) or silk to those who
had traditionally been able to afford the cost of such materials.

Not since the early thirteenth century, when the regulation
of clerical costume, the ban on priests wearing scarlet or
excessively luxurious cloth, was a leading feature of episcopal

legislation, had the fear been so clearly articulated that the lower orders were getting above themselves and that society was collapsing for lack of proper respect for rank: wastrels were rising whilst merchants were living like pedlars and lords as mere 'lads', as the English poem *Winner and Waster* chose to put it. The Scrope-Grosvenor case of 1380s, in which two leading families contended before the court of the King's constable for the right to bear the same coat of arms, and in which evidence was given by such celebrities as John of Gaunt, Geoffrey Chaucer and Owen Glyn Dwr, is itself an indication of the degree to which badges and outward symbols of rank were now being policed, to prevent the contamination of aristocracy by the lower orders, or the blurring of social distinction.

The livery badges of the fourteenth and fifteenth centuries – Richard II's white hart, a symbol apparently first adopted by his mother, the Lancastrian collar of 'S's, apparently adopted as early as the 1340s by Queen Philippa, John of Gaunt's mother, and representing the forget-me-not or '*souveyne vous de moi*', 'remember me' (an early and comparatively innocent use of the SS symbol) – can be interpreted as calls to obedience and order rather than as radical new departures. Nor was nostalgia confined to the political elite. In 1377, the peasants of southern England looked to Domesday Book and the eleventh-century customs of their manors as the origin of the 'Great Rumour' that villeinage was about to be abolished. The 'Law of Winchester' which Watt Tyler and the Peasants' Revolt of 1381 sought to reinstitute was probably this same Domesday law, since Domesday was known alternatively as the 'Book of Winchester'. Even the Lollards, for all their supposed radicalism, can be seen as deeply conservative, attempting to cut through the elaborations of late medieval religion towards a rediscovery of primitive, Biblical truths. Those who persecuted Lollardy via trial and inquisition themselves drew on memories of the twelfth-century Cathars and upon fears that England, in ancient times the home of the early-Christian heretic Pelagius, was about to return to its ancient British and heretical roots.

Buildings and fine arts

There is a sense by the fifteenth century, not just that Englishmen had more material possessions, a better diet than that of their predecessors, more luxurious furnishings, access to better supplied markets, but of England itself being increasingly cluttered up with the debris of the English past. Men and women expressed nostalgia for a heritage that they believed to be vanishing or crumbling around them even as they reached out to record or preserve it or to acquire the consumer goods and fashions of an increasingly commercialized age. The cathedrals and churches raised by the Normans, originally new and shocking reminders of a social revolution, had been transformed even by 1350 into venerable and ancient reminders of a long vanished past. The age of epic had ended. Lincoln Cathedral had been rebuilt three times since the Norman Conquest, its final incarnation completed in the reign of Henry III. Thereafter, from the 1250s, whilst the cathedral's masons repaired the old, and mended the damaged, there was no proposal to rebuild from scratch.

Partly this was the result of rising labour costs, which from the 1380s became positively prohibitive: estimates of the cost of building even a peasant cottage rose from 10s or 20s in the 1290s, to £3 for the simplest sort of dwelling by 1400, an instance of house-price inflation every bit as remarkable as that of the late twentieth-century property 'bubble'. Partly, however, it reflects a sense of respect for the past: the appreciation of a heritage that was no longer to be pulled down and improved, but was regarded as something precious, to be admired and preserved. Henceforth, although the old might be tampered with, as with the rebuilding of the naves of Canterbury and Winchester cathedrals, or Richard II's reroofing of Westminster Hall, it was already recognized that to build anew was not always to 'improve' upon what had gone before.

Abandoning the epic structures of the eleventh and twelfth centuries, challenging heaven in their height and scale, the later Middle Ages prized decoration and the sumptuous arts. Its greatest monuments are often on a modest or even a miniature scale: painted manuscripts and books of hours, or the remarkable gold and enamel toys exchanged as Christmas or New Year presents between kings, represented in England by the Dunstable swan, an exquisite gold livery badge perhaps associated with the Bohun earls of Hereford. The fifteenth century marked a high point in the painting of stained glass, and above all perhaps in the carving of alabaster. Beginning in the 1330s with the tomb of Edward II at Gloucester, alabaster, a distinctively English fine-grained form of gypsum quarried principally in Staffordshire and Derbyshire, became the stone of choice for the tomb effigies of kings, aristocrats and bishops. Whilst the very best stained glass continued to be imported into England from Burgundy, the Rhineland and especially from Normandy, rather than produced in the glass factories of the Weald of Kent, European buyers were only too keen to export English alabaster images of the saints, altar-pieces and other elaborately carved panels, a native English art, in its way just as remarkable as the bronze, ceramic and marble figures that Donatello or Lucca Della Robbia were in the process of fashioning for the churches, palaces and piazzas of fifteenth-century Florence. Pewter, made from an alloy 80 per cent tin and therefore dependent upon the Cornish tin deposits, used as an alternative to ceramics or glass for plates and drinking vessels, was another late-medieval export. Like the *Opus Anglicanum* of the Anglo-Saxons, these were mass-produced luxury goods, sumptuous arts that were distinctively English.

Digging up the past

Just as the mining of Cornish tin or Derbyshire alabaster was a semi-industrialized concern, so the digging up of the past was already, by the fifteenth century, a very ancient and respectable pursuit. Richard of Cornwall, the brother of King Henry III, had been licensed in the 1250s to excavate barrows and ancient graves in the west of England and to keep whatever treasure might be found. In the 1180s, King Henry II is said already to have ordered a search for the bones of King Arthur at Glastonbury, and these same bones were reburied there a century later by Edward I. It was perhaps from these Glastonbury excavations that Westminster Abbey claimed to have come into possession of King Arthur's seal, set in beryl, still being displayed in the 1480s. Again at Glastonbury, around 1400, a local monk named John wove a wonderful tale, in part copied from earlier histories of his abbey, in part newly spun, in which Glastonbury's claim to the relics of St Patrick was fiercely defended and in which King Arthur was revealed to be a direct descendant of Joseph of Arimathea, the attendant at Christ's burial who was said to have collected a portion of Christ's blood in a 'grail' identified as the cup used at the Last Supper.

According to legend, Joseph had travelled to England where he had founded Glastonbury Abbey in 63AD. This claim was of more than merely local significance. Since 1378, Christendom had been thrown into turmoil by the simultaneous election of two popes: one still based at Avignon commanding the allegiance of the kings of France, the other once again resident in Rome and recognized by the kings of England. To heal this 'Schism', a series of councils was held, in which the representatives of the various churches of Europe were seated and granted precedence according to the date at which their nations had first accepted the word of Christ. If Glastonbury had been founded as early as 63AD, then this would render the English Church the oldest in Europe, far senior to the French. Not surprisingly, French and Spanish churchmen sought to pour scorn upon Glastonbury's legend. The Glastonbury monks responded with a highly politicized exercise in archaeology, claiming to have excavated a tomb identified as belonging to

Joseph of Arimathea, the news of their find being communicated both to Henry V and to the Council of Siena in 1424.

Books, libraries and archives

It was not only at Glastonbury that a sense of the past was strongly felt. The most impressive and ancient of all English monuments, Stonehenge, in Wiltshire, had first been noticed in writing by Henry of Huntingdon and Geoffrey of Monmouth, who had suggested that it had been magically transported by Merlin from Ireland. Not until the fourteenth century, however, did illustrations and crude 'maps' of the stones begin to appear. Similar drawings were still being produced in the 1440s. At Bury St Edmunds and at St Albans, attempts were made to draw up 'Books of Benefactors', not merely listing but attempting physically to portray the chief figures of the monastic past, even down to highly Disneyfied drawings of King Offa or Cnut. Other written reminders of the past were assiduously preserved and copied. At St Albans, Thomas of Walsingham, the most significant chronicler of the early fifteenth-century, not only wrote his history as a deliberate continuation of the earlier work of Matthew Paris, but ended his career composing an *Epitome* of Norman history, in which he joined up the events of his own lifetime to the duchy's earliest chronicles, running from Rollo in 911 AD to Henry V's conquests after 1417.

A similar interest was shown in the old English past. Although it was immensely popular in the twelfth century, only two surviving manuscripts of Bede's *Ecclesiastical History*, the greatest of Anglo-Saxon books written in Latin, survive from the century after 1200. By contrast, no less than eighteen survive from the fourteenth century and a further eleven from the century after 1400. Bede himself was not canonized until 1935, but his grave at Durham was already, by 1400, being exhibited as a curiosity and potential shrine. Other English saints became the focus of revived attention. Requests had been made ever since the 1220s for the canonization of Osmund, first Norman bishop of Salisbury, but it was not until a further campaign of petitioning, in 1457, that the Pope officially recognized Osmund as a saint. At Winchester, the remains of the Anglo-Saxon St Swithun were translated to a major new shrine as late as 1476. Robert Grosseteste, bishop of Lincoln, whose merits as a saint had never been recognized by the papacy, was rediscovered in the 1360s by John Wycliffe and his followers, who assiduously read and recopied the manuscripts of Grosseteste's works that they found mouldering in the library of the Franciscan convent at Oxford, recognizing in Grosseteste one of the earliest and most outspoken critics of the Pope's claim to worldly rule.

As this story suggests, the libraries of medieval England were themselves increasingly piled high with the lumber of several centuries of literary and intellectual endeavour. In the fourteenth century, in an era when all books had to be consulted as handwritten manuscripts, many of them very rare, attempts were already being made by the Franciscans of England to compile a register listing all of the principal authors and texts required for study, a finding list cross-referenced to where precisely in England the books of these authors might be read. This guide, the so-called *Registrum Anglie*, was itself then used by Henry of Kirkstead, prior of Bury St Edmunds, who not only catalogued the more than 1,500 manuscripts that were already to be found at Bury, but compiled biographical and bibliographical registers of his own, listing as many monastic authors as were known to him with details of where, amongst more than 180 other English locations, their works might be consulted. Endeavours such as this, involving travel and communication amongst dozens of individual libraries, not only produced the first ancestors of Google and the properly annotated searching aid, but some of the earliest scholarly investigations of the identity of authors, the precise attribution of their works, in short exactly the sort of thing that medieval historians are still engaged in writing more than 600 years later.

Nor was it only monks who took to this sort of work. William of Worcester, the well-educated son of a Bristol saddle maker, secretary to Sir John Fastolf and hence involved with the Pastons in the execution of Fastolf's will, was an early humanist and rediscoverer of the classical past who learned Greek and translated Cicero into English. He also toured England in search of antiquities and topographical curiosities, copying out what he found into a series of note-books that very soon became valuable historical curiosities in their own right. At much the same time, John Rous of Warwick began writing his own antiquarian histories of the earls of Warwick (lavishly illustrated from tombs and seals), a history of the universities of Oxford and Cambridge (intended to disprove that the Greek mathematician Pythagoras was involved in the foundation of Cambridge), and a chronicle of the bishops of Worcester. Like William of Worcester, Rous deserves to rank as one of the first true anti-quaries in English history, as interested in the development of styles of armour as he was in recording historic monuments or the population of the villages through which he passed.

As early as the reign of King John, when a man named William 'Cucuel' is recorded taking receipt of chancery rolls dispatched from the itinerant court, the kings of England had an archivist. The task of maintaining the royal archive none-theless became ever more arduous and awesome as the thir-teenth century progressed and the mountains of parchment began to pile up. Already by the 1320s, when they were listed by the King's treasurer in a systematic 'array', the King's records were being treated as a vast time-capsule, none of them more venerable or more famous than Domesday Book. By the 1420s, the records of the twelfth or thirteenth centuries were of little or no use in the day-to-day business of government. Some were occasionally consulted. Most were left undisturbed from one end of a century to the next. The very fact, however, that they were not destroyed but kept, catalogued and arrayed tells us something important about fifteenth-century attitudes.

England was now officially a nation with a past, with its kings as the chief guardians and symbols of that heritage. With an interest in the past, and with antiquarianism came the deliberate collection of old things, not just as religious relics but merely because they were self-evidently 'old'. Richard Bury, bishop of Durham from 1333, author of the first surviving treatise on books as artefacts, scoured the second-hand book stalls of England in search of rarities. Autograph hunters are to be found as early as the 1390s, seeking out specimens of the handwriting of Abbot Thomas de la Mare of St Albans, 'copious and untidy but speedy', treasured in part because of the sanctity of the writer, in part as simple souvenirs. There was more than mere sentiment to such attitudes. Those who control the past generally possess the power to control the future. The processes of law, for example, in which the tracing of manorial descents, the verification of pedigrees and the proving or disproving of title occupied a central place, supplied a powerful incentive to historical research. It is no coincidence that one of the chief targets of the peasants of 1381 had been the burning of manorial records, and with them the proofs of hated servitude. It was by careful manipulation of the genealogical records of the royal family that such political coups as the Lancastrian seizure of power in 1399 and the Yorkist rebellion of the 1450s were brought to pass. In the fifteenth century, to adapt the words of T.S. Eliot, 'England was now and History'.

Music

Of all the arts, it is music which best conveys nostalgia and the fleeting nature of time. Thomas of Walsingham, at St Albans, besides writing on history, composed musical treatises in which he discussed such matters as the duration of notes and rhythmic modes. Archbishop Arundel, chief hammer of heretics, offered a passionate defence of music in the liturgy, arguing, against the Lollards, that singers and pipers kept up the spirits of pilgrims and that more pious insight could be obtained from listening to organs and good singers than from many sermons. The great stained glass windows of the Beauchamp chapel at Warwick, built in the 1440s, are cluttered not just with objects that display the luxury and consumerism of the fifteenth-century gentry but with such novel musical instruments as clavichords and harpsichords. After Agincourt, Henry V, whose father was himself a composer of religious music, commanded that no songs be made of his victories. Even so, such songs survive, commemorating his siege of Harfleur and Agincourt itself, this latter ('Our King went forth to Normandy, with grace and might of chivalry') being perhaps the first English 'pop' song, or rather the first English football 'chant' still known to us.

England by the 1420s had a music, a history and a sense of destiny that were distinctively her own. Time itself seemed no longer to march to a divine but to a human rhythm, measured by clocks, in musical notation, by regnal years, even by the rise and fall of English dynasties. In 1399, England could boast one of the oldest established royal dynasties, only the fifth (or the third if one allows that kings Cnut and Stephen were mere offshoots of the dynasties that they usurped) to have ruled England in the 600 years since King Alfred. By 1485, three further dynasties had come, and in two cases gone. Time itself was being cluttered up with names, dates and events. Amidst such a landscape, past certainties were to be treasured, no longer to be discarded as so much junk.

8

FROM RICHARD II TO RICHARD III,
1377–1485

Richard II

The coronation of Edward III's ten year-old grandson, Richard II caused delight to the chronicler Thomas Walsingham, latest successor to Matthew Paris as official historian at St Albans Abbey. According to Walsingham this was a day

> of joy and gladness…the long-awaited day of the renewal of peace and of the laws of the land, long exiled by the weakness of an elderly king and the greed of courtiers and servants.

There have been few more inaccurate predictions in English history. Richard II's coronation in July 1377 was in fact the beginning of the end for the Plantagenet dynasty, and ushered in one hundred years of slaughter at the elite end of society, culminating in the so-called Wars of the Roses after 1455. St Albans itself was to host not just one but two of the greater battles of these wars. There is a sense here of English history feeding upon itself. Several of the kings who ruled England after Edward III bear uncanny resemblances to kings already long dead: Richard II to Edward II, Henry V to Richard I, and Henry VI not just to Henry III but to Edward the Confessor.

Between the death of Edward III in June 1377 and the coronation of his grandson, Richard II, French and Spanish ships sacked the south coast of England, penetrating as far inland as Lewes, within a few miles of the site of the Battle of Hastings, burning Folkestone, Portsmouth, Dartmouth and Plymouth. It was in the midst of these attacks that Richard II was crowned, on 16 July, a Thursday. This was the first time since the hurried coronation of Henry III in 1216 that a King had not been crowned on a Sunday. Perhaps the chaos of the moment forced the government's hand. Perhaps, as Froissart hints, the coronation was hurried through amidst rumours that, otherwise, John of Gaunt, the King's uncle, might himself be crowned king. Coronation alone did not stem the crisis. From August into September 1377, the Isle of Wight was occupied by the French, Southampton was attacked and Poole was burned. Attacks upon the Isle of Wight continued into the 1380s, with sackings and the kidnapping of prominent citizens. Gravesend, only a few miles up the Thames from London, was burned by the French in 1380. By 1385, in alliance with the Scots, a French army was threatening to operate south of the Scots border whilst a French fleet proposed to attack England's southern coast, the first time since the reign of King John, and the dark days after Magna Carta, that England itself was so menaced.

Richard II's early years were thus overshadowed at first by warfare, then by the Peasants' Revolt of 1381, which revealed the fragility of royal authority. Richard acquitted himself well in the crisis of 1381. He was nonetheless entirely dependent upon a council, in which the servants of his late father, the Black Prince, coexisted uneasily with the great aristocrats and in particular with the king's uncles, John of

Gaunt, duke of Lancaster and Thomas of Woodstock, Duke of Gloucester. Like Edward II before him, Richard II found it impossible to keep his friendships within bounds. Without quite the scandal or passion that had attended Edward II's relations with Piers Gaveston, by 1384 Richard was so closely attached to Robert de Vere, Earl of Oxford, a young man five years his senior, that whispers began to spread at court. Sodomy was amongst the crimes with which Richard was eventually charged, albeit many years later and perhaps with scant justification. Earl Robert, meanwhile, was the latest in a line of impoverished members of the Vere family, of impeccable lineage, ennobled as long ago as the reign of Stephen, yet lacking the resources to maintain themselves in proper aristocratic state. Richard showered him with favours, including promotion as marquess, subsequently in 1386 as Duke of Ireland, the first time that a ducal title had been bestowed outside the immediate royal family.

Just as with Gaveston after 1307, Vere's promotion was resented by established figures at court. Vere himself lacked the political sense not to flaunt his good fortune. In particular, he seems to have poisoned the King's mind against John of Gaunt, raising the suspicion that Gaunt had set his own eyes upon the throne, either for himself or for his son, Henry Bolingbroke. Bolingbroke, at this stage Earl of Derby, was an almost exact contemporary of King Richard, who, in 1381, at the height of the peasant assault on London, whilst the King rode out to confront the rebels at Mile End, had been captured and threatened with death by the mob that invaded the Tower. Henry was saved only by the intervention of a servant whose bravery Richard II would soon have good cause to regret.

Tensions between Gaunt and the King came to a head on King Richard's first military campaign, in 1385 when he rode north to confront the Scots. Having burned Melrose Abbey and a series of targets between Newcastle and Edinburgh, Richard sought to end his campaign. Gaunt urged him to cross the Firth of Forth into the Highlands. Richard refused. By the time the army returned south, uncle and nephew were barely on speaking terms. A solution was devised. For nearly twenty years, Gaunt had been eager to pursue a claim to the throne of the Castile, acquired by his marriage to a daughter of the late King Pedro. It was with this Castilian claim in mind that treaties had been signed between England and Portugal, a Christian kingdom first established with the assistance of English crusaders in the 1140s, and thereafter a major centre for English trade. The Anglo-Portuguese treaties negotiated in 1373, renewed in 1386, initiated an alliance today still not broken after more than six hundred years.

These treaties ensured that Port wine was to become the favoured drink, and the downfall, of many an English gentleman. They also allowed John of Gaunt to lead an expeditionary force to northern Spain, now backed by the King in Parliament, only too anxious to rid himself of his overbearing uncle. Landing at La Coruña in Galicia, and therefore tracing out, like the Black Prince before him, much of the itinerary later followed by British armies in the wars against Napoleon, Gaunt failed to make good his claim to the Castilian throne, instead surrendering it in exchange for the marriage of his daughter to another of the claimants and a massive cash indemnity. He nonetheless managed conveniently to absent himself from England just as the crisis at the English court reached its climax. Furthermore, the Spanish pension paid to him each year throughout the 1390s added significantly to the resources available to him and his son in England.

In Gaunt's absence, an aristocratic coalition headed by the Duke of Gloucester and the earls of Arundel and Warwick, emerged to challenge the authority of the King's friends, targeting in particular Robert de Vere, Simon Burley and Michael de la de Pole, son of the Hull wool merchant whose career we have already encountered, appointed chancellor in 1383 and two years later created Earl of Suffolk. Pole was tarnished not only by his association with shady commercial transactions but through his failure to negotiate any effective peace with France. The French wars, indeed, had descended into tragi-comedy when the boneheaded bishop of Norwich, Henry Despenser, himself a grandson of Edward II's favourite Hugh Despenser the younger, had been entrusted with a major subsidy from the English Church and command of a 'crusade', authorized by the Pope who was at odds with the King of France. Landing at Calais in 1383, Despenser's 'crusade' had attacked Dunkirk and Ypres (names more usually associated with British warfare in the twentieth century), but had then beaten a hasty and humiliating retreat when the French King appeared on the scene.

The bishop had been impeached in Parliament for incompetence. His reputation as a man of God hardly improved when, on the Scots campaign of 1385, he was challenged to armed combat by the bishop of Galloway as a means of resolving the allegiances of England and Scotland within the papal Schism. It was this same bishop Despenser whose prosecution of Lollards, after 1399, was to lead to the burning of the first Lollard martyr, William Sawtre. As if to emphasize the multiplying associations between the reign of Richard II and that of Edward II, Despenser's infant nephew Thomas, later recognized as Lord Despenser, was married to a cousin of the King. Both the personalities and the issues of the 1320s seemed to haunt the politics of the 1380s.

In 1386, to resist a threat of invasion, Pole demanded an unprecedented subsidy from Parliament, four times the conventional assessment, intended to finance defence. Parliament responded by demanding Pole's removal from office. Confronted with these demands, the King declared that he would not dismiss so much as a scullion from his kitchen at Parliament's request. The issue of royal patronage and the King's ability to choose his own ministers and friends returned, as under Edward II, to the very centre-stage of political debate. As if to emphasize the parallels that might be drawn with the past, and as yet another reminder of the degree to which English history had become a self-referential phenomenon,

Richard is said to have threatened to seek aid from the French, no doubt thinking of Henry III, in the 1260s, seeking out the assistance of Louis IX in his own disputes over patronage against the English barons led by Simon de Montfort. Reminded by Gloucester and Arundel of the fate of Edward II, Richard once again resorted to past precedent, like Henry III in the 1260s, leading a great 'gyration' of England, avoiding Westminster and postponing his response to baronial demands by touring the country in an attempt to drum up support for his cause.

In November 1387, Gloucester, Arundel and the Earl of Warwick, later joined by Henry Bolingbroke and Thomas Mowbray (future Duke of Norfolk), launched a formal indictment of treason against five of the King's favourites, naming Pole, Vere and the Archbishop of York. The King himself was portrayed as a mere adolescent, victim of the adolescent's balance of humours which itself rendered him inconstant, lacking the 'virtue' ('*virtus*', implying the qual-ities of a full-grown man or '*vir*') that was expected of a ruler. Vere, widely regarded as no true '*vir*', responded by raising troops against these 'Lords Appellant'. On 20 December, his force was decisively defeated at Radcot Bridge on the Thames in Oxfordshire, site of a castle built for siege operations during the civil war of Stephen's reign and not twenty miles from Deddington, the site of Piers Gaveston's arrest in 1312. The Earl of Warwick who engineered Vere's downfall in 1387 was himself the grandson of the earl who, in 1312, had arranged the arrest and beheading of Gaveston. History cast a long shadow.

Vere fled into exile. Rumours circulated that the King was about to be deposed. Instead, in the so-called Merciless Parliament of 1388, the Lords Appellant arranged the impeachment and execution on charges of treason of eight of the King's ministers. Vere and Pole were sentenced in their absence. Burley and five others were beheaded despite impas-sioned appeals for leniency, with the Queen going down on her knees to plead for Burley's life, just as Richard II's grand-mother, Queen Philippa, had pleaded forty years earlier for clemency towards the burghers of Calais. Richard II neither forgave nor forgot the injury done to Burley, who had carried him on his shoulders as a ten-year-old boy to his coronation in 1377. On the precise spot of Burley's execution on Tower Hill, the King was later to have his revenge. In the meantime, and as with the earlier history of Edward II, the Appellants failed to put public duty before self-interest, or to agree in anything save their detestation of the executed ministers. Although in theory royal government was now put into commission, the King himself swiftly regained control over the conduct of his affairs.

The fact that revenge had now become the dominant charac-teristic of Richard's reign is perhaps surprising. Richard himself was a cultivated and by no means incompetent ruler. His marriage, in 1382, to Anne of Bohemia, daughter of the late Holy Roman Emperor, Charles IV, and sister of the emperor-elect, Wenceslas IV, King of Bohemia, brought him into contact with one of the most splendid courts in Europe. The style of Charles IV's court at Karlstein, south of Prague, was replicated in Richard's palaces and can be detected behind the self-image that Richard sought to project through such works of art as his 'coronation' portrait at Westminster Abbey, showing him enthroned in full majesty, his eyes staring with dispassionate intensity, like those of an icon of Christ, directly into the viewer's line of sight.

Besides the usual investment in luxury, embroidery and gilded toys, Richard's court was perhaps the first to have used, perhaps the first to have invented, pocket handker-chiefs: 'small pieces (of linen) to be given to the King to carry in his hand to dab and clean his nose', as his tailor's bill puts it, lacking any word for so unfamiliar a thing. New innova-tions in fashion, skin-tight hose, long pointed shoes, folly bells and even the cod-piece, speak of a court where conspicuous consumption and display were encouraged. The

Wilton Diptych, the most glorious of his surviving commissions, not only reveals Richard's devotion to the Virgin Mary, but his employment of symbols: the white hart (or 'Richart') badge, worn by each one of the eleven angels in attendance on the Virgin; the gold collar of broomcods (the seed pod of the broom plant) that Richard himself wears, and the broomcods scattered amongst harts across the King's robe, ultimately derived from the 'plante de genêt' or wild broom from which Richard's own 'Plantagenet' dynasty was named, more recently reimported from the court symbolism of Charles VI of France; the eagles and the flowers of rosemary with which the painting is scattered, symbols themselves of Anne of Bohemia and of Richard's links to the Holy Roman Empire. The technique of the painting is a combination of northern Gothic, laid over chalk on oak panels, but employing pigments bound with a medium of egg, and flesh tones under-modelled in green, themselves borrowed from the most advanced painting of the Italian *trecento*. This indeed, is one of the greatest works of pre-Renaissance art and a reminder that, under Edward III and Richard, English mercenaries were regularly employed in the wars of Florence and northern Italy. Bishop Despenser of Norwich, before promotion to his English diocese, had fought for the papacy in its wars against the Visconti rulers of Milan, a dynasty into which the second son of King Edward III had himself been married. Simon Burley, victim of the purge of 1388, had owned a copy of Giles of Rome's treatise on government, in which the King's duty to rule is presented as a divine obligation, ultimately beyond the constraint of mere earthly law. Machiavelli himself would have been at home in the English court politics of the 1390s.

If the Wilton Diptych directs us to the future, then it is also firmly anchored in the past. Richard himself is shown kneeling in the company of three saints: John the Baptist (to whom Richard and his grandfather, Edward III, displayed particular devotion), St Edmund of Bury and St Edward the Confessor.

The Confessor's shrine at Westminster played a major role in Richard's life: it was here that he had prayed and made offering before riding out to meet the peasant rebels at Smithfield in 1381, and it was here that he conducted candlelit visits by night for some of his more important diplomatic guests, including the Christian king of Armenia. The monks of Westminster Abbey regarded Richard as their greatest royal patron since Henry III, dedicating to him treatises on the history of the abbey, its rights of sanctuary, its Anglo-Saxon privileges, its crown jewels and regalia, its relics and in particular its relic of the Holy Blood, first granted by Henry III. Richard incorporated the Confessor's emblem, a cross patonce between five martlets, within his own heraldic coat of arms. It was at Westminster, in the rebuilding of William Rufus' great hall, that Richard invested the majority of the funds that he devoted to building.

Once again, it is important to notice here the reverence for the past: Westminster Hall was reroofed and refurbished, but it was neither razed nor rebuilt. History was now heritage. The clearest example of Richard's attachment to history comes through his devotion to the cult of Edward II. Murdered in 1327, Edward had attracted little interest over the next fifty years. Richard II, however, not only commissioned an enquiry into the miracles worked at Edward's tomb, but twice, in 1390 and again in 1397, sent embassies to the Pope, hoping to obtain official canonization for Edward as a saint. He also requested, equally unsuccessfully, that Archbishop Arundel consecrate him with the oil of St Thomas, supposedly delivered to Thomas Becket by divine intervention, first recorded in the reign of Edward II when Edward himself had sought to be anointed with it.

Like Edward II after 1312, Richard II after 1388 passed his time preparing revenge. The atmosphere at court veered from frosty towards terror. The death of Anne of Bohemia in 1394 was followed by an outpouring of royal grief in which the King is said to have ordered the demolition of his palace at

Sheen, only recently built and supplied with such luxuries and innovations as piped hot and cold water with large brass taps, with personal latrines for each bedroom. Nonetheless, the fact that Anne had never once fallen pregnant left the question of the succession still undecided. It also opened the way for a renewal of negotiations with France.

In 1396, Richard was betrothed to the young daughter of Charles VI, as part of a twenty-eight-year truce negotiated with the French.

Ireland

In the meantime, the King had led a military expedition into Ireland, intended to subdue the rebel and self-styled 'King of Leinster', Art (or Arthur, a name not without significance for Englishmen concerned about myths of the once and future king) MacMurrough. Richard thus became the first English king since John in 1210, and the last before James II in the 1680s, to visit his Irish dominions. The date of his crossing, in October 1394, was itself determined by history. October was far too late in the year for proper campaigning. It had none-theless been in October 1171 that King Henry II, the founder of Richard's dynasty, had first crossed to Ireland, landing like Richard in 1394, at Waterford. The relative success of his expedition, in which the Irish chieftains were made to swear fealty to Richard, removing their caps, belts and weapons and, on their knees, placing their hands between those of the King, contributed to a rise in Richard's confidence. On his return to England, he arranged for the reburial of Robert de Vere, who had died and been buried in exile at Louvain four years before, in the Vere family mausoleum in Essex. It might have struck contemporaries that Edward II, in the aftermath of his Scots campaign of 1314, had reburied Piers Gaveston, originally interred at Oxford, in great pomp at the Dominican Priory of King's Langley in Hertfordshire. Also in 1395, Richard made arrangements for his own burial at Westminster, requesting that his epitaph proudly declare 'He threw down all who violated the royal prerogative; he destroyed heretics and scattered their friends.' This great 'throwing down' was about to begin.

To his household, Richard had already recruited a loyal body of Cheshire archers; Cheshire had been part of his estate even before the death of Edward III and it had been to Cheshire that he already turned during the crisis of 1387. Whilst his archers slept in the same room with him, calling him 'Dycun', the tone for the rest of the court had changed. Exalted titles, an insistence that courtiers address Richard as 'majesty' or 'prince', marked the King's new aloofness. According to one chronicler, it became the King's custom to sit enthroned 'from dinner till vespers, talking to no one but watching everyone. When his eye fell on a courtier, regardless of rank, that person had to bend the knee towards the King.' The last sovereign to behave in such a way had been Empress Matilda, during her brief period of power in the 1140s, who had insisted on remaining seated whilst her lords stood and who, as a result, had been chased out of London for her arrogance.

Some historians have suggested that, by 1397, Richard was losing touch with reality, his paranoia and his isolation symptoms of mental instability. Those who caught sight of the King's dancing costume adorned with one hundred oranges of silver gilt, or his 'hanselyn' (perhaps another doublet) embroidered with water, rocks and leeches, and embellished with thirty whelks and mussels of silver gilt and fifteen cockles of white silver, might have been forgiven for supposing that the days of Caligula or Nero were come again. Even so, such luxurious self-indulgence does not in itself spell madness. If the King was mad, it is remarkable that his move against the Appellants, when it came, was so well-timed and executed.

In July 1397, without apparent warning, Richard ordered the arrest of the Duke of Gloucester and the earls of Arundel and Warwick. John of Gaunt, by now an old man, outwardly reconciled to the King since his return from Spain, stood mutely by. In Parliament, summoned that September under

the gaze of 200 of Richard's Cheshire archers, the three
Appellants were indicted for treason. Arundel was convicted
and carried to execution at precisely the same spot on Tower
Hill where Burley, the King's tutor, had been beheaded nine
years before. Gloucester, the King's uncle and the brother of
John of Gaunt, had already been promised that the King would
show him 'the same mercy as was shown to Burley'. In
Parliament it was announced that the duke had been carried off
to Calais where he had died; the suspicion, later confirmed as
fact, was that he had been stifled there under a feather bolster,
at Richard's command. Thomas Arundel, Archbishop of
Canterbury and brother of the disgraced earl, was exiled for
life, as was the Earl of Warwick, dispatched to that remotest of
wildernesses, the Isle of Man.

Rebellion

For those who remained, most notably for Thomas Mowbray,
now Earl of Norfolk, and Henry Bolingbroke, earl of Derby,
these were dangerous days. Although in theory pardoned for
their part in the events of 1388, neither of them could ignore
the signs of tyranny and paranoia at court. Mowbray mentioned
plots at court to Bolingbroke. Bolingbroke mentioned them to
his father, John of Gaunt, who in turn informed the King.
Mowbray and Bolingbroke quarrelled, not least because
Bolingbroke blamed Mowbray for the murder of his uncle,
Gloucester. The King insisted that a duel be fought, but then
just as suddenly cancelled his command, in September 1398,
imposing exile on both parties. Bolingbroke was promised that
he might seek his father's lands, should John of Gaunt die
during his absence overseas. In fact, at Gaunt's death, the
following February, the King seized the entire honour of
Lancaster into his own hands, disinheriting Bolingbroke.
Confident that he had dealt with the situation, Richard then
crossed once again to Ireland. Bolingbroke had little alternative but to act. He landed at Ravenspur in Holderness on 1
July 1399. The Duke of York, Richard and Bolingbroke's uncle

and the last surviving son of Edward III, threw in his lot with the rebellion. So did the Duke of Northumberland, Henry Percy, and his son, another Henry, known as 'Hotspur', perhaps on the understanding that Bolingbroke was merely demanding his personal rights and reform of the realm, more likely already aware that deposition was the only means by which the King could be silenced. The King himself returned from Ireland to Conway in north Wales, where he was met by Northumberland and promised that Bolingbroke, who would meet him at Flint, sought only his own inheritance. At Flint, Bolingbroke took the King captive, carrying him off to imprisonment at the Tower.

Henry IV

For the second time in the century, an aristocratic rebellion had imprisoned the King. Like Edward II in 1326, also taken captive in Wales, Richard II was kept out of the public gaze and, in secret, persuaded to abdicate. Those who 'received' his abdication, including Henry Bolingbroke and Archbishop Arundel, declared that Richard had gone voluntarily, surrendering his signet ring to Bolingbroke as a token of his desire that Bolingbroke succeed him as king. In all probability, there was nothing voluntary about it. Parliament accepted the fait accompli. A charge sheet was hastily prepared against the former King and his tyranny, and on 13 October, a Monday, clearly chosen because it was the greatest day in the liturgical year for the Westminster monks, the feast day of their own saint Edward the Confessor, Bolingbroke was crowned at Westminster as King Henry IV. For his coronation, Archbishop Arundel employed the very oil of St Thomas, first discovered by Edward II, prized by Richard II, and which henceforth was to be used at the coronation of at least three further English kings. Stored in a golden vessel shaped like an eagle, and said to have been given to St Thomas by the Virgin Mary, this substance in theory conferred even greater honour on the kings of England than was conferred on the kings of France by their own holy oil stored at Rheims, brought down from heaven by a mere dove not by an imperial eagle or by Christ's own mother. The coronation of 1399 was also quite possibly the first occasion when the stone of Scone, confiscated from the Scots a century earlier, was used in the inauguration of an English King. To crown so unlikely a king as Henry IV required every trick in the Westminster dressing-up box.

Richard II, meanwhile, was dispatched to Pontefract castle, within Henry's own honour of Lancaster. There he died, perhaps stifled like Gloucester, perhaps having starved himself to death. It was surely no coincidence that it had been at Pontefract that Edward II had condemned to death Henry's own ancestor, the first of the great Lancastrian rebels, Thomas of Lancaster. In 1387, almost at the moment of his joining the Lords Appellant in rebellion against the King, Henry Bolingbroke had named his own second son Thomas, the second figure in family history to bear the name Thomas of Lancaster. In his lifetime, Richard II had requested burial at Westminster. Henry IV ignored this wish and instead had Richard, his cousin, interred at the Dominican friary at King's Langley. The significance here was also plain enough. It was at King's Langley that Edward II had buried Piers Gaveston. In death, Richard was to join not his royal ancestors but a hated royal catamite, beheaded for his abuse of power. In an almost equally fitting echo of the past, at much the same time that Richard was buried, Thomas Lord Despenser, a great-grandson of another equally notorious favourite of Edward II, was seized in rebellion at Cardiff, carried off to Bristol and there executed by the mob. Truly, Richard II's had been a reign haunted by England's past.

For the English of the fourteenth century to have killed one king (Edward II), might be considered a misfortune. To have killed two began to look like deliberate carelessness. Henry IV might pose as God's anointed, his coronation timed to coincide with the feast day of the pacific Edward the

Confessor. But the Confessor's feast itself fell on the eve of the anniversary of the Battle of Hastings, 14 October, and Henry IV's accession itself marked almost as dramatic a debut for the new king as William of Normandy's victory of 1066. In 1327, Edward III, hustled on to the throne a few years or decades before his time, had at least been the son of the previous king, born in the purple. In 1399, by ending the rule of a dynasty more than two hundred and fifty years old, Henry IV proclaimed himself every bit as much a usurper as William of Normandy three centuries before.

Taking a short-term view, the problems of legitimacy that were to haunt fifteenth-century politics were the outcome of the Lancastrian revolution of 1399, ensuring that after Richard II no king could sleep soundly in his bed. Viewed in the longer term, the accession of Henry IV and his Lancastrian dynasty was itself the product of a slow slide towards violence and usurpation begun as long ago as the 1290s with the gathering pace of warfare on England's frontiers, the emergence of treason trials against leading subjects in which death was the inevitable sentence, and the incremental way in which revenge and the desire for vengeance were established as driving forces within aristocratic politics.

At the time of his accession, Henry IV's greatest strengths were his piety and his wealth. In the 1390s, as Earl of Derby, he had twice volunteered to crusade against the pagans of Lithuania. On the second occasion, when the campaign ended prematurely, he had travelled as a pilgrim to Jerusalem, the ultimate goal of all crusaders. As heir to the honour of Lancaster and the lands of John of Gaunt, he already had the prospect of an annual income of at least £12,000. Combined after 1399 with the estates of the crown, this rendered him perhaps the wealthiest man, in terms of his personal fortune, to have ruled England since the Conquest of 1066. This brought further problems, however, since it persuaded the Commons that Henry IV no longer had need of subsidies voted by Parliament. Indeed, it was widely supposed that, before ascending the throne, the new King had proclaimed his intention to live 'off his own', without the crippling taxes that for the past fifty years had poisoned relations between crown and taxpayers. If Henry made any such undertaking, then he very soon came to regret it.

From the shadows, both foreign and domestic issues emerged to tarnish Henry's claims to legitimacy. To the costs of maintaining the affinity of Lancastrian knights and retainers he had inherited from his father were now added those of the royal household. Henry's personal finances spiralled out of all control. Far worse, as early as January 1400, within only three months of his coronation, a plot emerged to kill the King and his sons and to restore the deposed Richard II. It was in the subsequent reprisals that Lord Despenser was murdered by the Bristol mob. Richard II's own demise, announced within a few weeks, was another immediate consequence of this threat to the new regime. The King's knights were put to good use in Scotland, in August 1400, when they were amongst a major force of over 15,000 men sent north in an attempt to persuade King Robert III to recognize Henry's title as king. For the rest, it was left to the Percys, for the past fifty years or more virtually independent rulers of the northern March, to impose order on the Scots, inflicting a major defeat upon Scots raiding parties at Homildon Hill in September 1402. Meanwhile, as early as September 1400, within only a month of his return from the north, Henry IV was confronted with rebellion in Wales.

Owen Glyn Dwr

Owen Glyn Dwr, distantly descended from the ancient princes of Deheubath, more closely allied to such English marcher families as Lestrange and Hanmer, and himself previously attached to the household of the fitzAlan earls of Arundel, declared himself 'prince of Wales', gathering together a small band of supporters and crackpots, complete with his own bard, a man named Crach Ffinant, 'the prophet'. The initial spur to his rebellion appears to have been rivalry with a local English lord. Deeper tensions underpinned its success, including long-standing Welsh resentment of the English monopolization of offices and the professions. What might have seemed a small gang of malcontents very soon swelled into a full-scale army, capable of sacking English border towns and declaring, with echoes of the 1290s, its determination to ensure 'the obliter-ation of the English language'. As in the 1290s, when the English king and his army appeared to defy the rebels, Owen and his men merely vanished 'into the woods'. English armies, as had been revealed in the reign of Edward I, in the short term were no match for native guerrilla resistance. By 1401, the Glyn Dwr revolt had spread across Wales. Welsh students at Oxford and Cambridge were said to be abandoning their studies, and Welsh labourers leaving English employment in order to swell the rebel ranks. Glyn Dwr himself laid siege to Carmarthen where his new standard, a golden dragon on a white field, was unfurled.

In the longer term, like previous Welsh risings, this was a doomed venture. The English control of the coastline, even despite such temporary setbacks as the Welsh seizure of Cardiff, Aberystwyth and Harlech, ensured that pressure could always be brought to bear. Unlike the Scots at Stirling Bridge or later at Bannockburn, Glyn Dwr's men never risked pitched battle with an English army, lacking either the desper-ation or the resources to inflict a defeat upon Henry IV that might have tipped the balance from rebellion into a full-scale revolt in the name of Welsh independence. Glyn Dwr himself could hardly claim the titles or bloodlines of a Robert de Bruce. Even as early as 1405, his fortunes were on the turn, although he continued to summon 'parliaments', to issue documents under his own princely seal dated according to the years of his reign, and for a further ten years, until his ultimate disap-pearance into legend after 1415 (the exact year of his death and its circumstances have never been securely established), to pose as a thorn in the flesh of English imperialism. As in Ireland, where from the 1360s the Statute of Kilkenny had enshrined earlier moves towards apartheid, forbidding English settlers to intermarry with the native Irish, to use the Irish language, or to have recourse to Irish law, one effect of Welsh intransigence was an even more draconian discrimination by the English against the Welsh. Meanwhile, the costs and the diversions of the campaign of Glyn Dwr, and the repeated failure to capture Glyn Dwr himself, mocked all claims by Henry IV to have brought peace or prosperity to the English people.

Furthermore, Glyn Dwr proved adept at concerting his efforts with those of the Scots, the French, the Irish, and most dangerously of all with Henry IV's domestic critics. In 1405, a French force some two and a half thousand strong landed at Milford Haven combining with the Welsh in raids into Worcestershire. The Welsh were still raiding into Merioneth in 1415, the year of Henry V's great victory at Agincourt. The Welsh revolt caused annual losses estimated as high as £8,500 to the King's Welsh estate, leave alone the costs of sending armies against Glyn Dwr in each year after 1401. By 1401, indeed, there were so many demands being made on the King's treasury that there was not even enough money to pay the messengers delivering them.

Battle of Shrewsbury

In the same year, a letter to the King, apparently from the former heretic, Bishop Repyndon of Lincoln, declared that 'joy has turned to bitterness...evils multiply themselves everywhere and hope of relief fades from the grieving hearts of men'. The Parliament of 1402 was the first since the deposition of Richard II to be asked to grant subsidies as well as to continue the customs duties on wool. In the following year, news reached the King of an alliance between the Percys, his erstwhile allies, and Glyn Dwr. The outcome was the first true battle to have been fought on English soil since Evesham in 1265. Outside Shrewsbury, on 21 July 1403, Henry IV met the Percys in force. The King himself was nearly killed, his standard hurled to the ground. His eldest son, the future Henry V, was seriously wounded by an arrow in the face. The younger Percy, 'Hotspur' was killed in the action. His uncle, the King's cousin, Thomas Percy, Earl of Worcester, was captured and executed. His father, Henry Percy, Earl of Northumberland, was tried and convicted of trespass rather than treason, and ultimately pardoned. Hotspur's body was carried off for burial at Whitchurch, but when rumours began to circulate that he had survived the battle, the King ordered that the body be exhumed and displayed in Shrewsbury market place, propped up between two mill stones. It was then ritually dismembered and its parts sent for display to the four corners of the realm. At the field of battle, over the common pit into which many hundreds of the slain had been thrown, the King endowed a chantry college, only the second such institution, since Battle Abbey built by William the Conqueror after Hastings, to have been founded by an English king on the site of his victory, and in this instance, as at Hastings, commemorating the victory by a King of England over an army of Englishmen.

Death of an Archbishop

The battle of Shrewsbury ended neither the Glyn Dwr rebellion nor the refusal of Henry IV's enemies to recognize Henry as legitimate king of England. Northumberland rebelled again in 1405, being joined by the Earl of Norfolk. For reasons that remain unclear but which perhaps derived from his kinship to the Percys, the rebellion was also joined by Richard Scrope, Archbishop of York, one of those churchmen who had previously striven hardest to justify the deposition of Richard II and the accession of the Lancastrian dynasty. At the first sign of the King's reaction, Northumberland fled, seeking refuge in Wales, then in Scotland, eventually being killed in 1408, his body posthumously quartered and his head sent for display on London Bridge. Scrope, however, paraded his continued defiance of the King. Like an earlier archbishop of York of the 1130s, leading out his militia in war against the Scots at the Battle of the Standard, he insisted on appearing armed and in armour, at the head of a private army of eight or nine thousand men. As this should remind us, like King Stephen in the 1130s, Henry IV after 1399 had been challenged first by the Scots, then by the Welsh, and now not only by English rebels but by English rebel bishops. History, as we have seen, has a tendency to repeat itself.

No match for the royal army sent against him, Archbishop Scrope then surrendered. He was carried off to Pontefract, the castle where Richard II had spent his last days five years before. Whilst the Archbishop of Canterbury, Thomas Arundel, sped northwards to plead for mercy, and whilst the King himself gave assurances that nothing untoward was about to happen, Scrope was condemned to death by a kangaroo court of laymen and lawyers and executed, at Clementhorpe, just outside the city of York. Five blows of the axe are said to have been required before his head was severed. He thus became the first English bishop to have suffered judicial execution since the foundation of the English Church nearly a millennium before, and the first bishop since Thomas Becket to have been killed, as it was assumed, at the direct order of an English king. The coincidence that both Henry II, the 'murderer' of Archbishop Becket, and Henry IV, the 'executioner' of Archbishop Scrope, shared the same name was not lost on contemporaries. A cult sprang up at York associated with the late archbishop and, by September 1406, measures had to be taken to cordon off Scrope's tomb in York Minster with high barriers. Henry IV, who had been anointed with Becket's oil at his coronation in 1399 and who had chosen to be buried in Canterbury Cathedral close to Becket's shrine, rather than amongst his Plantagenet ancestors at Westminster, had in effect re-enacted the circumstances of Becket's murder, if not in a cathedral then within easy sight of one. The precedent that his actions set, not least for the judicial execution of bishops on charges of treason (a charge to be levelled with bloody results throughout the sixteenth century), was a baleful one. Scrope's execution was followed by something approaching nervous collapse on behalf of the King.

For eight years after 1405, Henry IV retreated to the shadowed edges of English government. Various suggestions have been made as to the nature of his malady: mental illness, leprosy, ague, dropsy. Despite the bloated features displayed on his tomb effigy at Canterbury (itself carved from ultra-fashionable English alabaster), Henry IV himself had always been an ill-defined figure: keeping his own counsel, working from within the circle of his family and affinity rather than craving the theatre of public display. Whatever his personal feelings towards King Richard, for more than twenty years he had been schooled, blooded and closeted in the company of his royal cousin before, in 1399, springing his trap.

The sense of a mind moving in the dark, of hidden secrets, of beliefs at odds with received opinion, may have contributed to the suspicion with which the Church, after 1399, regarded Henry's court. As the chief price for continued backing of Henry's regime, Archbishop Arundel demanded royal support in the prosecution of heresy. The King himself, whatever his own opinion, had little alternative but to acquiesce. At moments of crisis meanwhile, Henry himself seems to have been quite happy to entertain calls for the disestablishment of the Church, the seizure of its revenues and their application to his own pressing financial needs. Another cry heard on these occasions was to have an equally long posterity: 'resumption', the demand that patronage unwisely distributed by earlier kings be clawed back to fill the gaping hole in public finance.

To judge from his own posterity, Henry IV was a highly capable man: all four of his sons, the future Henry V, Thomas of Lancaster, John duke of Bedford and Humphrey duke of Gloucester, were well-educated and active in politics or military affairs. It was to them, rather than to the usual run of place-men and ministers, that a great deal of the business of government was entrusted. In 1405, in a bizarre reversal of the history of the 1320s in which another, rather more famous

Thomas of Lancaster had been put to death at Pontefract, it was to his half-brother, Thomas, son of John of Gaunt and a veteran of the battle of Shrewsbury, that Henry had entrusted the trial and execution of Archbishop Scrope. Thomas' brother, Henry Beaufort, bishop in turn of Lincoln and then Winchester, was accepted as a leading figure within Henry IV's counsels. This was the politics of family and affinity imported to the very heart of royal government: a practical demonstration of the ways in which such family harmony, only dreamed about by Edward III, might tame discord and power the great engines of state. Between 1407 and 1410, the council ruled without once summoning Parliament.

Royal Family Tree

The problem was that to many, after 1399, no matter what harmony might reign within the house of Lancaster, this was simply the wrong family to lay claim to government. At the time of Richard II's deposition, the Beauforts – Thomas, Henry and their elder brother John – were the rankest of parvenus, illegitimate children born to John of Gaunt's liaison with a low-born governess, Katherine Swynford, legitimized and promoted as recently as 1397 as a result of pressure brought to bear by Gaunt upon a weakened papacy. More seriously for Henry IV, even if it had been agreed in 1399 that King Richard, the only surviving offspring of Edward III's eldest son, the Black Prince, must go, there were other members of the royal family considered to have equal or indeed superior claims to those of Henry Bolingbroke. To understand why this was so, we must take a painful but necessary glance at the royal family tree. If what follows seems all too much like the plot of a Verdi opera without the charm of the music, or indeed like a list of the characters assembled from a Dickens novel, with no real sense of what these people said or did, then such is the price that has to be paid for an understanding of English politics in the fifteenth century. This was the politics of the gang boss, or the

Godfather, in which everybody was related to everyone else and God help the person who forgot that their enemy was someone's else cousin or friend. It was also a period in which noblemen shunned autobiographical disclosure. Just as mafia bosses tend not to write their memoirs, so there is a risk that, lacking personal details or disclosures, the great aristocrats of fifteenth-century England fade into a monochrome blur: so many Percys, Beauforts or Somersets, accumulating wealth and notoriety but with precious little, save dull dates and events, to distinguish between them.

Even so, we must at least attempt to set out the dynastic problems here. Henry IV's father, John of Gaunt, was the third of Edward III's five sons to have survived infancy. The fourth and fifth such sons, Gaunt's younger brothers, Edmund of Langley, Duke of York, and Thomas of Woodstock, Duke of Gloucester, both had offspring including Edmund Langley's son, the future Edward, Duke of York. Edmund Langley himself was still alive in 1399, and had defected to Henry IV's cause almost immediately on Henry's landing. Being descended from sons of Edward III junior to Gaunt, neither line of descent via York or Gloucester immediately overshadowed Henry IV's claim to the throne. More worrying was the figure of John of Gaunt's elder brother, Henry IV's uncle, Lionel of Antwerp, the second of Edward III's sons, created Duke of 'Clarence', his new title itself redolent of English history, derived from the castle, town and honour of Clare in Suffolk, home to an Anglo-Norman dynasty which had gone on to acquire vast estates in Wales and Ireland, much of which now came to Lionel. Lionel had died in 1368, when the future Henry IV was not yet two years old, but he had left a child to succeed him, a daughter, Philippa, married to Edmund Mortimer, Earl of March, a great-grandson of the Mortimer who in the 1320s had been the favourite and lover of Queen Isabella, Edward III's mother.

Edmund Mortimer died in 1381. His son by Philippa, Roger Mortimer, did not come of age until 1394. Even so, given that King Richard II had no children to succeed him, there was already discussion as to the rights that this Roger, as the direct descendant of Lionel of Antwerp, the second eldest of Edward III's sons, might have to be considered heir to the throne. The fact that his claim had passed through the female line counted for relatively little in a realm whose kings had led England into the Hundred Years War on the basis of the claims of a woman, Queen Isabella, might transmit rights to the throne of France.

Roger Mortimer died in 1398, on the brink of arrest, leaving a seven-year-old son, Edmund Mortimer, in no position to lay claim to the throne when Richard II was deposed. Even so, the wealth of the combined Mortimer and Clare estates rendered their holders potentially powerful. Both in 1397, when Roger Mortimer had been acclaimed on his return from Ireland by followers wearing his colours of red and green, and in 1403 when the followers of Henry 'Hotspur' Percy, himself married to Roger Mortimer's sister, had apparently shouted 'Henry Percy King' at the height of the Battle of Shrewsbury, there were signs that the Mortimers might be promoted as rivals to the Lancastrian line, if not by themselves then by those who sought to exploit their claims for factional advantage. A brother of Roger Mortimer, captured in Wales by Glyn Dwr, even proposed to kidnap Edmund, the Mortimer heir, then in the custody of Henry IV and to carry him off as a figurehead to launch a Mortimer claim to the throne. The plot was foiled before the boy had been taken further west than Cheltenham. Even so, Edward, Duke of York, the King's cousin, was briefly imprisoned for his failure to disclose what he had known of such plots against the crown. Throughout his reign, Henry IV had to keep careful watch not only over Church and state but over the incubus within his own family, the Mortimer claim, that threatened to reveal all his own, or his sons' claims to legitimacy as mere artifice.

Young Prince Henry and the French Crisis

This in turn helps to explain why Henry IV's eldest son and heir, Henry V, was so anxious to prove both his legitimacy and his close relationship with God. If not the closest heir to Edward III, then Henry V could at least prove himself the claimant whom the Almighty was keenest to promote. Trained up in the wars against Glyn Dwr, wounded in the face at the Battle of Shrewsbury, Henry was already an experienced commander by the time that his father fell ill in 1405. Perhaps not the favourite amongst his father's sons, he nonetheless stepped forwards to play a significant role in the council that over the next few years attempted to reform royal finance, to deal with the situation that arose when the heir to the throne of Scotland, the future James I, was fortuitously captured by English sailors at sea, and to consider the options in France that opened up as the result of the emergence of serious factional fighting between supporters of the Duke of Burgundy and the Armagnac party that had previously gathered around the Duke of Orléans. These disputes themselves reflected the fact that the King of France, Charles VI, was incapable of governing himself let alone his realm. First seized with the symptoms of madness in the early 1390s, Charles had since suffered episodes in which he believed himself to be made of glass, fearful of sitting down for fear of breaking, able to recognize no one and capable of no serious work save for looking at picture books.

As early as 1411, Prince Henry was proposing to lead an English expedition to France in support of the Burgundian faction. To this end, and so that Henry IV might himself join his son, 'an old streamer of worsted worked with the arms of the King, St Edward and St George' was prepared for the King's sailing to Calais, a sailing which in the event did not take place. In the same year, spurred on by his uncle, Henry Beaufort, the Prince may even have suggested that Henry IV abdicate in his favour. If so, this was a suggestion that merely fuelled discord between father and son, with Henry IV's last years perhaps dominated by his rivalry with the Prince.

Henry V

We must beware taking our view of Henry V from William Shakespeare, Laurence Olivier or the music of Sir William Walton. In all probability, the last years of the old King were nothing like so gloomy, nor the breach with his eldest son anything like so serious, as Shakespeare's history plays suggest. When Henry IV died in 1413, Henry V nonetheless chose to look to other role models than his father. Those that he selected not only set the tone for a renewal of warfare in France but for his own much vaunted orthodoxy in all matters relating to the Church. There were to be no Lollard knights at Henry V's court, as revealed, almost immediately after his succession, by the disgrace and flight of Sir John Oldcastle and his fellow conspirators. The wounds of the past were, in so far as was possible, to be healed. In 1413, the year of his accession, Henry V removed the body of Richard II from its exile at King's Langley and had it reinterred in the royal mausoleum at Westminster where it had originally been intended to lie.

To France

Warfare, meanwhile, supplied a convenient means both to test God's favour and to distract his critics from the severe political and financial crises with which the Lancastrian dynasty was still plagued. Henry IV had left so little money in his treasury that his executors initially refused to serve in the execution of his will. In warfare, Henry V could hope to revive the spirit of Edward III, his great-grandfather. By transforming the Anglo-French dispute into something approaching a crusade by Englishmen against the forces of French evil, he might even revive the spirit of the long-vanished Richard I, by this time considered the very paragon of Christian knighthood, author of near-mythical feats including a propensity for eating the flesh of his Saracen foes. Above all, in a peculiar reversal of the circumstances of 1066, Henry V might emulate the success of William 'the

Conqueror', through military victories demonstrating that his right to rule came directly from God.

Unlike his father, Henry V's appearance is not certainly known to us. The closest that we come is a sixteenth-century panel portrait that historians suggest is based upon a contemporary study from the life. What is most striking here is the haircut: a 'pudding bowl', shaved clear above both ears and at the back of the skull, that would lead most modern youths to sue their barber but which, in days gone by, was meted out to schoolboys, like prunes and cold baths, as one of the penalties of a classical education. The last time that a haircut like this had been worn by a potential king of England was in the Bayeux Tapestry, when it was precisely the shaving clear of their ears and neck that had proclaimed the spartan qualities of England's Norman conquerors. Now, rather than a Norman conquering England, an English King, similarly shaved, would take an army of English conquerors into Normandy.

Moving with a combination of diplomacy and skilful propaganda, already displayed in the presentation of the Oldcastle rebellion as something hydra-headed and frightful rather than the sad piece of incompetence that it actually was, by the end of 1414, Henry had proclaimed his intention to act as the hammer of all heretics and hence as a Christian ruler every bit as loyal to the Church as the King of France. He next had to provoke a reaction from France. Like Bismarck in the 1860s, he had to start a war without appearing to have done so. Ambassadors were sent to France to demand the proper implementation of the terms of the Treaty of Brétigny agreed more than fifty years before, the restoration of territories which the Treaty had in theory guaranteed to the English, the payment of more than £250,000 still owing from the ransom of King Jean II captured at Poitiers (who had died still in English captivity in 1364), and, most outrageously of all, the marriage of Henry himself to Catherine of Valois, Charles VI's youngest daughter. When the French replied with an offer of partial compliance, Henry demanded the whole deal, which was inevitably refused. He could thus pose as the injured party, and from November 1414 persuade Parliament to grant the subsidies necessary to restart the war.

His strategy at this stage was so bold as to defy common sense. He would allow God and history to decide the right-eousness of his cause. In other words, he would simply repeat the campaign of Edward III that had culminated in the first of the great English victories, at Crécy in 1346. He would land in Normandy and from there lead a great '*chevauchée*' in arms across northern France in the direction of Calais, trusting that this would provoke the French king to a full-scale confron-tation in which, as at Crécy, God would once again prove himself an Englishman. Like all the greatest generals, Henry not only had a bold plan, but the good fortune to unfold that plan more or less exactly as proposed. Landing at Harfleur on 14 August 1415, late in the campaigning season, within six weeks Henry had used his cannon to pound the town into surrender. Contrary to various retellings of the story, he allowed no massacre of the local population. On the contrary, having hoisted the royal standard and the banner of St George, the red cross symbolizing his crusading intentions, he ordered all women and children rounded up and sent under conduct to the French garrison at nearby Lillebonne. There they were indeed raped, but by their fellow Frenchmen, not by Henry's soldiers. Harfleur itself was to be turned into a base for future operations, and to this end its records were systematically burned in the public square, so that no one might know who had owned what. The history of Normandy itself was to be rewritten by fire. The parallels here to the Peasants' Revolt and the deliberate burning of manorial records are obvious and worth pondering.

Agincourt
From Harfleur, with barely a glance at Rouen, the ducal capital to the south, Henry marched his army, by now already depleted by the effects of dysentery, across country in the

direction of Calais. There was no need for this march, other than to re-enact the Crécy campaign, and to provoke a response. The army might just as easily have returned to England from Harfleur as from Calais. Throughout September and October, ships arrived at Harfleur to disembark the cannon used in Henry's siege. Nor was pillage a motive: the ordinances that Henry laid down for his army strictly prohibited any looting save for food. Provocation was clearly the chief intention. It succeeded. A fortnight's march by more than 10,000 men, hurried along to begin with at the rate of nearly twenty miles a day, forced by the French presence on the north bank of the Somme to march inland a full twenty miles to the north-east of Paris before a crossing of the Somme could be effected, most of their nights spent camping in the open regardless of the weather, brought Henry and his men on 24 October near to the small hamlet of Agincourt, only a day or two's march from Calais itself. Here, they encountered the French army commanded by the twenty-one-year-old Duke of Orléans. Scenting a defeated enemy, and just as keen to wipe clean past humiliations as the English were keen to reinflict them, the duke determined upon battle.

That night it rained, transforming the recently ploughed fields into a quagmire. Either side of the fields lay woods, filled with English and Welsh archers. Not surprisingly, the French were in no hurry to attack. A large part of the morning was spent in parleys and reconnaissance. Growing impatient with the delay, and defying all of the tactics by which English armies had previously triumphed against the French, at around ten in the morning Henry ordered his army go on the offensive. The eight thousand or so English men-at-arms were outnumbered by the French, by quite what proportion has never been agreed, probably more like two-to-one than the six-to-one or even thirty-to-one that various of the chroniclers allege. Urging his troops forward through the sticking mud, Henry nonetheless ensured that his archers came within range of the French cavalry before the French themselves had made preparations for defence let alone for a charge. The outcome was panic, as the French vanguard was forced back into a packed melée of horses and men which itself then came under assault from English archery.

This was far from the battle portrayed by Shakespeare or Laurence Olivier: no French cavalry charge, no sudden unleashing of thousands of bowstrings, merely a grim half-run, half-stumble by men in armour from one pile of corpses to the next. The Duke of Suffolk, who had only succeeded to his titles on the death of his father a few weeks earlier, was killed in the fighting, as was the Duke of York, the King's cousin. Terrified by what might be waiting for them over the next few clods of earth, the English waded up the field, pole-axing Frenchman after Frenchman as they went. There was little thought of prisoners or ransoms. At around 1pm, during a lull in the slaughter, just as the English began to consider the possibility of ransoming survivors, a rumour went round that the French planned to counterattack. The King ordered the killing of whatever prisoners remained. The rumour was false. By modern historians, who most definitely were not there, the King's order has been branded a war crime. In reality, like Richard I at Acre, Henry V had little alternative but to think of the consequences should he face a hostile and regrouped army with large numbers of his own men guarding prisoners rather than free to fight. The battle was bloody enough on both sides, without our needing to view it through a prism of twentieth-century correctitude. By the same token, attempts entirely to exonerate Henry, by suggesting that the massacred prisoners numbered only a few hundred rather than the thousands claimed by his critics, are equally futile. All told, the battle lasted between two and three hours. As soon it was over, the rain came down once more.

Agincourt concludes the great trio of English victories in the Hundred Years War, ranking with Crécy and Poitiers as proof that it was the English who won the battles, even though it was the French who eventually won the war. In this stark paradox lies a fundamental truth. No matter how many times the French were defeated in battle, the war itself was not to be decided by a few brief hours of slaughter. At Agincourt, Henry V proved that his cause was just and that God was on his side. His victory was greeted with general celebration in England. By Parliament he was accorded the unprecedented honour of a lifetime grant of the customs on wool. Bishop Henry Beaufort, his cousin, proclaimed the invincibility of the English nation (unconsciously echoing claims that had been made earlier about the Normans after Hastings), comparing Henry to David and the great heroes of the Biblical Old Testament. In reality, in France, little else had changed. Normandy, save for Harfleur, was still in French hands. None of the demands made in 1414 had been met.

Normandy

The real genius of Henry V, and the real story of his success revealed itself not at Agincourt, but two years later, in 1417, when, using Harfleur as his base, he launched a campaign to conquer Normandy from the French. Agincourt was incidental to this great achievement. To launch a proper conquest, extraordinary efforts had to be made. As early as February 1417, orders went out that six wing feathers be plucked from every goose in twenty English counties and sent to the Tower of London for the flighting of arrows. In Parliament, to raise taxation, Henry Beaufort compared the King's labours over the past six Parliaments to God's creation of the world in six days. Even then, the crown jewels had to be pawned to secure loans, the greatest of them from Beaufort himself, the start of a process by which Beaufort, and his resources as bishop of Winchester, came to underwrite crown finance. By the 1430s, it was the bishop who in effect controlled the purse strings and hence the strategy of the Hundred Years War. In Normandy itself, Henry won a series of great victories. His cannon beat down the walls of the city of Caen. The city's population was deliberately massacred, in accordance with Biblical precedent,

and to warn other towns against resistance. Within a year, the
port of Cherbourg had fallen, with Cherbourg and Caen in
1418, as in 1944, crucial to the supply of English troops operating in Normandy. The duchy's capital, Rouen, was besieged
from July 1418 and in January 1419 surrendered, offering an
indemnity of £50,000.

The engines of the 1060s had been put into reverse. An
English King now seized the places of William the Conqueror's
birth and burial. The surrender of Caen to Henry V was itself
effected by a monk of the abbey of St-Etienne, William the
Conqueror's great Benedictine foundation, who is said secretly
to have shown the English how to penetrate the town's
defences. From the moment that Rouen fell, Henry V began to
invite the reissue of charters granted by his Norman and
Plantagenet ancestors to Norman beneficiaries. Such large
numbers of monasteries and private individuals queued up to
have their ancient charters confirmed that Henry V's 'Norman
Rolls' remain one of our richest sources of information for
grants made in the eleventh and twelfth, not just in the fifteenth
century. Once again, history loomed large.

Yet, rather than attempt to rebuild the landholding patterns
of the twelfth-century, to restore such families as Beauchamp
or Neville or Fitzalan to their ancestral estates, the King
encouraged an entirely new bonanza of land grants and land
grabbing amongst his captains and associates. As in other
colonial situations, most obviously as in the Roman conquests
of antiquity, Norman estates were bundled up and handed
over wholesale to the victors of 1418. The profits here were
immense. It was from these spoils of war, in part from rents
newly granted in Normandy, in part from his ransoming of
French prisoners, that a man like Sir John Fastolf, future patron
of the Paston family, acquired the resources to build a moated
castle for himself at Caister in Norfolk, to patronize scholars
and the Church, to establish himself as a Knight of the Garter
and as a great man within his county, and to build up his collections of manuscripts and carpets, tapestries and jewels: a vast

pile of bling purchased with the more than £20,000 that he is estimated to have gained from the conquest and colonization of Normandy and Maine. Fastolf's profits were exceptional even by the standards of a kleptomaniac age. Nonetheless, they speak of the wealth that might be made from England's old world colonies: a colonial land grab taking place across the English Channel, only seventy years before the rulers of Spain instituted a rather more famous land grab of their own, in the new worlds opening up across the Atlantic.

Dissolution of Alien Priories

At the same time as this new pattern of landholding in Normandy and the regions southwards towards the Loire was being established by English soldiers and settlers, an older pattern, lingering from the time of the Norman Conquest of the 1060s, was finally cleared away. From the eleventh century through to 1415, despite many alarms along the way, large numbers of Norman and French religious houses had retained property in England, the endowment of 'alien' priories which had continued to look to France for guidance and the appointment of their heads. Fears had long been expressed that such houses harboured spies and the enemy within, but it was left to Henry V to order their final destruction. Henry V's conquest of Normandy not only reversed the patterns of 1066, allowing an English army now to plunder the lands of the original plunderers of the eleventh century, but was accompanied by the deliberate obliteration of the last vestiges of Norman domination in England.

From the great disendowment of alien priories which followed, significant resources were redistributed to new collegiate foundations: to Winchester College, to Wykeham's New College at Oxford, to Archbishop Chichele's All Souls. Henry VI's great colleges at Eton and at Cambridge were endowed with a large part of the English estate formerly controlled by the Norman abbots of Bec, cradle of Lanfranc, Anselm and most of the Norman archbishops of Canterbury in the century after 1066. Henry V's own foundation of a Charterhouse for Carthusian hermits at Sheen in Surrey was granted the English estate of the Norman abbey of St-Evroult, once home to the Anglo-Norman chronicler Orderic Vitalis, first celebrator of William the Conqueror's union between England and Normandy. This dissolution of the alien priories, which was bitterly resented in France, marked a highly significant break with the past. Like the King's decision from 1417 to address all of his private correspondence in English rather than French or Latin, it suggests a new, chauvinistic approach to the relations between England and France.

Where once the Normans had colonized England, it was now Englishmen who filled the role of sahibs and proconsuls, directing an enterprise in France organized for English rather than mutual Anglo-Norman benefit. Henry V's dissolution of the alien houses also paved the way to other disendow-ments of Church land: to the closure of failing small priories in the 1480s from which new religious foundations such as Magdalen College Oxford reaped significant gains, and ulti-mately to a far more dramatic dissolution of religious houses, when Henry VIII and the reformers of the 1520s turned their attention not just to alien but to English monasteries, beginning with what remained of the small fry, later laying hands on the greater prizes, in all cases merely continuing a process that had already begun under Henry V. In this way, as in his personal puritanism, Henry V supplied an important model for the sixteenth-century Protestant reformers. Once again, the fifteenth century emerges as Janus-faced, looking both forwards and backwards in time, its own identity never entirely secure.

On to Paris

Henry V's victories did not cease with the conquest of Normandy. By July 1419, the King's brother, Thomas of Lancaster, had reconnoitered the gates of Paris itself. In all previous Anglo-French warfare, even in the twelfth century when the Plantagenets had pushed their authority far up the Seine, Paris itself had remained inviolate. Now, even Paris trembled. On 10 September 1419, the French dauphin, heir to King Charles VI, met with Duke John of Burgundy at Montereau, south-east of Paris. During their parley, the duke was assassinated, stabbed through the head, clearly with the dauphin's connivance, in a continuation of the Armagnac–Burgundian dispute. As a monk displaying the duke's remains to a later French king is said to have remarked, 'it was through the hole in this skull that the English entered France'. With the dauphin now disgraced at the French court, and with Burgundy forced into alliance with the English, Henry was able to negotiate an extraordinary conclusion to his wars. By the Treaty of Troyes, in May 1420, it was agreed that Henry would marry Catherine of Valois, daughter of Charles VI. On Charles' death, Henry or his son by Catherine would inherit the French crown. Meanwhile, he would serve as regent of France.

After besieging the dauphin's forces at Sens and Melun, on 1 December 1420, Henry entered Paris. Even the death of his brother, Thomas of Lancaster, killed fighting at Baugé in Anjou, the following March, could not disguise the extent of Henry's triumph. Baugé itself was a Scots rather than a French victory, fought by 4,000 Scots soldiers only newly arrived to assist their allies in France.

Henry's Marriage

For Henry, meanwhile, there was a brief period of honeymoon with his new bride. Harps, the traditional instrument of the Welsh and of Monmouth where Henry had been born, were ordered for Henry and Catherine to play. From a court and from camps that had been entirely male-dominated, Henry spent a few brief days, perhaps the first since his early childhood, in feminine society. Even here, his thoughts remained focussed upon dreams of empire and an imperial destiny. From the abbey of Coulombs near to Chartres, and as an aid to the conception of a son to succeed him, he borrowed a relic of Christ's foreskin, long treasured as a rather grisly aid to mothers who feared themselves barren.

Birth of an Heir and Death of the King

It remained only to deal with the last outposts of resistance in France, and to await the death of his father-in-law, Charles VI. In October 1421, Henry lay siege to Meaux. His son and only child by Catherine, the future Henry VI, was born at Windsor on 6 December, during the course of this siege, auspiciously enough at a castle from which it was prophesied that a new King Arthur would one day arise and on the feast day of St Nicholas, the patron saint of children. Meaux fell the following May. But the hardships of that winter, the effects of dysentery and his inability to ride, left Henry prostrate at Vincennes outside Paris where, on 31 August 1422, he died, ironically enough in the same château that, in the twentieth century, was to house the archives and hence the history of the modern French army. Charles VI of France died less than three months later, on 21 October. Had Henry V lived those extra fifty days he would have achieved the ambition of every English king, to be recognized not just as ruler of England but as legitimate heir to the throne of France. Instead, this honour passed to his son, Henry VI, barely ten months old. From an English perspective, defeat had only narrowly been snatched from the jaws of victory.

Henry V was the first English king since Richard I to have died on French soil. Like Richard I's, the reign of Henry had been brief but glorious: a mere seven years to set against Richard's ten. Richard had been only forty-one at his death, Henry an even more remarkable thirty-six, dying at the same age as Mozart and, by popular understanding, as Jesus Christ. From the time of Alexander the Great, a mere thirty-three years old at his death, all great heroes were expected to die young. Like Richard I, Henry had transformed his wars into a struggle between good and evil, to all intents as a crusade now fought against the French. As with Richard, the chaos that engulfed Henry's realm after his death, has tended to cast a roseate glow over his own reign and reputation, the last truly great king of England before the fall of night. Even in Henry's lifetime, the so-called *Gesta Henrici Quinti* ('The Deeds of Henry V') had sought to portray the King in heroic terms, as propaganda to recruit support for further war in France. By the 1430s, a life of Henry written at the request of his younger brother, Humphrey, Duke of Gloucester, was fostering a myth of the invincible warrior king. Henry V, like Richard I, had ascended from history into myth.

Problems caused by the King's Death

Yet as with Richard I, the problems that followed from Henry's reign were in many cases of the late King's making. Unlike Richard who left no children, Henry fathered a son, but a son barely ten months old and who was in no position to rule at the time of his father's death. Like Richard, Henry had spent the majority of his reign in foreign adventures, leaving England in the hands of regents and ministers. Whilst he lived, this council had governed effectively, far better indeed than had been the case with the council left to govern England during Richard I's crusade. Nonetheless, like Henry IV before him, Henry V had depended heavily upon his own Lancastrian family to prop up his regime. With his death, the tensions within this family for the first time began to spill over into open competition. Those who praise 'family values' should remember that families can prove not only supportive or benevolent institutions but destructive and bitterly divisive.

The reasons for the breakdown in Lancastrian harmony are clear enough. Henry left no written instructions for the government of either England or France after his death. Instead, it was taken for granted that his son, the young Henry VI, would be cared for by his uncles, Henry V's brothers, John, Duke of Bedford, and Humphrey, Duke of Gloucester. They in turn would govern with the assistance of their Beaufort kinsman, Henry Beaufort, bishop of Winchester, and Thomas Beaufort, Duke of Exeter. Bedford took charge of France. Gloucester and Henry Beaufort were left to squabble over who should have the greater say in England. The outcome was confusion, self-serving malice and a series of disputes within the council fit to rival any of those which had split the councillors of Richard I in the 1190s. Historians of the reign of Henry VI have frequently cited the warning rehearsed by Thomas of Walsingham (in fact directed towards the early years of Richard II): 'Woe unto thee, oh land whose king is a child', ultimately taken from the Bible (Ecclesiastes 10:16). They have not noticed that this same passage is followed in scripture by an equally significant warning against 'princes who dine together in the morning', in other words against counsellors whose squabbling or self-indulgence takes precedence over the national interest.

After 1422, the King's counsellors were far more of a threat to the stability of England than the tender age of the King himself. By 1425, Gloucester and Henry Beaufort were literally at daggers drawn, their armed retinues confronting one another on London Bridge. Bedford, who in France secured great victories against the dauphin, including a battle at Vernueil in 1424, which in some ways deserves to rival Agincourt, was forced to return to England to make peace. There were further disturbances in 1427 when the King's mother, Catherine of Valois, Henry V's widow still only in her mid-twenties, displayed an inclination to remarry. No mother of a ruling English king had remarried for the past four hundred years, for rather obvious reasons. Such a remarriage risked producing a second family which itself might have a claim to the throne. On the last occasion when a queen had taken a second husband, when Emma, the widow of King Aethelred, had been betrothed after Aethelred's death to the Danish usurper Cnut, this was precisely what had happened, with Cnut's offspring claiming precedence over Emma's sons by Aethelred, including the future King Edward the Confessor. Catherine of Valois's choice was definitely no King Cnut. As early as 1425, there were rumours that she was the lover of Edmund Beaufort, nephew of Henry Beaufort. Gloucester scotched any prospect of a Beaufort marriage by a statute in Parliament insisting that the King alone could consent to the remarriage of a dowager queen. Since Gloucester was the King's guardian, no such consent would be forthcoming. Instead, Catherine's attentions turned elsewhere.

Probably in 1430, and entirely in secret, she married a Welshman, a junior member of the royal household, named Owen Tudor. Later legend suggested that they had met at a court entertainment when an inebriated Tudor fell into her lap, or that her admiration for her future husband stemmed from having glimpsed him naked, bathing in a river. In France, it was rumoured that Owen was the bastard son of an alehouse keeper. In reality, he was sprung from a Welsh family of some distinction, albeit, like most such families, of dense and confusing genealogy. His ancestors could trace their descent from Ednyfed Fychan (Edynfed 'the Little'), steward in the 1230s, to Llywelyn the Great, prince of north Wales. In Welsh terms, Owen's family ranked amongst the upper gentry, with wide estates, alabaster tombs and all the trappings of gentility. In England, this counted for little, not only because the Tudors were related to Owen Glyn Dwr, whose rebellion for a time they had supported, but because the Glyn Dwr rebellion had itself encouraged disparagement and legal discrimination against the Welsh. Charles Dickens, was almost certainly paro-dying the pride and pretensions of families such as the Tudors when, in *Bleak House* (1852), he created the character of Mrs Woodcourt, with her verses quoted from '"Crumlinwallinwer" and the "Mewlinnwillinwodd" (if those are the right names, which I dare say they are not)' and her boasted descent from 'Morgan Ap-Kerrig'. In much the same way that the readers of Dickens were invited to sneer at the absurd Mrs Woodcourt, so the court of Henry VI sneered at the descent of Owen Tudor. What it did not do was deny that Owen Tudor had been legitimately married to the King's mother, or claim that the children of this marriage, Edmund born c.1430, and his younger brother, Jaspar, were bastards. On the contrary, when Catherine of Valois died in 1437, and the whole scandal for the first time came into the open, the Duke of Gloucester did his best to ruin Owen Tudor who for a period was placed under arrest at Newgate (from which, like so many prisoners from so many medieval prisons, he promptly escaped).

Not only did the court of Henry VI accept that Edmund and Jaspar were legitimate, but it seems to have raised no questions about their rather peculiar names. These names, however, and especially the choice of the name 'Edmund' for the elder son, may mask an even deeper family scandal, suggesting that Edmund Tudor was not the son of Catherine of Valois and Owen Tudor, but an illegitimate child born of the pre-existing affair between Catherine and Edmund Beaufort, Henry VI's cousin. The facts here remain unproved, although they are certainly bizarre. They carry us yet further into the Dickensian world of royal genealogy with its false identities and multiple plot-lines. What is beyond doubt is that the Tudors, Edmund and Jaspar, were well treated by Henry VI. In 1452, they were promoted to earldoms. In due course, Edmund Tudor was permitted to marry a daughter of another of the King's Beaufort cousins, John Beaufort, Duke of Somerset, the elder brother of Edmund Beaufort. This union produced a single child, born in 1457, three months after Edmund Tudor's sudden death from plague, and at a time when the child's mother, Lady Margaret Beaufort, was herself a mere thirteen years old. The son, christened Henry in honour of the King, was the offspring of perhaps the most significant teenage mother in English history. He will recur at the very end of our story, emerging, like the demon king in a pantomime, to claim the English throne.

In the meantime, and before we take flight from this maze of family relationships, there is one further kink in the Lancastrian family line which must be pointed out. We have already seen that the Mortimer descendants of Lionel, Duke of Clarence, the elder brother of John of Gaunt, possessed claims to be considered the senior heirs to Richard II and the main Plantagenet bloodline. At the very beginning of the reign of Henry V, just as the King had been about to embark for the Agincourt campaign, these claims had been asserted one again, when in the so-called Southampton Plot, the Earl of Cambridge, the King's cousin, had conspired to promote his brother-in-law, Edmund Mortimer, Earl of March, as King in Henry V's place. Edmund Mortimer himself had betrayed the conspiracy. Cambridge was executed. Nonetheless he left behind a son, named Richard, who in due course, following the deaths both of Edmund Mortimer, in 1425, and of Edward, Duke of York, killed at Agincourt, became heir to the joint Mortimer and York estates, descended on both his mother and his father's side directly from Edward III. By the 1430s, Richard, Duke of York, as this boy was styled, could pose as quite the most plausible of Henry VI's potential *competitora* for the English throne.

The same dynastic politics which had earlier brought strength to Kings Henry IV and V now threatened scandal and subsidence. The roots of the vast royal family tree spread so wide that they undermined the very claims upon which the house of Lancaster had been founded. Throughout the 1420s and early 1430s, whatever efforts Bedford made to prop up English rule in France were negated by the refusal of Gloucester to approve subsidies, by the ongoing rivalry between Gloucester and the Beauforts, and by the underlying problems of crown finance, caused chiefly by the decline in wool exports. Regardless of success or failure in war, crown revenues from customs and taxation had declined from an average of £70,000 in the 1360s to a mere £30,000. Even before the death of Henry V, the annual defence budget of £52,000, excluding the costs of war in France, had to be set against a total annual revenue for the crown of just £56,000, leaving in theory nothing whatsoever to pay for military operations beyond defence, and a mere £4,000 to cover the costs of the entire royal household and establishment. The mathematics here were not to be defied. The French enterprise was unsustainable. This did not prevent strenuous efforts being made to salvage it, any more than the mathematics of later empires, British, Nazi or Soviet as the case might be, persuaded their rulers that such empires were doomed.

In France itself, starved of supplies, their wages unpaid from year to year, the commanders around John, Duke of Bedford developed a stoicism fit to rival that of veterans of the German eastern front after Stalingrad. These were violent, professional soldiers, convinced that their own bravery and camaraderie were being sabotaged by politicians closer to the throne. Humphrey, Duke of Gloucester, and other such useless 'golden pheasants' might boast of their feats of arms, having dipped no more than a toe in the real fighting. Those left to face the heat of the day grew bitter and increasingly convinced that corruption on the home front was undermining their efforts.

Henry VI

The Dual Monarchy

Gestures and symbolism for a while might mask the underlying truth. Hurrying forward the date of the King's coronation, special celebrations were arranged in England in November 1429 and in France in December 1431, at which Henry VI, though still a boy, was ceremonially crowned and invested with his realms. At the coronation banquet in 1429, the full range of symbolism was deployed to broadcast the King's authority. Custards shaped into the leopards of England or the fleur-de-lys of France accompanied each course, and large pastry centre-pieces displayed the figures of St Edward the Confessor and St Louis (Henry VI's sainted English and French ancestors), St George of England and St Denys of France. Similar symbolism, including the re-enactment of significant scenes from recent history, was arranged for the

King's ceremonial landing at Calais, on 23 April 1430, the feast day of St George, and for his entry into Paris in December 1431, the first Sunday in Advent, prior to his coronation in the cathedral of Notre-Dame. Nonetheless, the very fact that this coronation took place in Paris rather than in the traditional coronation church of Rheims, and the fact that Henry was kept waiting for more than a year at Calais and Rouen before it was judged safe to escort him to Paris, revealed a harsher reality: English government was not only bankrupt but in the process of losing the military side of the war. English authority in France was no more substantial or long-lasting than the pastry delicacies at Henry's coronation feast.

Joan of Arc

The chief turning point here, the Lancastrians' Stalingrad, is generally reckoned to have occurred at Orléans in 1429. It involved an illiterate seventeen-year-old peasant girl from the far eastern frontiers of France, Joan of Arc. Convinced that she had been called upon to restore the dauphin, disinherited for the past ten years, to his rightful position as King, and that she was acting as the mouthpiece for voices, including those of saints Michael, Katherine and Margaret who chose to speak through her, Joan sought out the dauphin on the Loire. Whether genuinely convinced, or merely keen to manipulate her for political ends, various figures at the dauphin's court claimed to identify her as the *Pucelle* or 'Maid' whose restoration of France had been prophesied since the 1390s. Joan not only brought a new messianic spirit to the French resistance at Orléans, from where the English were compelled to withdraw, but forced the dauphin's hand, persuading him to lead a triumphal progress to Rheims. There, on 17 July 1429, having been greeted by crowds shouting 'Noel!', as if Christ himself were come again, he was crowned as King Charles VII.

It was this, more than anything, that persuaded the English political leadership to opt for almost immediate coronation of the seven-year-old Henry VI, as King both of England and France. Having been accorded an honoured place at the coronation of Charles VII, Joan herself was captured less than a year later, at Compiègne, north of Paris, attempting, as at Orléans, to bring her miraculous powers to bear upon an English siege. In 1431, at Rouen, she was tried, renounced her many sins, but then, two days later, changed her mind and claimed that once again her voices had spoken to her. The relapse into heresy was her undoing. She was publicly burned, her naked body exposed to the crowd before incineration, and the ashes thrown into the Seine.

The irony here is that Joan's spirit of prophecy, so significant to the revival of French morale, was one to which King Henry V, the chief author of that English conquest against which Joan had fought, had been peculiarly attuned. Perhaps precisely because he had passed so much of his life in the company of men, with barely a passing acquaintance with his mother or wife let alone with other women, Henry V had a peculiar respect for female spirituality, both in its power for good and its potential for evil. We have already considered the Church's wider scepticism about female saints and their supposed gifts of prophecy: from whom were such gifts derived, from God or from the Devil? Regardless of such reservations, and despite the suspicions that he is said to have entertained against his own step-mother, Queen Joan, accused after Henry IV's death of sorcery and traffic with hidden powers, Henry V had been an enthusiastic patron of religious women and in particular of the order of St Bridget of Sweden, introduced by the King to a new foundation at Syon Abbey on the opposite bank of the Thames to his Carthusian priory at Sheen. The nuns of Syon, who, like the Carthusians, continued to play a significant role in the religious life of Henry VI, popularized the prophetic 'Celestial Visions' of their foundress: emotion-charged images of Christ and his mother not dissimilar to the visions seen by the distinctly unofficial St Julian of Norwich. Joan of Arc with her voices and her visions was merely a militant embodiment of the spirit of prophecy first detected in Bridget.

The French Campaign Goes Sour

Even after the trial and 'martyrdom' of 'Saint' Joan, the rot in England's French empire might have been stopped. Bedford was a more than competent commander. Cardinal Beaufort was prepared to extend massive loans to the crown, more or less single-handedly propping up the English war effort from the revenues of his see of Winchester. The problem was that Beaufort and the council could not agree what these war efforts should involve. Moreover, other members of the royal family began to rise within the council, most notably Richard, Duke of York, appointed on Bedford's death as lieutenant and effective vice-regent in France, and Margaret of Anjou, daughter of René, Count of Anjou and titular King of Naples, an impoverished but well-connected French heiress, niece to King Charles VII, in 1444 married to Henry VI of England as part of attempts to broker an Anglo-French peace.

Neither Richard of York's appointment as lieutenant in France nor the King's French marriage did anything to stem the tide that was already running against English rule in France. The Anglo-Burgundian alliance which, for the past twenty years had been crucial to the maintenance of Henry V's French empire, collapsed in 1435, only a week after the death of Bedford. In 1436, before Richard of York had even taken up his appointment as Bedford's successor, Paris fell to the French, with the Bastille the very last English outpost to be surrendered. Attempts to negotiate a more permanent peace, not least through the marriage of Henry VI and Margaret, led only to accusations from veterans and hotheads alike that the spirit of Henry V was being betrayed. Whilst France fell, Richard of York haggled over whether he was to be titled 'regent and governor' or merely 'lieutenant general' of this disintegrating empire. As with all military disengagements, the problem was how to justify negotiating away territory that itself had been won only at a heavy cost in English blood.

A sense of England's historic destiny in this instance determined the choice of valiance and defeat rather than surrender and victory. In particular, the attempt to broker peace in the mid-1440s by the surrender of Maine, the region immediately to the south of Normandy, a crucial frontier zone since at least the time of William the Conqueror, ended in fiasco when what was intended as a surrender to René of Anjou, Henry VI's father-in-law, in practice turned out to involve a handover to Charles VII, de facto King of France. Veterans such as Sir John Fastolf, whose wages had not been paid throughout the 1420s and 30s but who instead had been compensated with grants of land in the conquered territories of Normandy and Maine, found themselves deprived of precisely those rewards which their stalwart defence over the past twenty years had appeared to guarantee. The sense of betrayal and resentment was palpable. Where the union established between Normandy and England after 1066 had lasted a century and a half, those who had dreamed of a similar enrichment of English settlers in Normandy after 1417 found their empire collapsing after barely thirty years.

In the meantime, the greatest of the armchair generals, Humphrey, Duke of Gloucester, was himself destroyed by a combination of family politics and court gossip. His first marriage, to a claimant to the county of Hainault, had ended in the late 1420s in farce and embarrassment, when his attempts to win back his wife's lands in Flanders resulted in military failure, a breach in Anglo-Burgundian relations and a declaration from the papacy that the marriage itself was illegal and therefore annulled. Duke Humphrey had promptly married his mistress, Eleanor Cobham, with whom, for the next ten years, he established a notably literary circle, with their country retreat near Greenwich, their salon of poets, historians and astrologers, and their collection of priceless books, many of them brought from Italy and shedding a

Renaissance glow of 'humanism' amidst Greenwich's rain and mud.

The problem lay with the astrologers. By 1440, with the King still unmarried and childless, and with Humphrey of Gloucester next heir to the throne, his duchess began to consult various of the most eminently respectable astrologers over the prospects for the King's health. The astrologers told her that Henry VI might suffer a severe illness in the summer of 1441. She also, no doubt with thoughts for her own childlessness, took advice from a wise woman named Margery Jourdemayne, known as 'the witch of Eye' and as 'an ancient pythoness', over what potions or charms might enable her to bear her husband a son and heir. Amidst the fevered atmosphere of Henry VI's court, when these precautions were disclosed, they were taken as proof of treasonable sorcery. Eleanor was sentenced to public penance, walking barefoot to three London churches on successive days carrying a taper, and thereafter to perpetual imprisonment. She died, more than ten years later, still a prisoner. The astrologers were drawn and quartered. Margery the witch was burned.

Duke Humphrey spent the remaining few years of his life as a disgraced and disgruntled presence about the court. His clashes with the Duke of Suffolk resulted, in 1447, in his arrest in a Parliament meeting in the de la Pole heartlands at Bury St Edmunds. His death, in custody, was blamed upon a stroke, but the official explanation was widely disbelieved. The spirit of Joan of Arc, and the hysteria that it had engendered, had themselves infected the processes of politics and the royal court. The books which Duke Humphrey helped import to England, and which still constitute one of the great treasures of the Bodleian Library in Oxford where many of them came to rest, shed not only the glow of the Italian Renaissance but a rather more sinister aura of plot and conspiracy. The spirit of the Borgias was wafted far north of the Alps.

In all of this, the King himself played a merely passive role. This passivity, more than anything else, helps to explain the breakdown in royal authority that gathered pace throughout the 1440s. Ten months old at the time of his succession, Henry VI had grown up as a sensitive and apparently intelligent spectator to the disputes that divided his uncles. Certain characteristics in the young king early began to attract notice, if not yet alarm. He was generous to a fault. He was inclined to pardon and to extend mercy. He disliked the taking of animal, let alone of human life. He was fastidious in his habits, shunning the company of women. As late as 1448, by which time he was in his mid-twenties and had been married for three years, the sight of men bathing naked in the hot water pools at Bath led him to demand that the local bishop intervene to put an end to such scandals. He was much given to the study both of religion and of the past, to meditation on the cross and the five wounds of Christ, to the avoidance of all travel on Sundays (apparently claiming precedent from the reign of the Anglo-Saxon King Edgar), and to a large part of that devotional programme that contemporaries knew as the '*devotio moderna*' ('the modern style of religion').

He had developed a particular veneration for King Alfred, founder of the West Saxon dynasty, and in 1442 even petitioned the papacy to have Alfred canonized as a saint. His enthusiasm here was perhaps derived from a shared interest in education. Amongst his earliest and most personal ventures as king were the endowment of a university at Caen in Normandy immediately after his French coronation in 1431, followed by his foundation of a school, Eton College in the shadow of Windsor Castle, and of an attached university college, King's at Cambridge, for whose endowment and government he showed particular concern. The university of Caen, within sight of the castle from which William of Normandy had planned his conquest of 1066, was one of the last, though by no means the least significant of the effects of the English occupation of Normandy.

Like many of the greatest benefactors of higher education, indeed like many of the most avid readers of history, Henry himself had attended neither school nor university, and could in no way be considered an 'educated' man.

Besides his interest in King Alfred, Henry showed equal devotion to the cult of St Edward the Confessor, turning the Confessor's feast days on 5 January and 13 October each year into major occasions within the royal calendar. Rather remarkably, having first met his bride, Margaret of Anjou, in 1445, Henry seems to have waited until January 1453, perhaps even until the precise feast of the Confessor's deposition on 5 January, to impregnate her with their only child, a son known as Edward of Lancaster, who was born on 13 October, the feast of the Confessor's translation and coincidentally the anniversary of the accession of the Lancastrian dynasty with the coronation of King Henry IV on 13 October 1399.

Henry VI was possessed of many qualities. The chief problem was that his private virtues very soon came to be seen as public vices. Generosity, forgiveness and mercy were all very well in a king, but they needed to be tempered with realism, force and justice. These qualities, the boy king signally lacked. One key here is supplied by Henry's choice of personal emblem, the antelope. Antelopes supporting the heraldic arms of England and France were already displayed at his French coronation in 1431, when Henry was only nine years old, presumably chosen not so much by the King himself as by his councillors and in particular by his overbearing uncles. In the bestiary (the medieval encyclopedia of animal lore), the antelope is portrayed as a creature so wild that hunters can only catch it when its saw-like horns become caught in the branches of trees. The moral that it teaches is that playing in the thickets of worldliness merely threatens to kill both body and soul: admirable sentiments no doubt, but hardly appropriate to the education of a king who, by necessity, should have had rather more familiarity with the thickets of worldliness than was the case with Henry VI.

As with so many aspects of fifteenth-century England, history loomed large over Henry VI's court. His devotion to the memory and the feast days of Edward the Confessor might in some senses remind us of an earlier English King, Henry III, himself a mere boy for the first ten years of his reign, thereafter regarded as pious but ineffectual. It might also suggest that England, by the 1440s, was coming to bear a marked resemblance to the England of the 1040s and the reign of Edward the Confessor himself. Like Henry VI's, the Confessor's court had been riven by faction and blood feud, with its greater families possessing landed and financial resources superior to those of the King, capable of buying up the support of many lesser men. Like Henry VI after 1422, Edward the Confessor had been orphaned at a tender age, and the remarriage of his French mother, Emma of Normandy, like the remarriage of Henry VI's mother, Catherine of Valois, had sown poisonous discord even within the English royal family. The Confessor's wife, Edith daughter of Earl Godwin, like Margaret of Anjou, Henry's Queen, was both mistrusted and seen as a far more effective politician than her husband.

In the eleventh century, England itself had stood on the brink of feudal anarchy, dominated by aristocratic privilege, tending towards the breakdown of public authority, in which the wishes of the few prevailed over the interests of the many. What historians of the fifteenth century are inclined to describe as 'bastard feudalism' might better be seen as the first true emergence in English history, at least since the eleventh century, of precisely those tendencies towards anarchy and aristocratic self-interest which the French have always regarded as typically 'feudal'. Once again, a sense of the past dominates a much later period, and behind the posturings of a Gloucester, a York or a Beaufort we can detect something of the spirit of Harold or Tostig, the Godwinsons, the Leofricsons and the warring dynasties of Northumbria.

What is perhaps most remarkable about the first twenty years of the reign of Henry VI is not their turbulence but the mere fact that the King's regime survived. Even amidst the farcical negotiations over Maine in the mid-1440s, through a piece of theatre splendidly stage-managed by William de la Pole, it had still been possible to persuade visiting ambassadors, come to prepare for Henry's marriage to Margaret of Anjou, that all was well with the Lancastrian court and that the King was a simple but sound figure, surrounded by a family, including his kind uncle Humphrey, who did him proud. It was this act of subterfuge more than anything else that earned Pole promotion as Duke of Suffolk. Three years later, Pole had engineered the arrest and death of Duke Humphrey. Worse still, in 1449, attempting to wipe clean the reputation for heedless pacifism which had dogged his negotiations over Maine, Pole lent his support to an English attack upon Brittany, led by Edmund Beaufort, Duke of Somerset, once reputed the lover of the King's mother. The attack only provoked the French to a full-scale declaration of war which in turn led to a swift collapse in English lordship. In October, Somerset surrendered Rouen, followed on 1 July 1450 by his surrender of Caen. By August, Cherbourg, the last English stronghold in Normandy, had fallen, and in the following year Charles VII launched an invasion of Gascony, taking Bordeaux in June and Bayonne, in the far south, two months later.

The effects of such humiliation, like the defeats in Algeria upon the French after 1950, or in Vietnam upon the Americans after 1970, threatened cataclysm. Even before the fall of Caen, Pole was impeached for treason, banished and then, when the ship in which he hoped to flee was intercepted by privateers off the Suffolk coast, beheaded in the name of the 'Community of the realm', an amorphous entity that had made its last major interventions in national politics as long ago as the 1260s. England itself was flooded with refugees from the Normandy settlement, and by veterans of the Normandy campaigns, convinced that corruption and mismanagement, very close to the throne, were to blame for the public's grievances. In January 1450, the bishop of Chichester was murdered by disgruntled soldiers who had waited too long for their pay. A few months later, so was the bishop of Salisbury, attacked at Mass by a mob of protestors, themselves perhaps the victims of a recent slump in the Wiltshire cloth industry caused by Burgundian embargoes on cloth exports. No one openly dared blame the King for these troubles, but in most minds it was self-evident that Henry VI was incapable of managing his own, let alone the nation's affairs. In particular, there were demands for the forced 'resumption' of the patronage and largesse which Henry had lavished upon ministers such as Pole and Somerset, and which had contributed to the perilous state of the crown's own finances.

Somerset's mishandling of the 1450 campaign led to temporary imprisonment on his return from France, and a permanent breach with Richard of York who held him to blame for the loss of Normandy and who seems to have considered it a matter of honour that Somerset be brought to account. A sense of honour slighted also inspired the actions of John Talbot, Earl of Shrewsbury, one of the most distinguished veterans of the war, a field commander for the past fifty years, perhaps first blooded at the battle of Shrewsbury in 1403, in almost permanent residence in Normandy since Henry V's reign, and, although a witness to the surrender of Rouen in 1449, by this stage aged well over sixty, determined to have his revenge.

Jack Cade

In the midst of these disasters, England itself erupted into chaos with a rebellion in Kent led by an obscure demagogue, Jack Cade. In the summer of 1450, Cade incited disturbances across the south-east, complaining against government malad-ministration and corruption. As in the Peasants' Revolt of 1381, though on this occasion drawing its membership from an upper level of peasantry and minor gentry who feared that their own property was threatened by the troubles of the past few years, the rebels camped on Blackheath on the outskirts of London. Dispersed by the threat that the King was about to ride out against them, they unleashed a series of royalist raids against west Kent: a home-brewed variety of the '*chevauchées*' previously employed by English armies in France. London itself seethed with outcry against corruption. The King fled to Kenilworth. The rebels sat in judgment upon his ministers, executing one or two of the smaller fry. As in 1381, it was the resistance of the propertied classes of London which brought an end to rebellion. Cade himself attempted flight into Sussex, where he was arrested and killed. His body was posthumously beheaded. If there were echoes of the reign of Edward the Confessor to the 1440s, then in 1450 then they were joined to echoes of 1381.

Loss of Aquitaine

In the midst of all this, a miracle seemed to present itself. The citizens of Bordeaux, resenting their new French rulers, took repossession of the city and its surrounding region in the name of Henry VI. John Talbot, veteran of the Norman wars, 'England's Achilles', led an expeditionary force from England. The disasters of the past few years seemed on the verge of solution. On 17 July 1453, attempting to bring assistance to the town of Castillon on the river Dordogne east of Bordeaux, Talbot threw his troops against what he assumed to be a weakly defended French position. It was in fact an artillery battery into which the French had retreated. Undaunted, and determined, Don Quixote-like to prove his honour, Talbot charged. As is the inevitable consequence of cavalry advancing directly into cannon, at Castillon as in the Charge of the Light Brigade almost exactly four hundred years later, shrapnel triumphed over horse-flesh. Talbot was killed, his death at the age of sixty-six a fitting symbol of the end of British empire in France and of the futility of much that in the previous century had passed for chivalry. Bordeaux fell to Charles VII in October. After almost exactly three hundred years united to the English crown, Aquitaine was no longer an English colony.

The Madness of King Henry

1453 was indeed a year of miracles. On 29 May, two months before Talbot's defeat at Castillon, Constantinople had fallen to the bronze cannon of the Ottoman Turks, bringing an end to a thousand-year-old civilization and to Christian empire in the East. On 13 October, the feast day of St Edward the Confessor, only a week after the fall of Bordeaux, Henry VI's queen gave birth to a son, christened Edward. In the same year, a Kentish man named William Caxton, perhaps troubled by the recent disturbances following Cade's revolt, moved his luxury goods business from London to Bruges. Following the lead of Johannes Gutenberg of Mainz, who in 1454 began distributing copies of a Bible, produced on a printing press using moveable metal type, the first great book to have been manufactured in this way and harbinger of a revolution in the distribution of learning that was to transform European intellectual life, Caxton subsequently set himself up as England's first printer-publisher. His first English book, the *Recuyell* (or 'collection', from the French recueil) *of the Historyes of Troye*, was printed in 1473, followed almost immediately with the *Game of Chess* printed the following year. It was to history, followed shortly afterwards by war-inspired board games, that English publishing owed its origins and its earliest profits.

In the meantime, as if in sympathy with the insanity of the times, King Henry VI went mad. As early as 1435, when news had been brought to him of the collapse of the Anglo-Burgundian alliance, the King is said to have wept in public. In the aftermath of Castillon, he entirely lost his reason. For several months he was unable to recognize his own family, or even to acknowledge the birth of his son. A sort of catatonic lethargy descended. It may have been genetic. He was, after all, the grandson of the mad King Charles VI of France. Yet the malady, if inherited, should then also have passed to his Tudor half-brothers, and his Valois cousins, which seems not to have been the case. His other grandfather, Henry IV, had suffered lengthy bouts of illness, though no attempt to prove Henry IV's insanity has succeeded. Whatever the cause, the King's madness mirrored the state of England as a whole.

Houses of York and Lancaster

By the summer of 1453, law and order were already collapsing in the English provinces. Disputes in East Anglia, between the followers of the Poles and those of the Mowbray dukes of Norfolk, or in Lancashire between the families of Stanley and Harrington, are only the most notorious, because the best documented of these spasms in the body politic. John Talbot, the hero of Castillon, had himself engaged in all manner of violence as an English landowner, from 1413 onwards. After 1450, the Talbots were at open war with the Berkeleys in Gloucestershire, imprisoning Lord Berkeley, seizing Berkeley Castle and demanding a large share of the Berkeley estate. There is a reminder here that even the chivalry of a Talbot could mask rather more violent impulses.

Moreover, as in the eleventh century, the further that social order broke down, the more people began to jockey for position, to seek refuge within the affinity of the great, or to build up vaster and vaster estates precisely because only through land and the income it afforded could a great man acquire an affinity large enough to see off his rivals. The fate of Sir John Fastolf, as recorded in the Paston letters, can be regarded as a symptomatic of a wider breakdown in the social fabric. Raids on Fastolf's estate by Pole and members of the court, culminated, after 1450, in an even more insidious series of attacks and occupations by Alice Chaucer, Pole's widow and a granddaughter of the poet. Fastolf turned for defence to the dukes of Norfolk and York. By Richard of York, partly in repayment of a loan, partly as compensation for his 'great labours and vexations' on York's behalf, he was given a spear-pointed diamond, listed by his executors as having been set in 'a very rich collar called in English "a White Rose"', valued at 4,000 marks: a most potent symbol of the degree to which the house of York, with its white rose, was now emerging as the only credible alternative to Henry VI and the Lancastrians with their collars of SSs.

The further Henry VI declined into imbecility, the more this highlighted the position of York as the only credible alternative if a King were to be found capable of ruling. Yet even after Henry went mad, York was slow to act. His determination to punish what he regarded as the cowardice of Somerset had already led to two earlier flirtations with rebellion, in 1450 when he had returned from Ireland without permission from the court to stir up Parliament against the governing council, and in 1452, when he had once again attempted to use Somerset's impeachment as a rallying cry for reform, in all probability hoping to secure his own recognition as next heir to the throne should Henry VI die childless. Even so, the penalties for treason, and the precedents set in the cases of Gloucester or Pole, were such that, only with reluctance would any politician demand a position at centre-stage. The breakdown in local order was matched to a fatal loss of confidence in central government. Even when York did move, in 1454, to accept a role as protector of the incapacitated king and as defender of the realm, the experiment was swiftly brought to an end, in part by the aggression of the Queen, who was determined that her own son, Edward of Lancaster, born in 1453, would now be recognized as heir to Henry VI, partly by the recovery of the King which, though only temporary, was used as a pretext to remove York from his office as protector.

Wars of the Roses

Too late to rescue the city of Paris in 1436, too cautious in 1441 to prosecute bold action against the French, too late in 1450 to play much role in the impeachment of Pole, when Richard did eventually act, in the summer of 1455 it was with excessive caution. At St Albans, in a battle fought between two more or less equal factions, he and his allies, headed by Richard Neville, Earl of Warwick, defeated a force in theory commanded by

Henry VI, Somerset and the Percy affinity from Northumberland. Somerset was killed. Henry VI, deserted and wounded in the neck, was escorted by York to St Albans Abbey where York submitted on bended knee, being restored thereafter as the King's protector.

The first battle which Henry VI had fought took place on English soil and was a defeat for the house of Lancaster. It resolved nothing save for the hatred between York and Somerset. Instead it set a dangerous precedent. Over the next thirty years, whenever a political faction considered its demands unsatisfied, trial by battle was the preferred method of solving the dispute. These wars, the so-called Wars of the Roses, in no way rivalled the wars earlier fought in France. There were to be no prolonged sieges, no great ravishing of the English countryside to compare with the horrors inflicted on northern France after 1340 or on Normandy from 1417. Instead, what ensued was a series of battles almost without a war: a curtain raiser at St Albans, followed by the first real act in 1459–61, a second act in 1469–71 and a violent but apparently final coda in 1483–5.

The battles themselves are poorly documented, for all that they and their sites have been pored over by military historians convinced that troop movements can be reconstructed, as if by magic, from a proper juggling with topography and the accounts that do survive. The overall outcome of each battle, by contrast, is not in doubt, the certainty here being supplied from the fact that virtually each encounter witnessed the death of a significant contingent of leaders or political players. These were literally killing fields, in which the chivalric games of joust and tournament turned into the most bitter sort of vendetta and blood feud. As each generation of players was carried dead from the pitch, another sprang up to take its place.

At St Albans in 1455, Somerset was killed. There followed a brief hiatus, with York's protectorate undermined by the Queen and by resistance to any resumption of royal patronage distributed over the past twenty years. Inconclusive encounters at the battles of Blore Heath and Ludlow in 1459, led to York's flight to Ireland, from where, like Harold Godwinson in the 1050s, he planned his return to power. At the Battle of Northampton in 1460, the King was once again taken prisoner by York's ally, Warwick, and by the Earl of March, York's eldest son. York himself returned from Ireland to be proclaimed protector and this time to be recognized as heir to the throne should Henry die. Still there was a reluctance to seize the throne itself, let alone to kill off Henry VI, in part perhaps because of compassion for Henry's prolonged childhood, minority and present incapacity, in part out of a more hard-headed reluctance to undermine, once again, the very basis of public or royal authority. Theologians, from the twelfth century onwards, had sanctioned the killing of tyrants. They had said nothing about killing the feckless or the childlike. Six months after Northampton, on 30 December at Wakefield, near Sandal in Yorkshire, Richard of York himself rode out to death on the battlefield. His head was displayed on the walls of the city of York dressed in a paper crown: a macabre use for the new medium of print.

Wakefield did not end the Yorkist rebellion. At the second Battle of St Albans in February 1461, a Yorkist defeat, Henry VI was released from captivity, only to be forced to flee into exile in Scotland after 29 March when the Earl of March, Richard of York's son, entered London, having defeated the western Lancastrian army at Mortimer's Cross, and thence proceeded to Towton (outside York) where yet another Yorkist victory was inflicted on the Lancastrians.

Edward IV and Henry VI

March himself had meanwhile been proclaimed King in London, taking the title King Edward IV. In each of these battles, lives were lost and much blood was spilled. Entire dynasties were obliterated: the Poles, the Beauforts, ultimately the Lancastrian dynasty itself. Towton was fought in a raging snowstorm, on Palm Sunday. A hundred and fifty years earlier, fighting on Palm Sunday had been so deplored that its punishment was a contributory factor in Edward I's conquest of Wales. Amidst the horrors of the 1460s, however, it went almost unremarked.

The death toll at Towton was exceptionally high, including the Earl of Northumberland and lords Clifford, Randolph, Dacre, Neville and Wells amongst the Lancastrian dead. After Mortimer's Cross, Owen Tudor, Henry VI's step-father, was taken to Hereford and beheaded, a mad woman combing his hair and placing a hundred candles around his severed head at the market cross. Both Edward of Lancaster, Henry VI's vengeful little son, aged a mere eight at the second Battle of St Albans, and Edward, Earl of March, the future Edward IV, only eighteen at the time of his victory at Towton, were blooded in these encounters, in effect as a lost generation of boy soldiers whose lives were now consecrated to war. This was tribal warfare, akin to the convulsions of African chieftainship, albeit fought under silk standards in the latest and most fashionable of plate armour. England had been riven by civil wars in the past, most notably during the 1140s under King Stephen. Stephen's reign, however, had witnessed only one pitched battle, at Lincoln in 1141, and virtually nothing by way of judicial execution of the aris-tocracy. After 1460, battles came thicker and faster than they had ever done before.

After Towton and for the first time in English history, there were now two rival kings, Edward IV and Henry VI, both anointed in Westminster, both claiming to be right successor to their royal ancestors. The irony is that one of these claimants, Henry VI, a direct descendant of King Edward I, was forced to seek refuge with the King of Scots, whilst the other, Edward IV, found himself threatened not so much by the rather feeble attempts at a Lancastrian come back, at the battles of Hedgeley Moor and Hexham in 1464, as by his own closest allies and indeed by his own brother. Although Henry VI was eventually taken prisoner by the

Yorkists, betrayed in July 1465 in Ribblesdale in Lancashire and thence conveyed as a prisoner to the Tower of London, there followed a second act to the drama.

George, Duke of Clarence, Edward IV's younger brother, rebelled with the assistance of the earl of Warwick, Richard Neville, making bizarre and common cause with Margaret of Anjou, Henry VI's queen. By the late 1460s, the continued operation of Queen Margaret's court in Scotland and later in France, and rumours of secret contacts between the Queen and the English aristocracy, led to a rash of arrests in which former Lancastrians were tried and executed. Warwick and Clarence declared their rebellion in 1469, with Clarence marrying Warwick's daughter at Calais on 11 July. They then launched an invasion of Kent defeating Edward IV's forces at the Battle of Edgcote on 26 July. Deserted by his men, Edward IV himself was taken captive and sent as a prisoner to Warwick Castle. For a few weeks, with two crowned kings now prisoners of state, Warwick and Clarence attempted to rule, in theory as representatives of Edward IV, in practice as usurpers even of the Yorkist claim. But Edward IV himself secured his release and by the end of October was once again in possession of London.

A pretence was maintained that peace would be restored. In reality, Warwick and Clarence had spilled too much blood to be left unpunished. Sensing their coming fate, they mounted a rebellion in Lincolnshire. Defeated at a battle fought near Empingham, they then fled to France from where they launched yet another invasion in September 1470, backed by Queen Margaret and by Henry VI's half-brother, Jaspar Tudor. It was now Edward IV's turn to flee into exile in Flanders. Henry VI was released from his imprisonment in the Tower and crowned for a second time on 3 October 1470. His second reign, described by contemporaries as his 'readeption', lasted barely six months. By April 1471, Edward IV was once again at the gates of London, having landed at Ravenspur in Yorkshire, at more or less precisely the same spot from which

Henry Bolingbroke, the founder of the Lancastrian dynasty, had in 1399 launched his bid to depose King Richard II.

Death of Henry VI

Henry VI was now processed through the city of London, dressed shabbily in a long blue gown, greeted with only lukewarm enthusiasm by his subjects. He was then forced to accompany King Edward to confront the Lancastrian army at the Battle of Barnet, fought on Easter Sunday in thick fog.

Here Warwick 'the Kingmaker' was killed. Henry was promptly returned to the Tower. After yet another Yorkist victory, at Tewkesbury on 4 May, the last of the Beaufort dukes of Somerset was captured and executed. Queen Margaret was captured and Edward of Lancaster, her eighteen-year-old son, killed. Henry VI was himself put to death within only a few hours of Edward IV's return from Tewkesbury to London, the official explanation being that he had died of 'pure displeasure and melancholy'. Edward IV, the anointed of God, had at last realized the necessity of killing his fellow anointed. Had his father, the Duke of York, been a little more ruthless in this respect, in the immediate aftermath of the first Battle of St Albans in 1455, or had Edward IV grasped this particular nettle after Henry VI's capture in 1465, the entire sorry story of the Wars of the Roses might never have been. As it was, the survival of both Henry VI and his eldest son, Edward of Lancaster, had served as a rallying cry to rebellion. With their deaths, the killing should in theory have ceased. For a while it seemed to have done so.

'Saint' Henry

Henry VI's body was conveyed for burial at Chertsey Abbey in Surrey, where it almost immediately began to attract claims of miraculous healing. In death, 'Saint' Henry proved a far more effective protector of his people than he had ever been in life. Indeed, to judge by the number of pilgrim badges collected by visitors to his shrine, the cult of Henry VI, the least royal of

English kings, soon came to rival that of Thomas Becket, the most anti-royal of English saints.

King Edward IV

Edward IV, having secured the throne, now sought to enjoy the fruits of his usurpation. In this he was hindered first and foremost by the disloyalty of his own family, and in particular of his younger brother George, Duke of Clarence, rewarded in Edward's first reign with a vast estate and provision for a household of 399 staff, grander even than that of the royal household, yet lured into rebellion against his brother by the prospect of marriage to a daughter of Richard Neville, Earl of Warwick.

In 1471, Clarence had in theory made his peace with the King, but his treason was never truly forgiven. As early as 1472, a dispute with the youngest of his three brothers, Richard, Duke of Gloucester, over the partition of the Neville estates, in which Richard was almost certainly the aggressor but in which Edward IV backed Richard against Clarence, swiftly degenerated into an open rift amidst accusations of abuse of power by all concerned. By 1477, not only had Clarence been implicated in the kidnapping and judicial murder of a maidservant, and accused of poisoning his wife, who had in fact died from the effects of childbirth, but also in charges of imagining the King's death by necromancy brought against Clarence's retainer, Thomas Burdet. Convicted for his involvement in these and other affairs, after a show trial that would have done credit to the henchmen of Josef Stalin, Clarence was executed in the Tower of London, apparently by drowning in a barrel of sweet Greek (or malmsey) wine. With fine hypocrisy, Edward IV paid for lavish funeral celebrations and a tomb at Tewkesbury Abbey. Where it had taken the Lancastrian dynasty nearly fifty years to collapse into rancour and self-interest, the house of York almost immediately fell to fighting within itself. These were men and women who simply did not behave as kings and queens were expected to behave.

Elizabeth Woodville

The King, Edward IV, although a competent enough politician and capable of generosity to his supporters, had already caused scandal as early as 1464 by secretly marrying Elizabeth Woodville, the widow of a Lancastrian knight who had died fighting for Henry VI at the second Battle of St Albans. By her first husband Elizabeth already had two sons, besides an entire quiver of brothers and sisters for whom Edward was persuaded to secure prestigious marriages. The Woodvilles, former servants of John, Duke of Bedford, were not the sort of people that kings were expected to marry. Worse still, the rumour circulated that Edward IV had already been contracted to marry another heiress at the time of his marriage to Elizabeth, so that even the legitimacy of the King's Woodville sons, including the future Edward V, born in 1470, was called into question.

Amidst such lawlessness, there was little further need for outlaws. The outlaws of the greenwood, indeed, either faded away or were subsumed within the contending affinities of the greater figures at court. Robin Hood himself went to war, in the person of Sir John Conyers who, calling himself 'Robin of Redesdale' or 'Robin Mend-All', played a significant role in harassing the northern Yorkists in 1469. Other figures from English myth were brought into commission, none more potent than King Arthur, adopted by Edward IV as his special protector, with Edward himself claiming to be the 'second Arthur' who would unite the kingdoms of Britain, fulfilling a prophecy made by the Angelic Voice to Cadwallader, last King of the Britons, at the end of Geoffrey of Monmouth's *History of the Kings of Britain*, itself first written down by Geoffrey of Monmouth during the earlier civil war of King Stephen's reign.

Sir Thomas Malory

It was as a hapless participant in the wars of the 1460s and 70s, bringing defeat with him to every party to which he changed sides, that the Warwickshire gentleman and outlaw, Sir Thomas Malory, began to assemble his own stock of Arthurian lore. Malory's *Morte d'Arthur*, in some ways the greatest of the medieval Arthurian cycles, was written between 1468 and 1470 whilst Malory languished in far from chivalric captivity as a prisoner of Edward IV in the Tower of London. It was published fifteen years later by William Caxton, on his printing press at the sign of the Red Pale in Westminster, becoming, together with Chaucer's *Canterbury Tales* published by Caxton in 1476, the very first English bestseller, its success all the more ironic given that the warfare of the 1470s was so very far from the polite and honour-ridden combat described in Malory's fantasies. Misappropriated from the Welsh, and clothed in fifteenth-century armour, Arthur became a hero for the modern age: doomed, drawn both to piety and to mass murder, an appropriately violent and confused national figurehead for violent and confusing times.

The Yorkists
Even here, and for all its illegitimacy and air of corruption, the Yorkist regime might have survived, not least had Edward IV made good his promises to reopen the war with France. As was remarked in Parliament, briefly revived as a forum to vote taxation to the crown, foreign adventures were the ideal way of re-establishing domestic harmony, channelling the more warlike impulses of the aristocracy into hostility towards a common foe. In just this way, Henry V's anti-French crusades after Agincourt had brought the royal family and the aristocracy to coalesce around a common military goal. Edward IV himself had been born at Rouen, in the final stages of the late Anglo-French war, the last king in English history to have been born on French rather than on English soil. In 1475, he set out to reopen the Hundred Years War, but it was a war that was promptly cancelled as a result of negotiations between Edward and the French king, Louis XI. Chivalry and heroism

were exchanged for an annual pension of £10,000 from the French court.

Money was now seen as Edward's chief goal, not honour or peace. Alchemy, the transformation of base metal into gold, and the restoration through alchemical harmony of a vanished golden age were perhaps already obsessions of a court itself given over to the worship of worldly goods. Like Merlin in the stories of King Arthur, the talented George Ripley, the King's principal alchemist, played an alarming role both as defender of the regime and as an interpreter of Arthurian history on the King's behalf. Even such Yorkist symbols as the white rose, the sun in splendour or the three crowns, had distinctive and widely recognized alchemical resonances. Whether this amounted to very much in practice, and whether Edward IV was truly a great patron of arcane science, the air of mystery which such writings conveyed certainly added to the intrigues of a court already suspected of licentiousness, moral and financial corruption and of trafficking with powers that were best left undisturbed.

Edward's Death and Richard of Gloucester

The atmosphere of Edward IV's court was of crucial significance in determining events after Edward's sudden death in 1483, at the age of forty. The cause of his death remains uncertain, but gluttony may well have been a contributing factor. For at least the past ten years, Edward had been running to fat. As with the obesity of William I in the 1080s, corpulence could be interpreted as the wages of sin: the outward mark of the criminal usurper. Through his management of men rather than institutions, through his sheer capacity to survive the outrageous fortunes of the 1460s, and through his careful husbanding of the crown's finances, Edward appeared to have restored at least some stability to English kingship. Government still functioned, both in the provinces and at the centre, albeit increasingly without any active role for Parliament, with authority mediated instead through local power-brokers and the favouring of one magnate faction against another. In the Midlands, Lord Hastings had been promoted to replace the Duke of Clarence as the King's chief enforcer. John de Vere, earl of Oxford, was deliberately ruined in order that his estates might be used to reward John Howard, himself settled into the shoes of the late Duke of Norfolk. The King had intervened in the local warfare fought out between the Stanley and the Harrington families in Lancashire. Above all, Edward IV had relied upon his younger brother, Richard, Duke of Gloucester, granted a large share of the estate that had formerly belonged to Richard Neville, Earl of Warwick, and a power base entirely his own in south Wales and the north of England. Throughout the 1460s, and in the face of the rebellions by Clarence and Warwick, Richard of Gloucester had remained loyal to Edward IV. In 1471, aged barely eighteen, he had taken a decisive lead in suppressing rebellion in Kent, executing the rebels' leader, in theory pardoned his crimes. When the citizens of York disputed the wisdom of admitting Edward IV to their city, Richard suggested killing them all and being done with it. Already, Richard displayed a very practical approach to murder. Thereafter, through the disgrace of the Veres and of his brother, Clarence, he had established an unassailable position for himself as the King's most trusted confident and as one of the richest men in England. He was also one of the best regarded. His probity, his loyalty, his espousal of morality and his patronage of puritan spirituality, his collection of books and his patronage of pious literature, all marked him out as a good man amidst a court of sinners. With an uncle such as Richard, it was supposed, the young sons of Edward IV would be shepherded to the throne in just the same way that John of Gaunt, in the end, had shepherded his nephew Richard II, or John, Duke of Bedford, uncle of Henry VI, had upheld the cause of his own royal ward. Richard, in accordance with historical precedent, was groomed to become the very best of royal uncles. He turned out to be the very worst.

Edward IV died at Windsor on 9 April 1483. His twelve-year-old son, Edward V, was then at Ludlow on the Welsh border. The coronation was set for 4 May. In the company of his mother's brother, Lord Rivers, the boy was brought southwards, the party diverting to Stony Stratford in Buckinghamshire in order to meet up with Edward's loving uncle, Richard. There, entirely contrary to what anyone had expected, Richard arrested Lord Rivers and other members of the Woodville affinity. The Woodvilles themselves were unpopular, regarded as upstarts glutted on the spoils of power. Richard had little difficulty in manipulating public opinion, and the affinity of the King's household, against them. By 10 June, he was writing to the city of York for assistance against Elizabeth Woodville, the former Queen, and her associates, claiming that they intended his murder.

Richard III and the Young Princes

Even now, it was assumed that, having dealt with these difficulties at court, Richard would serve as a loyal protector to his nephew, King Edward V, whose coronation was postponed to 22 June. Instead, on 13 June, Richard ordered the arrest and summary execution of Lord Hastings, the King's chamberlain, former manager of the royal household, loyal servant of the house of York, almost certainly because Hastings refused to cooperate with Richard in a plot to seize the throne. Obtaining custody of Edward V's younger brother, Richard of Woodstock, who had fled with his mother to the sanctuary of Westminster Abbey, Richard now committed both of his nephews to the Tower of London. They were never seen again. Whether or not they can be identified with the skeletons of two adolescent boys discovered in the Tower in 1674, by the end of June 1483, the two princes were either dead or awaiting their murderer's knock at the door. On 22 June, the date to which the coronation of Edward V had in theory been postponed, instead of a twelve-year-old King, the Londoners were confronted by Dr Ralph Shaw, one of Richard of Gloucester's tame clergyman, who at St Paul's Cross proclaimed Richard's own titles to be recognized as King, arguing that the princes in the Tower were bastards, the marriage of Edward IV to Elizabeth Woodville having been contracted against the spirit of canon law. There was a sound legal argument that might have been made here. In practice, it drew only the flimsiest of veils across usurpation and murder. By the time that Richard of Gloucester was crowned King on 6 July, the princes were probably already dead. If not, then they died in August, when an unsuccessful plot was unearthed to rescue them from the Tower.

It remains one of the more remarkable aspects of this story that Richard, potentially a loyal servant of the crown and protector to his royal nephews, should have preferred to seize their throne and, in the outcome, to die a hated usurper rather than a beloved uncle. Perhaps there was some kink in the Yorkist family DNA sufficient to explain the treachery first of Clarence, now of Richard, the younger brother. Perhaps Richard's morality was fiercer and more sincere than historians have been inclined to suppose; his sense of puritanism simply revolted at the spectacle of Edward V, son of a corrupt Woodville marriage, ascending the throne. Like many puritans, Richard perhaps found it easy to disguise his own self-interest as an act of public duty. After 1483, he did his best to popularize the cult of Henry VI, allowing for the removal of the late King's relics from Chertsey to Windsor Castle as a means of yet further blackening the moral reputation of his brother, Edward IV. Edward IV's mistress was forced to do public penance in the streets of London as if she were a common whore. Henry VI was reburied next to the effigy of Edward IV, whose late government was publicly declared to have been motivated by concupiscence with 'every good maiden and woman standing in dread to be ravished and defouled'. Richard emerged as neither the first nor the last in a series of self-consciously 'northern' politicians whose personal austerity and probity seemed to promise a return to core moral values.

Opposition to Richard

In the meantime, the stunned shock that Richard's usurpation caused very swiftly yielded place to revulsion and to a determination to remove him from the throne. The murder of Hastings had already robbed him of the support of the royal household, of precisely that power base that Edward IV had laboured so hard and at such expense to build up. In the provinces, Richard's own entrenched authority in Wales and northern England had inspired tensions with families such as the Percy dukes of Northumberland and the Stafford dukes of Buckingham. Buckingham, once Richard's closest ally, allowed to inherit Hastings' affinity but not his lands, most of which remained to Hastings' widow, now made common cause with the Woodvilles and with Lady Margaret Beaufort, mother of Henry Tudor. Their rebellion was swiftly crushed. Buckingham was executed. Nonetheless, from the autumn of 1483, Richard III was to have no peace and the English nothing save a pretence that the realm was safely established under his rule. Unlike any English King since Harold in 1066, Richard was left with no real function in government save to watch and to wait for an invasion that everyone knew to be approaching.

Henry Tudor

As with Harold and 1066, there is a false sense of inevitability to Richard III's reign. Its outcome is so well known that history itself is inverted so that the end may explain the beginnings. In reality, there was nothing inevitable about Richard's defeat. The only plausible alternative candidate to the throne to emerge after 1483, Henry Tudor, possessed a claim weaker even than William of Normandy's had been four hundred years before. William was a foreigner and a bastard. Henry Tudor was of Franco-Welsh ancestry, recently established in France and backed by French and Breton silver. Richard III, by contrast, was the brother of the late King and descended from the senior branch of the family of Edward III. Henry Tudor, a great-grandson of Charles VI, was more closely related to the French royal family than he was to the English, being merely a great-great-great-grandson of Edward III. On both sides, his descent had passed through the female line. The strength of the Tudor claim derived from no innate virtue but from the fact that, by 1483 and after two decades of fratricidal bloodshed, Henry Tudor was virtually the only alternative male claimant left standing. In exile, he was surrounded by a group of French and Breton opportunists rather similar to the French brigands who had gathered at the court of William of Normandy. No more than Richard III or Edward IV was Henry Tudor the sort of person that the English expected to have as king.

Not merely the circumstances but various of the names remained unchanged between the 1060s and the 1480s: John de Vere, Henry's chief ally, 13th earl of Oxford, was directly descended from the Veres, native to the Norman-Breton frontier, who had fought for the Conqueror, obtained land in Essex and Cambridgeshire and then risen through marriage to the Clares (themselves founders of the honour of Clarence) to become royal chamberlains under King Henry I. Like at least one of the armies at Hastings in 1066, Henry Tudor's army in 1485 marched under a dragon standard. Like William in 1066, Henry had no alternative but to bring his enemies to a decisive battle, if only to fulfil the prayer that he delivered to the Almighty on first landing, at Milford Haven, on Sunday 7 August 1485: 'Judge me, oh Lord, and determine my cause!' William of Normandy could not have expressed a better summary of the role of battle as divine trial, nor Edward III at Crécy, nor Henry V at Agincourt.

Battle of Bosworth

Like Hastings in 1066, the Battle of Bosworth of 22 August 1485, is misnamed. The great battle of 1066 was fought four miles from Hastings itself, on the ridge known as Senlac. Bosworth was certainly not fought at Market Bosworth but at an uncertain site, only in 2010 relocated by archaeologists from the traditional 'battlefield' on Ambion Hill to a position two miles away, straddling the Roman Road near Fenn Lane Farm, the discovery of a silver-gilt livery badge depicting Richard III's symbol, the boar, being not the least remarkable proof of this relocation. As this implies, Bosworth, unlike Hastings, is one of the least well-reported battles in medieval history. The distribution of the opposing armies, even the question of who actually fought and who stood aloof, remains to a large extent unanswered.

It is still possible to pinpoint similarities between 1485 and 1066. Richard III spent the months before Henry Tudor's landing, in Nottingham and its surrounding forests, like Harold Godwinson in the Bayeux Tapestry with his hawks and his hounds, or like the proverbial Robin Hood, pursuing what had been the sport of kings for many years before ever William of Normandy set foot in England. In 1066, poor communications and the inadequacy of the old Roman roads had disrupted contacts between north and south, so that William was able to land in Sussex whilst Harold was still busy in Yorkshire. In 1485, although on 11 August Richard had news of Henry Tudor's landing, and although by 19 August the authorities of the city of York were arranging to send eighty men to the King's assistance, poor communications ensured that this contingent, like many others, simply failed to arrive. The fact that the battle itself was fought in a marsh, either side of a Roman road, should itself indicate the degree to which England, even a thousand years after the departure of the last Roman legions, still belonged to a sub-Roman world, part cultivated, part still wilderness. Hastings had developed into a mass assassination attempt upon Harold and his body-guard gathered around the royal standard. Bosworth began as an attempt by Richard III to kill Henry Tudor before any serious blows had been struck, trampling the Tudor dragon underfoot in much the same way that one imagines Harold's dragon, shown in the Bayeux Tapestry, was trampled underfoot by the Normans.

Just as at Hastings, where Mowbrays and Veres and a host of families who were to dominate English politics for the coming four centuries were assembled, so at Bosworth gathered Percys and Stanleys and Howards, the coming men of the sixteenth and seventeenth centuries. Direct descendants of the Lord Stanley who fought at Bosworth served as prime minister and foreign secretary in the governments of Queen Victoria. Edward Stanley, seventeenth earl of Derby, was still serving as Secretary of State for War in 1924. Two of his sons were members of the British cabinet in 1938. One of them, Secretary of State for War in 1940, was still a government minister as late as 1945. Charles Howard, twentieth earl of Suffolk, died in 1941 as a bomb-disposal expert, posthumously awarded the George Cross. Miles Fitzalan-Howard, seventeenth duke of Norfolk, was still a major-general commanding British troops on the Rhine in 1965. The families which met at Bosworth in 1485 were to enjoy an ascendancy in English politics and military affairs just as great as that enjoyed by the Norman families which had fought at Hastings in 1066.

Here, however, the comparisons begin to run dry and the contrasts assert themselves. Harold was defended to the death by his men at Hastings, to such an extent that the entire flower of the English nobility was cut down in a single day. Richard III commanded no such allegiance. Two of the greatest forces gathered at Bosworth, in theory to support the King, either stood aloof, as seems to have been the case with Henry Percy, Duke of Northumberland, or actively threw in their lot with Henry Tudor, as may have been the case at Bosworth with Lord Stanley. Richard is said to have gone down shouting 'Treason! Treason! Treason!', an appropriate summary of the entire political malaise in which England had become embroiled. The only nobleman who died with him was John Howard, the most blatant of upstarts: until 1470 a mere Suffolk knight only later raised through marriage and affinity to the status and title of his former masters, the Mowbray dukes of Norfolk. After Hastings, it took William of Normandy a full three months to lay claim to the English throne. At Bosworth, at least according to legend, the crown or a coronet formerly worn by King Richard, was found on the field of battle and placed on Henry Tudor's forehead even as the last battlefield executions were taking place. William 'the Conqueror' marked the site of his battle with penance and the foundation of a great Benedictine Abbey. Henry Tudor, the future Henry VII, attempted no such commemoration of his victory. Far from founding a religious house, he was the father of a future king who was to suppress and squander the resources of every monastery in England.

England and the English: National Identity

The Battle of Bosworth did not put an end to medieval England any more than the Battle of Hastings brought the Middle Ages into existence. Traditions and institutions survived. Some, such as the Exchequer, are with us still. Others, such as the chronic willingness of the barons to resort to war, and the crown's inability to live off its own resources, were still determining factors behind the historical events for centuries still to come: the dissolution of the monasteries and the Protestant Reformation of the 1530s, for example, or the English Civil War a century later. History itself, by contrast to history books, does not divide easily into periods or clear-cut 'befores' and 'afters'. Like the shades of William of Normandy or Harold Godwinson hovering over the events at Bosworth Field, it tends to cast a shadow long after its actors have gone to their graves.

Nonetheless, if we cannot end here with a high note and a declaration that, in August 1485, on Bosworth Field, the modern or the early modern era was born, we can at least declare that by the time that Henry Tudor placed a crown upon his head, England had acquired both a history and a national identity. Wealth and the bounty of nature were England's birthrights, a consequence of geography, of the constant presence of the sea, and of the toil of those who first cleared the land, dug the mines and tilled the soil. From at least the age of Bede, as far back as the eighth century, came an idea of Englishness and of national destiny united under Christian kingship. For all of the shattering uncertainties and usurpations of the fifteenth century, the kingdom of England, unlike the kingdom of France or the empire of Germany, remained a united and indivisible whole.

From at least the eleventh century, and William of Normandy's victory at Hastings, a willingness to resort to violence and a determination to prove a God-given destiny through battle, had become defining characteristics of Englishness. From this emerged a state and an aristocracy themselves derived from warfare and the needs of organizing society for war. From the twelfth century, if not before, came a sense both of history and of irony. Nostalgia for past glories and a determination, at some future point, to rebuild a golden age, were combined with an ability to subvert the magniloquence of kings and to laugh at the very pomp that such nostalgia might otherwise encourage. The English, from their lands in France and later in Wales, Ireland and Scotland, had come to think of themselves as an imperial people, heirs to Arthur and to the Roman glories of the past. Deeply mistrustful of foreigners, they were themselves a nation of mongrels, half-breeds and polyglots, ruled after 1485 by Welshmen, dependent upon European trade and closely tied to the fortunes of France. The English were neither polite nor obedient. For all their claim to be doing God's work, they were as often engaged in spying or rebellion as in administering justice or in protecting their own much boasted liberties. They were a paradox awaiting description. Above all they were a people secure in their knowledge, even in their mythologizing of the past. They had come into possession of a history, and their past was never far distant from their present thoughts.

FURTHER READING

The guide to reading which follows is deliberately *not* intended as a series of footnotes, tracing each and every citation, but as a selection of books and articles that readers might explore, should they wish to dig more deeply into English medieval history. Readers keen to remark such things might care to notice how much of the following reading list draws upon work published since 1990 (a sign, not merely of the absurd dictates of the government's Research Assessment exercise, but of the degree to which medieval history now flourishes) and how many of the books cited here were published at Woodbridge, by Boydell and Brewer, thanks to the wholly beneficent influence of Richard Barber.

Historians traditionally divide their sources between the 'primary' (essentially those written or created at the time or purporting to supply a direct memory of past events) and the 'secondary' (those written by later scholars attempting to make sense of events already long past), and it is to the primary sources that I would first and foremost direct readers. The primary sources for medieval England were mostly written in Latin or French, though excellent translations exist for many of the more important. Selections of them can be found in the four medieval volumes of *English Historical Documents*, edited by D.C. Douglas, with the individual volumes covering the periods 500–1042, 1042–1189, 1189–1327 and 1327–1485 edited by Dorothy Whitelock, D.C. Douglas and George W. Greenaway, Harry Rothwell, and A.R. Myers. Complete, as opposed to selective, translations of various of the more important chronicles are available from the splendid series of Nelson's, later Oxford Medieval Texts, ranging from Bede's *Ecclesiastical History* (edited by Bertram Colgrave and R.A.B. Mynors) and the principal biography of Edward the Confessor, the *Life of King Edward who rests at Westminster* (edited by Rank Barlow), through to the *Chronica Majora* of Thomas of Walsingham (edited by John Taylor, Wendy R. Childs and Leslie Watkiss). Amongst sources written in Anglo-Saxon or English, see, for example, the excellent translations in the Penguin Classics editions of *Alfred the Great* (edited by Simon Keynes and Michael Lapidge), or Chaucer's *Canterbury Tales* (edited and translated into modern English by Nevill Coghill), or Langland's *Piers Plowman* (edited and translated by J.F. Goodridge). Amongst sources originally written in French, a special significance attaches to the so-called *History of William Marshal* (edited by Anthony J. Holden, Stewart Gregory and David Crouch, 3 vols, Anglo-Norman Text Society, 2002–6).

Since the proper edition and re-edition of primary sources remains one of the principal tasks of each generation of medieval historians, and since not all of the major sources edited in the nineteenth century have as yet been fully revised and re-edited for a more modern or critical audience, some sources remain available only in translations prepared in the Victorian era, most notably the great chronicles of Roger of Wendover and Matthew Paris (both translated for the Bohn Classics series by John Allen Giles) or the equally significant chronicles for the twelfth century (translated by Joseph

Stevenson in his multi-volume *Church Historians of England*, 1854–56). Others are readily available as Penguin Classics, as for example Geoffrey of Monmouth's *History of the Kings of Britain* (edited by Lewis Thorpe) or Gerald of Wales' *Journey Through Wales* (also edited by Thorpe), or Gerald's equally remarkable *History and Topography of Ireland* (edited by John J. O'Meara). For the administrative, as opposed to the literary or chronicle sources, readers may find it enlightening to dip into the massive runs of such series as the *Calendar of Patent Rolls* or *Calendar of Close Rolls* (both in sets of more than 100 volumes, published by HMSO, ongoing since the 1890s). If nothing else, readers will derive from even a glimpse of such sources an idea of the sheer scale on which the medieval evidences of English royal government have been preserved to us. The arts and artefacts of the Middle Ages constitute an equally rich 'primary' source. Here, particularly recommended, are the massive illustrated catalogues to the three great exhibitions of medieval art held in London since the 1980s: *English Romanesque Art 1066–1200*, edited by Sandy Heslop and others (London, Hayward Gallery 1984), *Age of Chivalry: Art in Plantagenet England 1200–1400*, edited by Jonathan Alexander and Paul Binski (London, Royal Academy 1987), and *Gothic: Art for England c.1400–1547*, edited by Richard Marks and others (London, Victoria & Albert Museum 2003).

As for the secondary sources, besides the individual works recommended below, chapter by chapter, the entire period is surveyed in three magnificent and massive volumes in the new Oxford History of England, by Robert Bartlett, *England under the Norman and Angevin Kings, 1075–1225* (Oxford 2000), Michael Prestwich, *Plantagenet England, 1225–1360* (Oxford 2005), and Gerald Harriss, *Shaping the Nation: England, 1360–1461* (Oxford 2005). Two other surveys have retained their status as classics: Christopher Brooke, *From Alfred to Henry III, 871–1272* (first published in 1961, still in print), and Maurice Keen, *England in the Late Middle Ages* (first published in 1973). Outside the Oxford series, the best of the modern overviews are those by Michael Clanchy, *England and its Rulers, 1066–1307*, 3rd edn (Oxford 2006); David Carpenter, *The Struggle for Mastery: Britain, 1066–1284* (London 2003); Miri Rubin, *The Hollow Crown: A History of Britain in the Late Middle Ages* (London 2005), and (with a welcome European dimension for the late Middle Ages, too often considered in Anglocentric isolation) John Watts, *The Making of Polities: Europe, 1300–1500* (Cambridge 2009). My own exploration of the subject would have been rendered impossible but for the existence of the new *Oxford Dictionary of National Biography*, edited by H.C.G. Matthew and Brian Harrison, 61 vols (2004, available in most decent libraries as an online resource at <http://www.oxforddnb.com>).

Chapter 1

Sir Frank Stenton's *Anglo-Saxon England* (first published in 1943, still in print in its latest edition) remains classic. For a sense of the wealth and sophistication of the Anglo-Saxons, the principal modern authority is James Campbell, whose collected essays are available in two volumes, *Essays in Anglo-Saxon History* (London 1986), and *The Anglo-Saxon State* (London 2000). He also served as principal editor of a very useful collection of studies *The Anglo-Saxons* (London 1982), notable not least for the fact that it introduces a general readership to the thinking of Patrick Wormald, the principal authority on Anglo-Saxon law. For the wealth of England, besides Campbell, see John R. Maddicott, 'Trade, Industry and the Wealth of King Alfred', *Past and Present*, 123 (1989), 3–51, with a subsequent debate in this same journal by Ross Balzaretti and Janet L. Nelson, *Past and Present*, 135 (1992), 142–63. For biographies of the principal figures, see Ann Williams, *Aethelred the Unready* (London 2003); M.K. Lawson, *Cnut: The Danes in England in the Early Eleventh Century* (London 1993); Frank Barlow, *Edward the Confessor*, 2nd edn (London 1997), and the still indispensable D.C. Douglas, *William the*

Conqueror (London 1964), with a particularly useful series of essays on the Confessor's reign, *Edward the Confessor: The Man and the Legend*, ed. Richard Mortimer (Woodbridge 2009). For events seen from the perspective of England's queens, see Pauline Stafford, *Queen Emma and Queen Edith* (Oxford 1997). Amongst individual topics considered, there is a wealth of information on medieval textiles in the journal *Medieval Clothing and Textiles* (Woodbridge 2005–). For elves, Karen L. Jolly, *Popular Religion in Late Anglo-Saxon England* (Chapel Hill 1996); for vampires, Geoffrey of Burton's *Life and Miracles of St Modwena*, ed. Robert Bartlett (Oxford 2002). For the structures of society, Robin Fleming, *Kings and Lords in Conquest England* (Cambridge 1991), and Emma Mason, *The House of Godwine* (London 2003). For the St Brice's Day massacre, Ann Williams, '"Cockes Amongst the Wheat": Danes and the English in the Western Midlands in the First Half of the Eleventh Century', *Midland History*, 11 (1986), 1–22. For pre-conquest Normandy, David Bates, *Normandy Before 1066* (London 1982), and for the Conqueror's family background, Elisabeth M.C. van Houts, 'The Origins of Herleva, Mother of William the Conqueror', *English Historical Review*, 101 (1986), 399–404. There is a wealth of material, several hundred essays all told, to be excavated from the annual publication of the Proceedings of the Battle Conference, *Anglo-Norman Studies* (Woodbridge 1978–), a series initiated by R. Allen Brown that has at last enabled scholars on both sides of the great divide of 1066 and on either side of the Channel to come together to discuss leading themes in both Anglo-Saxon and Norman history. For the Bayeux Tapestry, there are excellent colour reproductions by Wolfgang Grape, *The Bayeux Tapestry* (Munich 1994) and the more tradional David M. Wilson, *The Bayeux Tapestry* (London 1985). For the battle itself various studies are assembled by Stephen Morillo, *The Battle of Hastings: Sources and Interpretations* (Woodbridge 1996), complementing Morillo's monograph, *Warfare under the Anglo-Norman*

Kings, 1066–1135 (Woodbridge 1994). For the logistics of the 1066 campaign, the remarkable calculations of Bernard S. Bachrach, 'Some Observations on the Military Aspect of the Norman Conquest', *Anglo-Norman Studies*, 8 (1985), 1–25, are cited here with relish though not necessarily with complete confidence in their accuracy. For the suggestion that it was William of Arques, rather than William of Normandy, who visited England in 1051, I am indebted to Peter Davidson and to my Norman Conquest special-subject class at Norwich.

Chapter 2

An excellent selection of primary sources is available on the Norman Conquest in R. Allen Brown, *The Norman Conquest of England: Sources and Documents*, 2nd edn (Woodbridge 1995). Amongst the more approachable general accounts of this period, Brian Golding, see *Conquest and Colonisation: The Normans in Britain, 1066–1100* (Basingstoke 1994). For Norman identity, R.H.C. Davis, *The Normans and their Myth* (London 1976); W.L. Warren, 'The Myth of Anglo-Norman Administrative Efficiency', *Transactions of the Royal Historical Society*, 5th series 34 (1984), 113–32. For the burdens of society, Austin Lane Poole, *Obligations of Society in the 12th and 13th Centuries* (Oxford 1946), and the particularly illuminating discussion by Alan Cooper, *Bridges, Law and Power in Medieval England, 700–1400* (Woodbridge 2006). For the English after 1066, the fundamental study remains that by Ann Williams, *The English and the Norman Conquest* (Woodbridge 1995), with particular studies of the posthumous history of Harold and the Godwinsons by Alan Thacker, 'The Cult of King Harold at Chester', in *The Middle Ages in the North-West*, ed. T. Scott and P. Starkey (Oxford 1995), pp. 155–76, and Richard Sharpe, 'King Harold's Daughter', *Haskins Society Journal*, 19 (2008), 1–27. For the survival of Anglo-Saxon officers at the heart of William's administration, see Simon Keynes, 'Regenbald the Chancellor', *Anglo-Norman Studies*, 10 (1988), 185–222. The

Belet and Hose families discussed here emerge from my own research. For surnames, see J.C. Holt, *What's in a Name? Family Nomenclature and the Norman Conquest*, Stenton Lecture (Reading 1981), reprinted in Holt, *Colonial England 1066–1215* (London 1997). For Domesday, the best starting point remains V.H. Galbraith, *Domesday Book: Its Place in Administrative History* (Oxford 1974), though, more recently, see David Roffe, *Decoding Domesday* (Woodbridge 2007). For Domesday's 'tormented voices', Alan Cooper, 'Protestations of Ignorance in Domesday Book', in *The Experience of Power in Medieval Europe, 950–1350*, ed. Robert F. Berkhoffer and others (Aldershot 2005), pp. 169–81. For chivalry and the sense of English superiority over other British peoples, see various of the essays by John Gillingham, 'Conquering the Barbarians', and '1066 and the Introduction of Chivalry into England', collected in Gillingham, *The English in the Twelfth Century* (Woodbridge 2000), pp. 41–58, 209–31. For the coronation rite, Janet L. Nelson, 'The Rites of the Conqueror', *Anglo-Norman Studies*, 4 (1981), 117–32. For the upper end of society, see Robin Fleming's *Kings and Lords*, noted above, chapter 1, and F.M. Stenton, *The First Century of English Feudalism, 1066–1166*, 2nd edn (Oxford 1961); J.H. Round, *The King's Serjeants and Officers of State* (London 1911); Chris P. Lewis, 'The Early Earls of Norman England', *Anglo-Norman Studies*, 13 (1991), 207–23. For horses, there is a brief introduction by R.H.C. Davis, *The Medieval Warhorse* (London 1989), and more recently Ann Hyland, *The Medieval Warhorse: From Byzantium to the Crusades* (Stroud 1994), and Hyland, *The Warhorse, 1250–1600* (Stroud 1998). For the Varangians and contacts with Byzantium, John Godfrey, 'The Defeated Anglo-Saxons Take Service with the Eastern Emperor', *Anglo-Norman Studies*, 1 (1978), 63–74; Krijnie N. Ciggaer, 'England and Byzantium on the Eve of the Norman Conquest', *Anglo-Norman Studies,* 5 (1981), 78–96; Jonathan Shepherd, 'The English and Byzantium: A Study of

Their Role in the Byzantine Army in the Later Eleventh Century', *Traditio,* 29 (1993), 53–92. For the English and Anglo-Norman languages after 1066, Ian Short '"Anglice loqui nesciunt": Monoglots in Anglo-Norman England', *Cultura Neolatina,* 69 (2009), 245–62. For castles, the work of Robert Liddiard is fundamentally significant, including Liddiard, 'Castle Rising, Norfolk: A "Landscape of Lordship"', *Anglo-Norman Studies,* 22 (1999), 169–86, and *Landscapes of Lordship: Norman Castles and the Countryside in Medieval Norfolk, 1066–1200,* British Archaeological Reports British Series 309 (2000), with a good selection of essays by other hands ed. Liddiard as *Anglo-Norman Castles* (Woodbridge 2002). For a more traditional approach, and for some excellent aerial photography, R. Allen Brown, *English Castles,* 2nd edn (Woodbridge 2004); R. Allen Brown, *Castles from the Air* (Cambridge 1989). For hunting and the animal kingdom, I have relied heavily upon Naomi Sykes, 'Zooarchaeology of the Norman Conquest', *Anglo-Norman Studies,* 27 (2005), 185–97. For bunny-men and the misinterpretation of archaeological evidence, Tom Williamson, *Rabbits, Warrens and Archaeology* (Stroud 2007). For the Bayeux Tapestry, there is a useful selection of essays collected by Richard Gameson, *The Study of the Bayeux Tapestry* (Woodbridge 1997). For farming and the leasing of land, Reginald Lennard, *Rural England, 1086–1135* (Oxford 1959). For building, Eric Fernie, *Romanesque Architecture: Design, Meaning and Metrology* (London 1995). For the historiography and the Victorian debate, see Marjorie Chibnall, *The Debate on the Norman Conquest* (Manchester 1999), and (particularly useful not just for the eleventh but the twelfth century) Claire Simmons, *Reversing the Conquest: History and Myth in Nineteenth-Century British Literature* (New Brunswick 1990). Two 'Victorian' books nonetheless retain their cutting edge: John Horace Round, *Feudal England* (London 1895), and Frederick William Maitland, *Domesday Book and Beyond* (Cambridge 1897, reprinted with an introduction by J.C. Holt 1997). For short versus long hair, Robert Bartlett, 'Symbolic Meanings of Hair in the Middle Ages', *Transactions of the Royal Historical Society*, 6th series 4 (1994), 43–60.

Chapter 3

Besides the reading recommended for chapter 2, there are excellent overviews by Marjorie Chibnall in her surveys *Anglo-Norman England 1066–1166* (Oxford 1986) and *The World of Orderic Vitalis* (Oxford 1984). Individual biographies of the three kings considered here include Frank Barlow, *William Rufus* (London 1983); Judith A. Green, *Henry I: King of England and Duke of Normandy* (Cambridge 2006), and a rich haul of titles on King Stephen, amongst which R.H.C. Davis, *King Stephen, 1135–1154*, 3rd edn (London 1990), David Crouch, *The Reign of King Stephen, 1135–1154* (London 2000), and Edmund King, *King Stephen* (London 2010) can be particularly recommended. For other major players on the political scene, there are significant biographies by William M. Aird, *Robert Curthose* (Woodbridge 2008) and Marjorie Chibnall, *The Empress Matilda* (Oxford 1991). For an overview of royal biographical forms, see essays by Nicholas Vincent and others in *Writing Medieval Biography, 750–1250: Essays in Honour of Professor Frank Barlow*, ed. David Bates and others (Woodbridge 2006). The approach adopted here in respect of the legality of William's claims has been refined in opposition to that of George Garnett, *Conquered England: Kingship, Succession and Tenure, 1066–1166* (Oxford 2007). For the laws of Henry I, I depend upon forthcoming work by Nicholas Karn, and an excellent and approachable overview by John Hudson, *Land, Law and Lordship in Anglo-Norman England* (Oxford 1994). For the church, the best overview remains that by Frank Barlow, *The English Church, 1066–1154* (London 1979). For the posthumous life of Bede, see R.H.C. Davis, 'Bede After Bede' in Davis' collected essays, *From Alfred the Great to Stephen* (London 1991). For monasticism, the best survey remains that by David Knowles, *The Monastic Order in England*, 2nd edn (Cambridge 1966). For Anglo-Norman burials, Brian Golding, 'Anglo-Norman Knightly Burials', in *The Ideals and Practice of Medieval Knighthood*, ed. Christopher Harper-Bill and Ruth Harvey (Woodbridge 1986), pp. 35–48, with further details in Emma Cownie's *Religious Patronage in Anglo-Norman England, 1066–1135* (London 1998). For the rewriting of saints' lives after 1066, Paul Hayward, 'Translation-Narratives in Post-Conquest Hagiography and English Resistance to the Norman Conquest', *Anglo-Norman Studies*, 21 (1999), 67–93. For Lanfranc, the best introduction remains his own letters, *The Letters of Lanfranc, Archbishop of Canterbury*, ed. Helen Clover and Margaret Gibson (Oxford 1979). The same can be said for *The Letters of Saint Anselm of Canterbury*, ed. Walter Fröhlich, 3 vols (Kalamazoo 1990–94), although no reader should pass by the opportunity to explore Richard Southern's great biography, *Saint Anselm: A Portrait in a Landscape* (Cambridge 1990), or Southern's equally magnificent study of Eadmer, Anselm's biographer, *Saint Anselm and his Biographer* (Cambridge 1966). For the 'sortes', see George Henderson, 'Sortes Biblicae in Twelfth-Century England: The List of Episcopal Prognostics in Cambridge, Trinity College MS R.7.5', in *England in the Twelfth Century*, ed. Daniel Williams (Woodbridge 1990), pp. 113–35. My remarks on the Canterbury lavatories emerge from a discussion with Tim Tatton-Brown. For Peterborough, see Edmund King, *Peterborough Abbey 1086–1310: A Study in the Land Market* (Cambridge 1973). Pending the forthcoming work of Sandy Heslop, the only complete 'guide' to the seals of England's medieval kings remains the outdated series of images compiled by Alfred B. Wyon, *The Great Seals of England from the Earliest Period to the Present Time* (London 1887). Individual aspects of the reign of Henry I can be approached via the collected essays of C. Warren Hollister, *Monarchy, Magnates and Institutions in the Anglo-Norman World* (London 1986). An edition of the Pipe Roll for 1130, with

English translation, is about to appear via the Pipe Roll Society, ed. Judith Green. The 'Constitutio', ed. Stephen Church, is appended to the latest edition of *The Dialogue of the Exchequer*, ed. Emily Amt (Oxford 2007). For the judiciary, there is much detail in Ralph V. Turner, *The English Judiciary in the Age of Glanvill and Bracton, c.1176–1239* (Cambridge 1985). For the aristocracy in politics, the classic study remains that by David Crouch, *The Beaumount Twins: The Roots and Branches of Power in the Twelfth Century* (Cambridge 1986). For poisoning, the best work is now in French, but see meanwhile Josiah Cox Russell, 'Allegations of Poisoning in the Norman World' in his collected essays, *Twelfth Century Studies* (New York 1978), pp. 83–93. For William and the Jews of Norwich, pending the appearance of a new edition by Miri Rubin, see *The Life and Miracles of St William of Norwich by Thomas of Monmouth*, ed. Augustus Jessopp and Montague Rhodes James (Cambridge 1896), with a secondary study by Gavin I. Langmuir, 'Thomas of Monmouth: Detector of Ritual Murder', *Speculum*, 59 (1984), 820–46, and reflections on the racial or nationalistic context by Hugh M. Thomas, *The English and the Normans: Ethnic Hostility, Assimilation and Identity 1066–c.1220* (Oxford 2003). For the Cistercians and Ailred, the best introduction remains Walter Daniel's contemporary *Life of Ailred of Rievaulx*, ed. F.M. Powicke (London 1950, subsequently reprinted as an Oxford Medieval Text). For wool and the wool trade, although outdated in some respects, Eileen Power, *The Wool Trade in English Medieval History* (Oxford 1941) supplies the most readable introduction. For the feast days of Mary and their role in royal itineraries, see Nicholas Vincent, 'King Henry III and the Blessed Virgin Mary', in *The Church and Mary: Studies in Church History 39*, ed. R.N. Swanson (Woodbridge 2005), 126–46.

Chapter 4
For overviews of the Plantagenets, see Martin Aurell (trans. David Crouch) *The Plantagenet Empire, 1154–1224* (Harlow

2007); John Gillingham, *The Angevin Empire*, 2nd edn (London 2001), and Richard Mortimer, *Angevin England, 1154–1272* (Oxford 1994). There is only one modern biography of Henry II that can be wholeheartedly recommended, although it is a very long book: W.L. Warren, *Henry II* (London 1973). It can be supplemented with various of the essays collected as *Henry II: New Interpretations*, ed. Christopher Harper-Bill and Nicholas Vincent (Woodbridge 2007). For Henry II's marital infidelities, see Marie Lovatt, 'Archbishop Geoffrey of York: A Problem in Anglo-French Maternity', in *Records, Administration and Aristocratic Society in the Anglo-Norman Realm*, ed. Nicholas Vincent (Woodbridge 2009), pp. 91–123. For the question of precedence, see Nicholas Vincent, 'Did Henry II Have a Policy Towards the Earls?', in *War, Government and Aristocracy in the British Isles, c.1150–1500: Essays in Honour of Michael Prestwich*, ed. C. Given-Wilson and others (Woodbridge 2008), pp. 1–25. Amongst the most evocative primary sources for the court of Henry, see Walter Map, *De Nugis Curialium: Courtiers' Trifles*, ed. M.R. James, revised by C.N.L. Brooke and R.A.B. Mynors (Oxford 1983), and the *Magna Vita Hugonis: The Life of St Hugh of Lincoln*, ed. Decima L. Douie and David H. Farmer, 2 vols (Oxford 1985). For the King's hawks, Robin S. Oggins, *The Kings and their Hawks: Falconry in Medieval England* (New Haven 2004); Richard Almond, *Medieval Hunting* (Stroud 2003). For class and the emergence of aristocratic privilege, David Crouch, *The Image of Aristocracy in Britain, 1000–1300* (London 1992), and Crouch, *The Birth of Nobility: Constructing Aristocracy in England and France, 900–1300* (London 2005). There are two excellent modern biographies of Becket, each taking a very different approach to its subject: Frank Barlow, *Thomas Becket* (London 1987), and Anne Duggan, *Thomas Becket* (London 2004), whilst no one should pass by the opportunity to dip into Duggan's magnificent edition and translation of *The Correspondence of Thomas Becket, Archbishop of Canterbury,*

1162–1170, 2 vols (Oxford 2000). Much of the detail above is taken from Nicholas Vincent, 'The Murderers of Thomas Becket', *Bishofsmord im Mittelalter*, ed. N. Fryde and D. Reitz (Göttingen 2003), pp. 211–72, partly reprinted as *Becket's Murderers*, William Urry Memorial Lecture (Canterbury 2004). For aspects of the aftermath, see Nicholas Vincent, 'The Pilgrimages of the Angevin Kings of England 1154–1272', in *Pilgrimage: The English Experience from Becket to Bunyan*, ed. C. Morris and P. Roberts (Cambridge 2002), pp. 12–45; Hans Eberhard Mayer, 'Henry II of England and the Holy Land', *English Historical Review*, 97 (1982), 721–39; Christopher R. Cheney, *From Becket to Langton: English Church Government 1170–1213* (Manchester 1956). For heraldry, Adrian Ailes, *The Origins of the Royal Arms of England: Their Development to 1199* (Reading 1982), and Ailes, 'The Knight, Heraldry and Armour: The Role of Recognition and the Origins of Heraldry', in *Medieval Knighthood IV*, ed. Christopher Harper-Bill and Ruth Harvey (Woodbridge 1992), pp. 1–21. For English attitudes to Celtic subject peoples, see John Gillingham, *The English in the Twelfth Century* (Woodbridge 2000), esp. 41–58. For William of Malmesbury, Rodney M. Thomson, *William of Malmesbury* (Woodbridge 1987). For Wace, there is an accessible English translation by Glyn S. Burgess, *The History of the Norman People: Wace's Roman de Rou* (Woodbridge 2004). For Geoffrey of Monmouth, besides the various English translations of his *History*, see Gillingham, *The English in the Twelfth Century*, pp. 19–39. For aspects of the twelfth-century renaissance, the classic work remains that by Charles Homer Haskins, *The Renaissance of the Twelfth Century* (Cambridge Mass. 1927), to be supplemented, as an introduction, by various of the studies collected as Richard Southern, *Medieval Humanism and Other Studies* (Oxford 1970). For technology, a starting point is provided by Jean Gimpel, *The Medieval Machine* (New York 1976), with particular examples above drawn from J. D. North, 'Some Norman Horoscopes', in

Adelard of Bath: An English Scientist and Arabist of the Early Twelfth Century, ed. C. Burnett (London 1987), pp. 147–61. For Glastonbury and Arthurian lore, a starting point is supplied by Reginald F. Treharne, *The Glastonbury Legends* (London 1971), and various of the essays, especially that by Julia Crick, 'The Marshalling of Antiquity: Glastonbury's Historical Dossier', in *The Archaeology and History of Glastonbury Abbey*, ed. Lesley Abrams and James P. Carley (Woodbridge 1991). For Gerald of Wales, besides the translated works noted above in the general introduction to sources, see Robert Bartlett, *Gerald of Wales, 1145–1223* (Oxford 1982). For Ireland and *Laudabiliter*, see Anne Duggan, 'The Making of a Myth: Giraldus Cambrensis, "Laudabiliter", and Henry II's Lordship of Ireland', *Studies in Medieval and Renaissance History*, 3rd series 4 (2007), 107–70. For Grosseteste, see Richard Southern, *Robert Grosseteste: The Growth of an English Mind in Medieval Europe* (Oxford 1986). For the Gothic, see Otto von Simson, *The Gothic Cathedral* (London 1956), and Paul Binski, *Becket's Crown: Art and Imagination in Gothic England, 1170–1300* (New Haven 2004). For the wooden door at Westminster, see Warwick Rodwell, 'New Glimpses of Edward the Confessor's Abbey at Westminster', in *Edward the Confessor*, ed. Richard Mortimer (Woodbridge 2009), pp. 163–6. For the 'volvelles' of Matthew Paris, see Daniel K. Connolly, *The Maps of Matthew Paris* (Woodbridge 2009). For the senses, C.M. Woolgar, *The Senses in Late Medieval England* (New Haven 2006). For the king's evil, the classic study remains that by Marc Bloch, *The Royal Touch* (trans. J.E. Anderson, New York 1961). For leprosy, Carole Rawcliffe, *Leprosy in Medieval England* (Woodbridge 2006). For categorization, Nicholas Vincent, 'Two Papal Letters on the Wearing of the Jewish Badge, 1221 and 1229', *Jewish Historical Studies*, 34 (1997), 209–24. William fitz Stephen's description of London is translated in the relevant volume of *English Historical Documents*, ed. D.C. Douglas and George W. Greenaway. For Eleanor of Aquitaine, the best of the modern biographies are those by Ralph V. Turner, *Eleanor of Aquitaine* (London 2009) and Jean Flori (trans. Olive Classe), *Eleanor of Aquitaine* (Edinburgh 2007), though the details above are drawn from Nicholas Vincent, 'Patronage, Politics and Piety in the Charters of Eleanor of Aquitaine', in *Plantagenêts et Capétiens: confrontations et héritages*, ed. Martin Aurell and N.-Y. Tonnerre (Turnhout 2006), pp. 17–60.

Chapter 5

There are excellent modern biographies of Richard I, by John Gillingham, *Richard I* (New Haven 1999), and of King John by W.L. Warren, *King John* (London 1961), and Ralph V. Turner, *King John* (London 1994). For various aspects of John's reign, see also *King John: New Interpretations*, ed. Stephen D. Church (Woodbridge 1999). Crucial for the history of baronial politics is J.C. Holt's now classic *The Northerners* (Oxford 1961, 2nd edn 1992), a masterpiece of concision and insight. Holt's more technical handling of *Magna Carta*, 2nd edn (Cambridge 1992) can be supplemented by the less daunting Ralph V. Turner, *Magna Carta* (London 2003). For the chronology of the Plantagenet collapse in Normandy, and for much else besides, see Holt, 'The End of the Anglo-Norman Realm', *Proceedings of the British Academy* (1975), 223–65, and the later pages of Daniel Power, *The Norman Frontier in the Twelfth and Early Thirteenth Centuries* (Cambridge 2004). For Isabella, John's Queen, see 'Isabella of Angoulême: John's Jezebel', in *King John: New Interpretations*, ed. Church, pp. 165–219. My thoughts on the murder of Arthur are informed by discussion with Paul Binski. For the Jews of York, see R.B. Dobson, *The Jews of Medieval York and the Massacre of March 1190*, 2nd edn (York 1994), with a forthcoming volume of essays in preparation, ed. Sarah Rees Jones. For the division of England from Norman landholding, David Crouch, 'Normans and Anglo-Normans: A Divided Aristocracy?', in *England and Normandy in the Middle Ages*,

ed. David Bates and Anne Curry (London 1994), pp. 51–67.
For John's aliens, Nicholas Vincent, *Peter des Roches: An Alien
in English Politics, 1205–1238* (Cambridge 1996). For the inter-
minable debate over the relative wealth of England and France,
see the latest contribution, by Nick Barratt, 'The Impact of the
Loss of Normandy on the English Exchequer: The Pipe Roll
Evidence', in *Foundations of Medieval Scholarship: Records
Edited in Honour of David Crook*, ed. Paul Brand and Sean
Cunningham (York 2008), pp. 133–40. For inflation, the classic
exposition remains that by Paul D.A. Harvey, 'The English
Inflation of 1180–1220', *Past and Present*, 61 (1973), 3–30, with
alternative thoughts by Paul Latimer and Jim Bolton in *King
John: New Interpretations*, ed. Stephen Church. For gallies, see
John Gillingham, 'Richard I, Galley-Warfare and Portsmouth:
The Beginnings of a Royal Navy', in *Thirteenth Century
England VI*, ed. Michael Prestwich and others (Woodbridge
1997), pp. 1–15. For Langton, the details here are drawn from
Nicholas Vincent, 'Stephen Langton: Archbishop of
Canterbury', in *Etienne Langton: Prédicateur, bibliste et théol-
ogien*, ed. Nicole Bériou, Gilbert Dahan and others (Turnhout
2010). For the interdict, Christopher R. Cheney, *Pope Innocent
III and England* (Stuttgart 1976). For the prosecution of crime,
John Hudson, *The Formation of English Common Law*
(London 1996); John Bellamy, *Crime and Public Order in
England in the Later Middle Ages* (London 1973); A.J. Musson,
'Turning King's Evidence: The Prosecution of Crime in Late
Medieval England', *Oxford Journal of Legal Studies*, 19 (1999),
467–80. For prisons and imprisonment, Ralph B. Pugh,
Imprisonment in Medieval England (Cambridge 1968); Jean
Dunbabin, *Prison and Imprisonment in Medieval Europe,
c.1000–c.1300* (London 2002); Guy Geltner, *The Medieval
Prison: A Social History* (Princeton 2008). For the King's
knights and enforcers, Stephen D. Church, *The Household
Knights of King John* (Cambridge 1999). There is still no
standard biography of Henry III. F.M. Powicke, *King Henry
III and the Lord Edward*, 2 vols (Oxford 1947), is so prolix

than it can hardly be recommended save as a literary curiosity. For the early years of the reign, see David Carpenter, *The Minority of Henry III* (London 1990), with a magnificent selection of Carpenter's articles republished as Carpenter, *The Reign of Henry III* (London 1996). The account of the reign given here is based upon my survey, first published in German, as Nicholas Vincent, 'Heinrich III (1216–72)', in *Die englischen Könige im Mittelalter von Wilhelm dem Eroberer bis Richard III*, ed. Hanna Vollrath and Natalie Fryde (Munich 2004), pp. 102–29. The primary sources for Henry III's reign are dominated by Matthew Paris, of whose *Chronica Majora* there is a complete translation by J.A. Giles, noted above amongst general reading, and illustrated excerpts by Richard Vaughan, *The Illustrated Chronicles of Matthew Paris* (Stroud 1984). For the survival and flourishing of Magna Carta, John R. Maddicott, 'Magna Carta and the Local Community 1215–59', *Past and Present*, 102 (1984), 25–65. For papal and Italian influence, Nicholas Vincent, *The Letters and Charters of Cardinal Guala Bicchieri, Papal Legate in England 1216–1218* (Canterbury and York Society 1996). For Parliament, John R. Maddicott, *The Origins of the English Parliament 924–1327* (Oxford 2010), and various of the individual essays, by Maddicott, Paul Brand, Simon Payling and Chris Given-Wilson in *A Short History of Parliament*, ed. Clyve Jones (Woodbridge 2009). For the politics of Henry III's reign, besides Carpenter's collected essays, see R.C. Stacey, *Politics, Policy and Finance under Henry III, 1216–1245* (Oxford 1987). For the King's work at Westminster, Paul Binski, *Westminster Abbey and the Plantagenets* (New Haven 1995). For Henry III's relics and sacrality, Nicholas Vincent, *The Holy Blood: Henry III and the Westminster Blood Relic* (Cambridge 2001). For Simon de Montfort, John R. Maddicott, *Simon de Montfort* (Cambridge 1994). For Lewes and Evesham, David Carpenter, *The Battles of Lewes and Evesham 1264–65* (Keele 1987), and Olivier Laborderie, J.R. Maddicott and David Carpenter, 'The Last Hours of Simon de Montfort: A New Account', *English*

Historical Review, 115 (2000), 378–412. For various of the international aspects of the reign, see Bjorn K. Weiler, *Henry III of England and the Staufen Empire, 1216–1272* (Woodbridge 2006), and the essays collected as *England and Europe in the Reign of Henry III (1216–1272)*, ed. B.K.U. Weiler and I.W. Rowlands (Aldershot 2002). For Richard of Cornwall, the only reliable modern biography remains that by Noel Denholm-Young, *Richard of Cornwall* (Oxford 1947). For Matthew Paris' maps, with colour reproductions in the study by Daniel Connolly noted above, chapter 5, see also Paul D.A. Harvey, 'Matthew Paris's Maps of Britain', *Thirteenth Century England IV* (Woodbridge 1992), pp. 109–21.

Chapter 6

The history of the reigns of all three Edwards is dominated by the work of Michael Prestwich. For a masterly overview, see Prestwich, *The Three Edwards* (London 1980). For a richly insightful biography, Prestwich, *Edward I* (London 1988). For Edward II, Roy Martin Haines, *King Edward II* (London 2003), but with more exciting studies of the King's evil counsellors and tyranny, Natalie Fryde, *The Tyranny and Fall of Edward II, 1321–1326* (Cambridge 1979), and Nigel Saul, 'The Despensers and the Downfall of Edward II', *English Historical Review*, 99 (1984), 1–33, and a good selection of essays ed. Gwilym Dodd and Anthony Musson, *The Reign of Edward II: New Perspectives* (Woodbridge 2006). For Edward III, the best of the modern biographies are those by W. Mark Ormrod, *The Reign of Edward III: Crown and Political Society, 1327–1377* (London 1990), and (admirably for a general public) Ian Mortimer, *The Perfect King: The Life of Edward III, Father of the English Nation* (London 2006). Just as the essays published as *Anglo-Norman Studies* dominate the secondary literature on the eleventh and early twelfth centuries, so two sets of annual or bi-annual essay collections now dominate the period after 1200: *Thirteenth Century England*, ed. Peter Coss, Simon Lloyd and others

(Woodbridge 1986–), and *Fourteenth Century England*, ed. Nigel Saul and others (Woodbridge 2000–). For the English royal style, W. Mark Ormrod, 'A Problem of Precedence: Edward III, the Double Monarchy, and the Royal Style', in *The Age of Edward III*, ed. J.S. Bothwell (Woodbridge 2001), pp. 133–53. For Becket's oil, T.A. Sandquist, 'The Holy Oil of St Thomas of Canterbury', *Essays in Medieval History Presented to Bertie Wilkinson*, ed. T.A. Sandquist and M.R. Powicke (Toronto 1968), pp. 330–44. For the Order of the Garter, Lisa Jefferson, 'MS Arundel 48 and the Earliest Statutes of the Order of the Garter', *English Historical Review*, 109 (1994), 356–85, whose implications are not fully explored by Hugh E.L. Collins, *The Order of the Garter, 1348–1461* (Oxford 2000). For multilingualism, most of the examples cited here are borrowed from Susan Crane, 'Social Aspects of Bilingualism in the Thirteenth Century', *Thirteenth Century England VI*, ed. Michael Prestwich and others (Woodbridge 1997), pp. 103–15. For England's imperial destiny, R.R. Davies, *The First English Empire: Power and Identities in the British Isles 1093–1343* (Oxford 2000). For Higden's maps, Kathy Lavezzo, *Angels on the Edge of the World: Geography, Literature and English Community, 1000–1534* (Ithaca 2006). For the details here of Edward I's early years, Nicholas Vincent, 'The Politics of Church and State as Reflected in the Winchester Pipe Rolls, 1208–80', *The Winchester Pipe Roll and Medieval English Society*, ed. Richard Britnell (Woodbridge 2003), pp. 157–81; John R. Maddicott, 'Edward I and the Lessons of Baronial Reform: Local Government, 1258–80', in *Thirteenth Century England I*, ed. Peter Coss and Simon Lloyd (Woodbridge 1986), pp. 1–30. For public finance, Gerald L. Harriss, *King, Parliament and Public Finance in Medieval England to 1369* (Oxford 1975). For the Hundred Rolls, Sarah Raban, *A Second Domesday? The Hundred Rolls of 1279–80* (Oxford 2004). For the expulsion of the Jews, Robert R. Mundill, *England's Jewish Solution, 1262–1290: Experiment and*

Expulsion (Cambridge 1998). For the Riccardi, Richard W. Kaeuper, *Bankers to the Crown: The Riccardi of Lucca and Edward I* (Princeton 1973). For the Welsh wars, John E. Morris, *The Welsh Wars of Edward I* (Oxford 1901) can still be read with pleasure, with a magisterial overview of the history of Wales by Rees Davies, *The Age of Conquest: Wales, 1063–1415* (Oxford 2000). For Edward I's war machine, Michael Prestwich, *War, Politics and Finance under Edward I* (London 1972). For war in general, there are magnificent surveys by Matthew Strickland, *War and Chivalry: The Conduct and Perception of War in England and Normandy, 1066–1217* (Cambridge 1996), and Michael Prestwich, *Armies and Warfare in the Middle Ages: The English Experience* (New Haven 1996). For Edward's castles, the best guide remains *The History of the King's Works*, vols 1–2 (*The Middle Ages*), ed. H.M. Colvin and others (London 1963), with the relevant sections abstracted as A.J. Taylor, *The Welsh Castles of Edward I* (London 1986). For overviews of the history of Scotland, see both Geoffrey W.S. Barrow, *The Kingdom of the Scots* (London 1973) and A.A.M. Duncan, *Scotland: The Making of the Kingdom* (Edinburgh 1975). For Robert Bruce, the classic study remains that by Geoffrey Barrow, *Robert Bruce and the Community of the Realm of Scotland*, 3rd edn (Edinburgh 1988). For the crisis of 1297, Michael Prestwich, *Documents Illustrating the Crisis of 1297–8* (Camden Society, London 1980). For the English clergy, Jeffrey H. Denton, *Robert Winchelsey and the Crown, 1294–1313* (Cambridge 1980). For the mounting sense of crisis in the fourteenth century, Barbara W. Tuchman, *A Distant Mirror: The Calamitous 14th Century* (New York 1978) remains highly readable, and see also William Chester Jordan, *The Great Famine: Northern Europe in the Early Fourteenth Century* (Princeton 1996), here using some of the ecological data from Robert S. Gottfried, *The Black Death: Natural and Human Disaster in Medieval Europe* (London 1983). For the English experience of famine, see John R.

Maddicott, *The English Peasantry and the Demands of the Crown, 1294–1341*, Past and Present Supplement 1 (1975). For yields, I depend upon figures supplied to me by Bruce Campbell, and compare the website at <http://www. cropyields.ac.uk>. For the death penalty, Henry Summerson, 'Attitudes to Capital Punishment in England, 1200–1350', *Thirteenth Century England VIII*, ed. Michael Prestwich and others (Woodbridge 2001), pp. 123–33; Summerson, 'Suicide and the Fear of the Gallows', *Journal of Legal History*, 21 (2007), 49–56; J.G. Edwards, 'The Treason of Thomas Turberville, 1295', *Studies in Medieval History Presented to Frederick Maurice Powicke*, ed. R.W. Hunt and others (Oxford 1948), pp. 296–309. For the mounting violence precipitated by Edward I, Matthew Strickland, 'Treason, Feud and the Growth of State Violence: Edward I and the "War of the Earl of Carrick", 1306–7', in *War, Government and Aristocracy in the British Isles c.1150–1500*, ed. Chris Given-Wilson and others (Woodbridge 2008), pp. 84–113. For the baronial politics of Edward II's reign, John R. Maddicott, *Thomas of Lancaster, 1307–1322* (Oxford 1970); J.R.S. Phillips, *Aymer de Valence, Earl of Pembroke, 1307–1324* (Oxford 1972). Pending the appearance of a full-scale biography of Gaveston, see Pierre Chaplais, *Piers Gaveston: Edward II's Adoptive Brother* (Oxford 1994). For Edward's supposed homosexuality, see the essays by W. Mark Ormrod and Ian Mortimer in *The Reign of Edward II*, ed. Dodd and Musson (Woodbridge 2006), pp. 22–60. For one of the principal primary sources, see the *Vita Edwardi Secundi: The Life of Edward the Second*, ed. Wendy R. Childs (Oxford 2005). For the medical history here, I depend upon discussion and assistance supplied by Carole Rawcliffe, and see Rawcliffe, *Medicine and Society in Late Medieval England* (Stroud 1995). For Mortimer and Isabella, Ian Mortimer, *The Greatest Traitor: The Life of Sir Roger Mortimer, 1st Earl of March, Ruler of England, 1327–1330* (London 2003). For Edward II after 1327, Roy Martin Haines, 'The "Afterlife" of Edward of

Caernarvon', *Transactions of the Bristol and Gloucestershire Archaeological Society*, 114 (1996), 65–86. For horse lists, Andrew Ayton, *Knights and Warhorses: Military Service and the English Aristocracy under Edward III* (Woodbridge 1994). For the Countess of Salisbury, Antonia Gransden, 'The Alleged Rape by Edward III of the Countess of Salisbury', *English Historical Review*, 87 (1972), 333–44. There is a modern biography of Wykeham by Virginia Davis, *William Wykeham: A Life* (London 2007). For the Church, the best overview remains that by W.A. Pantin, *The English Church in the Fourteenth Century* (Cambridge 1955). For English sanctity, and revealing comparisons with Italy, see Robert Brentano, *Two Churches: England and Italy in the Thirteenth Century*, 2nd edn (Berkeley 1988). For the most notorious of the bishops, John Aberth, *Criminal Churchmen in the Age of Edward III: The Case of Bishop Thomas de Lisle* (Philadelphia 1996). For monastic diet, see the wonderfully detailed portrait built up by Barbara F. Harvey, *Living and Dying in England, 1100–1540: The Monastic Experience* (Oxford 1993). For the origins of the schools of Oxford, see the official *History of the University of Oxford*, vol.1: *The Early Schools*, ed. Jeremy Catto (Oxford 1984), especially the essay by Richard Southern, and also the more provocative suggestions of R.H.C. Davis, 'The Ford, the River and the City', in Davis, *From Alfred the Great to Stephen* (London 1991), pp. 281–91. For Cambridge, I depend upon my own essay on the thirteenth-century bishops of Ely, in *Ely: Bishops and Diocese, 1109–2009*, ed. Peter Meadows (Woodbridge 2010). For discussion of founders' kin, I am indebted to Scott Mandelbrote and Christopher Brooke. No student of fourteenth-century bureaucracy can avoid the massive endeavours of T.F. Tout, *Chapters in the Administrative History of Medieval England*, 6 vols (Manchester 1920–33), which incidentally offer a far from negligible broader history of the period. For archery, Matthew Strickland and Robert Hardy, *The Great Warbow: From Hastings to the Mary Rose* (Stroud

2005). Amongst the many histories of the Hundred Years War, for a short summary, Christopher Allmand, *The Hundred Years War* (Cambridge 1988); for something a great deal longer and still ongoing, Jonathan Sumption's massive history has thus far reached 1399 in three volumes: *Trial By Battle*; *Trial by Fire*, and *Divided Houses* (London and Philadelphia 1990–2009). For Crécy, *The Battle of Crécy, 1346*, ed. Andrew Ayton and Philip Preston (Woodbridge 2005). For St George's, *St George's Chapel Windsor in the Fourteenth Century*, ed. Nigel Saul (Woodbridge 2005). For chivalry, the outstanding study by Maurice Keen, *Chivalry* (London 1984), and more recently, Keen, *Origins of the English Gentleman: Heraldry, Chivalry and Gentility in Medieval England, c.1300-c.1500* (Stroud 2002), with its counterpoint in Peter R. Coss, *The Lady in Medieval England, 1100–1500* (Stroud 1998). For Calais in the English Parliament, H.F. Chettle, 'The Burgesses for Calais, 1536–58', *English Historical Review*, 50 (1935), 492–501. For contemporary accounts of the Black Prince's campaigns, see *The Life and Campaigns of the Black Prince*, ed. Richard Barber (London 1979), and the selections from Froissart's *Chronicles*, trans. and ed. Geoffrey Brereton (Penguin Classics, first published 1968). Amongst a host of books on the Black Death, see most recently, and in starkest contrast, Ole J. Benedictow, *The Black Death, 1346–1353: The Complete History* (Woodbridge 2004) (arguing the traditional 'Bubonic' option) and Samuel K. Cohn, *The Black Death Transformed: Disease and Culture in Early Renaissance Europe* (London 2001) (arguing from a revisionist standpoint). Hard going, but underpinning the remarks here on the legal consequences, is Robert C. Palmer, *English Law in the Age of the Black Death, 1348–1381* (Chapel Hill 1993), with a response from Anthony Musson, 'New Labour Laws, New Remedies? Legal Reaction to the Black Death "Crisis"', in *Fourteenth Century England I*, ed. Nigel Saul (Woodbridge 2000), pp. 73–88, and with other consequences considered by

Paul Binski, *Medieval Death: Ritual and Representation* (London 1996); Jacques Rossiaud (trans. Lydia G. Cochrane), *Medieval Prostitution* (Oxford 1988), and always, in the background, the classic study by Johan Huizinga, *The Waning of the Middle Ages* (first English translation 1924). For Edward III, building and display after 1350, James Sherborne, 'Aspects of Court Culture in the Later Fourteenth Century', in Sherborne, *War, Politics and Culture in Fourteenth-Century England*, ed. Anthony Tuck (London 1994), pp. 171–94. For the return of plague, Robert Gottfried, *The Black Death* (London 1983), already cited. For diet and living standards, Christopher Dyer, *Standards of Living in the Later Middle Ages*, 2nd edn (Cambridge 1998), and Dyer's collected essays, *Everyday Life in Medieval England* (London 1994). For 1376, George Holmes, *The Good Parliament* (Oxford 1975), with a particularly insightful recent study by Gwilym Dodd, 'A Parliament Full of Rats? Piers Plowman and the Good Parliament of 1376', *Historical Research*, 79 (2006), 21–49.

Chapter 7
Besides the incomparable Gerald Harriss, *Shaping the Nation*, listed above amongst general reading, there is Maurice Keen's survey, *English Society in the Later Middle Ages* (London 1990). For chess, see Richard Eales, 'The Game of Chess: An Aspect of Medieval Knightly Culture', *The Ideals and Practice of Medieval Knighthood*, ed. Christopher Harper-Bill and Ruth Harvey (Woodbridge 1986), pp. 12–34. For the aristocracy, Chris Given-Wilson, *The English Nobility in the Late Middle Ages* (London 1987); James Bothwell, *Edward III and the English Peerage* (Woodbridge 2004), and Bothwell, *Falling from Grace: Reversal of Fortune and the English Nobility, 1087–1455* (Manchester 2008). For Chaucer's Franklin, Joseph A. Bryant, 'The Diet of Chaucer's Franklin', *Modern Language Notes*, 63 (1948), 318–25; Gordon H. Gerould, 'The Social Status of Chaucer's Franklin', *Proceedings of the Modern*

Language Association, 41 (1926), 262–79; Nigel Saul, 'The Social Status of Chaucer's Franklin: A Reconsideration', *Medium Aevum*, 52 (1983), 10–26. For church monuments, a starting point is Nigel Saul, *Death, Art and Memory in Medieval England: The Cobham Family and their Monuments, 1300–1500* (Oxford 2001). For the statute of labourers and other Edwardian legislation, Scott L. Waugh, *England in the Reign of Edward III* (Cambridge 1991). For sergeants-at-arms, Richard Partington, 'Edward III's Enforcers: The King's Sergeants-at-Arms in the Localities', in *The Age of Edward III*, ed. James S. Bothwell (Woodbridge 2001), pp. 89–106. For criminal gangs, a thirteenth-century example is considered by Michael Clanchy, 'Highway Robbery and Trial by Battle in the Hampshire Eyre of 1249', in *Medieval Legal Records Edited in Memory of C.A.F. Meekings*, ed. R.F. Hunnisett and J.B. Post (London 1978), pp. 25–61, and for the fourteenth century, see L. G. Stones, 'The Folvilles of Ashby-Folville, Leicestershire, and their Associates in Crime', *Transactions of the Royal Historical Society*, 5th series 7 (1957), 117–36; Maurice Keen, *The Outlaws of Medieval Legend*, 2nd edn (London 2000). For the robbery of the Tower, Paul Doherty, *The Great Crown Jewels Robbery of 1303* (London 2005). Langland's *Piers Plowman* is available in numerous modern versions, including that by J.F. Goodridge. For chantry chapels, Howard Colvin, 'The Origin of Chantries', *Journal of Medieval History*, 26 (2000), 163–73. My account of the battle of Poitiers comes from Richard Barber's translations for *The Life and Campaigns of the Black Prince*, as above, chapter 6. For hand guns and gunpowder, Malcolm Vale, 'New Techniques and Old Ideals: The Impact of Artillery on War and Chivalry at the End of the Hundred Years War', *War, Literature and Politics in the Late Middle Ages*, ed. C.T. Allmand (Liverpool 1976), pp. 57–72. For Chaucer's knight, the debate between Terry Jones, *Chaucer's Knight: The Portrait of a Medieval Mercenary* (London 1980), and Maurice Keen, 'Chaucer's Knight, the English Aristocracy and the

Crusade', in *English Court Culture in the Later Middle Ages*, ed. V.J. Scattergood and James W. Sherborne (London 1983), pp. 45–61, with an overview by Lee Patterson, *Chaucer and the Subject of History* (Madison 1991). For indentures, the introduction to 'Private Indentures for Life Service in Peace and War, 1278–1476', ed. Michael Jones and Simon Walker, *The Camden Miscellany 32*, Camden Society 5th series 3 (1994), and Simon Walker, *The Lancastrian Affinity 1361–1399* (Oxford 1990). For Bastard Feudalism, the classic statement remains that by K.B. McFarlane, 'Bastard Feudalism', *Bulletin of the Institute of Historical Research*, 20 (1945), reprinted in his collected essays, *England in the Fifteenth Century* (London 1981), and see *The McFarlane Legacy: Studies in Late Medieval Politics and Society*, ed. Richard H. Britnell and A.J. Pollard (Stroud 1995); Michael Hicks, *Bastard Feudalism* (London 1995), and, for the earlier period, the debate between David Crouch, Peter Coss and David Carpenter, 'Bastard Feudalism Revised', *Past and Present*, 131 (1991), 165–203; David A. Carpenter, 'The Second Century of English Feudalism', *Past and Present*, 168 (2000), 30–71. For William Marshal, David Crouch, *William Marshal: Knighthood, War and Chivalry, 1147–1219*, 2nd edn (London 2002). For William and Michael de la Pole, E.B. Fryde, *William de la Pole: Merchant and King's Banker* (London 1988); J.S. Roskell, *The Impeachment of Michael de la Pole Earl of Suffolk in 1386 in the Context of the Reign of Richard II* (Manchester 1984). For Bodiam, Charles Coulson, 'Some Analysis of the Castle of Bodiam, East Sussex', in *Medieval Knighthood IV*, ed. Christopher Harper-Bill and Ruth Harvey (Woodbridge 1992), pp. 51–107. For Pulteney, Chaucer and Whittington, the *Oxford Dictionary of National Biography*, and S.L. Thrupp, *The Merchant Class of Medieval London (1300–1500)* (Chicago 1948); Caroline M. Barron, 'Richard Whittington: The Man Behind the Myth', in *Studies in London History Presented to Philip Edmund Jones*, ed. A. E. J. Hollaender and W. Kellaway (London 1969), pp. 197–248. For bells, the best modern study is in French, but see J.M.A.F. Smits van Waesberghe, *Cymbala: Bells in the Middle Ages* (Rome 1951), and the chapter on 'Copper Alloys' by Claude and John Blair, in *English Medieval Industries: Craftsmen, Techniques, Products*, ed. John Blair and Nigel Ramsay (London 1991), pp. 81–106. For the Pastons, besides the various editions of their letters, with a useful selection by Roger Virgoe, *Illustrated Letters of the Paston Family* (London 1989), see Colin Richmond, *The Paston Family in the Fifteenth Century*, 3 vols (Cambridge/Manchester 1990–2001). For the Neville correspondence, J. and L. Stones, 'Bishop Ralph Neville, Chancellor to King Henry III and his Correspondence: A Reappraisal', *Archives*, 16 (1984), 227–57. For pilgrim and other badges, Brian Spencer, *Pilgrim Souvenirs and Secular Badges* (Woodbridge 2010). For the classic modern statement of fifteenth-century affinity, see Christine Carpenter, 'The Beauchamp Affinity: A Study of Bastard Feudalism at Work', *English Historical Review*, 95 (1980), 514–32. For the land market, Christine Carpenter, *Locality and Polity: A Study of Warwickshire Landed Society, 1401–1499* (Cambridge 1992); Simon Payling, *Political Society in Lancastrian England: The Greater Gentry of Nottinghamshire* (Oxford 1991). For the Beauforts, G.L. Harriss, *Cardinal Beaufort* (Oxford 1988); Michael K. Jones and Malcolm G. Underwood, *The King's Mother: Lady Margaret Beaufort, Countess of Richmond and Derby* (Cambridge 1992). For the peasantry, Barbara A. Hanawalt, *The Ties That Bound: Peasant Families in Medieval England* (Oxford 1986); For ale and ale houses, Judith Bennett, *Ale, Beer and Brewsters in England* (Oxford 1996). For my remarks on disease, I have relied heavily on a forthcoming paper by Carole Rawcliffe. For pardons, Naomi D. Hurnard, *The King's Pardon for Homicide Before 1307* (Oxford 1969). For labour, its regulation and reward, I have relied heavily upon the papers collected as *The Problem of Labour in Fourteenth-Century England*, ed. James Bothwell, P.J.P. Goldberg and W. Mark Ormrod (Woodbridge 2000), especially those by Christopher Dyer, Richard Emmerson, P.J.P.

Goldberg, Chris Given-Wilson, Stephen Knight and Derek Pearsall. For the Luttrell Psalter, Michael Camille, *Mirror in Parchment: The Luttrell Psalter and the Making of Medieval England* (London 1998). For peasant obligations and the ending of serfdom, R.H. Hilton, *The Decline of Serfdom in Medieval England*, 2nd edn (London 1983); Mark Bailey, *The English Manor, c.1200–1500* (Manchester 2002). For protest, John R. Maddicott, 'Poems of Social Protest in Early Fourteenth-Century England', in *England in the Fourteenth Century*, ed. W. Mark Ormrod (Woodbridge 1986), pp. 130–44. For political interventions before 1300, David Carpenter, 'English Peasants in Politics, 1258–67', in Carpenter, *The Reign of Henry III*, pp. 309–48. Several of the examples of violence here are taken from James B. Given, *Society and Homicide in Thirteenth-Century England* (Stanford 1977). For animal maiming, see a modern comparison, John E. Archer, *By a Flash and a Scare: Incendiarism, Animal Maiming and Poaching in East Anglia, 1815–1870* (Oxford 1990). For 1381, still indispensable are the collections of essays ed. R. Barrie Dobson, *The Peasants' Revolt of 1381* (London 1970), and R.H. Hilton, *Bond Men Made Free: Medieval Peasant Movements and the English Rising of 1381*, new edition with introduction by Christopher Dyer (London 2003). For Corpus Christi, Miri Rubin, *Corpus Christi* (Cambridge 1990). For the 'Parlement of Fowles', W. Mark Ormrod, 'Murmur, Clamour and Noise: Voicing Complaint and Remedy in Petitions to the English Crown, c.1300–c.1460', in *Medieval Petitions: Grace and Grievance*, ed. Ormrod and others (Woodbridge 2009), pp. 135–55. For Wycliffe, still the best short biography is that by K.B. McFarlane, *John Wycliffe and the Beginnings of English Nonconformity* (London 1952), since supplemented by the massive researches of Anne Hudson and Margaret Aston: Hudson, *The Premature Reformation: Wycliffite Texts and Lollard History* (Oxford 1988); Aston, *Lollards and Reformers: Images and Literacy in Late Medieval Religion* (London 1984); *Lollardy and Gentry in the Later Middle Ages*, ed. Margaret

Aston and Colin Richmond (Stroud 1997). For the prehistory of English heresy, H.G. Richardson, 'Heresy and the Lay Power under Richard II', *English Historical Review*, 51 (1936), 1–28. The 'horrid cross' is taken from Paul Binski's *Becket's Crown*. The appalling story of Stephen le Pope from Ronald Hutton, *The Pagan Religions of the Ancient British Isles* (Oxford 1991). My discussion of the religious role of women is informed by Nancy Caciola, *Discerning Spirits: Divine and Demonic Possession in the Middle Ages* (Ithaca 2006). There are translations of both Julian of Norwich's *Revelations of Divine Love* and *The Book of Margery Kempe* in the Penguin Classics series, ed. Clifton Wolters and B.A. Windeatt. For humoral theory, I rely upon Bettina Bildhauer, *Medieval Blood* (Cardiff 2006) and Christopher D. Fletcher, *Richard II: Manhood, Youth and Politics, 1377–99* (Oxford 2008). For Walsingham, J.C. Dickinson, *The Shrine of Our Lady at Walsingham* (Cambridge 1956). For the Wilton Diptych, Dillian Gordon, *Making and Meaning: The Wilton Diptych* (London 1993). For burning as punishment, Nicholas Vincent, 'Simon of Atherfield (d.1211): A Martyr to his Wife', *Analecta Bollandiana*, 113 (1995), 349–61. For Oldcastle and his associates, K.B. McFarlane, *Lancastrian Kings and Lollard Knights* (Oxford 1972). For persecution as social good, Ian Forrest, *The Detection of Heresy in Late Medieval England* (Oxford 2005). For spies and spying, J.O. Prestwich, 'Military Intelligence under the Norman and Angevin Kings', in *Law and Government in Medieval England and Normandy: Essays in Honour of Sir James Holt*, ed. George Garnett and John Hudson (Cambridge 1994), 1–30; J.R. Alban and C.T. Allmand, 'Spies and Spying in the Fourteenth Century', in *War, Literature and Politics in the Late Middle Ages*, ed. C.T. Allmand (Liverpool 1976), pp. 73–101. For attacks on foreigners, John L. Leland, 'Aliens in the Pardons of Richard II', *Fourteenth Century England IV*, ed. J.S. Hamilton (Woodbridge 2006), pp. 136–45. For the processes of outlawry and sanctuary, Given, *Society and Homicide*, and W.C. Jordan,

'A Fresh Look at Medieval Sanctuary', in *Law and the Illicit in Medieval Europe*, ed. Ruth Mazo Karras and others (Philadelphia 2008), 17–32. For Shrewsbury's 'Grope Cunt Lane', first recorded in 1304, also noting examples at London, Oxford, Wells and York, Margaret Gelling, *The Place-Names of Shropshire: Part Four, Shrewsbury Town and Surburbs* (Nottingham, English Place Name Society 2004), 5. For the Southwark stews, Martha Carlin, *Medieval Southwark* (London 1996), and Ruth Mazo Karras, *Common Women: Prostitution and Sexuality in Medieval England* (Oxford 1996). For Robin Hood, the classic introduction remains that by J.C. Holt, *Robin Hood*, 2nd edn (London 1989), with a further study forthcoming by David Crook. For harpers, minstrels and jesters, Constance Bullock-Davies, *Menestrellorum Multitudo: Minstrels at a Royal Feast* (Cardiff 1978); John Southworth, *Fools and Jesters at the English Court* (Stroud 1998). For woodworking, forestry, alabaster, pewter and the glass trade, see the relevant chapters in *English Medieval Industries*, ed. John Blair and Nigel Ramsay, with the discussion of woodland resources here informed by the work of Paul Warde, *Ecology, Economy and State Formation in Early Modern Germany* (Cambridge 2006). For maps, *Local Maps and Plans from Medieval England*, ed. R.A. Skelton and P.D.A. Harvey (Oxford 1986). For coal, Mark Arvanigian, 'Regional Politics, Landed Society and the Coal Industry in North-East England, 1350–1430', in *Fourteenth Century England IV*, ed. J.S. Hamilton (Woodbridge 2006), pp. 175–91. For the Lancastrian badge, Doris Fletcher, 'The Lancastrian Collar of Esses: Its Origins and Transformations Down the Centuries', in *The Age of Richard II*, ed. J.L. Gillespie (Stroud 1997), pp. 191–204. For my ideas on nostalgia, I am indebted to discussion with Paul Binski. For the Glastonbury legends and Joseph, James P. Carley, 'A Grave Event: Henry V, Glastonbury Abbey, and Joseph of Arimathea's Bones', in *Culture and the King: Essays in Honor of Valerie M. Lagorio*, ed. M.B. Shichtman and J.P. Carley (Albany 1994), pp. 129–48. For

Thomas of Walsingham, besides the modern edition and translation of his *Chronica Majora*, noted above, see James G. Clark, *A Monastic Renaissance at St Albans: Thomas of Walsingham and his Circle, c.1350–1440* (Oxford 2004). For the late-medieval translations of saints' relics, see B.J. Nilson, *Cathedral Shrines of Medieval England* (Woodbridge 1998). *The Registrum Anglie* is ed. Richard H. and Mary A. Rouse (London 1991). For the fifteenth-century antiquaries, Antonia Gransden, 'Antiquarian Studies in Fifteenth-Century England', *Antiquaries Journal*, 60 (1980), 75–97. For autographs, V.H. Galbraith, 'The Literacy of the Medieval English Kings', *Proceedings of the British Academy*, 21 (1935), 201–38. For music, Andrew Wathey, *Music in the Royal and Noble Households in Late Medieval England* (New York 1969); *Music as Concept and Practice in the Late Middle Ages*, ed. Reinhard Strohm and Bonnie J. Blackburn (Oxford 2001). For the Beauchamp chapel, Alexandra Buckle, '"Fit for a King": Music and Iconography in Richard Beauchamp's Chantry Chapel', *Early Music*, 38 (2010), 3–20.

Chapter 8

The political narrative is informed by A.J. Pollard, *Late Medieval England 1399–1509* (Harlow 2000). Disclosing the extent to which the history of fifteenth-century England, like that of ancient Judea, is structured according to the lives of its good and bad kings, the standard royal biographies are those by Nigel Saul, *Richard II* (London 1997); Ian Mortimer, *The Fears of King Henry IV* (London 2007); C.T. Allmand, *Henry V*, 2nd edn (London 1997); Bertram Wolffe, *Henry VI* (London 1983); R.A. Griffiths, *The Reign of King Henry VI* (London 1981) and by Charles Ross, *Edward IV*, 2nd edn (London 1997), and Ross, *Richard III* (London 1981). For attacks on the Isle of Wight, S.F. Hockey, *Insula Vecta: The Isle of Wight in the Middle Ages* (Chichester 1982). For the navy, N.A.M. Rodger, *The Safeguard of the Sea: A Naval History of Britain, 660–1649* (London 1997). For Richard II, besides Nigel Saul's magnificent life, there are two collections of extremely valuable essays, *Richard II: The Art of Kingship*, ed. Anthony Goodman and James L. Gillespie (Oxford 1999), and *The Age of Richard II*, ed. James L. Gillespie (Stroud 1997) as well as Christopher Fletcher's *Richard II: Manhood, Youth and Politics* (noted above, chapter 7). For Bishop Despenser, Margaret Aston, 'The Impeachment of Bishop Despenser', *Bulletin of the Institute of Historical Research*, 38 (1965), 127–48; Kelly DeVries, 'The Reasons for the Bishop of Norwich's Attack of Flanders in 1383', in *Fourteenth Century England III*, ed. W. Mark Ormrod (Woodbridge 2004), pp. 155–65, and for his nephew, Martyn Lawrence, '"Too Flattering Sweet to be Substantial"? The Last Months of Thomas, Lord Despenser', *Fourteenth Century England IV*, ed. J.S. Hamilton (Woodbridge 2006), pp. 146–58. For the 'Merciless Parliament', and for Richard's adolescence, Fletcher, *Richard II*. For the handkerchief, George B. Stow, 'Richard II and the Invention of the Pocket Handkerchief', *Albion*, 27 (1995), 221–35. For court culture, Gervase Mathew, *The Court of Richard II* (London 1968). For the Wilton Diptych, Dillian Gordon, *Making and Meaning: The Wilton Diptych* (London 1993); *The Regal Image of Richard II and the Wilton Diptych*, ed. Dillian Gordon, Caroline Barron and others (London 1997), and Shelagh Mitchell, 'Richard II and the Broomscod Collar: New Evidence from the Issue Rolls', *Fourteenth Century England II*, ed. Chris Given-Wilson (Woodbridge 2002), pp. 171–80. For the atmosphere at court, Nigel Saul, 'Richard II and the Vocabulary of Kingship', *English Historical Review*, 110 (1995), 854–77. For Richard in Ireland, James L. Gillespie, 'Richard II: King of Battles', in *The Age of Richard II*, ed. Gillespie (Sutton 1997), pp. 139–64. For the coronation oil, J.W. McKenna, 'The Coronation Oil of the Yorkist Kings', *English Historical Review*, 82 (1967), 102–4. For Henry IV's Accession, *Henry IV: The Establishment of the Regime, 1399–1406*, ed. Gwilym Dodd and Douglas Biggs (Woodbridge 2003). For the Welsh, R.R. Davies, *The Revolt of Owain Glyn Dwr* (Oxford 1995). For the Scrope rebellion, Peter McNiven,

'The Betrayal of Archbishop Scrope', *Bulletin of the John Rylands University Library*, 54 (1971–72), 173–213. For Henry V, in addition to Allmand's magnificent biography, see the collection of essays ed. Gerald L. Harriss, *Henry V: The Practice of Kingship* (Oxford 1985), and the contemporary life of the King, the *Gesta Henrici Quinti: The Deeds of Henry the Fifth*, ed. Frank Taylor and J.S. Roskell (Oxford 1975). For the Lollard knights, besides McFarlane, *Lancastrian Kings*, see Peter McNiven, *Heresy and Politics in the Reign of Henry V: The Burning of John Badby* (Woodbridge 1987). For the Agincourt campaign, Anne Curry, *The Battle of Agincourt, 1415* (Stroud 2000); Curry, *Agincourt: A New History* (Stroud 2005); Juliet Barker, *Agincourt: The King, the Campaign, the Battle* (London 2005). The briefer account by John Keegan, *The Face of Battle*, 2nd edn (London 2004) retains its value, with splendid surrounding detail by Ian Mortimer, *1415: Henry V's Year of Glory* (London 2009). For the ensuing conquest of Normandy, Juliet Barker, *Conquest: The English Kingdom of France 1417–1450* (London 2009); C.T. Allmand, *Lancastrian Normandy, 1415–1450* (Oxford 1983). For the profits of war, K.B. McFarlane, 'The Investment of Sir John Fastolf's Profits of War', *Transactions of the Royal History Society*, 5th series 7 (1957), 91–116. For the end of the alien houses, D.J.A. Matthew, *The Norman Monasteries and their English Possessions* (Oxford 1962). For Christ's foreskin, Nicholas Vincent, *The Holy Blood* (Cambridge 2001). For the minority of Henry VI, John Watts, *Henry VI and the Politics of Kingship* (Cambridge 1996). For Catherine of Valois and the Tudor marriage, Ralph A. Griffiths and Roger S. Thomas, *The Making of the Tudor Dynasty*, 2nd edn (Stroud 2005), and for the suggestions over the paternity of Edmund Tudor, Gerald Harriss, *Cardinal Beaufort*. For general remarks as to the evidential poverty and general uselessness of the fifteenth-century English aristocracy, see McFarlane, *England in the Fifteenth Century* (London 1981), and Colin Richmond, 'Identity and Morality: Power and Politics During the Wars of the Roses', in *Power and Identity in the Middle*

Ages: Essays in Honour of Rees Davies, ed. H. Pryce and J. Watts (Oxford 2007), pp. 226–41. For the Southampton Plot, T.B. Pugh, *Henry V and the Southampton Plot of 1415* (Southampton 1988). For the use of imagery and propaganda, J.W. McKenna, 'Henry VI of England and the Dual Monarchy: Aspects of Royal Political Propaganda, 1422–32', *Journal of the Warburg and Courtauld Institutes*, 28 (1965), 145–62. For Joan of Arc, the most recent biography is by Larissa J. Taylor, *The Virgin Warrior: The Life and Death of Joan of Arc* (London 2009). For Richard of York, P.A. Johnson, *Duke Richard of York, 1411–1460* (Oxford 1988). For the trial of Duke Humphrey's wife, R.A. Griffiths, 'The Trial of Eleanor Cobham: An Episode in the Fall of Duke Humphrey of Gloucester', *Bulletin of the John Rylands Library*, 51 (1969), 381–99. For Duke Humphrey as humanist, Alessandra Petrina, *Cultural Politics in Fifteenth-Century England* (Leiden 2004) and the exhibition catalogue, *Duke Humfrey and English Humanism in the Fifteenth Century* (Bodleian Library Oxford 1970). For the piety of Henry VI, Roger Lovatt, 'A Collector of Apocryphal Anecdotes: John Blacman Revisited', in *Property and Politics: Essays in Later Medieval English History*, ed. T. Pollard (Gloucester 1984), pp. 172–97. For his dynastic awareness, R.A. Griffiths, 'The Sense of Dynasty in the Reign of Henry VI', in Griffiths, *King and Country: England and Wales in the Fifteenth Century* (London 1991), pp. 83–101. For the Cade rebellion, I.M.W. Harvey, *Jack Cade's Rebellion of 1450* (Oxford 1991). For Talbot, A.J. Pollard, *John Talbot and the War in France, 1427–1453* (London 1983). For Caxton, N.F. Blake, *Caxton and His World* (London 1969). For the Wars of the Roses, amongst a wealth of alternatives, see Christine Carpenter, *The Wars of the Roses* (Cambridge 1997). For George, Duke of Clarence, Michael A. Hicks, *False, Fleeting, Perjur'd Clarence: George Duke of Clarence, 1449–78*, 2nd edn (Bangor 1992), and for Richard Neville, Earl of Warwick, Hicks, *Warwick the Kingmaker* (Oxford 1998). For the posthumous cult of Henry VI, Leigh Ann Craig, 'Royalty, Virtue, and Adversity: The Cult of King Henry VI', *Albion*, 35

(2003), 187–209. For Malory, illuminated by recent perform-
ances by the Royal Shakespeare Company, see P. J. C. Field, *The
Life and Times of Sir Thomas Malory* (Cambridge 1993), with
the *Morte d'Arthur* edited (by Janet Cowen) as a Penguin
Classic. For alchemical interests at the court of Edward IV,
Jonathan Hughes, *Arthurian Myths and Alchemy: The Kingship
of Edward IV* (Stroud 2002). For Richard III, besides the
standard biography by Charles Ross, see Rosemary Horrox,
Richard III: A Study of Service (Cambridge 1989), with a wealth
of illuminating detail by Colin Richmond, '1485 and All That, or
What was Going on at the Battle of Bosworth?', in *Richard III:
Loyalty, Lordship and Law*, ed. P. W. Hammond (London 2000),
pp. 199–242. For Bosworth, Michael Bennett, *The Battle of
Bosworth*, 2nd edn (Stroud 1993). For the relocation of the battle
site, readers are advised to keep an eye on cyberspace, meanwhile relying upon such reports as that at <http://news.bbc.co.
uk/1/hi/england/leicestershire/8523386.stm>.

INDEX